PROFICIENT

C

PROFICIENT

C

The Microsoft® guide to

intermediate and advanced C programming

AUGIE HANSEN

PUBLISHED BY
Microsoft Press
A Division of Microsoft Corporation
16011 N.E. 36th Way, Box 97017, Redmond, Washington 98073-9717

Library of Congress Cataloging in Publication Data
Hansen, Augie
Proficient C.
Includes index.
1. C (Computer program language) I. Title.
QA76.73C15H367   1987   005.13′3   86-31109
ISBN 1-55615-007-5

Printed and bound in the United States of America.

     4 5 6 7 8 9 FGFG 8 9 0 9 8

Distributed to the book trade in the
United States by Harper & Row.

Distributed to the book trade in
Canada by General Publishing Company, Ltd.

Distributed to the book trade outside the
United States and Canada by Penguin Books Ltd.

Penguin Books Ltd., Harmondsworth, Middlesex, England
Penguin Books Australia Ltd., Ringwood, Victoria, Australia
Penguin Books N. Z. Ltd., 182-190 Wairau Road, Auckland 10, New Zealand

British Cataloging in Publication Data available

This book is dedicated to my parents, who worried throughout my child-hood and teenage years that I would electrocute myself in my electronics laboratory, and to my family, Doris, Lindsey, Reid, and Corri. They all mean much more to me than I can ever tell them using mere words.

Contents

SECTION V Appendixes

Acknowledgments

Working with the management and staff at Microsoft Press has been a distinct honor and a rewarding experience in many ways. I am impressed by the dedication, skill, and knowledge of all the individuals that I have dealt with either directly or indirectly during the development and preparation of *Proficient C.*

The person who is responsible for suggesting this book to me is Claudette Moore. She helped me pare down the original outline to something manageable, provided all the needed software, arranged for Microsoft experts to answer my questions, and kept things moving in the right direction.

Marie Doyle had the primary responsibility for editing the manuscript. She has been tireless in her efforts to obtain consistency and accuracy of the material and to ferret out my hidden assumptions. Thanks also to Dori Shattuck who participated in the early editing of the project.

I am indebted to Jeff Hinsch for poring over all the figures and source listings, testing all programs to verify correct operation, and working with me at some pretty strange hours to transfer files electronically.

Jim Beley has been involved throughout the project. He was best known to me as the hit man ("Just calling to check on our schedule . . . "), but his efforts and those of his staff are essential to the preparation and delivery of a book. Jim made many helpful suggestions along the way to improve the book and assure its timely delivery.

I also wish to thank Reed Koch, who reviewed the manuscript and contributed many useful comments and suggestions on the manuscript and the programs.

Many other individuals who have devoted themselves to this project will probably never be known to me by name. I appreciate their efforts nonetheless.

Introduction

Building a house that someone is willing to live in is quite an undertaking. The process starts with a good design that makes sense in the context of its surroundings and proceeds to completion through a series of carefully planned steps. Throughout the process, the builder must select the right materials and must employ the right tools to shape and join those materials.

A computer programmer faces a similar challenge. He or she needs good tools and needs to use them as effectively as a craftsperson in any other profession or trade. Rather than hammers and saws, the programmer needs assemblers, compilers, linkers, debuggers, and many other specialized tools. In addition, the computer programmer can benefit from the work of others by examining and using collections of ready-to-use program modules.

Objectives of This Book

Proficient C is a book for programmers. It is primarily about writing programs that are good tools for programmers. It demonstrates the use of C in the development of nontrivial applications, so we will not waste any time solving the Fibonacci series or calculating factorials. Although programs that do such things are instructive, they are of little value to us in building our tools.

Proficient C presents proven techniques for developing programs that solve real problems. Now, any person with a modicum of business sense knows that a problem is simply an opportunity in disguise, and some programmers have been astute enough to detect this connection and turn it into piles of hard cash. Whether or not money is your motivation for programming is unimportant; if you are going to program for any reason, you should try to do it well. This book is designed to help you do just that.

We will focus on creating building blocks—reusable modules that have wide applicability. Being frugal with our time and energy, we will use existing modules, such as those in the standard libraries that accompany most C compilers, as much as possible. And, of course, we will use our own modules again and again as we develop increasingly sophisticated programs.

Intended Audience

Programmers with at least a modest level of experience in some high-level language or assembly language will have an easy time going through this book. A working knowledge of C or a similar language (such as Pascal, ALGOL, Modula 2, or Ada) is assumed. Those readers without such experience will be best served by first reading an introductory text on C. Several good beginner- and intermediate-level C books are listed at the end of this introduction.

I don't share the opinion that BASIC programmers are somehow crippled by the experience of programming in BASIC, but I admit that many will find some of the concepts embodied in C to have an alien feel. Topics like indirection and recursion don't become immediately clear to most programmers who encounter them for the first time. Study and practice are required in order to become comfortable with them.

Hardware

All functions and programs in this book were developed and tested in an MS-DOS environment on an AT&T PC6300, and in a PC-DOS environment on an IBM PC/AT. The programs will probably also work on other compatible hardware that runs MS-DOS version 2.00 or later. With suitable compilers, many of the programs in this book that are not dependent upon specific PC features can easily be ported to other hardware and operating systems. That's one of the many beauties of C.

You are well advised to have as much primary and secondary storage as possible. A comfortable amount of random access memory (RAM) is 512 kilobytes. This allows room for a RAM disk to speed some operations. A hard disk is also recommended. These recommendations are based on the fact that most modern C compilers in the PC marketplace are large and are usually accompanied by massive libraries of standard functions. C compilers will function on less well-endowed systems, but the cost is usually diminished performance.

Software

Many of the programs in this book require MS-DOS or PC-DOS, version 2.00 or later. For the most part, I will refer to DOS in the generic sense. I will use the terms MS-DOS and PC-DOS in contexts where the difference is noticeable. (There are very few of these, limited mostly to a few external commands that may be available in one version and not in another.)

A good text editor is critical to success in large programming projects. You can use the DOS EDLIN editor if you're a bit of a masochist, but I recommend that you acquire a good programmer's editor like EDIX (Emerging Technology Consultants, Inc.), Brief (Solution Systems), or Epsilon (Lugaru Software, Ltd.). You may also use Microsoft Word, WordStar, or any other word processor that permits files to be saved in a straight ASCII (unformatted) form.

Without a C compiler, of course, this book will be of little value to you. The programs were written using Microsoft C, version 4.00, but other C compilers can be used instead. I have tried to minimize the use of features of one compiler that would prevent the use of others of comparable capability. Appendix B describes several other C compilers and what, if anything, must be done to compile the programs presented in this book using those compilers.

The DOS linker (LINK) provided with the operating system is used to combine object files and library modules into executable programs. A version of the linker that understands DOS pathname conventions is a necessity. Microsoft provides updated versions of the linker with all of its language products.

Organization

Section I describes the C compiler system and presents some views on program development. In Chapter 1, we look at the proposed ANSI standard for C and at compilers that attempt to track this moving target. Chapter 2 explores ways in which program development can be made more of a science than an art. Chapter 3 shows how C is used in a DOS setting with emphasis placed on effective use of the DOS command-line and environment variables.

Section II describes standard libraries and interfaces. Chapter 4 focuses on the use of the many existing functions in the standard C libraries. In Chapter 5, we explore the low-level interface to DOS from our C programs. Although not portable to other operating systems, such as UNIX/XENIX, these functions are important for certain classes of programs running on the PC. Additional functions built on top of the standard libraries are used at a higher level to manage the all-important user/machine interface. These functions are the topic of Chapter 6. In Chapter 7, we automate program configuration, but allow the user to override the automatic settings in various ways.

Section III presents a useful set of file-oriented programs. Chapter 8 provides several UNIX-like file and directory utilities, including an LS program to list a directory in special formats, a TOUCH command to assist the MAKE program maintainer, and an RM command. This orientation to basic file utilities leads to the development of a versatile print command (PR) in Chapter 9. Chapter 10 deals with ways of viewing the contents of non-ASCII files.

Section IV switches gears, leaving the realm of line-oriented programs to address the issues of screen-oriented programs. Chapter 11 introduces the concept of a buffered screen interface, and the concept is brought to fruition and expanded upon in Chapter 12, which covers screen-management functions. Chapter 13 describes an interface package that uses the much-maligned ANSI device driver provided with DOS. Chapter 14 presents a visual means of viewing files.

Other Books on C

Many introductory-level C books crowd the shelves in bookstores, with most of the books introduced in the past four or five years due to the rapidly increasing popularity of PCs and to the "discovery" that C is an extremely compliant and versatile computer programming language. Here is a list of some C books that my students and I have found to be valuable learning aids.

The C Primer, 2nd Edition, by Les Hancock and Morris Krieger (McGraw-Hill, 1985), is noted for its gentle introduction to programming in C. The use of flowcharts and examples based on models familiar to everyone makes this an easy-to-read and enjoyable book.

Programming in C, by Stephen G. Kochan (Hayden, 1983), has been my mainstay as a teaching book for beginning programmers. It covers the essentials of C without getting bogged down in superfluous detail.

C Primer Plus by Mitchell Waite, Stephen Prata, and Donald Martin (SAMS, 1984), is replete with corny but memorable examples and illustrations. It is a comprehensive book that gets a bit deeper into C language than some of the other beginners' books.

In addition to these introductory books, you may want to take a pass through *Variations in C* by Steve Schustack, another C book from Microsoft Press (1985). It is oriented toward developers of business applications and is loaded with advice on good programming style and many very useful examples.

And every C programmer should have a copy of the ubiquitous *The C Programming Language* by Brian Kernighan and Dennis M. Ritchie (Prentice-Hall, 1978). Although it is somewhat dated now, it is a treasure trove of C lore and law and is still considered the standard reference on the C language.

Notational Conventions

The following notational conventions apply to the text and examples in this book:

▶ DOS program names are shown in capital letters (DIR, TYPE). The names of programs we develop are treated the same way (PR, VE, NOTES) when the executable program is being referred to.

▶ Names of C functions, variables, and keywords are shown in italics (*environ, fgets( ), main( ), #define*). This same treatment is given to the names of source and object files (*myprog.c, myprog.obj*) and user-supplied function, constant, and variable names.

▶ Command syntax follows these conventions:

ITEM	CONVENTION	EXAMPLE
literal text	roman type	cmd
placeholders	italic type	cmd *option*
repeat item	ellipses	cmd *file* . . .
optional item	square brackets ([])	cmd [*opts*] *file*
logical OR	vertical bar (|)	cmd [*a* | *b*] *file* . . .

Special Offer
COMPANION DISKS TO PROFICIENT C

Microsoft Press has created two COMPANION DISKS to Augie Hansen's PROFICIENT C that are essential resources for anyone who wants to forego the drudgery of typing (and the time required to find and correct those inevitable typing errors) and begin using the book's C programs immediately. Choose the COMPANION DISK that best suits your needs:

Source Code Disk for PROFICIENT C
In addition to the source code for all the programs found in PROFICIENT C (approximately 8,000 lines), this disk contains all the MAKE files used to compile and link the specialized parts of the large programs.

Executable Programs Disk for PROFICIENT C
This disk contains all the stand-alone, executable programs in the book. Also included are the precompiled libraries built for the programs: BIOS, DOS, ANSI, video, and utility routines. Each precompiled library is provided in small, compact, medium, and large memory modules so that you can incorporate the code developed in PROFICIENT C immediately into a program.

In addition, the Executable Programs disk includes Appendix D in ASCII text file form. This file is a comprehensive reference guide to all the routines presented in this book, and is included to assist you in developing your own reference materials as you add to and customize PROFICIENT C routines.

If you have any questions about the files on the disks, you can send your written queries or comments directly to author Augie Hansen, Omniware, P.O. Box 37048, Denver, Colorado, 80237.

The COMPANION DISKS are only available directly from Microsoft Press. To order, use the special bind-in card at the back of the book. If the card has already been used, you can send $15.95 for each disk ordered (California residents add $0.96 and Washington State residents add $1.29 sales tax per disk) to: Microsoft Press, PROFICIENT C COMPANION DISKS OFFER, 13221 SE 26th, Suite L, Bellevue, WA 98005. Add $1.00 per disk for domestic postage and handling; $2.00 per disk for foreign orders. Payment must be in U.S. funds. You may pay by check or money order (payable to Microsoft Press), or by American Express, VISA, or MasterCard; please include both your credit card number and the expiration date. Allow four weeks for delivery.

SECTION I

Getting
Started

The C Compiler System 1

The tradition of C, originally established in its UNIX context, has had a profound effect on the programming environments of a vast range of machine types and sizes and has influenced the gamut of computer operating systems. Whether you program on an S-100-bus 8080 system running CP/M or on a CRAY-2 hosting a version of UNIX System V, or nearly anything in between, there is probably a C compiler system available for your environment.

In this chapter, we will briefly describe the proposed American National Standards Institute (ANSI) standard for C, some emerging standards for operating systems, and extensions of those that affect our C programming. Then we'll get a brief overview of the Microsoft C Compiler, its various memory models, and C programming support tools.

Standards and Compatibility

Anything that survives the test of time and that is likely to have a wide base of support is a candidate for standardization. As standards evolve, de facto or otherwise, we face the issue of compatibility with the standard. So it is with C.

Proposed ANSI-Standard C

The first attempt at standardizing C was the distribution of the "C Reference Manual" written by Dennis M. Ritchie, the author of C. The "C Reference Manual" was published as an appendix to the book *The C Programming Language* by Brian Kernighan and Dennis M. Ritchie. For many years, this book has been the only generally available description of C. However, since the "C Reference Manual" was promulgated, there have been numerous changes to C that are not supported by all C compiler suppliers, so portability among computer systems, and even among compilers on the same computer system, has been diminished.

The /usr/group Committee produced the "UNIX 1984 Standard" document to attempt standardization of the UNIX operating system. One major aspect of the /usr/group proposal is a standard set of library routines. Many of the recommendations, but not all of them, have been incorporated into AT&T's "System V Interface Definition," which defines a standard base for, among other things, the Operating System Services and Other Library Routines, the two major components of the standard library for C. The current de facto standard for C is the UNIX System V implementation by AT&T.

In recent years, the American National Standards Institute's Technical Committee on the C Programming Language—Committee X3J11—has been working to produce the first official American National Standard for C. Committee X3J11 is composed of members from various industrial companies, educational institutions, and government agencies.

The proposed ANSI standard for C is an attempt to "promote portability, reliability, maintainability, and efficient execution of C language programs on a variety of computing systems." The draft standard uses the "C Reference Manual" and the "UNIX 1984 Standard" as base documents for the language and the library, respectively.

The following list describes some of the features that have been added to C or changed since its original description and points out some of the implications of the new features and changes.

- ▶ The *enum* type specifier has been added, giving C an enumeration data type.

- ▶ The *void* keyword can be applied to functions that do not return a value. A function that does return a value can have its return value cast to *void* to indicate to the compiler (and *lint,* under UNIX/ XENIX) that the value is being deliberately ignored.

▶ Structure handling has been greatly improved. The member names in structure and union definitions need not be unique. Structures can be passed as arguments to functions, returned by functions, and assigned to structures of the same type.

▶ Function declarations can include argument-type lists (function prototyping) to notify the compiler of the number and types of arguments.

▶ Hexadecimal character constants can be expressed using an introductory \x followed by from one to three hexadecimal digits (0—F). Example: 16 decimal=\x10, which can be written as 0x10 using the current notation.

▶ The # in preprocessor directives can have leading white space (any combination of spaces and tabs), permitting indented preprocessor directives for clarity. In addition, new preprocessor directives have been added:

```
#if defined (expression)
#elif (expression)
```

Standard Run-Time Library Routines

The standard libraries that accompany most C compilers are standard because we accept them as such, not because of any law. Over many years and millions of lines of C source code, programmers have evolved a set of often-used routines that have been polished and packaged into libraries. Some of the routines, such as *read( )* and *write( )*, provide system-level services and are essentially our hooks into the underlying operating system. Other routines—string-handling functions and macros, for example—are part of the external subroutine library. (In Chapter 4, we will examine some representative standard library functions and present examples of their uses in programs.)

In the last few years, some new additions have been made to the standard libraries. Among them are a set of buffer-management routines, some new string-handling routines, improved I/O error reporting, and additional debugging support routines. The proposed ANSI standard specifies a basic set of system-level and external routines.

Microsoft C, Version 4.00

The Microsoft C Compiler, version 4.00, adheres closely to the proposed ANSI standard. I will briefly describe the compiler system and its features, to set the stage for the programs that follow. Appendix A provides a detailed description.

The Microsoft C Compiler is a three-pass optimizing compiler. The passes are named C1, C2, and C3. These passes could be called directly, but in practice they should not be. We use one of the control programs MSC and CL to invoke them for us. MSC is the primary compiler control program. With MSC, the linker must be called separately to combine program object files and library modules into an executable program. CL is similar in operation to the UNIX/XENIX C compiler control program *cc*. It invokes both the compiler passes and the linker, as needed, to produce an executable program.

The Microsoft C Compiler uses DOS environment variables to locate libraries and header files in special disk directories. These are normally set to *lib* and *include,* respectively. The compiler will use a designated temporary area on disk if the variable *TMP* is defined. The temporary area can be a virtual disk to speed disk-intensive processing.

If the machine used at run time has a math coprocessor, the coprocessor is used automatically. Floating-point emulation is used if no coprocessor is installed. Thus, it is not necessary to have separately compiled versions of the same program for differently configured systems.

The material in this book was developed on personal computers running MS-DOS and the Microsoft C Compiler, version 4.00. But many of the programs presented here can be moved with little or no change to other hardware, other operating systems, and other C compilers. Appendix B describes several other major C compilers and how they can be used to compile the programs in this book.

The primary areas that preclude unqualified portability to other environments are related to the occasional use of special keys on the PC keyboard, to screen updating via BIOS and direct-access routines, and to the use of other hardware elements of the PC, such as built-in timers and reserved memory areas. Where possible, dependencies on PC hardware have been avoided. One of the goals of the book is to show off some of the marvelous capabilities of the PC and the Microsoft C Compiler, so by design, some of the material is not portable to other environments without some changes.

Memory Models and Uses

Microsoft C supports programs up to one megabyte in size. It provides five primary memory models plus some extensions that let you produce mixed memory models to meet special needs. The memory models are defined by the following table:

MODEL	SIZES		
	Code	*Data*	*Arrays*
small	64 KB	64 KB	64 KB
medium	1 MB	64 KB	64 KB
compact	64 KB	1 MB	64 KB
large	1 MB	1 MB	64 KB
huge	1 MB	1 MB	>64 KB

Support Tools

When we talk about a C compiler, we usually implicitly include a set of support tools that make up a working C compiler system. We'll now examine some of the important support tools that enhance the C programming environment.

LINK, the DOS Linker Regardless of what language you program in, you will use the DOS LINK program, the object linker provided with DOS. Depending upon which version of DOS and which language product you have, you may have to upgrade to a newer version of the linker. The linker must understand DOS pathnames and, when used with the Microsoft C Compiler, must be able to access the values in DOS environment variables that point to the library and include file directories.

The version of LINK that is used to link the programs in this book is version 3.51. It was shipped with the version 4.00 C compiler. This version of LINK provides a single-level overlay-linking capability that permits memory space to be shared sequentially by several program modules. Earlier versions of LINK, back to version 3.12, will also work, but they do not have the overlay capability of the 3.51 version. I chose not to use overlays in this book, so there is no requirement for an overlay linker.

LIB, the Object-File Library Maintainer A library in the computer programming context is a collection of compiled or assembled functions. The functions in a given library are typically related to each other by some common factor, such as the role they serve in handling one major programming task. LIB is provided with Microsoft language products. It allows us to create, organize, and maintain run-time libraries.

The linker calls on various libraries to resolve external names during a linker session. The linker automatically looks for the standard C library (*slibc.lib, mlibc.lib,* and so on) for the appropriate memory model. It looks in the current directory unless the DOS environment variable LIB tells it to look elsewhere, or you provide a list of other libraries to search.

We will make extensive use of the libraries provided with our compilers, and we will create some libraries of our own. (Our library strategy is documented in Chapter 2.) Nearly all of the service routines we write in this book will end up in an object library somewhere. Appendix D summarizes all object library functions developed in this book.

MAKE, the UNIX-Style Program Maintainer Any repetitive task begs to be automated. MAKE is an automated program maintainer that emulates the basic behavior of the UNIX MAKE program. I will present information on the use of MAKE in building some of the programs in this book. Because my programs, even some of the simple ones, are usually broken into a number of small modules, it is important to have a tool that takes most of the drudgery out of maintaining the programs as changes are made to them during the development and lifetime maintenance periods.

MAKE performs its magic by applying rules, both built-in and user-supplied, to keep each object file up to date with its sources. The user-supplied rules reside in a "makefile" that lists all the modules of a program; the dependencies of objects on sources, header files, and libraries; and the recipe for how to connect the pieces. MAKE is equally able to control documentation projects and other activities that manage groups of disk files.

The next chapter describes the design and development process espoused in this book and shows the relationships of the various activities involved in building a program. MAKE plays an important role in the process.

CodeView, the Symbolic Debugger

With the release of version 4.00 of the Microsoft C Compiler, Microsoft unleashed CodeView, a spectacular window-oriented, source-level symbolic debugger.

Anyone who has done even a modest amount of programming knows the sense of frustration that accompanies a bug hunt. A program that should take a couple of hours to design, write, and test can cost you many hours of anguish because of a subtle, hard-to-find bug. CodeView has the debugging capabilities and operating features needed to shrink the debugging task down to manageable proportions.

The debugger is a logical extension of the DOS DEBUG program and Microsoft's SYMDEB, so knowledgeable users of those programs will find CodeView very easy to learn. Using multiple windows, CodeView allows you to view source code, disassemble object code, and monitor program variables, CPU registers, and the stack. Figure 1-1 is a sample CodeView screen that reveals some of the primary features of the debugger.

CodeView works on color or monochrome systems, can handle a 43-line EGA (enhanced graphics adapter) screen, and supports both mouse and keyboard user interfaces.

MASM, the Macro Assembler

The Microsoft C Compiler produces object files in the Microsoft object format, so there is no need to run a separate assembler pass. For information about MASM and ASM, see *Advanced MS-DOS* by Ray Duncan, Microsoft Press, 1986.

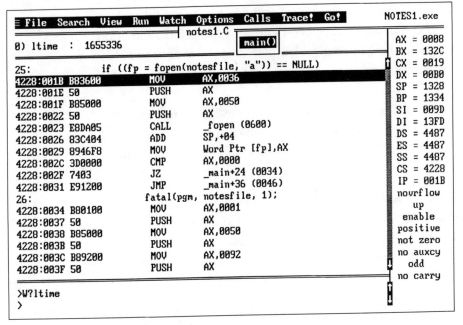

```
≡ File  Search  View  Run  Watch  Options  Calls  Trace!  Go!        NOTES1.exe
┌──────────────────────────── notes1.C ────────────────────              AX = 0008
0) ltime  :  1655336                    │ main() │                       BX = 132C
                                                                         CX = 0019
25:              if ((fp = fopen(notesfile, "a")) == NULL)               DX = 00B0
4228:001B B83600       MOV       AX,0036                                 SP = 1328
4228:001E 50           PUSH      AX                                      BP = 1334
4228:001F B85000       MOV       AX,0050                                 SI = 009D
4228:0022 50           PUSH      AX                                      DI = 13FD
4228:0023 E8DA05       CALL      _fopen (0600)                           DS = 4487
4228:0026 83C404       ADD       SP,+04                                  ES = 4487
4228:0029 8946F8       MOV       Word Ptr [fp],AX                        SS = 4487
4228:002C 3D0000       CMP       AX,0000                                 CS = 4228
4228:002F 7403         JZ        _main+24 (0034)                         IP = 001B
4228:0031 E91200       JMP       _main+36 (0046)                         novrflow
26:              fatal(pgm, notesfile, 1);                                 up
4228:0034 B80100       MOV       AX,0001                                  enable
4228:0037 50           PUSH      AX                                      positive
4228:0038 B85000       MOV       AX,0050                                 not zero
4228:003B 50           PUSH      AX                                      no auxcy
4228:003C B89200       MOV       AX,0092                                   odd
4228:003F 50           PUSH      AX                                      no carry

>W?ltime
>
```

FIGURE 1-1 │ *Sample CodeView screen display*

Program Development 2

Program development means different things to different people. The particular interpretation often depends on whether the question is asked of a programmer who always works independently or one who normally functions as a member of a team.

Whether done by an independent programmer or a team of programmers, program development is a blending of art and science and is an iterative process. For anything but trivial projects, we rarely know exactly how we will do the job before actually starting to do it. We can usually make some good guesses, but there is often an element of discovery involved. As long as something is learned each time through the loop, and as long as mistakes are not repeated, we will likely make some headway.

The science part is somehow keeping ourselves headed in the right direction, capturing needed information during the course of a project, and effectively applying what is learned. The art is in knowing what to try when all else fails and in being able to conjure up the correct data structures and algorithms to solve seemingly intractable problems.

There is usually at least one approach to solving a problem that makes the task easier than do other approaches. Experience and imagination are your two most important allies in pursuit of this approach. The experience need not be all yours, either—try to borrow existing ideas and adapt them to your purpose if there is a reasonable fit. And be pleased to have other programmers borrow your ideas—it's a sure sign of success.

Guiding Principles

During the past 10 years or so, I have had the good fortune to be both an observer and a participant on solo and group programming efforts. As a technical writer and publications supervisor, I was able to see the good, the bad, and the ugly aspects of very large programming efforts. As a developer, I saw firsthand how the development process can be made to work well and how it can be made to fail pitifully.

The consistent and careful application of structured design and the incremental development of both programs and the documents that describe them are critical factors in the success of programming projects. I suspect that the exact method used has less bearing on the outcome of a project than does the fact that the participants consciously attempt to control what is going on rather than just letting it happen.

This book encourages a heavy dependence on the development of reusable modules. The concept of creating reusable modules—essentially stockpiling programming pieces—seems obvious in retrospect, but it was quite a revelation to a generation of programmers 10 to 15 years ago. The standard library is a wonderful example of the concept coming to fruition. There is something elegant about a function that, for example, copies a string onto the end of another string and returns a pointer to the start of the resulting string. Variations of this technique pervade the standard library and give us options in using the library routines that we would not have if the routines had been designed in a less general way.

The point here is that we should keep an eye focused on the future use of what we are doing now. First, strive to get something working, but don't quit too soon. Refine it, generalize it, and make it available for future use, both by yourself and by others. The extra time spent in this endeavor will be paid back many times over in saved project time. Also, don't neglect to document what you do, both in comments within the sources and in separate manual-style documentation.

The Development Cycle

The first step in the development cycle is determining what must be done. This is the problem-definition phase and is the time when we determine the user's needs, investigate the operating environment, and try to get a feel for the boundary conditions that will influence our design.

The next phase, program design, is anything but a straightforward process. We need to keep our minds open to many alternatives. We should attempt paper designs, perhaps written in pseudocode, which is a human-language description disguised as program code. Our hope is that at least one of the paper designs will lead to a solution that can be implemented. A major objective at this stage is to produce a language-independent solution to the problem at hand so that we have options later, in terms of choosing a language that best fits the circumstances.

When we have what we believe is a workable solution, we can select a language and start coding. I prefer to use C because of its compactness and versatility, but I sometimes use Pascal, Assembler, or BASIC in my work. The choice should be based on factors such as the "lingua franca" of the host environment (local custom), whether any work has already been done on the problem in a particular language (invested value), and whether any of the current investment is worth saving (sometimes it isn't). But telling a hundred assembly-language programmers that from to-day forward all work will be in C is potentially risky business. It might be easier to learn yet another assembly language!

The next phase of the program-development cycle is an important one that is often overlooked. Testing should be planned right along with development, and should be done either by the programmer of the item to be tested or by an associate working closely with the programmer. As soon as the code is done, there should be a way to exercise it to see that the program does what it is supposed to do, doesn't do anything it shouldn't, and protects itself from possible adverse effects of unwanted inputs.

It is not too hard to check a program for correct behavior in the presence of *expected* inputs. This is, of course, important. But the behavior of a program in the face of *unexpected* inputs is equally important. Writing a program that defends itself well is a bit of a challenge and requires a somewhat perverse mentality on the part of the programmer and the tester.

Checking boundary conditions, handling errors promptly and correctly, and generally just being on guard for the conditions that could make your program crumble is something that requires discipline and practice. Be sure to check the return codes from routines that flag errors. Standard library I/O routines are particularly good about telling you when something goes wrong (full disk, bad filename, and so forth). Don't let this vital information fall on the floor.

As I said earlier, the program-development process is an iterative one. At any point in the process, don't be afraid to pull the plug and start over if you find yourself traveling the wrong path. If necessary, go to completion, refine the original definition, and do the job again until it's right. You'll be glad you did.

Our Local Environment

For the purposes of our development work in this book, we will set up some directories for header files and libraries. The hardware and software assumptions listed in the Introduction apply. We will use the Microsoft recommendations for the standard run-time libraries and supplied header-file locations. Any header and library files that we create will be placed in the new directories *include**local* and *lib**local,* respectively. This practice precludes one of our homegrown files from clobbering one of the files provided with the compiler if we accidentally use the same name. It also collects all of our own files together for convenient access.

We will be preparing several header files as we go on through this book. For now, we'll start with the file *std.h,* which contains some basic information needed by many of our C source files.

In addition to defining some often-used constants, *std.h* contains a definition of a Boolean data type (using the *enum* type specifier) and some aliases for standard data types that have long names (*unsigned short,* for example). I used to use these often, but as my typing speed increased, I began to use the original names. Feel free to use whatever you find most natural (or easiest to type).

We can use the preprocessor to retrieve our local header files in a way that is consistent with the approach used for standard header files.

The preprocessor directive

#include <local\std.h>

tells the preprocessor to read in the text of the file \include\local\std.h because we previously set the DOS environment variable INCLUDE to \include.

```
/*
 *       std.h
 */

/* data type aliases */
#define META      short
#define UCHAR     unsigned char
#define UINT      unsigned int
#define ULONG     unsigned long
#define USHORT    unsigned short

/* Boolean data type */
typedef enum {
        FALSE, TRUE
} BOOLEAN;

/* function return values and program exit codes */
#define OK        0
#define BAD       1
#define SUCCESS 0
#define FAILURE 1

/* infinite loop */
#define FOREVER while (1)

/* masks */
#define HIBYTE  0xFF00
#define LOBYTE  0x00FF
#define ASCII   0x7F
#define HIBIT   0x80

/* lengths */
#define MAXNAME 8
#define MAXEXT  3
#define MAXLINE 256
#define MAXPATH 64

/* special number */
#define BIGGEST 65535
```

Similarly, our local library directory will eventually contain a utility library, *util.lib,* a pair of operating-system interface libraries, *dos.lib* and *bios.lib,* and several other special-purpose libraries. The linker must always be given the correct name for the directory that contains the library files. We will arrange for this to be done automatically by using a makefile that includes pathname specifiers for the required directories. Then we'll let MAKE do all the hard work. Isn't high tech wonderful?

Now it's time to do some programming. We begin in Chapter 3 with an examination of how our C programs interact with the MS-DOS system.

The DOS-to-C Connection 3

DOS is, of course, the very popular and widely used operating system for the IBM PC and other personal computers that have a comparable 16-bit architecture. *Proficient C* is designed to help you write C programs in a DOS environment.

To obtain the greatest benefit from our PCs, we must understand both the C language and the DOS environment in which we program. In addition, we would like to exploit the similarities among DOS, UNIX, and XENIX for some classes of programs, especially those that don't require the use of specialized hardware or direct screen access.

From the beginning, DOS has had some features in common with UNIX and its many descendants, including XENIX. Among these similarities are basic aspects of command syntax (*copy from to,* rather than the "backward" approach of CP/M); the use of a common "file" orientation for all data streams, including the console (keyboard and screen) and the printer; and a batch-processing capability (.BAT files under DOS and shell scripts under UNIX). Starting with version 2.00, the operating system acquired many more features that are reminiscent of those provided by UNIX. Among the new features were a hierarchical file system and related support for a hard disk, installable device drivers for customization, a user-controllable environment, and input/output (I/O) redirection. These important features added greatly to the power and flexibility of DOS.

In this chapter, we will examine I/O redirection, command-line processing, and access to the DOS environment. Some aspects of each of these topics will be involved in the construction of the programs that are presented in the remainder of this book.

Proficient C makes extensive use of the routines in the C run-time library. In this chapter, we use only a few of the more common library routines. A detailed discussion of the C run-time library is presented in the next chapter (Chapter 4). We defer discussion of device drivers until Chapter 13.

Input/Output Redirection and Piping

By way of a few simple examples, we will quickly review some of the basics of input and output and set the stage for considerably more detailed work using the I/O features of the C run-time library, a marvelous collection of prepackaged routines.

Program I/O is based on the concept of standard streams: standard input (*stdin*), standard output (*stdout*), and standard error (*stderr*). The *stdin* stream is usually "connected" to the keyboard, and both the *stdout* and *stderr* are usually connected to the screen. Under DOS, both *stdin* and *stdout* can be redirected to other devices, but *stderr* always goes to the screen.

Because all references to I/O devices are treated like files under DOS, we can make ad hoc changes in the source or destination of data being processed by a program. The output of the DIR command, for example, normally goes directly to the screen (*stdout*). But with a minor change to the command line, we can send the directory listing directly to a printer by redirecting the DIR command's standard output. The command

```
dir > prn
```

tells DOS to feed the data that DIR normally sends to the console screen to the default printer device instead. Thus, the standard output of DIR is redirected.

We can similarly redirect input to a command. The DOS MORE command is a good example. MORE is classified in the DOS manual as a *filter*—a program that is designed to read from the standard input device, perform a transformation of some kind on that input, and produce some output on the standard output device. The transformation performed by MORE is to parcel out the input it receives in screen-sized chunks. MORE can be used as the termination of a *pipeline*—a series of programs connected to each other by a pipe, symbolized by the vertical bar (|). The

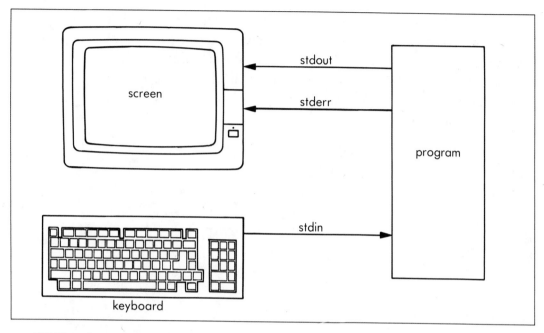

FIGURE 3-1 | *Default standard I/O streams*

DOS pipe is actually implemented as a pair of redirections. The output of one program is redirected to a specially named disk file, which then becomes the input to the next program in the pipeline.

The ability to join individual programs into custom-designed collections via the pipe mechanism is an important consideration in the design of an operating system. We can easily plug the output of one program into the input of another to perform special processing. To control the output of the TYPE command, for example, we issue the following command:

```
type myfile.txt | more
```

This command will display no more than a full screen of text at a time, allowing the user to page through the text at a leisurely pace rather than see the text flash by and scroll off the screen before it can be read.

The same effect can be achieved by redirecting input to MORE using the command

```
more < myfile.txt
```

We have redirected the standard input of MORE in this case.

To illustrate the use of redirection and piping techniques, here is a program called CP, which is a highly simplified version of the DOS COPY command. It is written as a filter in that it copies its standard input (*stdin*) to its standard output (*stdout*) one character at a time. Strictly speaking, however, CP is not a filter, because it simply passes its input to its output without modification.

```
/*
 *      cp -- a simplified copy command
 */

#include <stdio.h>

main()
{
        int ch;

        while ((ch = getc(stdin)) != EOF)
                putc(ch, stdout);
        exit(0);
}
```

This program should look familiar to anyone who has studied C programming at any level. Although very simple, CP allows us to copy a file from one place in a file system to another with ease. It has some serious limitations that we will address as we proceed through this chapter—for one thing, CP does no error checking, so it depends on DOS to do that work on its behalf. In addition, CP takes no filenames on the command line, so all input must be via redirection, which requires extra typing.

CP simply gathers a single character at a time from the standard input and checks to see whether it is the *EOF* (end-of-file) indicator. If the input is not *EOF*, it is immediately sent to the standard output. If *EOF* is detected, the processing loop terminates, and so does the program.

EOF is defined in *stdio.h* as -1. This is why the character-storage location *ch* is declared to be an *int* instead of a *char* data type. Since *char* can be signed or unsigned (depending on system implementation), we must always be prepared to detect the *EOF* flag to terminate the copying process.

The *getc( )* and *putc( )* library routines are implemented as macros and are defined in *stdio.h*. They are fast and use the standard I/O library user-buffering scheme. A buffer of *BUFSIZ* bytes (512 bytes in the Microsoft C implementation) is used for reading and writing operations. When *getc( )* attempts to read past the end of an input stream, it returns *EOF*.

There are several ways to use CP. Simply typing *CP* on the DOS command line causes the program to take input from the keyboard and display a copy of it on the console screen. You will see the text you type twice, once as you type it, because DOS is echoing your input, and a second time after you type a carriage return to end your input. User input may be terminated by typing Ctrl-Z followed by a carriage return.

```
C>cp
This is a line of text.
This is a line of text.
^Z

C>
```

To copy the contents of a file to the screen, you type the command

CP < *filename*

just as you would with the MORE command. To create a new file (or update an existing file), you can type

CP >> *newfile*

and CP will copy your keyboard input into *newfile* until you type Ctrl-Z (the DOS end-of-file marker).

Although this simple program is useful, it would be much more versatile if it could accept optional parameters on the invocation command-line, such as the names of files to process, and control information to tailor the processing to meet user needs. The next section explores the use of command arguments and applies them in several demonstration programs.

Command-line Processing

A program's invocation command line may contain optional arguments in addition to the program name. The *main( )* function of a C program is usually written in such a way as to look first for optional arguments and then for filenames or other parameters.

Under UNIX, the convention is to start optional arguments with a leading dash. DOS, however, uses a forward slash (/) to specify options, or what are commonly referred to as *switches.* (UNIX uses the forward slash as the pathname separator. Since DOS was not originally so close in spirit to UNIX as it is now, DOS's use of the forward slash as a switch flag is for-givable. However, this choice made it necessary to use something else for a separator in pathnames when they were introduced in DOS version 2.00, so DOS designers decided to use the backslash (\ ) as the pathname sepa-rator.) I have elected to use the leading dash as an option flag, but you can easily modify the code to allow the use of /, or to accept either form, as is done in the Microsoft C Compiler programs.

Arguments are passed to our programs by the C run-time startup function. A count of arguments, *argc,* and an array of pointers to charac-ter strings, *argv,* are passed as arguments to *main( )* (along with *envp,* which we'll look at in detail shortly). If a program needs to access the arguments, it must include *argc* and *argv* in the definition of its *main( )* function:

```
main(argc, argv)
int argc;
char *argv[];
{
        /* function body */
}
```

Figure 3-2 depicts how the command line and its components are managed in memory. The command line can be thought of as having two components: the command name itself (available within C programs only under DOS version 3.00 and later) and the command "tail," which may contain optional arguments such as filenames or input data. Only the command-name component is required by DOS. The command-line text, if present, is obtained from the DOS command-line tail. Information in the tail may be optional or required, based on the design of the program being executed.

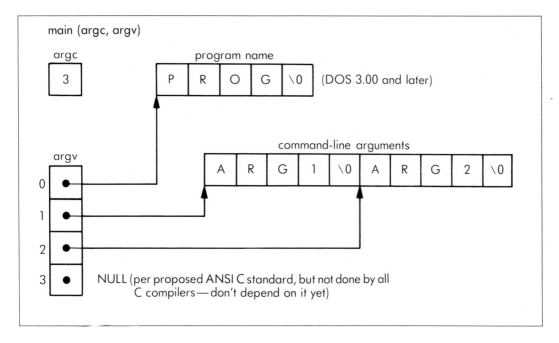

FIGURE 3-2 | *Command-line arguments*

Note the declaration of *argv* in the template for the *main( )* function shown above. The declaration

    char *argv[ ];

says that *argv* is an "array of type pointer to type *char.*" This declaration may also be written as

    char **argv;

which says that *argv* is a "pointer to a pointer to type *char.*" The net result is the same, but these are not identical declarations.

Program Name

The name used to invoke a program under DOS version 3.00 and later is available to the program as *argv[0]* (or *argv, if the pointer has not been moved). Earlier versions of DOS do not save the name used to invoke a program, so most C compilers for DOS substitute a dummy value, such as a null string or *c.* Being able to retrieve the invoking name can be very useful at times, so if our programs detect the use of DOS version 3.00 or later, we will let them use the name to their advantage.

How can the name be used? For one thing, when many programmers are producing programs in diverse locations for the same family of machines and operating systems, it is likely that the same name will be used for two or more programs that come into general distribution. We might like to be able to rename one of two identically named commands to avoid problems. This is easy to do if we have the source code, but it might not work if all we have is the executable program. Moreover, some programs (usually copy-protected programs) will not run if called by a different name. Another problem occurs when a program is renamed because, in most cases, the program name is hard-coded into error and help messages. So if we renamed CP.EXE to CPY.EXE, we might still get an error message like *cp: can't open file.txt,* which isn't nearly as useful as one that displays the currently used program name.

In Chapter 7, we'll find other uses for the command name. And throughout the programs in this book, where it makes sense to do so, we will try to obtain the invoking program name for use in error and help messages.

Ambiguous Filenames

Microsoft C provides a set of functions to handle the processing of wildcard characters in the formation of ambiguous filenames. Four object files are provided, one for each major memory model, and they may be placed in the default library directory for convenient access. The *ssetargv.obj* file is used with small-model programs; the *csetargv.obj, msetargv.obj,* and *lsetargv.obj* files are used with compact-, medium-, and large-model programs, respectively.

The *setargv( )* function expands wildcard characters in the command-line tail according to DOS rules (see the DOS manual for details) and passes them to the program in the form of an argument list. It is then up to the program to sift through the argument list it receives and separate optional arguments from filename arguments.

Accessing the Command Line

The following program shows how to access command-line arguments, including the program name. The REPLAY program first assumes that it will be called by the name *replay* but, just in case, it checks to see which version of DOS it is running under. If the DOS major number, obtained from the _osmajor global variable defined in *stdlib.h,* has a value of at least 3, REPLAY calls *getpname( )* to extract the filename part of the full pathname passed by DOS. If the user renames REPLAY.EXE to something else—say ARGLIST.EXE—then the program will issue the correct name when it displays the banner line just before displaying the arguments, if any, found on the command line.

```
/*
 *      replay -- echo the command-line arguments
 *      to standard output
 */

#include <stdio.h>
#include <stdlib.h>
#include <local\std.h>

main(argc, argv)
int argc;
char **argv;
{
        int i;
        char **p;
        static char pgm[MAXNAME + 1] = { "replay" };

        void getpname(char *, char *);

        /* get program name from DOS (version 3.00 and later) */
        if (_osmajor >= 3)
                getpname(*argv, pgm);

        /* check for arguments */
        if (argc == 1)
                exit(1);        /* none given */

        /* echo the argument list, one per line */
        p = argv;
        printf("%s arguments:\n\n", pgm);
        for (--argc, ++argv; argc > 0; --argc, ++argv)
                printf("argv[%d] -> %s\n", argv - p, *argv);
        exit(0);
} /* end main() */
```

Notice a few things in this demonstration program. We test for the presence of arguments (*if (argc == 1)*) and quit with a nonzero exit code if there are none. An argument count of 1 means that only the command name was typed on the DOS command line. This simple precaution prevents us from printing a banner line and nothing more, which would look kind of silly.

The temporary pointer *p* is declared as a pointer to a pointer to a character and is assigned the initial value of *argv*. When we enter the loop, *argv* is incremented so that it points past the command-name string to the first optional argument. Each time through the loop, *argv* gets incremented, so *argv − p* in the body of the loop yields the number of the current argument and *∗argv* yields the argument string. We could just as easily have incremented *p* while leaving *argv* stationary, which would require the argument-number calculation to be reversed (*p − argv*).

The *pgm* character array is large enough to hold an eight-character name plus a terminating null character. It must be declared *static* so that it can be initialized to the expected name. We put a name in the array so that if none is available from the operating system, we'll still have one to work with—although there is a small risk that it may be the wrong one, if someone has changed the program name.

If *_osmajor* is 3 or more, we call *getpname( )* to grab the base program name out of the pathname string, which may be anything from a simple filename to a full or relative pathname, complete with drive specifier and extension. (DOS allows pathnames for programs in version 2.00 and later. For the purposes of this book, earlier versions of DOS are considered to be obsolete.)

Here is the code for *getpname( )*:

```
/*
 *      getpname -- extract the base name of a program from the
 *      pathname string (deletes a drive specifier, any leading
 *      path node information, and the extension)
 */

#include <stdio.h>
#include <ctype.h>
```

(continued)

```
void getpname(path, pname)
char *path;     /* full or relative pathname */
char *pname;    /* program name pointer */
{
        char *cp;

        /* find the end of the pathname string */
        cp = path;      /* start of pathname */
        while (*cp != '\0')
                ++cp;
        --cp;           /* went one too far */

        /* find the start of the filename part */
        while (cp > path && *cp != '\\' && *cp != ':' && *cp != '/')
                --cp;
        if (cp > path)
                ++cp;   /* move to right of pathname separator */

        /* copy the filename part only */
        while ((*pname = tolower(*cp)) != '.' && *pname != '\0') {
                ++cp;
                ++pname;
        }
        *pname = '\0';
}
```

The program-name pointer, *pname*, accesses an array in the calling function that is large enough to hold the *filename* part (eight characters) of a valid DOS *filespec*, plus the terminating null byte.

The *getpname( )* function receives the full pathname of a file (*path*), immediately sets *cp* to the start of *path*, finds the terminating null byte, and backs up one position. It then moves backward to the start of the filename, which is marked by the beginning of *path* if the name is a simple filename, or by one of the accepted separators (:, \, or /). Notice that the backslash has to be escaped (\ \) to turn off its special meaning. The last thing *getpname( )* does is copy the filename part to *pname*, stopping when it sees a dot or a null byte. (It is customary in programming to refer to a single . as a *dot*.)

The *getpname( )* function is one we will use often, so it should be put in a place where it can be retrieved easily. We will now start accumulating useful object modules in a library of our own called *util.lib*, which will reside in a directory called \ *lib* \ *local* on the default disk drive. (Users of other compilers may need to make some adjustments if their compilers do not allow this.) The function is first compiled using the command

```
msc getpname;
```

and then the object file, *getpname.obj*, is added to the utility library
by typing

```
lib \ lib \ local \ util  + getpname;
```

Any time we need to use this function, we add the library path to the list of libraries to be searched by LINK.

We can automate the process by using MAKE with a script in a makefile routine such as the following one I assembled for the REPLAY program (the use of the MAKE program maintainer is explained in Chapter 1):

```
# makefile for the REPLAY program

LIB=c:\lib
LLIB=c:\lib\local

replay.obj:      replay.c
        msc $*;

replay.exe:      replay.obj $(LLIB)\util
        link $* $(LIB)\ssetargv, $*, nul, $(LLIB)\util;
```

This makefile, called *replay.mk*, is invoked using the command

```
make replay.mk
```

The MAKE program will take care of the details of recompiling objects and relinking the needed program modules to produce a new executable program. This example is the paradigm for all the programs that follow. Simple programs will be presented with specific compile and link descriptions; I will present makefiles for the more complex programs in later chapters.

Pointers and Indirection

The source code presented thus far uses quite a few pointers. Many programmers who are new to C language (and, for that matter, quite a few who are not so new to it) have problems with the declaration and application of pointers. Indeed, I have seen entire books written about C programming that sidestep the issue of pointers by using indexed arrays almost exclusively. That may seem a good way to minimize the difficulty one experiences in learning C, but it robs the programmer of one of C's most powerful capabilities and is really an unnecessary limitation.

If you are having problems with pointers, try to visualize a pointer declaration in the following way. (We'll use a pointer to a character here because it is commonly encountered.) The line

```
char *cp;
```

declares a character pointer. Place your finger tip over the *cp* part of the declaration and see what's left (*char* *). Read this as "*cp* is a pointer (the *) to a character storage location (the *char*)." In an expression, then, the unadorned *cp* yields a storage location that holds a pointer to (the address of) a character. If, however, you cover the *cp* grouping, you are left with the type *char.* This says that when you see *cp* in an expression, it yields a character storage location. You can retrieve the value stored there and may assign a character value into the storage location.

Look back through the source for *getpname( ),* which is loaded with examples of the variable *cp* used in both contexts. Once you feel comfortable with single indirection, as this is called, try the same thing with double indirection, such as you encounter with the declaration of the argument vector:

```
char **argv;
```

The illustration in Figure 3-3 on the next page may help to clarify this a bit. If it doesn't come easily to you, don't give up on it. A little practice will make it clear. You have to get a picture in mind of what's happening.

In Chapter 6, we will examine user/machine interfaces further. We will introduce a variety of ways of handling command-line arguments and talk about *getopt( ),* an AT&T library routine that attempts to standardize command-line syntax.

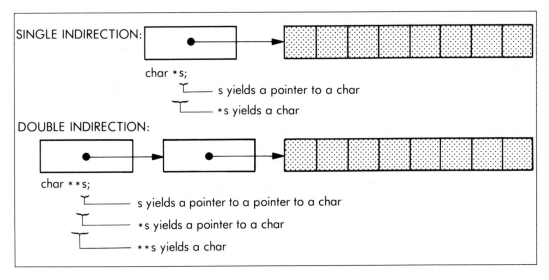

FIGURE 3.3 | *Pointers and indirection*

DOS Environment Variables

Another way to get data into a program or to modify a program's behavior is by using variables that are maintained in the DOS environment. To see which variables are in the environment and what their values are, type

set

at the DOS prompt and view the listing. All environments contain the values of COMSPEC and PATH. On my system, the environment list looks like this:

```
COMSPEC=C:\COMMAND.COM
PATH=C:\DOS;C:\BIN;C:\PWP;C:\WP;
PROMPT=$p$g
PWPLIB=c:\pwp
INCLUDE=c:\include
LIB=c:\lib
TMP=c:\
CONFIG=c:\config
FGND=cyan
BKGND=blue
BORDER=blue
```

From the DOS command line or from within a batch file, a user can add variables to the operating environment by using the SET command. The command

```
set var = val
```

instructs DOS to add the variable *var* to the environment and assign it the value *val*. Within a batch file, the value of the DOS environment variable *var* can be obtained by using the construct %*var*%. The following batch file, SHOW.BAT, does this to display the values set for foreground and background colors (see Chapter 13 to find out how these values can be used):

```
echo off
echo FGND = %FGND%
echo BKGND = %BKGND%
```

The initial *echo off* is used to silence DOS, which displays each line in a batch file before processing it, unless it's told not to. (The default really ought to be echoing off, and many enterprising programmers have patched COMMAND.COM for each version of DOS to disable this echoing.)

COMMENT

The amount of environment space reserved by DOS (prior to version 3.2) is only 160 bytes. You may want to expand the default space by using SETENV, a utility program supplied with version 4.00 of the Microsoft C Compiler. Some other commercial software products include a program called ENVSIZE, or something similar, but not all C compilers have such a utility.

We want to be able to selectively read DOS environment variables into our C programs, and we may even want to change them during the execution of our programs. The library functions *getenv( )* and *putenv( )* allow us to do both of these tasks. The functions use an environment pointer to gain access to the DOS environment.

The Environment Pointer

Access to the DOS environment is obtained through the global
variable *environ,* or the *main( )* function argument *envp.* The header file
stdlib.h declares the environment pointer as

```
extern char **environ
```

Thus, *environ* is an array of pointers to environment strings.

To add a third argument to *main( )* to obtain a pointer to the environment, you would use the following form:

```
main(argc, argv, envp)
int argc;
char *argv[];
char *envp[];
{
      . . .
}
```

If *envp* is declared as an argument to *main( )*, both *argc* and *argv* also must
be declared because of the way C function arguments are processed.
Note that the declarations for *argv* and *envp* could be written

```
char **argv;
char **envp;
```

because these are functionally identical to the previous declarations.

The *envp* argument to *main( )* is simply a copy of *environ* at the time
the program began execution. If subsequent changes are made to the environment, the global *environ* variable is kept current, but the value of
envp, which is local to *main( )*, is not.

Reading from the DOS Environment To read the value of a DOS variable
into a C program, use the *getenv( )* function, which returns a pointer to a
character string if the variable is defined, or returns *NULL* if it is not.

The following test program, SHOWENV, accepts a list of strings from
the user and checks each in turn to see if it is the name of a currently defined environment variable. If it is, SHOWENV displays the string and its
value. If not, SHOWENV displays the message "var not defined" and moves
on to the next string, if any. If no arguments are given to the command,
SHOWENV prints out the entire environment list.

```
/*
 *      showenv -- display the values of any DOS variables
 *      named on the invocation command line
 */

#include <stdio.h>
#include <stdlib.h>
#include <string.h>
#include <local\std.h>

main(argc, argv, envp)
int argc;
char **argv;
char **envp;
{
        register char *ep;
        static char pgm[MAXNAME + 1] = { "showenv" };
        extern void getpname(char *, char *);

        /* use an alias if one is given to this program */
        if (_osmajor >= 3)
                getpname(*argv, pgm);

        /* if no arguments, show full environment list */
        if (argc == 1)
                for (; *envp; ++envp)
                        printf("%s\n", *envp);
        else {
                /*
                 * treat all args as DOS variable names and
                 * display values of only specified variables
                 */
                ++argv; /* skip past command name */
                --argc;
                while (argc > 0) {
                        if ((ep = getenv(strupr(*argv))) == NULL)
                                fprintf(stderr, "%s not defined\n", *argv);
                        else
                                printf("%s=%s\n", *argv, ep);
                        ++argv;
                        --argc;
                }
        }
        exit(0);
}
```

The library function *strupr( )* is applied to the string being processed, because DOS always converts the variable name to uppercase letters before saving it in the environment. If *strupr( )* were not used, no match would be found if the user typed the string arguments in lowercase letters.

Writing to the DOS Environment The process of modifying the DOS environment list is analogous to reading it, except that the *putenv( )* function is called. A return value of 0 indicates success and −1 indicates failure, usually due to a lack of memory in which to write the modified environment. The program SETMYDIR attempts to add the variable *MYDIR* to the DOS environment by calling *putenv( )*.

```
/*      setmydir -- try to change the DOS environment      */

#include <stdio.h>
#include <stdlib.h>
#include <local\std.h>

main(argc, argv)
int argc;
char **argv;
{
        register char **p;
        static char var[] = { "MYDIR" };
        static char pgm[MAXNAME + 1] = { "setmydir" };
        extern void fatal(char *, char *, int);
        extern void getpname(char *, char *);

        /* use an alias if one is given to this program */
        if (_osmajor >= 3)
                getpname(*argv, pgm);

        /* try to add the MYDIR variable to the environment */
        if (putenv("MYDIR=c:\\mydir") == -1)
                fatal(pgm, "Error changing environment", 1);

        /* display the environment for this process */
        for (p = environ; *p; p++) {
                printf("%s\n", *p);
        }
        exit(0);
}
```

Please note that *putenv( )* modifies the environment in which the current process is running (the environment inherited is a copy from DOS), but it does not change the original DOS environment. To observe this, compile the SETMYDIR program. Then run a SET command to list the starting environment (assuming you don't already have a *MYDIR* variable), run the SETMYDIR program, then run the SET command again. You'll see the *MYDIR* variable come into existence while the program is running, then it will disappear when the program stops executing.

> # CAUTION
>
> *Be careful to assign values into the environment correctly. The form of the SET command is rigid. No white space (space, tab) is permitted on either side of the equal sign. If spaces or tabs are inserted, neither* getenv() *nor the* %var% *batch-file mechanism will recognize that the variable is defined.*

The ability to modify the environment passed to a running program is important. A program can, for example, set up its own private PATH so that it can access its own set of commands while running, without disturbing the user's normal environment, which is restored when the program terminates.

That's about it for the DOS-to-C connection via command lines and environment variables. We'll be using these connections extensively in our programs, so spend some time getting familiar with the techniques and routines described in this chapter.

In the next chapter we will take a much closer look at some of the standard library routines that are part of the run-time library of the C compiler package.

SECTION II

Standard Libraries and Interfaces

Using Standard Libraries 4

C has no built-in input/output capabilities; all I/O operations are handled by external functions. Neither does C have any built-in string-handling facilities or mathematical functions. This is not a deficiency, but rather it is a benefit that permits each C compiler implementation to use features and capabilities of the host hardware and operating system, while presenting the same external interface to programs. All such facilities are external to C and are handled by routines (functions and macros) that typically reside in special libraries, which are collections of often-used routines.

The UNIX heritage of C has produced a large body of ready-to-use routines that have successfully made the trip to DOS despite some significant differences in the underlying operating systems and their supporting environments. The routines mask the differences by providing a clean, consistent, and fairly well-documented interface to programs.

In this chapter, we will explore a small selection of the hundreds of routines in the standard C run-time library and use them to construct some simple but useful programs. Other library routines will be introduced in later chapters as the need for them arises.

Why Use Libraries?

Simply put, the standard libraries give us a reasonable degree of program portability, provide consistent and predictable interfaces, and, most important, reduce programming effort. Out of the millions of lines of C code that have been written over the years, certain operations have been programmed over and over again. Just a few obvious examples include: opening and closing files; reading and writing characters; detecting errors and displaying relevant messages; splitting, concatenating, and copying strings; and managing a hierarchy of directories and files.

In the standard libraries, many of these operations have been highly refined for speed, flexibility, and applicability to a wide range of situations. I prefer to use something that exists, if it works, rather than start from ground zero. Therefore, this book will concentrate on using the run-time library provided with the compiler wherever the library routines will do the job. We will develop mid-level and high-level routines that depend on standard libraries to carry out the low-level work. In all but a few special cases, we will avoid creating new low-level functions—it is simply not necessary most of the time.

The portability issue is often the basis of religious debate, something I wish to avoid because it is a waste of valuable time and energy. The portability I strive for in the C programs in this book is that needed to move a program among the various MS-DOS and PC-DOS systems, to extensions of the DOS environment such as Windows, and to a lesser degree, to XENIX and other UNIX-like systems. In some cases, I will sacrifice portability to achieve a high level of performance under raw DOS because that's what will "sell" best for a given application.

To go for complete DOS/UNIX transparency requires that some of the nicer features of a PC must be forsaken so that programs will run on any terminal type that can be connected to a multi-user system. In particular, this usually means saying good-bye to the use of function keys, arrow keys, attractive line-drawing characters, and fast screen updates. Going for the best performance on a PC usually means sacrificing portability to UNIX for such screen-intensive applications as a programmer's editor.

However, careful design can minimize the effects of most of the differences between DOS and UNIX. The use of standard libraries goes a long way toward ensuring DOS/UNIX portability because of the effort Microsoft and other C compiler vendors have placed on providing compatible libraries. The differences among vendors' libraries usually occur in PC-specific low-level interfaces. Although I will discourage the use of such PC-specific functions in programs designed for general use, they are the subject of Chapter 5 and will be used in some of our programs.

Exception Handling

Some days, things just don't seem to go right. Ever had one of those? Well, programs have days like that, too. As programmers, we have a responsibility to our programs to build in some way of dealing with unexpected events. This is called *exception handling* and is an essential component in the development of commercial-quality programs.

Exception handling has two parts: detection and recovery. The standard library functions attempt to detect errors and inform calling functions about them. It is up to us to build in the appropriate recovery procedures, even if that simply means giving up on a task, which is sometimes all we can do.

One of the more common error conditions is the absence of a needed file. The *fopen( )* function, for example, tries to open a named file. If asked to open a nonexistent file for reading, *fopen( )* returns *NULL* instead of a valid file pointer. What's the appropriate response to this error condition? At the very least, we may want to inform the user about the missing file. If the error occurs in a loop that is processing a list of files, we may choose to print a brief but informative message ("file XYZ.C not found") to *stderr* before moving on to the next name in the list. In other circumstances, it may be best to print the message and terminate processing with an ERRORLEVEL (exit code), to tell DOS that something is wrong.

Standard Library Error Functions

A set of standard library functions assists us with exception handling. A global variable, *errno*, holds the number of the most recent error. This number is used as an index into an array of error messages, *sys_errlist*. (The message associated with error number 0 is "Error 0," a catchall for errors not described elsewhere.) Rather than access *errno* and *sys_errlist* directly, we can call on *perror( )* to print the error message to the standard error output. The manual page summary of *perror( )* is:

```
#include <stdlib.h>
void perror(string);
char *string;
```

where *void* indicates that there is no return value and *string* is a pointer to a message that we provide.

COMMENT

Compilers that do not adhere completely to the proposed ANSI C standard may not support the void *data type (or lack of type, in this case) for functions. It may be necessary to use the following* typedef *to compensate for this deficiency:*

```
typedef int void;
```

Calls to void *functions will actually return an integer that can safely be ignored.*

The output of *perror( )* is the string we provided, followed by a colon, a space, the text of the system message for the most recent error, and a trailing newline, all sent to *stderr*. Thus, the statement

```
perror("File error");
```

if triggered by an attempt to open a nonexistent file for reading, produces the following output on the screen:

```
File error: No such file or directory
```

Appendix A of the *Microsoft C Compiler Library Reference Manual* lists the *errno* symbolic constants used under MS-DOS, the message text for each, and a description of each error. The DOS error messages are necessarily a subset of the error messages used by UNIX and XENIX. See your own C compiler library documentation for a detailed description of each error and message.

Ambiguous Return Values Two macros, *ferror( )* and *feof( )*, are used to resolve an ambiguity that is produced by certain standard library routines: Because they are designed to return a pointer to a character, functions like *fgets( )* (which we will use in an example shortly) must return *NULL* to indicate either that an error has occurred or that the end of the file has been reached. We need to take additional steps to determine which condition caused the *NULL* return value before we take any action.

The manual page summary of *ferror( )* is

```
#include <stdio.h>
int ferror(stream);
FILE *stream;
```

where *stream* must be the file or stream associated with the *NULL-*
returning routine. The summary for *feof( )* is the same except for the
macro name. The *ferror( )* macro returns a nonzero value to indicate that
an error condition exists and *feof( )* returns a nonzero value if the end of
the file has been reached, thus resolving the ambiguity of the *NULL* value.

The following code fragment illustrates a way of handling the ambiguous return:

```
              .
              .
              .
errcount = 0;
while ((s = fgets(line, BUFSIZ, fp)) != NULL) {
        /* process the line */
              .
              .
              .
}
if (ferror(fp)) {
        perror("Read error");
        clearerr(fp);
        if (++errcount >= MAX_ERR) {
                fprintf(stderr, "Too many errors\n");
                exit(1);
        }
}
              .
              .
              .
```

Notice the use of *clearerr( )* in the preceding fragment. Once an error occurs in a stream, the error indication remains until the stream is
closed or until the indication is intentionally cleared by using either *clear-
err( )* or *rewind( )*. In the foregoing example, we clear the error indication
and allow some maximum number of errors (*MAX_ERR*) before giving up.
On the other hand, if the *NULL* is the result of having reached the end of
the file, we fall through to other processing.

A common programming procedure is to display an error message and then call *exit( )* to flush output buffers and return to the operating system with an exit code that indicates an abnormal termination. For convenience, we will package these statements into a function called *fatal( )*, which displays the program name, the message text, and a newline. This will usually provide enough information to the user to help determine the cause of the abnormal exit.

```
/*  fatal -- issue a diagnostic message and terminate  */

#include <stdio.h>
#include <stdlib.h>

void fatal(pname, mesg, errlvl)
char *pname;      /* program name */
char *mesg;       /* message text */
int errlvl;       /* errorlevel (exit code) */
{
        fputs(pname, stderr);     /* display error message */
        fputc(':', stderr);
        fputc(' ', stderr);
        fputs(mesg, stderr);
        fputc('\n', stderr);

        /* return to DOS with the specified errorlevel */
        exit(errlvl);
}
```

The *fatal( )* function doesn't return to the calling function, hence the *void* return type. The *errlvl* value should be nonzero—a small positive integer—to indicate an abnormal termination. The specific values used for *errlvl* should be documented in a manual page for the program.

Operating System Interrupts Another type of exception is an interrupt from the operating system, usually caused by the user pressing Ctrl-Break or Ctrl-C. The library function *signal( )* can be used to control how such interrupts are handled. The summary for *signal( )* is

```
#include <signal.h>
int (*signal(sig, func))( );
int sig;
int (*func)( );
```

This bizarre-looking declaration is not a misprint. The line

int (*func)( );

declares a pointer to a function that returns an integer. This is not the same as

int *func ( );

which declares a function that returns a pointer to an integer. The declaration of *signal( )* also is a pointer to a function that returns an integer.

The only value for *sig* permitted under DOS is SIGINT, #*defin*ed in the *signal.h* header file. SIGINT is the DOS Ctrl-Break interrupt. Other signals, including SIGHUP (hangup) and others that apply under the multitasking UNIX and XENIX operating system, currently have no meaning under DOS.

One of three responses to the interrupt can be specified in the *func* argument. A value of *SIG_IGN* causes the interrupt to be ignored. We might choose to ignore the DOS Ctrl-Break interrupt during all or a portion of the lifetime of a program to prevent the user from aborting some critical operation. For example, it is unwise to let the user break out of a text editor without first presenting the opportunity of saving changes that were made to the editing buffer—it could be that the user was fumbling for, say, Ctrl-D to move the cursor right and hit Ctrl-C by mistake. I know, I've done it myself!

Second, a *func* value of *SIG_DFL* causes the running program to abort upon receipt of the interrupt, closing all open files and returning control to DOS. Buffers are not flushed. This is usually what will happen if you don't use *signal( )*, unless you are using DOS functions that ignore Ctrl-Break by design (see Chapter 5).

A third type of response is to provide a pointer to a signal-handling function. This is referred to as *signal catching* and is more of an art than a science. The safest method of signal catching simply cleans up any work in progress and makes a graceful exit. It either accepts the default treatment or, in a few cases, simply ignores the interrupt.

A return value of −1 from *signal( )* flags an error, *errno* = *EINVAL,* which says that the *sig* argument is invalid. This identifies a programming problem that should be corrected before any user ever sees the program.

Time Functions

The standard library provides several routines for retrieving and converting time values. The UNIX *ctime* subroutine package and the *time( )* system call are available as functions in the Microsoft C run-time library for DOS. Because these functions have received very little attention in books about DOS, we will give them a moment in the spotlight.

The *time( )* function returns the number of seconds that have elapsed since 00:00:00 GMT (Greenwich mean time) on January 1, 1970. This date and time is called the *epoch*. GMT is now officially called Universal time (UT), but the use of the term GMT is likely to continue indefinitely, just as *core* is still used to mean main memory, even if it's all solid state. File-modification times and other times and dates that are visible to the user are presented as local time values.

The declaration of *time( )* is

```
#include <time.h>
long time(timeptr);
long *timeptr;        /* (usually NULL) */
```

The *time( )* function takes a pointer to *long* as an argument and produces a *long* return value. The argument can always be the *NULL* pointer. Before C had a *long* data type, it was necessary to provide a suitable buffer for the time value. Passing the address of the buffer synthesized a "call by reference" (C uses "call by value" for parameter passing). Now the application of *time( )* simply assigns the return value to a *long* integer.

Time Conversions

The *long* time value is wonderful for the computer, but we humans don't often tell someone what time it is as a number of seconds since the epoch. A more convenient notation for us is a character string that spells out, at least as abbreviations, what the date and time are. We need some convenient way to make a conversion from the *long* value to a character string. We also have to deal with Universal time and local time and with the complications of daylight saving time.

Figure 4-1 shows the relationships of the *time( )* function and the functions that constitute the *ctime* subroutine package. Two functions, *gmtime( )* and *localtime( ),* can be used to convert values from the *long* result of *time( )* to time structure pointers. The DOS time structure template, *struct tm,* defines a set of variables of type *int* that can hold hour, minute, second, month, day, and year values, plus a flag for daylight saving time and numbers for day-of-week and day-of-month calculations. This time structure template is defined in the file *time.h.*

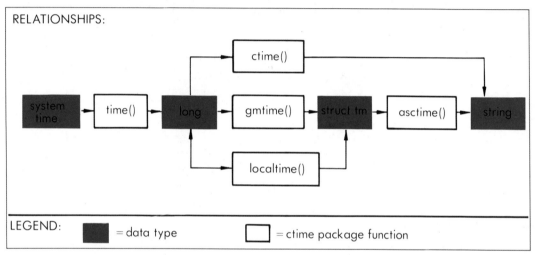

RELATIONSHIPS:

LEGEND:　■ = data type　　　□ = ctime package function

FIGURE 4-1 | *Time and date functions and variables*

　　　Time and date information in the structure is easy to access and use, but it is still not suitable for human consumption. Both *gmtime( )* and *localtime( )* return pointers to a time structure. The declarations for these functions are

```
#include <time.h>
struct tm *gmtime(time);
long *time;
struct tm *localtime(time);
long *time;
```

CAUTION

These two functions use a single statically allocated structure. Any call to one of these functions, therefore, will overwrite the result of any previous call to either function.

While *gmtime( )* always returns a direct conversion of the time value
returned by *time( )*, *localtime( )* does some additional adjustments to compensate for the difference between GMT and the time zone set into the
DOS environment via the *TZ* variable. If *TZ* is not explicitly set (it usually
isn't), then Pacific time is used. I am willing to wager that nearly every PC
running DOS today thinks it is in Redmond, Washington! We'll see shortly
how you can tell your PC where it really is, but first we need to examine
how to convert the time structure data into strings we can read and
understand.

Creating Strings The function *asctime( )* takes a pointer to the time
structure and converts the structure members to a 26-byte string. The format of the string is

```
Sat Jul 12 13:05:33 1986 \n \0
```

where \n is a newline character and \0 is the terminating null byte. Each
character should be surrounded by single quotes to show that it is a character constant. Rather than clutter the displayed string, I'll just ask you to
imagine the quotes there.

The function *ctime( )* provides a shortcut for creating a local time
string. It takes a *long* time result from *time( )* and returns a pointer to a
character string of the format described above. Its declaration is

```
#include <time.h>
char *ctime(time);
long *time;
```

CAUTION

The character string pointed to by ctime( ) *is the same
statically allocated string pointed to by* asctime( ). *A call
to one of these routines destroys the result of any previous
call to* either *of them.*

Time Zones Now on to the subject of time zones. A DOS environment
variable called *TZ* can be set to reflect the time zone in which a PC is operating. Adding a line like

```
set TZ=MST7MDT
```

to my AUTOEXEC.BAT file tells DOS that my machine is running in the mountain time zone, that there is a 7-hour difference between mountain standard time and Greenwich mean time, and that daylight saving time is honored in this zone. Several other variables are also maintained by the *ctime( )* subroutine package. They can all be updated by a call to *tzset( )* (or to *asctime( )*, which calls *tzset( )*). These variables are

VARIABLE	MEANING
int daylight;	Daylight savings time flag
long timezone;	Difference from GMT in seconds
char *tzname[];	*timezone* strings

If a daylight string is set in the TZ variable, *daylight* is set to a nonzero value. The value of *timezone* is the difference in seconds between local standard time and GMT. The variable *tzname* is an array of pointers to character strings. The first (*tzname[0]*) is a pointer to the three-letter string for the standard time zone and the second (*tzname[1]*) is a pointer to the daylight string (e.g., MDT) if one was specified. The last element (*tzname[2]*) is a *NULL* pointer that typically terminates an array of pointers. If no TZ setting is done at boot time, the *ctime* package uses *PST8PDT* as a default.

   When compiled and run, the following little program, TIMEDATA, shows some of the time-related values for your system. Don't be surprised to see Pacific time zone data even if that is not your "home" time zone.

```
/*
 *      timedata -- time zone and time value tests
 */

#include <stdio.h>
#include <time.h>

main()
{
        long now;
        struct tm *tbuf;
```

(continued)

```
        /* get TZ data into global variables */
        tzset();

        /* display the global time values */
        printf("daylight savings time flag = %d\n", daylight);
        printf("difference (in seconds) from GMT = %ld\n", timezone);
        printf("standard time zone string is %s\n", tzname[0]);
        printf("daylight time zone string is %s\n", tzname[1]);


        /*
         *  display the current date and time values for
         *  local and universal time
         */
        now = time(NULL);
        printf("\nctime():\t%s\n", ctime(&now));
        tbuf = localtime(&now);
        printf("local time:\t%s\n", asctime(tbuf));
        tbuf = gmtime(&now);
        printf("universal time:\t%s\n", asctime(tbuf));

        exit(0);
}
```

Here is an example of the output of TIMEDATA taken from my system in Denver, Colorado:

```
daylight savings time flag = 1
difference (in seconds) from GMT = 25200
standard time zone string is mst
daylight time zone string is mdt

ctime():        Mon Feb 16 06:19:33 1987

local time:     Mon Feb 16 06:19:33 1987

universal time: Mon Feb 16 13:19:33 1987
```

If you accept the Pacific default for *timezone* while operating in a different time zone, there is usually no harm done. The effect of not setting *TZ* is that you are fibbing about the local time, which will cause DOS to have an incorrect notion of what GMT is. For example, had I let *TZ* default to *PST8PDT* and set local time correctly for Denver, the system value for GMT would be off by one hour.

However, problems might occur for systems connected into wide-area networks that must keep accurate track of file-modification times and various other timed events, possibly while crossing several time zones. In such cases, all connected systems should have the correct time zones set in the *TZ* variable and agree on what the value of GMT is.

Getting a time-and-date string is a first step for us in the development of a program called NOTES, a simple electronic diary. But we will also need a way of creating and modifying files before we can assemble a working prototype, so let's talk about that next.

Basic File and Character I/O Functions

Much of what we will do in the rest of this book will involve some interaction with disk files. There are many standard I/O routines in the C run-time library that deal with files on various levels. In this section, we will review some of the more frequently used functions. Then we will create a useful demonstration program.

The run-time library provides access to disk files and other I/O streams using DOS file handles. These functions—*open( )*, *close( )*, *read( )*, *write( )*, *lseek( )*, and so on—are analogous to the UNIX system calls of the same names that use file descriptors. These functions are unbuffered from a user's perspective, although the operating-system kernel may anticipate read operations and delay write operations to minimize disk-head movement, and improve I/O efficiency.

Buffered I/O

Another level of file access is the set of standard library subroutines that do buffered I/O. The functions *fopen( )*, *fclose( )*, *fgetc( )*, *fputc( )*, *fgets( )*, and *fputs( )* are representative of this level and are used extensively in the programs in this book. These functions use a file pointer that points to a structure of type *FILE*. The *FILE* structure template is defined in *stdio.h*, the header file that is included in all source files that use standard I/O library functions.

All file-access functions will be covered at one time or another in programs later in the book. For now, we'll concentrate on the buffered I/O

library functions. By way of example, here is a fairly typical use of the
standard run-time library in a program called NOTES, which lets us keep
an electronic notebook or diary. This first version, NOTES1, is a simplified
prototype.

```
/*
 *      notes1 -- add an entry to a "notes" text file
 *
 *      version 1: appends new data to NOTES.TXT in the
 *      current directory -- uses local date/time stamp
 *      as a header for each new entry
 */

#include <stdio.h>
#include <stdlib.h>
#include <time.h>
#include <local\std.h>

main()
{
        FILE *fp;
        static char notesfile[MAXPATH + 1] = { "notes.txt" };
        char ch;
        long ltime;
        static char pgm[MAXNAME + 1] = { "notes1" };

        extern void fatal(char *, char *, int);

        /* try to open notes file in current directory */
        if ((fp = fopen(notesfile, "a")) == NULL)
                fatal(pgm, notesfile, 1);

        /* append a header and date/time tag */
        ltime = time(NULL);
        fprintf(stderr, "Appending to %s: %s\n",
                notesfile, ctime(&ltime));
        fprintf(fp, "%s\n", ctime(&ltime));

        /* append new text */
        while ((ch = getchar()) != EOF)
                putc(ch, fp);
```

(continued)

```
    /* clean up */
    if (fclose(fp))
            fatal(pgm, notesfile, 2);
    exit(0);
}
```

This program, although rather simple and not yet fully developed, is immediately useful in its current form. It takes input from the keyboard and appends it to a "notesfile" in the current directory. The program is invoked by typing NOTES on the DOS command line. Each new session starts by placing a blank line and a date/time stamp at the end of the data file, currently hard-coded into the program as *NOTES.TXT*. Text input is simply typed at the keyboard and terminated by the user typing a Ctrl-Z (end-of-file) character on a line by itself.

This simple version of NOTES allows no options. If you make an error while inputting text, you must back up and correct it before moving off the line. To edit the *NOTES.TXT* file, you must leave the NOTES program and call upon some text-editing program. We will embellish the NOTES program with additional features in later chapters, but for now we will accept its limitations and treat it as a learning aid.

The call to *fopen( )* is interesting. The function will open the named file for appending if the file already exists, or it will silently create the file if it doesn't exist. The call returns a valid *FILE* pointer if the file is opened successfully, or *NULL* to flag an error. (Attempting to open a directory, for example, produces an error.) Our program must be prepared to deal with errors. Therefore, at the risk of having our programs look like LISP source code, we will always test the return value of I/O functions. To ignore this extra bit of work is not simply bad programming practice; it can be dangerous. A program that fails without a whimper is not apt to inspire strong feelings of trust in its users.

The declaration of *fopen( )* is

```
#include <stdio.h>
FILE *fopen(pathname, type);
char *pathname;
char *type;
```

The pathname argument may be a simple filename and optional extension, or a full or relative pathname with an optional leading drive specifier. The *type* argument is one of the following:

ARGUMENT	MEANING
r	Open for reading (file must exist)
w	Open for writing (create or truncate)
a	Open for appending (create if necessary)
r+	Open for both reading and writing (the file must exist)
w+	Open for both reading and writing (create or truncate)
a+	Open for reading and appending (create if necessary)

The optional + within the type string specifies update mode, in which both reading and writing are allowed. The file pointer must be set by an intervening call to *fseek( )* or *rewind( )* when switching between read and write operations or vice versa.

Unlike UNIX and XENIX, which use a single newline (NL) character to terminate a text line, DOS uses a carriage-return character (CR) plus a linefeed (LF) character. The codes to NL and LF are identical (ASCII code 10), so you will usually see the DOS end-of-line treatment described as CR/NL, but it is really CR/LF. Technically, LF moves down a line but retains the same column position, so a CR is needed to get back to the first column. The NL code convention achieves the two tasks in a single operation, saving a byte per line in ordinary text files. Both methods of terminating a line are allowed by the ANSI standard (see Chapter 13 for more information about ANSI standards).

In addition to a different end-of-line treatment, DOS uses an explicit Ctrl-Z (ASCII code 26) to mark the end of a file. (Under UNIX and XENIX, the end-of-file condition is sensed when an attempt is made to perform an operation beyond the last position in a file, which is known because an exact size is maintained for each disk file.)

The conventions just described for DOS text files do not apply to binary files (executable program files, for example), which can contain any arbitrary bit patterns in any position. For binary files, all bits are significant, and an accurate file size must be maintained by DOS so it knows where the end of the file is.

To maintain compatibility with existing C programs, UNIX text-file conventions are used within C programs under DOS. When a file is opened, the differences are specified by a text (t) or binary (b) flag appended to the *type* argument to *fopen( )*, or by the global *_fmode* translation-mode variable if neither t nor b is explicitly specified. The default for *_fmode* is text-translation mode.

We can use separate statements for the processing and the error-detection phases of each call to a library routine:

```
FILE *fp

fp = fopen(notesfile, "a");
if (fp == NULL)
        fatal(pgm, notesfile, 1);
```

This is rarely done, however. You are more likely to see this written in the condensed form (shown in *notes1.c,* on page 52) which is the de facto convention for embedding assignments that is used by many, but by no means all, C programmers:

```
FILE *fp

if ((fp = fopen(notesfile, "a")) == NULL)
        fatal(pgm, notesfile, 1);
```

Don't let "convention" sway you, however. Use whichever form looks pleasing to your eye. Just be sure the statements are logically correct and that error conditions are checked and responded to in a reasonable way.

The *getchar( )* and *putc( )* calls are actually macros defined in *stdio.h.* These calls tend to work somewhat faster than the equivalent functions, *fgetchar( )* and *fputc( ),* because they expand to in-line code and eliminate the function-call overhead associated with true functions. However, if we had many calls to *putc( )* and *getchar( )* (which is just *getc( )* with *stdin* specified as the stream), we would save some space by using the functions because the code for the function only has to appear one time in the object file, rather than once for each call to the macros.

Rather than clutter this chapter with information that is available to you in the C compiler's *Library Reference Manual,* we'll just refer to that document (or the equivalent for other C compilers) for more details and move on to some other interesting topics that are essential to the development of our programs.

Process Control Functions

A process is an environment in which a program executes. When you run the NOTES.EXE program, for example, DOS allocates an *instruction* segment, a *user data* segment, and a *system data* segment. It then initializes the instruction and data segments from the program and starts execution.

The Microsoft C run-time library provides a group of functions for controlling the execution of processes from within a process. The easiest to use is *system( )*, which takes a program-name argument (may be a full or relative pathname) and runs the named program as a subprocess. When the subprocess terminates, control is returned to the calling process. The declaration of *system( )* is

```
#include <process.h>
int system(string);
char *string;
```

where the string argument is the name of a built-in DOS command or an external program that must be in the current directory or be accessible via the PATH variable. DOS must be able to find and load COMMAND.COM to service the *system( )* call. A return of −1 indicates an error.

A simple example of the *system( )* function in use is the following code fragment that calls a text editor from within a running process:

```
        .
        .
        .
if (system("EDIX") == -1) {
        perror("System error");
        /* error recovery procedure */
        .
        .
        .
}
```

An error return could be caused by the absence of a valid COMMAND.COM file or by the inability of DOS to find the EDIX.EXE file with the information provided by the *system( )* call plus the current value of PATH.

The *exec( )* and *spawn( )* families of process-control functions are more complicated to use, but they provide considerably more versatility. The two families have much in common and each has six members. The base function name—*exec,* for example—takes a one- or two-letter suffix to fully specify the function's behavior. Thus, the *exec( )* function names are *execl( ), execle( ), execlp( ), execv( ), execvp( ),* and *execve( ).* The symbols appended to the base function names have these meanings:

SUFFIX	MEANING
l	Uses a NULL-terminated list of arguments
v	Uses a variable list of arguments
e	Receives an environment pointer
p	Searches PATH to find program files

Rather than show all six function declarations for each of the families, we'll look at one representative function of each. Both of these functions automatically pass along a copy of the current environment to the child process. Here is the declaration for *execl( )*:

```
#include <process.h>
int execl(pathname, arg0, arg1, . . ., argn, NULL);
char *pathname;
char *arg0, *arg1, . . .,*argn;
```

The declaration for *spawnvp( )* is

```
#include <process.h>
int spawnvp(modeflag, pathname, argv);
int modeflag;
char *pathname;
char *argv[ ];
```

The *exec( )* family always overlays the current process (parent) with a new process (child) that destroys the parent, so it is impossible to return from an *exec( )* function call. The *spawn( )* family, however, runs the subprocess with an action determined by the *modeflag* parameter. A value of *P_WAIT* causes the parent process to suspend execution while the child runs. When the child process terminates, control is returned to the parent. A *spawn( )* call with a *modeflag* value of *P_OVERLAY* produces the same effect as the equivalent *exec( )* function call.

Arguments are handled differently for the fixed-list (l) and variable-list (v) versions of these functions. The fixed-list version is used when we know in advance how many arguments will be presented. We place a *NULL* argument after the last argument we want to pass, to tell the *exec( )* or *spawn( )* function that the list is complete. In the variable-list version of the functions, a pointer to an argument list is passed. The argument list is handled just like the *argv* of a program's *main( )* function, which was described earlier in this section.

The first argument in a fixed list (*arg0*) or a variable list (*argv[0]*) is usually a copy of the *pathname* argument. Other values will not cause an error, but *NULL* should not be used in the first position of a fixed list: The *NULL* would effectively hide the remainder of the list from the child process, since a *NULL* argument marks the end of the list. Recall that under DOS version 3.00 and later, the program name is available to the child as *arg0* or *argv[0]*.

Here is an example of the *spawnvp( )* function in action. It is used to run a text editor as a subprocess. If an EDITOR environment variable is defined, its string value is used as the program name. If EDITOR is not defined, NOTES uses the DOS EDLIN program. The editor is given the name of the current *notesfile* as an argument. This update to the NOTES program also adds an alternative way of terminating input (using a dot alone on a line like the UNIX *mail* program) and a way of ignoring the Ctrl-Break interrupt so that a user cannot garble the *NOTES.TXT* file by interrupting it in the middle of text entry.

```
/*
 *      notes2 -- add a date/time stamped entry to a
 *      "notes" data file.  Allow user to optionally
 *      edit the data file upon completion of the entry.
 */

#include <stdio.h>
#include <stdlib.h>
#include <time.h>
```

(continued)

```
#include <signal.h>
#include <process.h>
#include <local\std.h>

/* length of date/time string */
#define DT_STR   26

main(argc, argv)
int argc;
char **argv;
{
        int n;              /* number of lines added */
        int exitcode = 0;
        FILE *fp;
        static char notesfile[MAXPATH + 1] = { "notes.txt" };
        static char editname[MAXPATH + 1] = { "edlin" };
        char ch;
        char dt_stamp[DT_STR];
        char *s;
        long ltime;
        static char pgm[MAXNAME + 1] = { "notes2" };

        extern void fatal(char *, char *, int);
        extern void getpname(char *, char *);
        static int addtxt(FILE *, FILE *);

        if (_osmajor >= 3)
                getpname(*argv, pgm);

        /* locate the "notes" database file and open it */
        if (argc > 1)
                strcpy(notesfile, *++argv);
        else if (s = getenv("NOTESFILE"))
                strcpy(notesfile, s);
        if ((fp = fopen(notesfile, "a")) == NULL)
                fatal(pgm, notesfile, 1);

        /* disable Ctrl-Break interrupt */
        if (signal(SIGINT, SIG_IGN) == (int(*)())-1)
                perror("Cannot set signal");

        /* append a header and date/time tag */
        ltime = time(NULL);
```

(continued)

```
        strcpy(dt_stamp, ctime(&ltime));
        fprintf(stderr, "Appending to %s: %s", notesfile, dt_stamp);
        fprintf(fp, "\n%s", dt_stamp);

        /* add text to notes file */
        if ((n = addtxt(stdin, fp)) == 0) {
                fputs("No new text", stderr);
                if (fclose(fp))
                        fatal(pgm, notesfile, 2);
                exit(0);
        }
        else
                fprintf(stderr, "%d line(s) added to %s\n", n, notesfile);
        if (fclose(fp))
                fatal(pgm, notesfile, 2);

        /* optionally edit text in the notes file */
        fprintf(stderr, "E + ENTER to edit; ENTER alone to quit: ");
        while ((ch = tolower(getchar())) != '\n')
                if (ch == 'e') {
                        if (s = getenv("EDITOR"))
                                strcpy(editname, s);
                        if ((exitcode = spawnlp(P_WAIT, editname, editname,
                                        notesfile, NULL)) == -1)
                                fatal(pgm, editname, 3);
                }
        exit(exitcode);
}


/*
 *      addtxt -- append new text to notes file
 */
static int addtxt(fin, fout)
FILE *fin, *fout;
{
        int ch;
        int col = 0;    /* column */
        int n = 0;      /* number of lines added */

        while ((ch = fgetc(fin)) != EOF) {
                if (ch == '.' && col == 0) {
                        ch = fgetc(fin); /* trash the newline */
                        break;
```

(continued)

```
        }
        fputc(ch, fout);
        if (ch == '\n') {
                col = 0;
                ++n;
        }
        else
                ++col;
    }
    return (n);
}
```

The source listing for NOTES contains a few things we haven't shown before. First, the *signal()* function is used to disable the Ctrl-Break input from the keyboard. Since *signal()* returns a pointer value of −1 on errors instead of the usual *NULL*, we need to use the strange-looking cast of the value on the right side of the comparison. The *(int(*)())* −1 is needed because the C compiler expects a pointer to an integer.

Second, the dot (.) is used to terminate data input. This involves a slight complication. A dot usually does not occur in free text as the first character of a line, but it may occur anywhere else. We depend on this, and check that the current position is the beginning of a line and that the input character is a dot before terminating data entry.

Third, the EOF signal (a typed Ctrl-Z) may be used anywhere to halt data entry. It should, however, be used only on a line by itself. If *Ctrl-Z* is typed following some text on a line, some programs will not accept the line because it is not properly terminated. Programs should be written to handle this situation, but many insist that each line in a text file end with a CR/LF combination and may fail in unpredictable ways if a line dead-ends without the expected termination.

The next program, *RUN_ONCE*, is a bit of a novelty, but it has a purpose in some restricted circumstances. Let's say you have an office setting in which computer users with very limited experience are expected to run a single program, perhaps an integrated database-spreadsheet-word processor-blender-and-kitchen-sink program. You want the system to come up running this program and you also want to prevent the users from exiting to DOS. If they quit the catchall program, the *RUN_ONCE* program tells them to turn off the power and then it locks up the machine.

```
/*
 *      run_once -- run a program one time and then
 *      "hang" the system to prevent unwanted use
 */

#include <stdio.h>
#include <stdlib.h>
#include <process.h>
#include <local\std.h>

main(argc, argv)
int argc;
char *argv[];
{
        extern void fatal(char *, char *, int);

        ++argv;         /* skip over the program name */

        /* run the specified command line [pgmname arg(s)] */
        if (spawnvp(P_WAIT, *argv, argv) == -1)
                fatal("run_once", "Error running specified program", 1);
        fprintf(stderr, "Please turn off the power to the computer.\n");

        FOREVER         /* do nothing */
                ;
}
```

After compiling this program, try running it on your favorite text editor or some other program. For example,

```
run_once word myfile.doc
```

loads and executes the *RUN_ONCE* program, which spawns Microsoft Word with MYFILE.DOC as an argument. When the user quits Word, the system displays the exit message and appears to be dead. A reboot is required to restart the system. If the *RUN_ONCE* program is embedded in the AUTOEXEC.BAT file, it will prevent the users from doing anything except what is planned for them by whoever sets up the system. (This is easily defeated by someone who knows DOS. All that is required is to load a floppy disk with another copy of DOS that does not have the *RUN_ONCE* program installed. But someone who knows this probably knows how to use DOS anyway.)

Other Library Functions

We have barely scratched the surface of the standard run-time library provided with the Microsoft C compiler. Our purpose has been to describe some representative library routines and to illustrate their use in real programs. As we develop programmer's utilities and other programs in the remainder of this book, we will introduce more of these routines in context.

The functions and macros we have looked at so far are portable, with little or no change, to various versions of DOS and to UNIX-based operating systems. The next chapter delves into functions that are tied intimately to DOS and are therefore not easily ported to other operating environments. Although they lack portability, the functions are important for programs that need to obtain the highest level of performance possible from a PC.

PC Operating System Interfaces 5

For me, one of the joys of working with a personal computer, after having spent years working on time-sharing systems over slow-speed data lines, is the incredible responsiveness of the PC in terms of screen updates. To "paint" a 24-line screen at 9600 bps (bits per second) typically takes about 4 seconds—not too bad, really. But at the more common 1200 bps used by most dial-up connections, a complete paint job takes closer to 16 seconds. Paging through a document or a source list at this speed becomes a bit of a chore, and one quickly learns how to use regular expression searches, small window sizes, and other tricks to minimize the time it takes to find the material of interest.

In contrast, using one of the slowest methods available on a PC, the DOS print-character function call, painting a full 25-line screen takes only about 4 seconds. By using BIOS routines intelligently, one often can do the job in less than half a second. Using direct screen access, the updates become virtually instantaneous. The PC has spoiled me, and it is really hard to go back to dial-up operations: It feels like the whole world has been put into slow motion.

In this chapter, we'll explore methods of managing screen displays via the DOS and BIOS interrupt services. The methods used here are not portable to UNIX and XENIX, and the BIOS routines are not even guaranteed to be portable to some nominally IBM-compatible hardware.

This material is presented to acquaint you with some of the techniques used in commercial-quality programs. The mark of such programs is how well they serve the user's needs. Among the needs I hear most often expressed, the following are related to screen and system configuration:

▶ The program must work on any compatible machine, regardless of the configuration (disks, display type, and so forth).

▶ The screen must be updated quickly—no growing old waiting around for the next frame.

▶ If both color/graphics and monochrome display systems are installed, it must be possible to choose which to use.

▶ There must be no flickering, blizzard effect, or other visual "noise" at any time.

Using DOS and BIOS routines, we can satisfy these needs almost completely. Only the first one is a problem because some machines were designed in a way that limits their BIOS compatibility. As a developer, I want to maximize the audience, so I address such machines by using the ANSI device driver, which is covered in Chapter 13.

The routines in this chapter cover needed functions that are not already handled by the standard run-time library, with a few exceptions. In those few cases, a function is presented that duplicates a system function because that function may not be available in the library of other C compilers. A case in point is *kbhit( )*: The function *keyready( )* performs the same function for those whose libraries don't have *kbhit( )* available.

We begin with an overview of the DOS and BIOS access routines in the standard library. These routines are the low-level access functions upon which our interface routines are built. Then we will write a program that shows how to use many of the routines we develop. The routines presented here are not a complete set; they are the high-use routines that we will need shortly. Other routines will be added to the DOS and BIOS libraries as we need them in later chapters.

System Interface Functions

The C run-time library provided with Microsoft C contains several low-level system-access functions. We will use three of them as a basis for our DOS and BIOS interfaces: *bdos( )*, *int86( )*, and *intdos( )*.

The functions *int86x( )* and *intdosx()* are used in programs that use long addresses. They behave just like their *int86( )* and *intdos( )* counterparts, but they take an additional argument that specifies segment registers used in forming long addresses. The segment register values can be obtained by using the *segread( )* function.

The file *dos.h* in the *include* directory contains several structure and union definitions that are needed by the system access functions. If you are not comfortable using C unions, here is a good example of how they may be used.

```
/*
 * dos.h
 *
 * Defines the structs and unions used to handle the input and output
 * registers for the DOS interface routines defined in the V2.0 to V3.0
 * compatibility package.  It also includes macros to access the segment
 * and offset values of MS C "far" pointers, so that they may be used by
 * these routines.
 *
 * Copyright (C) Microsoft Corporation, 1984, 1985, 1986
 */


/* word registers */

struct WORDREGS {
        unsigned int ax;
        unsigned int bx;
        unsigned int cx;
        unsigned int dx;
        unsigned int si;
        unsigned int di;
        unsigned int cflag;
        };


/* byte registers */

struct BYTEREGS {
        unsigned char al, ah;
        unsigned char bl, bh;
        unsigned char cl, ch;
        unsigned char dl, dh;
        };
```

(continued)

```
/* general purpose registers union - overlays the corresponding word and
 * byte registers.
 */

union REGS {
        struct WORDREGS x;
        struct BYTEREGS h;
        };

/* segment registers */

struct SREGS {
        unsigned int es;
        unsigned int cs;
        unsigned int ss;
        unsigned int ds;
        };

/* dosexterror struct */

struct DOSERROR {
        int exterror;
        char class;
        char action;
        char locus;
        };

/* macros to break MS C "far" pointers into their segment and offset
 * components
 */

#define FP_SEG(fp) (*((unsigned *)&(fp) + 1))
#define FP_OFF(fp) (*((unsigned *)&(fp)))

/* function declarations for those who want strong type checking
 * on arguments to library function calls
 */

#ifdef LINT_ARGS        /* argument checking enabled */

#ifndef NO_EXT_KEYS     /* extended keywords are enabled */
int cdecl bdos(int, unsigned int, unsigned int);
int cdecl dosexterr(struct DOSERROR *);
```

(continued)

```
int cdecl intdos(union REGS *, union REGS *);
int cdecl intdosx(union REGS *, union REGS *, struct SREGS *);
int cdecl int86(int, union REGS *, union REGS *);
int cdecl int86x(int, union REGS *, union REGS *, struct SREGS *);
void cdecl segread(struct SREGS *);
#else                     /* extended keywords not enabled */
int bdos(int, unsigned int, unsigned int);
int dosexterr(struct DOSERROR *);
int intdos(union REGS *, union REGS *);
int intdosx(union REGS *, union REGS *, struct SREGS *);
int int86(int, union REGS *, union REGS *);
int int86x(int, union REGS *, union REGS *, struct SREGS *);
void segread(struct SREGS *);
#endif  /* NO_EXT_KEYS */


#else

#ifndef NO_EXT_KEYS      /* extended keywords are enabled */
int cdecl bdos();
int cdecl dosexterr();
int cdecl intdos();
int cdecl intdosx();
int cdecl int86();
int cdecl int86x();
void cdecl segread();
#else                     /* extended keywords not enabled */
void segread();
#endif  /* NO_EXT_KEYS */

#endif  /* LINT_ARGS */
```

The header file defines two structures for the CPU registers and flags.
The first is *struct WORDREGS:*

```
/* word registers */

struct WORDREGS {
        unsigned int ax;
        unsigned int bx;
        unsigned int cx;
        unsigned int dx;
        unsigned int si;
        unsigned int di;
        unsigned int cflag;
        };
```

The second structure is *struct BYTEREGS:*

```
/* byte registers */

struct BYTEREGS {
        unsigned char al, ah;
        unsigned char bl, bh;
        unsigned char cl, ch;
        unsigned char dl, dh;
        };
```

A composite word/byte register data structure is made by overlaying the two structures, like this:

```
/* general purpose registers union - overlays the corresponding word and
 * byte registers.
 */

union REGS {
        struct WORDREGS x;
        struct BYTEREGS h;
        };
```

The union *REGS* lets us access the registers either as bytes (AL, AH, and so on) or as words (AX, BX, and so on). We can also access the system carry flag as a word register. It is unfortunate that we don't have similar access to the zero flag.

Now that we have the data structures in mind (or at least on paper), we can examine the primary system-access routines. Each is presented here with a manual-page summary and a brief description. In the next two sections, we will apply these functions to the task of creating our DOS and BIOS libraries. Any file that calls the following functions must include the header file *dos.h* by using the line

    #include <dos.h>

Here are the system-level functions:

```
int bdos(dosfn, dosdx, dosal);
int dosfn;                       /* function number */
unsigned int dosdx;              /* DX register value */
unsigned int dosal;              /* AL register value */
```

The *bdos( )* function is a DOS function interface that loads the DX and AL registers with values provided by the caller and then executes an INT 21H. Following the DOS function call, the value of the AX register is returned to the caller.

The uses of *bdos( )* are limited to DOS function calls that take arguments in either or both of the DX and AL registers (or none at all) and that do not use the carry flag to indicate errors. To minimize function-call overhead, we will use *bdos( )* in some keyboard functions and recommend its use for macros or for in-line code within a program.

```
int int86(intno, inregs, outregs);
int intno;                      /* interrupt number */
union REGS *inregs;             /* register values on call */
union REGS *outregs;            /* register values on return */
```

The *int86( )* function is a general-purpose interface routine that gives us nearly complete access to the full range of software interrupts. The function sets up the registers according to the caller's wishes and executes the specified interrupt. Upon return from the function call, *int86( )* fills *outregs* with the current register values and the value of the system carry flag, which will have a nonzero value if an error has occurred.

We will use *int86( )* to call BIOS routines for video and keyboard access and to check equipment and memory information. We also could use it to access DOS functions, but *intdos( )* does the job faster.

```
int intdos(inregs, outregs);
union REGS *inregs;             /* register values on call */
union REGS *outregs;            /* registers values on return */
```

The *intdos( )* function is just like the *int86( )* function except that it is designed to make DOS function calls directly and does not require an interrupt number. The INT 21H interrupt number is effectively hard-coded into *intdos( )*. The same input and output register behavior is observed as for *int86( )*.

The declaration of the register arguments to *int86( )* and *intdos( )* shows them as pointers. The union and structure definitions in *dos.h* do not reserve storage; they simply describe the needed storage requirements. We must declare storage in our routines by a statement like

union REGS *inregs, outregs;*

This statement allocates automatic storage for the unions. We then can load values into *inregs*, make the needed function call, and extract data from *outregs*. (There is nothing sacred about the names *inregs* and *outregs*. Use anything that seems appropriate, but ideally the names should be descriptive.) The *int86( )* and *intdos( )* functions need the addresses of the unions. A call to *intdos( )* looks like this:

```
intdos(&inregs, &outregs);
```

We can access elements of the structures either as bytes or as words. To load a value into AL, for example, we use the byte-oriented approach:

```
inregs.h.al = value;
```

To read the results of a function from the DX register, we use the word-oriented approach:

```
value = outregs.x.dx;
```

Next, we will put these system-level library functions to work for us in two important libraries in our growing collection of function libraries.

DOS Library Routines

The DOS library is composed of only a few routines that supplement the standard run-time library, which is very complete in its coverage of disk, keyboard, date/time, and many other functions. The routines presented here are primarily for the benefit of those who are using C compilers with libraries that do not fully support the DOS interface.

A local header file, *doslib.h,* contains constants used to specify DOS interrupts and the function numbers for calls to INT 21H, the DOS "umbrella" interrupt.

```
/*
 *      doslib.h
 */

/* DOS interrupts */
#define PGM_TERMINATE   0x20
#define BDOS_REQ        0x21
#define TERMINATE_ADDR  0x22
#define CB_EXIT_ADDR    0x23
```

(continued)

```
#define CRITICAL_ERR      0x24
#define ABS_DISK_READ     0x25
#define ABS_DISK_WRITE    0x26
#define PGM_TERM_RES      0x27

/* DOS functions -- usually placed in ah register for C86 calls */
#define PGM               0x0
#define KEYIN_ECHO_CB     0x1
#define DSPY_CHAR         0x2
#define AUX_IN            0x3
#define AUX_OUT           0x4
#define PRNT_OUT          0x5
#define KEYIN_ECHO        0x6
#define KEYIN             0x7
#define KEYIN_CB          0x8
#define DSPY_STR          0x9
#define KEYIN_BUF         0xA
#define CH_READY          0xB
#define GET_CH            0xC
#define DISK_RESET        0xD
#define SELECT_DISK       0xE
#define OPEN_FILE         0xF
#define CLOSE_FILE        0x10
#define FIRST_FM          0x11
#define NEXT_FM           0x12
#define DELETE_FILE       0x13
#define READ_SEQ          0x14
#define WRITE_SEQ         0x15
#define CREATE_FILE       0x16
#define RENAME_FILE       0x17
        /* 0x18 reserved */
#define CURRENT_DISK      0x19
#define SET_DTA           0x1A
#define DFLT_FAT_INFO     0x1B
#define FAT_INFO          0x1C
        /* 0x1D - 0x20 reserved */
#define READ_RANDOM       0x21
#define WRITE_RANDOM      0x22
#define FILE_SIZE         0x23
#define SET_INT_VEC       0x25
#define NEW_PGM_SEG       0x26
#define RAND_BLK_READ     0x27
```

(continued)

```
#define RAND_BLK_WRITE    0x28
#define PARSE_FILENAME    0x29
#define GET_DATE          0x2A
#define SET_DATE          0x2B
#define GET_TIME          0x2C
#define SET_TIME          0x2D
#define TOGGLE_VERIFY     0x2E
#define GET_DTA           0c2F
#define DOS_VERSION       0x30
#define PGM_TERM_KEEP     0x31
        /* 0x32 reserved */
#define CB_CHECK          0x33
        /* 0x34 reserved */
#define GET_INTR          0x35
#define GET_FREE_SPACE    0x36
        /* 0x37 reserved */
#define INTL_INFO         0x38
#define MKDIR             0x39
#define RMDIR             0x3A
#define CHDIR             0x3B
#define CREAT             0x3C
#define OPEN_FD           0x3D
#define CLOSE_FD          0x3E
#define WRITE_FD          0x40
#define UNLINK            0x41
#define LSEEK             0x42
#define CHMOD             0x43
#define IOCTL             0x44
#define DUP               0x45
#define FORCE_DUP         0x46
#define GET_CUR_DIR       0x47
#define ALLOC             0x48
#define FREE              0x49
#define SET_BLOCK         0x4A
#define EXEC              0x4B
#define EXIT              0x4C
#define WAIT              0x4D
#define FIND_FIRST        0x4E
#define FIND_NEXT         0x4F
        /* 0x50 - 53 reserved */
#define VERIFY_STATE      0x54
        /* 0x55 reserved */
#define RENAME            0x56
#define FILE_MTIME        0x57
```

(continued)

DOS Version Number

Under Microsoft C, the header file *stdlib.h* defines the global variables _osmajor and _osminor. These variables receive the DOS major and minor version numbers when a program starts running. The numbers may be used to verify that the version of DOS is capable of supporting features required by a program. For example, programs that use pathnames require DOS version 2.00 or later. The simple block of code added to the program provides low-cost insurance and alerts the user that it's time to upgrade.

```
if (_osmajor < 2) {
        fprintf(stderr, "Need DOS 2.00 or later\n");
        exit(1);
}
```

Another way to get the version number is to ask DOS for the number. The function *ver( )* does the job.

```
/*      ver -- get the MS-DOS (or PC-DOS) version number      */

#include <local\doslib.h>

/****************************************************************************
 * For MS-DOS versions prior to 2.00, the low byte (AL) of the return value is zero.
 * For versions 2.00 and beyond, the low byte is the major version number and the
 * high byte (AH) is the minor version number.
 ***************************************************************************/

int ver()
{
        return(bdos(DOS_VERSION, 0, 0));
}
```

The *ver( )* function uses *bdos( )* to get the version number from DOS. It returns the return value from *bdos( )*, which is the value in the AX register. AL holds the major version number and AH holds the minor version number. For versions of DOS prior to version 2.00, the returned major number is 0.

Keyboard Functions

The run-time library includes a couple of functions that read from and test the keyboard buffer. This section presents some alternative functions that do essentially the same jobs and which can easily be modified for use with other compilers.

To gather the user's input, we can call the run-time library function *getch()*. It reads the next available character from the keyboard buffer and responds to a Ctrl-Break. If there is nothing ready to read, it waits until there is. This operation is called a "blocking read" because the machine simply marks time while waiting for the user to type something. If the user presses Ctrl-Break, *getch()* executes the Ctrl-Break handler.

The function *getkey()* also does a blocking read. However, it differs from *getch()* in a few ways. First, it ignores Ctrl-Break. This prevents a user from breaking out of a program at a critical point that might damage files or data stored in memory. Second, *getkey()* checks the value of the keyboard code. If the code is a null byte ($\backslash 0$), it gets the next character code, bitwise-ORs it with 0x100 (which has the same effect as adding 256), and returns the modified value. This value can be compared against the constants that are defined in *keydefs.h* to determine what key was pressed. The defined values include most of the keys and combinations of keys on the keyboard.

Here is the source code for *keydefs.h*:

```
/*      keydefs -- values for special keys on IBM PC and clones      */

#define XF       0x100      /* extended key flag */

#define K_F1     59 | XF    /* function keys */
#define K_F2     60 | XF
#define K_F3     61 | XF
#define K_F4     62 | XF
#define K_F5     63 | XF
#define K_F6     64 | XF
#define K_F7     65 | XF
#define K_F8     66 | XF
#define K_F9     67 | XF
#define K_F10    68 | XF
```

(continued)

```
#define K_SF1    84 | XF        /* shifted function keys */
#define K_SF2    85 | XF
#define K_SF3    86 | XF
#define K_SF4    87 | XF
#define K_SF5    88 | XF
#define K_SF6    89 | XF
#define K_SF7    90 | XF
#define K_SF8    91 | XF
#define K_SF9    92 | XF
#define K_SF10   93 | XF

#define K_CF1    94 | XF        /* control function keys */
#define K_CF2    95 | XF
#define K_CF3    96 | XF
#define K_CF4    97 | XF
#define K_CF5    98 | XF
#define K_CF6    99 | XF
#define K_CF7   100 | XF
#define K_CF8   101 | XF
#define K_CF9   102 | XF
#define K_CF10  103 | XF

#define K_AF1   104 | XF        /* alternate function keys */
#define K_AF2   105 | XF
#define K_AF3   106 | XF
#define K_AF4   107 | XF
#define K_AF5   108 | XF
#define K_AF6   109 | XF
#define K_AF7   110 | XF
#define K_AF8   111 | XF
#define K_AF9   112 | XF
#define K_AF10  113 | XF

#define K_HOME   71 | XF        /* cursor keypad (NumLock off; not shifted) */
#define K_END    79 | XF
#define K_PGUP   73 | XF
#define K_PGDN   81 | XF
#define K_LEFT   75 | XF
#define K_RIGHT  77 | XF
#define K_UP     72 | XF
#define K_DOWN   80 | XF
```

(continued)

```
#define K_CHOME 119 | XF        /* control cursor keypad */
#define K_CEND  117 | XF
#define K_CPGUP 132 | XF
#define K_CPGDN 118 | XF
#define K_CLEFT 115 | XF
#define K_CRGHT 116 | XF


#define K_CTRLA 1              /* standard control keys */
#define K_CTRLB 2
#define K_CTRLC 3
#define K_CTRLD 4
#define K_CTRLE 5
#define K_CTRLF 6
#define K_CTRLG 7
#define K_CTRLH 8
#define K_CTRLI 9
#define K_CTRLJ 10
#define K_CTRLK 11
#define K_CTRLL 12
#define K_CTRLM 13
#define K_CTRLN 14
#define K_CTRLO 15
#define K_CTRLP 16
#define K_CTRLQ 17
#define K_CTRLR 18
#define K_CTRLS 19
#define K_CTRLT 20
#define K_CTRLU 21
#define K_CTRLV 22
#define K_CTRLW 23
#define K_CTRLX 24
#define K_CTRLY 25
#define K_CTRLZ 26


#define K_ALTA  30 | XF        /* alternate keys */
#define K_ALTB  48 | XF
#define K_ALTC  46 | XF
#define K_ALTD  32 | XF
#define K_ALTE  18 | XF
#define K_ALTF  33 | XF
#define K_ALTG  34 | XF
#define K_ALTH  35 | XF
#define K_ALTI  23 | XF
```

(continued)

```
#define K_ALTJ   36 | XF
#define K_ALTK   37 | XF
#define K_ALTL   38 | XF
#define K_ALTM   50 | XF
#define K_ALTN   49 | XF
#define K_ALTO   24 | XF
#define K_ALTP   25 | XF
#define K_ALTQ   16 | XF
#define K_ALTR   19 | XF
#define K_ALTS   31 | XF
#define K_ALTT   20 | XF
#define K_ALTU   22 | XF
#define K_ALTV   47 | XF
#define K_ALTW   17 | XF
#define K_ALTX   45 | XF
#define K_ALTY   21 | XF
#define K_ALTZ   44 | XF

#define K_ALT1        120 | XF  /* additional alternate key combinations */
#define K_ALT2        121 | XF
#define K_ALT3        122 | XF
#define K_ALT4        123 | XF
#define K_ALT5        124 | XF
#define K_ALT6        125 | XF
#define K_ALT7        126 | XF
#define K_ALT8        127 | XF
#define K_ALT9        128 | XF
#define K_ALT0        129 | XF
#define K_ALTDASH     130 | XF
#define K_ALTEQU      131 | XF

#define K_ESC         27        /* miscellaneous special keys */
#define K_SPACE       32
#define K_INS         82 | XF
#define K_DEL         83 | XF
#define K_TAB         K_CTRLI
#define K_BACKTAB     K_CTRLO

#define K_CTRL_PRTSC  114 | XF  /* printer echoing toggle */

#define K_RETURN      13        /* return key variations */
#define K_SRETURN     13
#define K_CRETURN     10
```

This is the source code for *getkey( )*:

```
/*      getkey -- return a code for single combo keystrokes
 *      - returns a unique code for each keystroke or combination
 *      - ignores "Ctrl-Break" input      */

#include <dos.h>
#include <local\std.h>
#include <local\doslib.h>
#include <local\keydefs.h>

int getkey()
{
        int ch;

        /* normal key codes */
        if ((ch = bdos(KEYIN, 0, 0) & LOBYTE) != '\0')
                return (ch);

        /* convert scan codes to unique internal codes */
        return ((bdos(KEYIN, 0, 0) & LOBYTE) | XF);
}
```

To determine whether a key has been pressed, we would use the run-time library function *kbhit( )*, which returns a nonzero value if a code is available in the keyboard buffer, indicating that at least one key has been pressed. The function *keyready( )*, presented next, does the same job.

```
/*      keyready -- non-zero if the keyboard buffer has any codes waiting      */

#include <dos.h>
#include <local\doslib.h>

int keyready()
{
        union REGS inregs, outregs;

        inregs.h.ah = CH_READY;
        intdos(&inregs, &outregs);
        return (outregs.h.al);
}
```

The *kbhit( )* or *keyready( )* function should be called *before* an attempt is made to read the keyboard. This produces a "nonblocking read." If nothing is ready, the program can do something useful while it waits for the user to press a key. That something should be broken up into brief allocations of work (i.e., sending a character to the printer), so that the keyboard provides a timely response to user input. There is, however, no good reason to put the entire computer to sleep waiting for user input. The following code fragment shows a way to handle keyboard processing and a background task:

```
.
.
.
int k, getkey(), keyready();    /* keyboard functions */
int do_task(TASK);              /* task dispatcher */
TASK taskp;                     /* task pointer */
.
.
.
while (1) {
        /* get user's input */
        if (keyready()) {
                k = getkey();
                switch (k) {
                case K_ESC:
                        do_exit();
                .
                .
                .
                }
        /* do background task */
        do_task(taskp);
}
.
.
.
```

For example, if the task dispatcher is calling a routine that dumps characters into a printer spooling buffer, the printer appears to run continuously while not burdening the main program at all. User commands and input will be honored immediately. Other background tasks might include doing a hard disk-to-tape backup, checking timed alarms, and running a sprinkler system.

The makefile, *dos.mk*, automatically builds the library *dos.lib*:

```
# makefile for the DOS library
LINC = c:\include\local
LLIB = c:\lib\local

# --- inference rules ---
.c.obj:
        msc $*;

# --- objects ---
OBJS = getkey.obj keyready.obj ver.obj

# --- compile sources ---
getkey.obj:      getkey.c $(LINC)\std.h $(LINC)\doslib.h $(LINC)\keydefs.h

keyready.obj:    keyready.c $(LINC)\doslib.h

ver.obj:         ver.c $(LINC)\doslib.h

# --- create and install the library ---
$(LLIB)\dos.lib: $(OBJS)
        del $(LLIB)\dos.lib
        lib $(LLIB)\dos +$(OBJS);
```

BIOS Library Routines

The ROM BIOS in a PC offers a wide range of services that we can use to our advantage. We will write routines that let us determine how the host computer is configured, control the cursor, check the status of special keyboard keys (such as Caps Lock and Num Lock), and read and write characters and video attributes anywhere on the screen.

The header file *bioslib.h* contains the constants needed to call various BIOS interrupts and services by symbolic names.

```
/*      bioslib.h      */

#define PRINT_SCRN      0x05    /* BIOS interrupts */
#define TOD_INIT        0x08
#define KEYBD_INIT      0x09
```

(continued)

```
#define DISK_INIT          0x0E
#define VIDEO_IO           0x10
#define EQUIP_CK           0x11
#define MEM_SIZE           0x12
#define DISK_IO            0x13
#define RS232_IO           0x14
#define CASS_IO            0x15
#define KEYBD_IO           0x16
#define PRINT_IO           0x17
#define TOD                0x1A
#define VIDEO_INIT         0x1D
#define GRAPHICS           0x1F


#define SET_MODE           0        /* video routine numbers */
#define CUR_TYPE           1        /* (placed in register AH before a BIOS interrupt 10H */
#define CUR_POS            2
#define GET_CUR            3
#define LPEN_POS           4
#define SET_PAGE           5
#define SCROLL_UP          6
#define SCROLL_DN          7
#define READ_CHAR_ATTR     8
#define WRITE_CHAR_ATTR    9
#define WRITE_CHAR         10
#define PALETTE            11
#define WRITE_DOT          12
#define READ_DOT           13
#define WRITE_TTY          14
#define GET_STATE          15
#define ALT_FUNCTION       18       /* EGA only */
#define WRITE_STR          19       /* AT only */


#define RESET_DISK         0        /* disk routine numbers */
#define DISK_STATUS        1
#define READ_SECTOR        2
#define WRITE_SECTOR       3
#define VERIFY_SECTOR      4
#define FORMAT_TRACK       5


#define KBD_READ           0        /* keyboard routine numbers */
#define KBD_READY          1
#define KBD_STATUS         2
```

Equipment Determination Functions

We'll start with a pair of functions that help us determine what equipment is installed in a PC and how much memory it has.

The first of these functions, *equipchk( )*, uses BIOS interrupt 11H to determine what devices are installed. A structure is used to hold the data obtained by *equipchk( )*, which declares the structure globally and fills it when called. Other functions can also access the data if they contain the following external definition:

```
extern struct EQUIP Eq;
```

Here is the source code for *equip.h* and *equipchk( )*.

```
/*      equip.h -- header for equipment determination/inventory      */


struct EQUIP {
        short   disksys,        /* 1 if disks installed */
                game_io,        /* 1 if game i/o adapter installed */
                nprint,         /* number of printer ports */
                nrs232,         /* number of serial ports */
                vmode,          /* initial video mode (from switches) */
                ndrive,         /* number of disk drives (from switches) */
                basemem;        /* amount of base memory in Kbytes */
};
```

```
/*      equipchk -- get equipment list      */

#include <dos.h>
#include <local\bioslib.h>
#include <local\equip.h>

struct EQUIP Eq;

int equipchk()
{
        union REGS inregs, outregs;

        /* call BIOS equipment check routine */
        int86(EQUIP_CK, &inregs, &outregs);
        /* extract data from returned data word */
        Eq.nprint = (outregs.x.ax & 0xC000) / 0x8000;
```

(continued)

```
        Eq.game_io = ((outregs.x.ax & 0x1000) / 0x1000) ? 1 : 0;
        Eq.nrs232  = (outregs.x.ax & 0x0E00) /0x0200;
        Eq.ndrive  = ((outregs.x.ax & 0x00C0) / 0x0040) + 1;
        Eq.vmode   = (outregs.x.ax & 0x0030) / 0x0010;
        Eq.basemem = ((outregs.x.ax & 0x000C) / 0x0004) + 1;
        Eq.disksys = outregs.x.ax & 0x0001 == 1;
        return (outregs.x.cflag);
}
```

To find out whether a game port is installed, call *equipchk( )* and then look at the *game_io* member of the structure.

```
#include <local\equip.h>
extern struct EQUIP Eq;
        .
        .
        .
if (equipchk())
        /* handle the error */;
if (Eq.game_io == 1)
        printf("Game adapter installed\n");
```

Although *equipchk( )* can tell us how much memory is installed on the main system board, it cannot help us get the total installed memory value. The *memsize( )* function calls BIOS interrupt 12H to get the system memory size, including any memory in the I/O channel on adapter cards (exclusive of display memory and that which is not contiguous with the main system-board memory).

```
/*      memsize -- get memory size      */

#include <dos.h>
#include <local\std.h>
#include <local\bioslib.h>

int memsize()
{
        union REGS inregs, outregs;

        return (int86(MEM_SIZE, &inregs, &outregs));
}
```

The size of main memory is reported as a 16-bit integer that represents the total number of kilobytes found.

Keyboard Status

Older PC keyboards did not have status lights on the Caps Lock
and Num Lock keys. It is helpful to the user if the status of these keys is
reported on the screen in applications in which the status is important.
The same holds true for the Ins key and, in some situations, the Scroll
Lock key. Also, we can use the status of the Shift, Ctrl, and Alt keys to alter the meaning of the function keys to do other jobs.

The *kbd_stat( )* function lets us obtain the needed information. It
calls BIOS interrupt 16H, service 2 (status), and returns the value of the AL
register. The header file *keybdlib.h* contains definitions of masks that are
used to test the return value from *kbd_stat( )* to determine which keys
were pressed.

```
/*       keybdlib.h       */


#define KBD_READ         0           /* keyboard routine numbers */
#define KBD_READY        1
#define KBD_STATUS       2


#define KS_RSHIFT        0x0001   /* bit masks for keys and states */
#define KS_LSHIFT        0x0002
#define KS_CONTROL       0x0004
#define KS_ALT           0x0008
#define KS_SL_STATE      0x0010
#define KS_NL_STATE      0x0020
#define KS_CL_STATE      0x0040
#define KS_INS_STATE     0x0080
```

```
/*       kbd_stat -- return the keyboard status word (bit-significant)       */

#include <dos.h>
#include <local\bioslib.h>
#include <local\keybdlib.h>


unsigned char kbd_stat()
{
        union REGS inregs, outregs;
```

(continued)

```
        inregs.h.ah = KBD_STATUS;
        int86(KEYBD_IO, &inregs, &outregs);
        return ((unsigned char)(outregs.h.al));
}
```

Video Access

One of the most frequently used ROM BIOS interrupts is 10H, the access point for video services. We will use many of these services in our programs.

The header file *video.h* contains some data structures used to hold important video-mode and cursor data. It also contains definitions of color and attribute values, special and drawing-character codes, and constants used by the mode and cursor structures.

```
/*      video.h     */

/* current video state/mode information */
extern short Vmode;
extern short Vwidth;
extern short Vpage;

#define MAXVMODE  17

/* video limit tables */
extern short Maxrow[MAXVMODE];
extern short Maxcol[MAXVMODE];
extern short Maxpage[MAXVMODE];

/* active display */
#define MONO    1
#define COLOR   2

/* cursor modes */
#define CURSOR_OFF      0
#define CURSOR_ON       1

/* installed display adapters */
#define MDA     1
#define CGA     2
#define EGA     4
```

(continued)

```
/* --- video modes --- */
/* CGA modes */
#define CGA_M40        0
#define CGA_C40        1
#define CGA_M80        2
#define CGA_C80        3
#define CGA_CMRES      4
#define CGA_MMRES      5
#define CGA_MHRES      6
/* MDA mode */
#define MDA_M80        7
/* PCjr modes */
#define PCJR_CLRES     8
#define PCJR_CMRES     9
#define PCJR_CHRES     10
/* modes 11 and 12 are not currently used */
/* EGA modes */
#define EGA_CMRES      13
#define EGA_CHRES      14
#define EGA_MHRES      15
#define EGA_EHRES      16


/* miscellaneous video masks */
#define CMASK   0x00FF    /* character mask */
#define AMASK   0xFF00    /* attribute mask */


/* attribute modifiers */
#define BRIGHT 8
#define BLINK  128


/* primary video attributes */
#define BLU    1
#define GRN    2
#define RED    4


/* composite video attributes */
#define BLK      0
#define CYAN    (BLU | GRN)            /* 3 */
#define MAGENTA (BLU | RED)           /* 5 */
#define BRN     (GRN | RED)           /* 6 */
#define WHT     (BLU | GRN | RED)     /* 7 */
#define GRAY    (BLK | BRIGHT)
#define LBLU    (BLU | BRIGHT)
```

(continued)

```
#define LGRN     (GRN | BRIGHT)
#define LCYAN    (CYAN | BRIGHT)
#define LRED     (RED | BRIGHT)
#define LMAG     (MAG | BRIGHT)
#define YEL      (BRN | BRIGHT)
#define BWHT     (WHT | BRIGHT)
#define NORMAL   WHT
#define REVERSE 112


/*      drawing characters -- items having two numbers use
 *      the first number as the horizontal specifier       */


/* single-line boxes */
#define VBAR1    179
#define VLINE    179     /* alias */
#define HBAR1    196
#define HLINE    196     /* alias */
#define ULC11    218
#define URC11    191
#define LLC11    192
#define LRC11    217
#define TL11     195
#define TR11     180
#define TT11     194
#define TB11     193
#define X11      197


/* double-line boxes */
#define VBAR2    186
#define HBAR2    205
#define ULC22    201
#define URC22    187
#define LLC22    200
#define LRC22    188
#define TL22     204
#define TR22     185
#define TT22     203
#define TB22     202
#define X22      206


/* single-line horizontal & double-line vertical boxes */
#define ULC12    214
#define URC12    183
```

(continued)

```
#define LLC12    211
#define LRC12    189
#define TL12     199
#define TR12     182
#define TT12     210
#define TB12     208
#define X12      215


/* double-line horizontal & single-line vertical boxes */
#define ULC21    213
#define URC21    184
#define LLC21    212
#define LRC21    190
#define TL21     198
#define TR21     181
#define TT21     209
#define TB21     207
#define X21      216


/* full and partial blocks */
#define BLOCK    219
#define VBAR     219     /* alias */
#define VBARL    221
#define VBARR    222
#define HBART    223
#define HBARB    220


/* special character-graphic symbols */
#define BLANK         32
#define DIAMOND       4
#define UPARROW       24
#define DOWNARROW     25
#define RIGHTARROW    26
#define LEFTARROW     27
#define SLASH         47
```

The primary functions in interrupt 10H are those used to get the current video state data (mode, screen width, and visual page) and to set the video mode.

The *getstate( )* function invokes video service 15 to get the values of the video mode, the screen width (redundant information, because the mode number implies a width, but screen width is directly accessible), and the visual page number. Although the IBM Technical Reference manual calls this the *active* page, it is really the *visual* page. To be consistent with the way BASIC defines pages, the active page is defined as the one being written to and the visual page as the one being viewed. The page number returned by service 15 is the visual page. Most of the time, the visual and active page numbers are the same.

```
/*      getstate -- update video state structure      */

#include <dos.h>
#include <local\std.h>
#include <local\bioslib.h>

/* current video state/mode information */
short Vmode;
short Vwidth;
short Vpage;

/*      video tables -- these tables of video parameters use a value of -1
 *      to indicate that an item is not supported and 0 to indicate that an
 *      item has a variable value.      */

/* video limit tables */
short Maxrow[] = {
        25, 25, 25, 25, 25, 25, 25,     /* CGA modes */
        25,                             /* MDA mode */
        25, 25, 25,                     /* PCjr modes */
        -1, -1,                         /* not used */
        25, 25, 25, 43                  /* EGA modes */
};

short Maxcol[] = {
        40, 40, 80, 80, 40, 40, 80,     /* CGA modes */
        80,                             /* MDA mode */
        -1, 40, 80,                     /* PCjr modes */
        -1, -1,                         /* not used */
        80, 80, 80, 80                  /* EGA modes */
};

short Maxpage[] = {
        8, 8, 4, 4, 1, 1, 1,            /* CGA modes */
        1,                              /* MDA mode */
        0, 0, 0,                        /* PCjr modes */
```

(continued)

```
        -1, -1,                          /* not used */
        8, 4, 1, 1                       /* EGA modes */
};

int getstate()
{
        union REGS inregs, outregs;

        inregs.h.ah = GET_STATE;
        int86(VIDEO_IO, &inregs, &outregs);

        Vmode = outregs.h.al;
        Vwidth = outregs.h.ah;
        Vpage = outregs.h.bh;
        return (outregs.x.cflag);
}
```

Because *getstate( )* contains the declarations of the video structures, it should be called before you use the other video functions (*clrscrn( )*, *clrw( )*, *scroll( )*, and *setctype( )*) that use the data in those structures.

The *setvmode( )* function is used to set the video mode. It cannnot be used, however, to switch from one adapter to another. That task must be handled in another way, which is described in Chapter 11. The mode numbers are defined in *video.h*. The mode number presented to *setvmode( )* is not value-checked.

```
/*      setvmode -- set the video mode (color/graphics systems only)     */

#include <dos.h>
#include <local\std.h>
#include <local\bioslib.h>


/***********************************************************
* mode #         description
* -------------  -------------------------------
* PC MODES:
*       0        40x25 Mono text (c/g default)
*       1        40x25 Color text
*       2        80x25 Mono text
*       3        80x25 Color text
*       4        320x200 4-color graphics (med res)
```

(continued)

```
*         5          320x200 Mono graphics (med res)
*         6          640x200 2-color graphics (hi res)
*         7          80x25 on monochrome adapter
*
* PCjr MODES:
*         8          160x200 16-color graphics
*         9          320x200 16-color graphics
*        10          640x200 4-color fraphics
*
* EGA MODES:
*        13          320x200 16-color graphics
*        14          620x200 16-color graphics
*        15          640x350 mono graphics
*        16          640x350 color graphics (4- or 16-color)
***********************************************************/

int setvmode(vmode)
unsigned int vmode;       /* user-specified mode number */
{
        union REGS inregs, outregs;

        inregs.h.ah = SET_MODE;
        inregs.h.al = vmode;     /* value not checked */
        int86(VIDEO_IO, &inregs, &outregs);

        getstate();      /* update video structure */
        return (outregs.x.cflag);
}
```

For the IBM Monochrome Adapter and for the standard Color Graphics Adapter (CGA) in any of its graphics modes, only page 0 is valid. On the CGA, the 40-column text modes permit up to eight screen pages in display memory and the 80-column text modes up to four screen pages. On the Enhanced Graphics Adapter (EGA), page ranges are a function of the mode as follows: mode 13, 0 through 7; mode 14, 0 through 3; modes 15 and 16, 0 and 1.

The job of setting the visual page falls to *setpage( )*. The page-number argument must be valid for the current video mode because its value is not checked.

```
/*      setpage -- select "visual" screen page for viewing
 *      (the "active" page is the one being written to)       */

#include <dos.h>
#include <local\std.h>
#include <local\bioslib.h>
#include <local\video.h>


int setpage(pg)
int pg; /* visual screen page number */
{
        union REGS inregs, outregs;

        /* check page number against table */
        if (Maxpage[Vmode] > 0 && (pg < 0 || pg >= Maxpage[Vmode]))
                return (-1);

        /* change the visual page */
        inregs.h.ah = SET_PAGE;
        inregs.h.al = pg;
        int86(VIDEO_IO, &inregs, &outregs);
        return (outregs.x.cflag);
}
```

Next we have four functions that are used for cursor control. Two of them, *readcur( )* and *putcur( )*, deal with cursor positioning. The other two, *getctype( )* and *setctype( )*, are used to determine the cursor shape and to set it to a particular shape, respectively.

The function *readcur( )* gets the cursor position for a specified page and passes back the row and column position data to the calling routine.

```
/*      readcur -- pass back the cursor position (row, col)        */

#include <dos.h>
#include <local\std.h>
#include <local\bioslib.h>


unsigned int readcur(row, col, pg)
unsigned int *row;        /* current row */
unsigned int *col;        /* current column */
unsigned int pg;         /* screen page */
{
        union REGS inregs, outregs;
```

(continued)

```
        inregs.h.ah = GET_CUR;
        inregs.h.bh = pg;

        int86(VIDEO_IO, &inregs, &outregs);

        *col = outregs.h.dl;            /* col */
        *row = outregs.h.dh;            /* row */

        return (outregs.x.cflag);
}
```

The *row* and *col* arguments are pointers to simulate "call-by-reference" parameter passing, which allows *readcur( )* to pass back more than a single value by directly accessing the storage locations of the variables in the calling function.

The *putcur( )* function moves the cursor to an absolute screen location on the specified screen page. The specified row, column, and screen-page values are not checked.

```
/*      putcur -- put cursor at specified position (row, col)      */

#include <dos.h>
#include <local\std.h>
#include <local\bioslib.h>

unsigned int putcur(r, c, pg)
unsigned int
        r,      /* row */
        c,      /* column */
        pg;     /* screen page for writes */
{
        union REGS inregs, outregs;

        inregs.h.ah = CUR_POS;
        inregs.h.bh = pg & 0x07;
        inregs.h.dh = r & 0xFF;
        inregs.h.dl = c & 0xFF;

        int86(VIDEO_IO, &inregs, &outregs);

        return (outregs.x.cflag);
}
```

The cursor on a PC screen is a "hardware cursor" formed by one or more raster scan lines in the cell at the current cursor position. The cursor always blinks. A hardware cursor is available only in text modes and not in graphics modes, although it is quite easy to fabricate one in software.

To determine the starting and ending scan lines for the cursor, we use *getctype( )*. The function uses the same video service as *readcur( )* but returns cursor type data, not position data. We can use *getctype( )* in a program to save the starting and ending scan lines so that we can restore them with *setctype( )* before the program terminates.

```
/*      getctype -- pass back cursor type info (scan lines)      */

#include <dos.h>
#include <local\std.h>
#include <local\bioslib.h>

#define LO_NIBBLE        0x0F

int getctype(start_scan, end_scan, pg)
int *start_scan;          /* starting scan line */
int *end_scan;            /* ending scan line */
int pg;                   /* "visual" page */
{
        union REGS inregs, outregs;

        inregs.h.bh = pg;
        inregs.h.ah = GET_CUR;

        int86(VIDEO_IO, &inregs, &outregs);

        /* end_scan = low 4 bits of cl */
        *end_scan = outregs.h.cl & LO_NIBBLE;

        /* starting_scan = low 4 bits of ah */
        *start_scan = outregs.h.ch & LO_NIBBLE;

        return (outregs.x.cflag);
}
```

The inverse operation, setting the cursor type, is a bit more difficult than finding out what type it is. The job is done by *setctype( )*. The *setctype( )* function sets the starting and ending scan lines to the values

given by its arguments. It is incumbent upon the calling function to specify correct values for the prevailing display mode.

```
/*       setctype -- set the cursor start and end raster scan lines       */

#include <dos.h>
#include <local\bioslib.h>

#define LO_NIBBLE        0x0F
#define CURSOR_OFF       0x2
#define MAXSCANLN        15

int setctype(start, end)
int start;        /* starting raster scan line */
int end;          /* ending raster scan line */
{
        union REGS inregs, outregs;

        inregs.h.ah = CUR_TYPE;
        inregs.h.ch = start & LO_NIBBLE;
        inregs.h.cl = end & LO_NIBBLE;
        if (start >= MAXSCANLN) {
                inregs.h.ah |= CURSOR_OFF;
                inregs.h.al = MAXSCANLN;
        }
        int86(VIDEO_IO, &inregs, &outregs);

        return (outregs.x.cflag);
}
```

The video functions described next are used to read and write characters and attributes in any video mode, and dots—individual pixel
values—in graphics modes only.

The function *readca( )* gets the character and video attribute of the
character cell at the cursor position without regard for the video mode.
This is a neat trick in graphics modes when you realize that, to do this, the
BIOS video routine has to do a pattern-matching operation on the displayed image to find out what the character is.

```
/*      readca -- read character and attribute at current position      */


#include <dos.h>
#include <local\std.h>
#include <local\bioslib.h>

int readca(ch, attr, pg)
unsigned char *ch;
unsigned char *attr;
unsigned int pg;          /* screen page for reads */
{
        union REGS inregs, outregs;

        inregs.h.ah = READ_CHAR_ATTR;
        inregs.h.bh = pg;                    /* display page */

        int86(VIDEO_IO, &inregs, &outregs);

        *ch = outregs.h.al;                  /* character */
        *attr = outregs.h.ah;                /* attribute */

        /* return the value in AX register */
        return (outregs.x.cflag);
}
```

When we are operating in one of the graphics modes, we can read
the values of individual picture elements—pixels, or dots. The function
readdot( ) returns the color number for the pixel at the specified row and
column coordinates.

```
/*      readdot -- read the value of a pixel (in graphics mode only)      */


#include <dos.h>
#include <local\std.h>
#include <local\bioslib.h>

int readdot(row, col, dcolor)
int row, col;
int *dcolor;     /* pointer to dot color */
{
        union REGS inregs, outregs;
```

(continued)

```
        inregs.h.ah = READ_DOT;
        inregs.x.cx = col;
        inregs.x.dx = row;
        int86(VIDEO_IO, &inregs, &outregs);
        *dcolor = outregs.h.al;

        return (outregs.x.cflag);
}
```

The allowed row and column values depend on the selected graphics mode:

MODE	ROW RANGE	COLUMN RANGE
4	0-319	0-199
5	0-319	0-199
6	0-639	0-199
13	0-319	0-199
14	0-639	0-199
15	0-639	0-349
16	0-639	0-349

The function *writec( )* writes a character or a string of identical characters, starting at the current cursor position. It does not change the cursor position. The number of repetitions must not cause the function to write past the end of the current line.

This function is particularly handy for quickly drawing lines and boxes on the screen. We will also use it as a building block in functions that manipulate higher-level objects, such as text strings that are presented in fixed-length fields and scrolling windows.

```
/*      writec -- write a character only (leave attribute undisturbed)      */

#include <dos.h>
#include <local\std.h>
#include <local\bioslib.h>

int writec(ch, count, pg)
unsigned char ch;        /* character */
```

(continued)

```
int count;              /* repetitions */
int pg;                 /* screen page for writes */
{
        union REGS inregs, outregs;

        inregs.h.ah = WRITE_CHAR;
        inregs.h.al = ch;
        inregs.h.bh = pg;
        inregs.x.cx = count;
        int86(VIDEO_IO, &inregs, &outregs);

        return (outregs.x.cflag);
}
```

The *writeca( )* function is the same as *writec( )*, except that it also
writes the video attribute at the same location or region.

```
/*      writeca -- write character and attribute to the screen    */

#include <dos.h>
#include <local\std.h>
#include <local\bioslib.h>

int writeca(ch, attr, count, pg)
unsigned char ch;       /* character */
unsigned char attr;     /* attribute */
int count;              /* number of repetitions */
int pg;                 /* screen page for writes */
{
        union REGS inregs, outregs;

        inregs.h.ah = WRITE_CHAR_ATTR;
        inregs.h.al = ch;
        inregs.h.bh = pg;
        inregs.h.bl = attr;
        inregs.x.cx = count;
        int86(VIDEO_IO, &inregs, &outregs);

        return (outregs.x.cflag);
}
```

To simulate the printing behavior of a simple terminal, use the *writetty( )* function to place characters on the screen. This function writes characters only, but it also does newline and screen-scrolling operations.

```
/*      writetty -- write to screen using TTY interface    */

#include <dos.h>
#include <local\std.h>
#include <local\bioslib.h>

int writetty(ch, attr, pg)
unsigned char ch;        /* character */
unsigned char attr;      /* video attribute */
int pg;                  /* screen page for writes */
{
        union REGS inregs, outregs;

        inregs.h.ah = WRITE_TTY;
        inregs.h.al = ch;
        inregs.h.bl = attr;
        inregs.h.bh = pg;
        int86(VIDEO_IO, &inregs, &outregs);

        return (outregs.x.cflag);
}
```

The *writedot( )* function writes a dot of the specified color at the row and column position passed as arguments. Valid color numbers are a function of the current graphics mode:

MODE	COLOR NUMBERS
4, 5, 10	0-3
6	0 and 1
8, 9, 13, 14	0-15
15	0-1
16	0-4 or 0-15

If bit 7 of the AL register is a 1, the dot color is exclusive-ORed (XOR) with the current dot color value.

```
/*      writedot -- display a dot at the specified position      */

#include <dos.h>
#include <local\std.h>
#include <local\bioslib.h>

int writedot(r, c, color)
int r, c;         /* row and column cordinate */
int color;        /* dot (pixel) color */
{
        union REGS inregs, outregs;

        inregs.h.ah = WRITE_DOT;
        inregs.h.al = color;
        inregs.x.cx = c;
        inregs.x.dx = r;
        int86(VIDEO_IO, &inregs, &outregs);

        return (outregs.x.cflag);
}
```

The following miscellaneous video functions are used to clear the current screen page, or a portion of it, scroll a region of the screen up or down, set the graphics palette or text border color, and write video attributes.

The *clrscrn( )* function uses the BIOS video scroll routine to initialize the visual screen page. The *clrw( )* function clears a window of specified dimensions on the visual screen page.

```
/*      clrscrn -- clear the "visual" screen page      */

#include <dos.h>
#include <local\std.h>
#include <local\bioslib.h>
#include <local\video.h>

int clrscrn(a)
unsigned int a;         /* video attribute for new lines */
{
        union REGS inregs, outregs;
```

(continued)

```
        inregs.h.ah = SCROLL_UP;
        inregs.h.al = 0;                    /* blank entire window */
        inregs.h.bh = a;                    /* use specified attribute */
        inregs.h.bl = 0;
        inregs.x.cx = 0;                    /* upper left corner */
        inregs.h.dh = Maxrow[Vmode] - 1;   /* bottom screen row */
        inregs.h.dl = Maxcol[Vmode] - 1;   /* rightmost column */
        int86(VIDEO_IO, &inregs, &outregs);

        return (outregs.x.cflag);
}
```

```
/*      clrw -- clear specified region of "visual" screen page      */

#include <dos.h>
#include <local\std.h>
#include <local\bioslib.h>

int clrw(t, l, b, r, a)
int t;          /* top row of region to clear */
int l;          /* left column */
int b;          /* bottom row */
int r;          /* right column */
unsigned char a; /* attribute for cleared region */
{
        union REGS inregs, outregs;

        inregs.h.ah = SCROLL_UP;  /* scroll visual page up */
        inregs.h.al = 0;          /* blank entire window */
        inregs.h.bh = a;          /* attribute of blank lines */
        inregs.h.bl = 0;
        inregs.h.ch = t;          /* upper left of scroll region */
        inregs.h.cl = l;
        inregs.h.dh = b;          /* lower right of scroll region */
        inregs.h.dl = r;
        int86(VIDEO_IO, &inregs, &outregs);

        return (outregs.x.cflag);
}
```

The *palette( )* function serves two purposes. In text modes, it sets the screen border color. In graphics modes, it sets the color palette from which drawing colors are selected.

```
/*        palette -- set graphics color values or border color        */

#include <dos.h>
#include <local\bioslib.h>

int palette(id, color)
unsigned int id, color;
{
        union REGS inregs, outregs;

        inregs.h.ah = PALETTE;
        inregs.h.bh = id;
        inregs.h.bl = color;
        int86(VIDEO_IO, &inregs, &outregs);

        return(outregs.x.cflag);
}
```

To scroll the entire visual screen page or a rectangular portion of it up or down, use *scroll( )*. The function takes a signed number: negative numbers scroll lines down the screen, nonzero positive numbers scroll lines up, and zero initializes the specified region. Vacated lines are set to blanks in the specified attribute.

```
/*        scroll -- scroll a region of the "visual" screen
 *        page up or down by n rows (0 = initialize region)        */

#include <dos.h>
#include <local\std.h>
#include <local\bioslib.h>

int scroll(t, l, b, r, n, a)
int t;  /* top row of scroll region */
int l;  /* left column */
int b;  /* bottom row */
```

(continued)

```
int r;  /* right column */
int n;  /* number of lines to scroll */
        /* sign indicates direction to scroll */
        /* 0 means scroll all lines in the region (initialize) */
unsigned char a;/* attribute for new lines */
{
        union REGS inregs, outregs;

        if (n < 0) {
                /* scroll visual page down n lines */
                inregs.h.ah = SCROLL_DN;
                inregs.h.al = -n;
        }
        else {
                /* scroll visual page up n lines */
                inregs.h.ah = SCROLL_UP;
                inregs.h.al = n;
        }
        inregs.h.bh = a;        /* attribute of blank lines */
        inregs.h.bl = 0;
        inregs.h.ch = t;        /* upper-left of scroll region */
        inregs.h.cl = l;
        inregs.h.dh = b;        /* lower-right of scroll region */
        inregs.h.dl = r;
        int86(VIDEO_IO, &inregs, &outregs);

        return (outregs.x.cflag);
}
```

The next function is really a composite of two BIOS video services. To change the attribute of a range of character positions without disturbing the characters, use *writea( )*. This function reads the character and attribute at each affected position and writes back the same character in the new attribute while leaving the current cursor position unchanged.

```
/*      writea -- write attribute only to screen memory (faked by
 *      reading char and attr and writing back the original
 *      character and the new attribute at each position)      */

#include <local\std.h>
```

(continued)

```
int writea(a, n, pg)
unsigned char a;/* video attribute */
int n;          /* number of positions to write */
int pg;         /* screen page */
{
        int i;
        int status;
        unsigned short chx, attrx;
        unsigned short r, c;

        /* get starting (current) position */
        status = 0;
        status = readcur(&r, &c, pg);
        for (i = 0; i < n; ++i) {
                status += putcur(r, c + i, pg);
                status += readca(&chx, &attrx, pg);
                status += writeca(chx, a, 1, pg);
        }

        /* restore cursor position */
        status += putcur(r, c, pg);

        return (status);
}
```

Demonstration Program

Now that we have a collection of DOS and BIOS interface routines, what can we do with them? Perhaps the best way to answer the question is to demonstrate their use in a program. A vehicle for showing off some of the routines is CURSOR, a program that magnifies the current cursor and lets us change its shape. CURSOR is proof that carefully written and applied BIOS video routines can produce startlingly fast screen manipulation—not instantaneous, but fast enough for commercial applications.

Before examining the source code for CURSOR, we will prepare several functions that are built on the current set of BIOS video routines. The functions *put_ch( )*, *putstr( )*, and *drawbox( )* can be viewed as a layer above the *writec( )* and *putcur( )* functions of the BIOS library just described. They provide often-used capabilities that are not provided in a convenient way by the primary BIOS functions.

The *put_ch( )* function displays a single character at the current cursor position and then advances the cursor to the next position. The name includes the underscore to distinguish *put_ch( )* from *putch( )*, a standard console I/O routine in the Microsoft run-time library. The *putstr( )* function displays a text string and advances the cursor to the next displayable position. Combining these two functions and several of the low-level BIOS functions in *drawbox( )* lets us create fine-ruled boxes for highlighted text and graphic elements of our screens. The *drawbox( )* function uses the single-line drawing characters of the IBM extended-ASCII character set. We could also use double-line and other combinations of line-drawing characters to produce distinctive boxes, as we will do in later chapters.

Here are the C source listings for *put_ch( )*, *putstr( )*, and *drawbox( )*:

```
/*      put_ch -- display a character in the prevailing video
 *      attribute and advance the cursor position      */

#include <local\video.h>

int put_ch(ch, pg)
register char ch;
int pg;
{
        int r, c, c0;

        readcur(&r, &c, pg);
        writec(ch, 1, pg);
        putcur(r, ++c, pg);
        return (1);
}
```

```
/*      putstr -- display a character string in the prevailing
 *      video attribute and return number characters displayed      */

int putstr(s, pg)
register char *s;
```

(continued)

```
unsigned int pg;
{
        unsigned int r, c, c0;

        readcur(&r, &c, pg);
        for (c0 = c; *s != '\0'; ++s, ++c) {
                putcur(r, c, pg);
                writec(*s, 1, pg);
        }
        putcur(r, c, pg);
        return (c - c0);
}
```

```
/*      drawbox -- create a box with IBM line-drawing characters      */

#include <local\video.h>

int drawbox(top, lft, btm, rgt, pg)
int top, lft, btm, rgt, pg;
{
        int i;
        int x;  /* interior line length for top and bottom segments */

        x = rgt - lft - 1;

        /* draw the top row */
        putcur(top, lft, pg);
        put_ch(ULC11, pg);
        writec(HBAR1, x, pg);
        putcur(top, rgt, pg);
        put_ch(URC11, pg);

        /* draw the sides */
        for (i = 1; i < btm - top; ++i)
        {
                putcur(top + i, lft, pg);
                put_ch(VBAR1, pg);
                putcur(top + i, rgt, pg);
                put_ch(VBAR1, pg);
        }
```

(continued)

```
        /* draw the bottom row */
        putcur(btm, lft, pg);
        put_ch(LLC11, pg);
        writec(HBAR1, x, pg);
        putcur(btm, rgt, pg);
        put_ch(LRC11, pg);
}
```

Now we can write *cursor.c*. The goal is to design a program that
presents a magnified view of the cursor and that allows us to interactively
adjust the cursor shape. The source for CURSOR is quite long. It is one of
several programs I wrote to test the DOS and BIOS interface functions.
The program shows how the DOS and BIOS interface functions are used in
a working example. By writing "driver" programs as I wrote the interface
functions, I was able to both anticipate what functions might be needed
and test the functions as they were written.

The pseudocode for CURSOR shows how the program works.

```
get video information
save current attribute/color values
draw basic screen (header, cursor image, instructions)
while (key is not RETURN)
        switch selection modes on left or right arrow
                clear start/stop selection pointer
                display new pointer
        adjust scan line position on up or down arrow
                clear current scan-line pointer
                calculate new pointer value
                update cursor image display
                        (scan lines, pointers)
set new cursor type
restore original attribute/color
clear screen
```

This simple description does not reveal a few details in the calculations needed to accurately display images for cursors on various types of
hardware. For example, CURSOR automatically adjusts the displayed image to compensate for 80- and 40-column screen widths, and differing

numbers of scan lines and widths in cursors on IBM monochrome display
systems (9 by 14) and color/graphics systems (8 by 8). The C source, which
shows how these details are handled, is in the file *cursor.c*.

```c
/*      cursor -- interactively set cursor shape      */

#include <dos.h>
#include <stdlib.h>
#include <local\video.h>
#include <local\keydefs.h>

/* additional drawing characters (others are defined in video.h) */
#define DOT     254
#define NO_DOT  196
#define D_POINT 31
#define R_POINT 16
#define L_POINT 17

/* dimensions of the help frame */
#define BOX_Y   6
#define BOX_X   30

/* upper-left row and column of big cursor */
int Ulr, Ulc;
int Mid;

/* cursor scan-line-selection modes */
typedef enum { STARTSCAN, ENDSCAN } CMODE;

int main()
{
        int i, j, ch;
        int start, end;
        int height, width;
        static char spoint[] = { "Start\020" }; /* contains right pointer */
        static char epoint[] = { "\021Stop" };  /* contains left pointer */
        static char title[] = { "CURSOR: Control cursor shape (V1.0)" };
        unsigned char
                oldattr,        /* video attribute upon entry */
                headattr,       /* video attribute of header */
                attr,           /* primary video attribute */
                standout;       /* highlighting video attribute */
        CMODE mode;
```

(continued)

```
static void drawdspy(int, int, int, int, int);
static void drawstart(int, char *);
static void drawend(int, int, char *);
static void drawactive(int, int, CMODE);
static void showhelp(int, int);
static void writestr(char *, int)

/* get video information and initialize */
getstate();
Mid = Vwidth / 2;
readca(&ch, &oldattr, Vpage);   /* preserve user's video attribute */
getctype(&start, &end, Vpage);  /* and cursor shape */
headattr = (WHT << 4) | BLK;

/* set parameters based on video mode (default = CGA) */
height = width = 8;       /* use an 8 by 8 block character cell */
attr = (BLU << 4) | CYAN | BRIGHT;
standout = YEL;
if (Vmode == MDA_M80) {
        /* uses a 14 by 9 dot block character cell */
        height = 14;
        width = 9;
        attr = NORMAL;
        standout = BWHT;
}
setctype(height + 1, height + 1);       /* cursor off */

/* basic text and layout */
Ulr = 2;
Ulc = Mid - width / 2;
clrscrn(attr);
putcur(0, 0, Vpage);
writeca(' ', headattr, Vwidth, Vpage);
putcur(0, Mid - strlen(title) / 2, Vpage);
writestr(title, Vpage);
showhelp(Ulr + height + 1, Mid - BOX_X / 2);

/* interactively select cursor shape */
mode = STARTSCAN;
drawdspy(start, end, standout, width, height);
drawstart(start, spoint);
drawend(end, width, epoint);
```

(continued)

```
        drawactive(height, width, mode);
        while (1) {
                switch (ch = getkey()) {
                case K_UP:
                        /* move up one scan line */
                        if (mode == STARTSCAN)
                                drawstart(start--, "       ");
                        else
                                drawend(end--, width, "       ");
                        break;
                case K_DOWN:
                        /* move down one scan line */
                        if (mode == STARTSCAN)
                                drawstart(start++, "       ");
                        else
                                drawend(end++, width, "       ");
                        break;
                case K_LEFT:
                        /* starting scan-line-selection mode */
                        mode = STARTSCAN;
                        drawactive(height, width, mode);
                        continue;
                case K_RIGHT:
                        /* ending scan-line-selection mode */
                        mode = ENDSCAN;
                        drawactive(height, width, mode);
                        continue;
                case K_RETURN:
                        /* set the new cursor shape */
                        setctype(start, end);
                        clrscrn(oldattr);
                        putcur(0, 0, Vpage);
                        exit(0);
                }

                /* make corrections at cursor image boundaries */
                if (start < 0)
                        start = 0;
                else if (start > height)
                        start = height;
```

(continued)

```
            if (end < 0)
                    end = 0;
            else if (end >= height)
                    end = height - 1;

            /* show updated cursor shape and pointers */
            drawdspy(start, end, standout, width, height);
            drawstart(start, spoint);
            drawend(end, width, epoint);
    }
        exit(0);
} /* end main() */



/*      drawdspy -- draw a magnified image of a cursor with the currently active
 *      scan lines depicted as a sequence of dots and inactive lines depicted as
 *      straight lines */

static void drawdspy(s, e, a, w, h)
int s;  /* starting scan line */
int e;  /* ending scan line */
int a;  /* video attribute */
int w;  /* width */
int h;  /* height */
{
        int i;

        /* display an exploded image of each scan line */
        for (i = 0; i < h; ++i) {
                putcur(Ulr + i, Ulc, Vpage);
                if (s >= h)
                        /* cursor is effectively off */
                        writeca(NO_DOT, a, w, Vpage);
                else if ((s <= e && i >= s && i <= e) || /* a full block */
                        (s > e && (i <= e || i >= s)))   /* a split block */
                        writeca(DOT, a, w, Vpage);
                else
                        /* outside start/end range */
                        writeca(NO_DOT, a, w, Vpage);
        }
```

(continued)

```
} /* end drawdspy() */



/*      drawstart -- display a pointer to the displayed starting
 *      scan line in the magnified cursor image */

static void drawstart(s, sp)
int s;          /* starting scan line number */
char *sp;       /* visual pointer to the displayed starting scan line */
{
        putcur(Ulr + s, Ulc - strlen(sp), Vpage);
        putstr(sp, Vpage);
} /* end drawstart() */



/*      drawend -- display a pointer to the displayed ending
 *      scan line in the magnified cursor image */

static void drawend(e, w, ep)
int e;          /* ending scan line number */
int w;          /* width of the cursor image */
char *ep;       /* visual pointer to the displayed ending scan line */
{
        putcur(Ulr + e, Ulc + w, Vpage);
        putstr(ep, Vpage);
} /* end drawend() */

static void drawactive(h, w, m)
int h, w;
CMODE m;
{
        int col;

        /* clear active selector row */
        putcur(Ulr - 1, Ulc, Vpage);
        writec(' ', w, Vpage);

        /* point to active selector */
        col = (m == STARTSCAN) ? 0 : w - 1;
        putcur(Ulr - 1, Ulc + col, Vpage);
        writec(D_POINT, 1, Vpage);
} /* end drawactive() */
```

(continued)

```
/*      showhelp -- display a set of instructions about the
 *      use of the cursor program in a fine-ruled box */

static void showhelp(r, c)
int r, c;        /* upper-left corner of help frame */
{
        static char title[] = { " Instructions " };
        extern int drawbox(int, int, int, int, int);

        /* fine-ruled box */
        clrw(r, c, r + BOX_Y, c + BOX_X, (WHT << 4) | GRN | BRIGHT);
        drawbox(r, c, r + BOX_Y, c + BOX_X, Vpage);

        /* centered title */
        putcur(r, c + (BOX_X - strlen(title)) / 2, Vpage);
        putstr(title, Vpage);

        /* display symbols and text using brute-force positioning */
        putcur(r + 2, c + 2, Vpage);
        put_ch(LEFTARROW, Vpage);
        put_ch(RIGHTARROW, Vpage);
        putstr("  Change selection mode", Vpage);
        putcur(r + 3, c + 2, Vpage);
        put_ch(UPARROW, Vpage);
        put_ch(DOWNARROW, Vpage);
        putstr("  Select scan lines", Vpage);
        putcur(r + 4, c + 2, Vpage);
        put_ch(L_POINT, Vpage);
        put_ch(LRC11, Vpage);
        putstr("  Set shape and exit", Vpage);
} /* end showhelp() */



/*      writestr -- write a string in the prevailing video attribute      */

static void writestr(s, pg)
char *s;                /* string to write */
unsigned int pg;        /* screen page for writes */
{
        unsigned int r, c, c0;
```

(continued)

```
        readcur(&r, &c, pg);
        for (c0 = c; *s != '\0'; ++s, ++c) {
                putcur(r, c, pg);
                writec(*s, 1, pg);
        }
        /* restore cursor position */
        putcur(r, c0, pg);
} /* end writestr() */
```

The makefile, *bios.mk*, automatically builds the library *bios.lib*. The makefile for CURSOR is contained in *cursor.mk*:

```
# makefile for the BIOS library
LINC = c:\include\local
LLIB = c:\lib\local


# --- inference rules ---
.c.obj:
        msc $*;


# --- objects ---
O1 = clrscrn.obj clrw.obj drawbox.obj equipchk.obj getctype.obj getstate.obj
O2 = kbd_stat.obj memsize.obj palette.obj putcur.obj putstr.obj put_ch.obj
O3 = readca.obj readcur.obj readdot.obj scroll.obj setctype.obj setpage.obj
O4 = setvmode.obj writea.obj writec.obj writeca.obj writedot.obj writetty.obj


# --- compile sources ---
clrscrn.obj:    clrscrn.c $(LINC)\bioslib.h $(LINC)\std.h

clrw.obj:       clrw.c $(LINC)\bioslib.h $(LINC)\std.h

drawbox.obj:    drawbox.c $(LINC)\video.h

equipchk.obj:   equipchk.c $(LINC)\bioslib.h $(LINC)\equip.h

getctype.obj:   getctype.c $(LINC)\bioslib.h $(LINC)\std.h

getstate.obj:   getstate.c $(LINC)\bioslib.h $(LINC)\std.h

kbd_stat.obj:   kbd_stat.c $(LINC)\bioslib.h $(LINC)\keybdlib.h
```

(continued)

```
memsize.obj:    memsize.c $(LINC)\bioslib.h $(LINC)\std.h

palette.obj:    palette.c $(LINC)\bioslib.h

putcur.obj:     putcur.c $(LINC)\bioslib.h $(LINC)\std.h

putstr.obj:     putstr.c $(LINC)\bioslib.h

put_ch.obj:     put_ch.c $(LINC)\bioslib.h

readca.obj:     readca.c $(LINC)\bioslib.h $(LINC)\std.h

readcur.obj:    readcur.c $(LINC)\bioslib.h $(LINC)\std.h

readdot.obj:    readdot.c $(LINC)\bioslib.h $(LINC)\std.h

scroll.obj:     scroll.c $(LINC)\bioslib.h $(LINC)\std.h

setctype.obj:   setctype.c $(LINC)\bioslib.h

setpage.obj:    setpage.c $(LINC)\bioslib.h $(LINC)\std.h $(LINC)\video.h

setvmode.obj:   setvmode.c $(LINC)\bioslib.h $(LINC)\std.h

writea.obj:     writea.c $(LINC)\std.h

writec.obj:     writec.c $(LINC)\bioslib.h $(LINC)\std.h

writeca.obj:    writeca.c $(LINC)\bioslib.h $(LINC)\std.h

writedot.obj:   writedot.c $(LINC)\bioslib.h $(LINC)\std.h

writetty.obj:   writetty.c $(LINC)\bioslib.h $(LINC)\std.h

# --- create and install the library ---
$(LLIB)\bios.lib:    $(O1) $(O2) $(O3) $(O4)
        del $(LLIB)\bios.lib
        lib $(LLIB)\bios +$(O1);
        lib $(LLIB)\bios +$(O2);
        lib $(LLIB)\bios +$(O3);
        lib $(LLIB)\bios +$(O4);
        del $(LLIB)\bios.bak
```

```
# makefile for CURSOR program

LLIB=c:\lib\local

cursor.obj:     cursor.c
      msc $*;

cursor.exe:     cursor.obj $(LLIB)\bios.lib  $(LLIB)\dos.lib
      link $*, $*, nul, $(LLIB)\bios $(LLIB)\dos;
```

When you run the CURSOR program some computers will exhibit unexpected behavior as a function of the installed hardware. The AT&T PC6300, for example, does not permit "split" cursors (the stop scan line is less than the start scan line). CURSOR will allow you to fashion a split cursor, but on the 6300, it disables the cursor instead. Also, I have not modified the program to work with EGA-compatible boards. EGA boards use different numbers of scan lines per character cell than CGA boards operating in the same (or equivalent) modes.

Before moving on to user interfaces, we will add one more function to the BIOS video library. The *writemsg( )* function is not used in this chapter, but it is called by a user-input function in Chapter 6. It displays a two-part message in a fixed field and leaves the cursor at its current position. The design of *writemsg( )* lets us concatenate strings visually and prevents them from extending beyond the available display area. In addition, if the resulting string does not completely fill the display field, *writemsg( )* pads the field with spaces in the prevailing attribute to clear any residue from the previous contents of the field.

```
/*      writemsg -- displays a message in a field of the prevailing video attribute
 *      and returns the number of displayable message characters written; truncates
 *      the message if it's too long to fit in the field */

#include <stdio.h>
#include <local\std.h>
```

(continued)

```
int writemsg(r, c, w, s1, s2, pg)
int r, c, w ;
char *s1, *s2;
int pg;
{
        int n = 0;
        char *cp;

        /* display first part of the message */
        if (s1 != NULL)
                for (cp = s1; *cp != '\0' && n < w; ++n, ++cp) {
                        putcur(r, c + n, pg);
                        writec(*cp, 1, pg);
                }

        /* display second part of the message */
        if (s2 != NULL)
                for (cp = s2; *cp != '\0' && n < w; ++n, ++cp) {
                        putcur(r, c + n, pg);
                        writec(*cp, 1, pg);
                }

        /* pad the remainder of the field, if any, with spaces */
        if (n < w) {
                putcur(r, c + n, pg);
                writec(' ', w - n, pg);
        }
        return (n);
}
```

Recommendations

We need to address a few library management issues. In my work and in this book, I have elected to keep the number of functions at one per file except in rare circumstances where two or more functions have a symbiotic relationship. The cost of doing this is increased disk use. Although most of the source files are less than 500 bytes in size, they each require from 2 to 8 KB of storage capacity on a typical hard disk. The amount used is a function of the block or cluster size of the disk, which is in turn a function of its capacity and the version of DOS used to format the disk.

The primary advantage of separate functions in libraries is that the linker program adds the object code only for the functions used in a program, thus avoiding the possibility of dragging in a lot of unneeded instructions.

The alternative—packaging related functions in a single object module in a library—can be effective too, as long as the functions so grouped are likely to be used together in a program. We could, for example, group the *getctype( ), setctype( ),* and other cursor-related functions in a single object module because they are usually employed together, as in the CURSOR example.

The issue of compatibility across a wide range of machines deserves comment. To obtain the broadest PC compatibility for your programs, use the higher-level DOS function calls. They are often slower and less versatile than the BIOS functions, but programs built on them can be run on virtually any machine that runs DOS.

Using BIOS interfaces will erode your market a little, but probably not enough to fret about for more than a few seconds. If a large enough market exists for a non-compatible machine (the Zenith Z-100, for example), you can create a customized version of the program because the dependencies can be limited to a few interface library functions.

Compatibility of PC/DOS-based programs to UNIX and XENIX is another matter. Some fundamental differences in architecture make transporting a program developed under DOS on a PC to a UNIX-based system difficult, but not impossible. The primary difficulty is that users in a multi-user environment are typically not using the console; they are connected by dial-up or hard-wired lines to the host computer. Those connections are a bottleneck that reduces the available "bandwidth" of the user interface to a tiny fraction of what a typical PC has available on a dedicated machine. Despite this difficulty, most programs can be written for portability between DOS and UNIX/XENIX. In fact, I have done most of my development work under XENIX and then converted to DOS afterward.

Going from DOS to UNIX is tougher because I tend to take advantage of all that the PC and DOS offer for program performance reasons. To gain some needed portability to UNIX, we can use the *Termcap/Curses* virtual terminal interface packages that permit UNIX to work with just about any alphanumeric video terminal. *Termcap* is a set of low-level functions that get terminal information from a database of terminal capabilities and provide control over cursor positioning and other video terminal functions.

Curses is a high-level screen-management package that provides optimization of cursor movements and control over displayed text, video attributes, and keyboard interactions. Curses also supports buffers that are larger than the screen and provides modest windowing features.

It is outside the scope of this book to provide detailed information on Termcap/Curses software. You may want use the virtual-terminal interface in your programs for one important reason: A program written under DOS on a PC using a Curses interface for screen management is easily ported to UNIX/XENIX. Give it a shot. A very good Curses implementation for the PC from Aspen Scientific works well with Microsoft C and other C compilers under DOS and is compatible with UNIX System V Curses. Lattice offers a non-optimizing version of Berkeley Curses as an adjunct to its C compiler. Other Curses implementations are available, but I have not tested them.

There is much more to the DOS/BIOS interface than we have covered in this chapter. As we need additional functions, we can use what we have done so far as models for the needed functions. Next, we look at one of the most important aspects of any program—the user interface.

The User Interface 6

The user interface has received a lot of attention in recent years. Human factors engineering (ergonomics)—the endeavor that is one part each of engineering, science, and "black magic"—is best known for dealing with such topics as how to design safe, comfortable car seats and how to lay out the cockpit of a jet aircraft. However, it also offers much information about how people use machines that have neither wheels nor wings. Although by no means a dissertation on human factors engineering, this chapter focuses on the primary points of contact between the computer and the user—the keyboard, the display screen, and the speaker—and on how to use these communications pathways effectively.

As programmers, we must consider both the application and the audience for the application. In addition, we need to know about the environment in which a program is to be used, in order to provide the best possible match between the program and its intended users. Some programs lend themselves to a command-oriented type of operation. Frequently used tools that may become components of pipeline commands are examples of this category. Other programs are well suited to windowing and menus, or at least benefit from their use. Programs that are infrequently used and that may involve complex step-by-step procedures fall into this category. Still other programs can successfully blend the two approaches or switch easily between them. In Chapter 13, we will develop a program that provides convenient screen control with instructions from either the DOS command line or a simple menu of commands. The mode of operation depends on how the program is called.

The use of pleasing visual effects and appropriate sound can do a lot to enhance both the appeal and the utility of a program. However, effectively using visual effects and sound in programs is no less an art than playing a musical instrument. Later in this chapter, we will explore the use of sound and text-oriented visual effects in our programs. But we will start with a view toward standardizing the way programs gather and process command-line options. Then we will develop some timer functions that are needed to do several important jobs.

Standard Command-line Processing

The standard user interface of unadorned UNIX/XENIX and DOS is the command line. One of the major modes of communication from the user to a program is via command-line options and other arguments. For years, there has been a need to standardize command-line option processing by programs in order to provide a clean and consistent user interface. This was evident long before CP/M and DOS were conceived in the fertile minds of their developers; the problem exists in Multics, UNIX, XENIX, and many other minicomputer and mainframe operating systems. Here is an example of the problem.

Under UNIX, command-line options are introduced by a leading dash (-). An option letter selects a particular program option and may require an option argument. Therefore, -w80 might be used to select a page width (w) of 80 columns when used with a printer program. The option argument—*80*, in this case, but other values may be allowed—must be entered if the w option letter is used.

An early version of UNIX (Version 7 in commercial circles) requires that options to the print command, *r*, be invoked individually, each having its own option flag and letter. Thus, printing a file in multiple columns without the usual header and footer lines requires a command constructed according to the following template:

pr -2 -t *filename*

in which the -2 and -t arguments specify the desired options, and *filename* is the lone filename argument.

Later versions of UNIX, starting with the release of System III, permit the option letters to be combined and introduced by a single option flag, so a command of the form

pr -2t *filename*

does precisely the same job as the first one shown. A command typed according to the older specification (separate option flags) is also allowed.

To complicate matters, some programs enforce the requirement that option letters that take arguments must have a space or tab between the letter and the argument while other programs require no white space (*-w 80* vs *-w80,* for example). These variations are the result of no small amount of anarchy among the developers and are the source of the confusion from which standards eventually evolve.

So why should this matter to DOS programmers and users? Well, for one thing, DOS resembles UNIX in many ways and emulates many UNIX features and principles. For another, the same kinds of problems already exist under DOS. Some commands take option switches, usually indicated by the forward slash (/), but some programs accept the dash (-) as well. The option switches usually are placed after the command name but before any filenames, yet some commands require that option switches follow everything else on the command line. Still other programs don't care where the option flags and arguments go—they simply scan the entire command line before doing anything.

Under recent versions of UNIX and XENIX, a utility function named *getopt( )* is used to process option flags and arguments in a consistent way. The *getopt( )* function can be used by any DOS program that accepts command-line options and arguments. We will apply it to a sample utility program, CAT, which concatenates files (one or more) onto the standard output stream.

Figure 6-1 on the next page shows us how *getopt( )* takes command lines and sensibly parses options and arguments. We have already seen in Chapter 3 how information in the DOS command tail is made available to a program via the *argc* and *argv* parameters to the *main( )* function and how a program can be written to use the information in the command tail. We have not yet, however, agreed on a format for commands.

For the programs in this book, we will present command lines according to a common template. The command name always appears first (this is an operating system requirement), followed by options, if any, followed by other data, typically filenames, if any. Options are introduced by a leading dash. Such a template works well for most of the commands we will encounter. However, with the more complicated commands, we probably will provide a menu-style interface instead of a command-oriented interface.

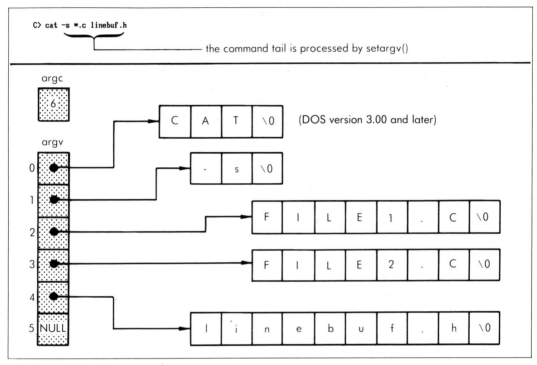

FIGURE 6-1 | *Expanding ambiguous filename specifications*

Ambiguous filename arguments are expanded automatically by the *setargv* routine if it is included in the link list. The argument vector array, *argv,* contains pointers to strings in memory. The DOS command tail is everything that follows the command name on the DOS command line, including the initial space or tab that separates the first option or argument from the command name. Although the DOS command tail is limited to 128 bytes, ambiguous file names can be expanded to produce effective command tails of much greater length. The figure illustrates what the pointers and strings would look like for the command line

cat -s *.c linebuf.h

if the current directory contains the two C source files, *file1.c* and *file2.c,* the header file *linebuf.h,* and possibly other files. Consider what this command might produce if invoked in a directory with many C source files.

The two C source-file names are stored with all letters converted to uppercase because DOS always converts to uppercase when it expands names. The -s option and the header file name are stored as literal copies because no expansions are required. The command name, available only under DOS 3.00 and later versions, is presented with all letters converted to uppercase regardless of how they are typed by the user, again because of a DOS convention.

The following source for *getopt( )* was provided by AT&T. It is the current version of *getopt( )* that is available from the AT&T UNIX System Toolchest.

```
/*
 *        Copyright (c) 1984, 1985 AT&T
 *        All Rights Reserved
 *
 *        ----- Author's Note -----
 *        getopt() is reproduced with permission of the AT&T UNIX(R) System
 *        Toolchest. This is a public domain version of getopt(3) that is
 *        distributed to registered Toolchest participants.
 *        Defining DOS_MODS alters the code slightly to obtain compatibility
 *        with DOS and support libraries provided with most DOS C compilers.
 */

#define DOS_MODS

#if defined (DOS_MODS)
        /* getopt() for DOS */
#else
#ident  "@(#)getopt.c   1.9"
#endif


/*      3.0 SID #      1.2     */
/*LINTLIBRARY*/
#define NULL    0
#define EOF     (-1)
```

(continued)

```
/*
 *      For this to work under versions of DOS prior to 3.00, argv[0]
 *      must be set in main() to point to a valid program name or a
 *      reasonable substitute string.   (ARH, 10-8-86)
 */
#define ERR(s, c)        if(opterr){\
        char errbuf[2];\
        errbuf[0] = c; errbuf[1] = '\n';\
        (void) write(2, argv[0], (unsigned)strlen(argv[0]));\
        (void) write(2, s, (unsigned)strlen(s));\
        (void) write(2, errbuf, 2);}

#if defined (DOS_MODS)
/* permit function prototyping under DOS */
#include <stdlib.h>
#include <string.h>
#else
/* standard UNIX declarations */
extern int strcmp();
extern char *strchr();
/*
 *      The following line was moved here from the ERR definition
 *      to prevent a "duplicate definition" error message when the
 *      code is compiled under DOS.  (ARH, 10-8-86)
 */
extern int strlen(), write();
#endif

int     opterr = 1;
int     optind = 1;
int     optopt;
char    *optarg;

int
getopt(argc, argv, opts)
int     argc;
char    **argv, *opts;
{
        static int sp = 1;
        register int c;
        register char *cp;
```

(continued)

```
        if(sp == 1)
                if(optind >= argc ||
                    argv[optind][0] != '-' || argv[optind][1] == '\0')
                        return(EOF);
                else if(strcmp(argv[optind], "--") == NULL) {
                        optind++;
                        return(EOF);
                }
        optopt = c = argv[optind][sp];
        if(c == ':' || (cp=strchr(opts, c)) == NULL) {
                ERR(": illegal option -- ", c);
                if(argv[optind][++sp] == '\0') {
                        optind++;
                        sp = 1;
                }
                return('?');
        }
        if(*++cp == ':') {
                if(argv[optind][sp+1] != '\0')
                        optarg = &argv[optind++][sp+1];
                else if(++optind >= argc) {
                        ERR(": option requires an argument -- ", c);
                        sp = 1;
                        return('?');
                } else
                        optarg = argv[optind++];
                sp = 1;
        } else {
                if(argv[optind][++sp] == '\0') {
                        sp = 1;
                        optind++;
                }
                optarg = NULL;
        }
        return(c);
}
```

The following synopsis and description of *getopt( )* are based on its observed behavior under UNIX System V, Release 2, the current UNIX standard. If we use this standard, programs developed under DOS that do not employ any hardware-dependent code will be readily transportable to UNIX/XENIX (and vice versa).

The *getopt( )* function receives an argument count and an array of pointers to argument strings (usually copies of the *argc* and *argv* parameters of *main( )*) and a string variable that is a list of allowable option flags. Single letters (uppercase and lowercase letters are unique) and single-digit numbers are acceptable option letters. If a valid option letter in the list is followed by a colon, *getopt( )* expects to find a following option argument.

In addition to the parameters passed to the function, the interface to *getopt( )* involves three global variables. The *optind* variable, the option index, is an integer that is initialized to 1; it keeps track of which option is currently being processed. A character pointer, *optarg,* is set to *NULL* unless the option being processed takes an argument, in which case *optarg* points to what should be the required argument. The third global variable is *opterr.* It is initialized to 1, which causes *getopt( )* to report errors such as an option flag that is not a member of the passed list or a missing argument. Our programs can shut off error messages from *getopt( )* by setting *opterr* to 0. Although *optind* and *optarg* must be declared as external variables in our programs, we need to declare *opterr* only if we intend to change its value.

> ## COMMENT
>
> *The UNIX and XENIX manual pages for* getopt( ) *contain an error. The value of* optind *does not default to 0. It is initialized to 1. Also, previous versions of* getopt( ) *emitted error messages when* opterr *was 0. The latest versions of* getopt( ) *have reversed the sense of the* opterr *variable and emit error messages if* opterr *is 1 (the default value).*

The pseudocode for *getopt( )* reveals the complexities of handling user input in a general way. The primary difficulty is in parsing optional arguments that may or may not be separated from the associated option letter by white space.

```
index to first argument following command name (done before the first call to getopt())
if (no arguments OR
  arg not an option OR
  flag without option letter)
        return EOF
else if (special end-of-options indicator)
        skip over argument
        return EOF
if (option letter not in option string)
        if (opterr is non-zero)
                print error message
        return '?'
if (option letter followed by ':' in option string)
        if (option argument found)
                set optarg to start of argument
                return option letter
        else
                if (opterr is non-zero)
                        print error message
                return '?'
else
        set optarg to NULL
        return option letter
```

To show how the *getopt( )* function is used in practice, we will now
write a program that uses *getopt( )* in its simplest form. Later in this chapter and in other chapters, we will use *getopt( )* in more complex argument-
processing situations.

The CAT program, presented next, uses *getopt( )* to process a single
option. CAT is used to concatenate files. It accepts a list of zero or more
files and produces a continuous data stream on its output. If only a single
file is named, CAT simply lists the file's contents on the screen. Figure 6-2
on the next page is the manual page for CAT.

NAME

       CAT — concatenate file

FORMAT

       cat [-s] [d: [path [filename [.ext]]] ...]

DESCRIPTION

       The CAT command accepts the -s option (silent), which tells the
program not to complain about missing files (this may be useful
in batch files). If no filenames are specified, CAT reads from the
standard input. DOS wildcard characters (? and ∗) may be used to
specify ambiguous filenames.

EXAMPLES

       Display the contents of a single file.

       cat hello.c

       Concatenate all C source files in the current directory into a
single source file.

       cat ∗.c >program.c

       Create a new file with text typed by the user.

       cat >myfile.txt
       This is a test.
       ^Z

FIGURE 6-2 | *Manual page for CAT*

The source for CAT follows:

```
/*
 *      cat -- concatenate files
 */

#include <stdio.h>
#include <stdlib.h>
#include <local\std.h>

main(argc, argv)
int argc;
char **argv;
```

(continued)

```
{
        int ch;
        char *cp;
        FILE *fp;
        BOOLEAN errflag, silent;
        static char pgm[MAXNAME + 1] = { "cat" };

        extern void getpname(char *, char *);
        extern int fcopy(FILE *, FILE *);
        extern int getopt(int, char **, char *);
        extern int optind;
        extern char *optarg;

        /* use an alias if one is given to this program */
        if (_osmajor >= 3)
                getpname(*argv, pgm);

        /* process optional arguments, if any */
        errflag = FALSE;
        silent = FALSE;
        while ((ch = getopt(argc, argv, "s")) != EOF)
                switch (ch) {
                case 's':
                        /* don't complain about non-existent files */
                        silent = TRUE;
                        break;
                case '?':
                        /* say what? */
                        errflag = TRUE;
                        break;
                }
        if (errflag == TRUE) {
                fprintf(stderr, "Usage: %s [-s] file...\n", pgm);
                exit(1);
        }

        /* process any remaining arguments */
        argc -= optind;
        argv += optind;
        if (argc == 0)
                /* no file names -- use standard input */
                if (fcopy(stdin, stdout) != 0) {
                        fprintf(stderr, "error copying stdin");
```

(continued)

```
                    exit(2);
            }
            else
                    exit(0);

    /* copy the contents of each named file to standard output */
    for (; argc-- > 0; ++argv) {
            if ((fp = fopen(*argv, "r")) == NULL) {
                    if (silent == FALSE)
                            fprintf(stderr, "%s: can't open %s\n",
                                    pgm, *argv);
                    continue;
            }
            if (fcopy(fp, stdout) != 0) {
                    fprintf(stderr, "%s: Error while copying %s",
                            pgm, *argv);
                    exit(3);
            }
            if (fclose(fp) != 0) {
                    fprintf(stderr, "%s: Error closing %s",
                            pgm, *argv);
                    exit(4);
            }
    }

    exit(0);
}
```

CAT duplicates its input stream on its output stream by calling *fcopy( )*. The input comes from files named on the command line or from *stdin* if no files are named. Output is to the standard output stream, *stdout*. Therefore, CAT is minimally a filter. The transformation it performs is to merge data streams into a single sequential output stream. CAT is most frequently used to list the contents of one file on the console screen or to combine a group of files into a single file. It may be used as the source node of a pipeline command, either taking its input from named files or the console.

Following is the C source for *fcopy( )*.

```
/*
 *       fcopy -- copy input stream (fin) to output stream (fout)
 *       and return an indication of success or failure
 */

#include <stdio.h>

int fcopy(fin, fout)
FILE *fin, *fout;
{
        int errcount = 0;
        char line[BUFSIZ];
        char *s;

        while ((s = fgets(line, BUFSIZ, fin)) != NULL)
                if (fputs(s, fout) == EOF)
                        ++errcount;
        if (ferror(fin))
                ++errcount;
        return (errcount);        /* 0 if all went well */
}
```

Since both *getopt( )* and *fcopy( )* are going to be useful in other programs, add them to the utility library.

Now that we have a function that lets us process command lines in a consistent way, we can move on to other aspects of the user-machine interface. We will now look at methods of producing machine-independent time measurements and delays.

Timing Functions

The routines and programs in this and the next subsections show how to time events, produce time delays, and create sounds. All depend in some way upon the PC's built-in timer circuits. We begin with a program called TIMER, which uses some of the *ctime* subroutines in the standard library that we examined in Chapter 4.

TIMER is an external program that lets us time intervals from the DOS command level and from within batch files. The program is handy for timing events lasting from a few seconds to a few days. It is not suitable for shorter intervals because of the way it is implemented. A typical use consists of starting a timer, running a program or performing a task, and then calling the timer again to check the elapsed time. Figure 6-3 is the manual page for TIMER, and its source code is in *timer.c*.

NAME

TIMER—provide timing data for up to four events

SYNOPSIS

timer [-efs#]

DESCRIPTION

TIMER uses command-line options to select program actions. The option letters may be combined following a single option flag (-) or invoked separately. If the f option is combined with other options, it must be last. These options are honored by TIMER:

Option	Meaning
-s	Start (or restart) a timer
-e	Display or record elapsed time
-f file	Record the output of the TIMER command in *file*
-#	The # symbol is a numeric parameter in the range of 0 to 3 that selects one of the four timers. If no number is specified, TIMER uses 0 by default.

EXAMPLES

Start the default timer:

timer -s

Restart timer 0 and record the output in the file *project.dat:*

timer -s -f project.dat

NOTES

TIMER uses the intra-application communication area to hold starting times for each of the timers. If another program uses the same memory locations, timer data could be corrupted. When asked to produce an elapsed time, TIMER tries to detect corrupt data and outputs an error message rather than a time value.

FIGURE 6-3 | *Manual page for TIMER*

The source for TIMER follows:

```
/*
 *        timer -- general purpose timer program; uses the
 *        PC's intra-application communication area (ICA) as
 *        a time and date buffer
 */

#include <dos.h>
#include <stdio.h>
#include <stdlib.h>
#include <string.h>
#include <time.h>
#include <memory.h>
#include <local\std.h>

#define NBYTES        16
#define ICA_SEG       0x4F
#define MAXTNUM       3
#define TIMEMASK      0x3FFFFFFF
#define FLAGBIT       0x80000000
#define IDBIT         0x40000000

main(argc, argv)
int argc;
char *argv[];
{
        int ch;
        char *cp;
        int tn;                   /* timer number */
        int errflag;              /* error flag */
        int eflag;                /* elapsed time flag */
        int sflag;                /* start timer flag */
        char dest[MAXPATH + 1];   /* destination file name */
        char timestr[MAXLINE];    /* buffer for elapsed time string */
        long now;                 /* current time */
        long then;                /* previously recorded time */
        FILE *fout;
        unsigned long tdata[MAXNUM];

        struct SREGS segregs;

        static char pgm[MAXNAME + 1] = { "timer" };
```

(continued)

```
static void usage(char *, char *);
extern char interval(long, char *);
extern void getpname(char *, char *);
extern int getopt(int, char **, char *);
extern int optind, opterr;
extern char *optarg;

if (_osmajor >= 3)
        getpname(*argv, pgm);

/* process optional arguments */
fout = stdout;
tn = 0;
errflag = eflag = sflag = 0;
while ((ch = getopt(argc, argv, "0123ef:s")) != EOF) {
        switch (ch) {
        case 'e':
                /* report elapsed timing */
                ++eflag;
                break;
        case 'f':
                /* use specified log file or stream */
                strcpy(dest, optarg);
                if ((fout = fopen(dest, "a")) == NULL) {
                        fprintf(stderr, "%s: Cannot open %s\n",
                                pgm, dest);
                        exit(1);
                }
                break;
        case 's':
                /* start (or restart) timing an interval */
                ++sflag;
                break;
        case '0':
        case '1':
        case '2':
        case '3':
                /* use specified timer */
                tn = ch - 0x30;
                break;
        case '?':
                /* bad option flag */
                ++errflag;
                break;
```

(continued)

```
                }
        }
        argc -= optind;
        argv += optind;

        /* check for errors */
        if (errflag > 0 || argc > 0)
                usage(pgm, "Bad command line option(s)");

        segread(&segregs);

        /* report current date and time */
        now = time(NULL);
        fprintf(fout, "%s", ctime(&now));

        /* control and report timer data */
        if (eflag) {
                /* report elapsed time for specified timer */
                movedata(ICA_SEG, 0, segregs.ds, tdata, NBYTES);
                then = tdata[tn];
                if ((then & FLAGBIT) != FLAGBIT || (then & IDBIT) != IDBIT) {
                        fprintf(stderr, "Timer database corrupted or not set\n");
                        exit(1);
                }
                interval(now - (then & TIMEMASK), timestr);
                fprintf(stdout, "Elapsed time = %s\n", timestr);
        }
        if (sflag) {
                /* start (or restart) specified timer */
                movedata(ICA_SEG, 0, segregs.ds, tdata, NBYTES);
                tdata[tn] = (now & TIMEMASK) | FLAGBIT | IDBIT;
                movedata(segregs.ds, tdata, ICA_SEG, 0, NBYTES);
        }
        fputc('\n', fout);

        exit(0);
}

/*
 *      usage -- display a usage message and exit
 *      with an error indication
 */
```

(continued)

```
static void
usage(pname, mesg)
char *pname;
char *mesg;
{
        fprintf(stderr, "%s\n", mesg);
        fprintf(stderr, "Usage: %s [-efs#]\n", pname);
        fprintf(stderr, "\t-e \tshow an elapsed time (must use start first)\n");
        fprintf(stderr, "\t-f file\tappend output to specified file\n");
        fprintf(stderr, "\t-s \tstart (or restart) an interval timer\n");
        fprintf(stderr, "\t-# \tselect a timer (0 to 3; default is 0)\n");
        exit(2);
}
```

The source for TIMER illustrates a slightly more complicated use of *getopt( )* than we saw in the CAT program. In addition to handling more option flags, TIMER has one option flag that requires an argument. The option -f takes an argument that specifies a filename; if -f is present, the next argument is presumed to be the required argument. The user can insert extra white space characters between the option flag and the argument, but it's not required. When *getopt( )* detects the -f option, it immediately sets *optarg* to point to the start of the argument string. The program calling *getopt( )* then interprets the argument.

The TIMER program uses a special area in memory that is called the intra-application communications area (ICA). The ICA resides in an area of memory (addresses 4F0–4FF hex) that is reserved by DOS. The ICA is a mere 16 bytes in length, but it's big enough to store four *long* integers, one for each of four separate timers. Few commercial programs use the ICA, but TIMER should protect itself against corruption of its data. Therefore, each timer value is represented by the lower 30 bits (0–29) of a four-byte *long*. The top two bits are used for status and identification purposes. The ID bit, bit 30, must be a logical value of 1. The most significant bit, bit 31, is also set to a logical value of 1 to indicate that a timer value has been stored. If these bits do not have the correct values, attempts to show an elapsed time produce an error message.

The *time( )* library function returns a *long* integer that is the number of seconds since the epoch (00:00:00 on January 1, 1970 for *ctime* sub-routines). There are 31,536,000 seconds in a normal year (add one day, 86,400 seconds, for a leap year). Using the first 30 bits of a *long* to hold the time value gives us a range of 34 years, so TIMER will function correctly until 2004—by which time I hope to have a new computer and operating system. We can extend the span to 68 years by not using a separate ID bit, but that increases our risk of returning incorrect elapsed time values if some other program happens to use the ICA.

TIMER is a small-model program because it requires little code space and even less data space. However, the ICA is in the BIOS segment, not the program's data space. TIMER uses the *movedata( )* library function to read and write data in the ICA. Because *movedata( )* requires two segmented addresses, TIMER also calls the *segread( )* library function to get the data segment register value. The other address needed by *movedata( )* is in the BIOS data segment. I chose to use 0x4F as the segment value (*ICA_SEG*) and an offset of 0 for the ICA, but these can be reversed if you prefer.

When the -e flag is given, TIMER calls *interval( )* with the number of seconds between "now" and when the timer was started. The saved timer is not altered. The *interval( )* function translates the elapsed seconds into ASCII text using the form *hh:mm:ss*. If no timer number is specified, timer 0 is used. The user may restart an interval timer by using the -s (start) option along with the timer number.

```
/*
 *      interval -- report the interval given in seconds as
 *      a human-readable null-terminated string
 */

#include <stdio.h>

char *
interval(seconds, buf)
long seconds;
char *buf;
{
        int hh, mm, ss;
        long remainder;

        /* calculate the values */
        hh = seconds / 3600;
        remainder = seconds % 3600;
```

(continued)

```
    mm = remainder / 60;
    ss = remainder - (mm * 60);
    sprintf(buf, "%02d:%02d:%02d\0", hh, mm, ss);

    return (buf);
}
```

I have found TIMER to be most useful for recording work time against project accounts in my consulting practice and also as a means of measuring program execution times. Using the -f option, all data that would normally appear on the console screen is instead appended to the named file, which becomes a handy record of activities. When testing program execution speeds, I minimize the effects of disk loading times by setting up a virtual disk for the batch file, the TIMER program, and the data file. Everything else is run from a hard disk or a floppy disk so that loading and access times for the program will be taken into account. This beats using a stopwatch and ink on paper.

The PC Timer and Time Delays

Following is a brief description of the timer circuits in the PC and a look at some of the internal programs that keep track of time in various ways. Refer to Figure 6-4 while reading through this description. The figure shows the basic elements of the PC's timer and speaker-control circuits. We can ignore the speaker elements (shaded boxes) for now and concentrate our attention on the clock signal generator and timer/counters 0 and 1.

The primary clock rates for the system unit and peripheral interfaces are derived from a high speed crystal-controlled oscillator, an 8284A device. One of the output signals is divided down to 1.19318 megahertz (MHz) and is fed to the 8253-5 timer/counter on the CLK input of all three channels. (An 8254-2 timer/counter circuit is used in the PC/AT.) Channel 1 is used to refresh main memory; we should not alter this channel in any way. Channel 2 will be described when we cover sound generation. Of primary interest to us now is channel 0, which is used to provide a system-wide timer interrupt (interrupt 8). This interrupt is called a clock tick.

A clock tick occurs at a rate of about 18.2 per second, or one approximately every 55 milliseconds. The number of ticks per second is the timer

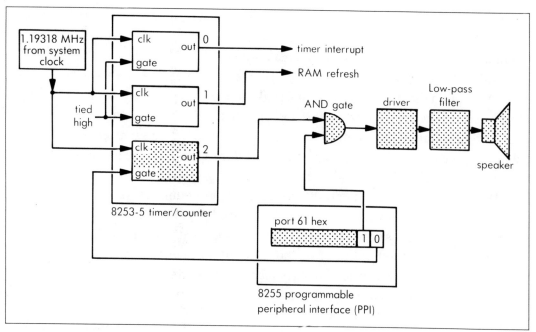

FIGURE 6-4 | *Timer and speaker control circuits*

input clock rate, 1.19381 MHz, divided by 65536, which is the divisor on timer channel 0. Other divisors may be used to produce different interrupt frequencies.

Each timer/counter channel contains a 16-bit counter, a pair of 8-bit latches to hold the starting count, a pair of 8-bit output latches, and control logic. Each input clock pulse decrements the value held in the 16-bit counter until the value is 0. Setting a count of FFFF hex gives us a divisor of 65535, which is one less than needed. If, however, we set the starting count to 0, the first input clock pulse will cause the counter to go from 0 to 65535 (0−1= −1; all bits set to logical 1). This technique produces an effective divisor of 65536, the correct value, because the counter is treated as an unsigned integer. Consult the Intel timer/counter documentation for more information on how it works and how it may be programmed.

The ticks are used by the ROM BIOS to update the time-of-day (TOD) clock, which is stored as the number of ticks since midnight. Therefore, any program that modifies the count on timer channel 0 must compensate for the change to maintain the tick rate seen by BIOS. We can use the same 18.2 ticks per second as the basis of some machine-independent timing functions to produce delays and to create sound.

We may want to build delays into our programs for a variety of reasons. A program that has a banner frame (I like to call it the "ego frame") must be seen to be appreciated, so it is appropriate to hold it on screen for a few seconds. Automated "slide shows" need controllable delays between frames to pace the presentation. Accurate short-duration delays are also needed to produce audible sound effects.

When there was only a single PC model, many programmers were not too careful about how time delays were produced. We often depended upon the characteristics of the machine by using loops that went through the right number of iterations to waste the required time. Of course, faster processors and higher clock rates in many of the newer computers have shrunk delays produced this way to as little as an eighth of their former selves. We are now in need of a way to produce reliable, machine-independent time delays.

The *delay( )* function uses the computer's timer to generate delays that are consistent with the entire family of IBM PCs and portable to most compatible machines. In order to produce the required waiting period, the *delay( )* function converts the specified period into a number of timer ticks. It does so by multiplying the period by *TICKRATE,* which is defined in *timer.h* in the *include**local* directory. It then adds that amount to the current number of clock ticks obtained from the time-of-day counter and stores the sum. Then *getticks( )* is called repeatedly by *delay( ).* The *delay( )* function exits when the value returned by *getticks( )* equals or exceeds the target value.

The *getticks( )* function queries the TOD clock and returns the current time of day as a count of clock ticks. One modification is made when the TOD clock rolls over from one day to the next: Since the TOD clock count is reset to zero and a flag is set to indicate the day increment, the *getticks( )* function adds a day's worth of ticks (1,573,040 [1800B0 hex]) to the count it returns if the flag is nonzero. Since all machines in the IBM product line (and most compatibles) use the 1.19381 MHz timer clock rate, the delay period is the same on all of the machines and is totally independent of the CPU speed and master clock rate of the machine.

The following files contain the sources for the header file, *timer.h,* and the functions *delay( )* and *getticks( ):*

```
/*
 *       timer.h -- header for timer control routines
 */


/* timer clock and interrupt rates */
#define TIMER_CLK       1193180L
#define TIMER_MAX       65536L
#define TICKRATE        TIMER_CLK / TIMER_MAX

/* timer port access for frequency setting */
#define TIMER_CTRL      0x43
#define TIMER_COUNT     0x42
#define TIMER_PREP      0xB6
```

```
/*
 *       delay -- provide a delay of ** approximately ** the
 *       specified duration (resolution is about 0.055 second)
 */

#include <local\timer.h>

void
delay(d)
float d;/* duration in seconds and fractional seconds */
{
        long ticks, then;
        extern long getticks();

        /* convert duration to number of PC clock ticks */
        ticks = d * TICKRATE;

        /* delay for the specified interval */
        then = getticks() + ticks;
        while (1)
                if (getticks() >= then)
                        break;
}
```

```
/*      getticks -- get the current BIOS clock ticks value      */

#include <dos.h>

#define BIOS_DATA_SEG   0x40
#define TIMER_DATA      0x6C
#define TICKS_PER_DAY   0x01800B0L

long getticks()
{
        static long total = 0;  /* accumulated count of timer ticks */
        long count;             /* current BIOS TOD count */
        long far *lp;           /* far pointer */
        /* set up the far pointer to the BIOS TOD counter */
        FP_SEG(lp) = BIOS_DATA_SEG;
        FP_OFF(lp) = TIMER_DATA;
        while (1) {              /* read the TOD count */
                count = *lp;
                if (*lp == count)
                        break;  /* two matching TOD readings */
        }
        /* correct for clock roll-over, if necessary */
        total = (count < total) ? count + TICKS_PER_DAY : count;
        return (total);
}
```

The *delay( )* function has general applicability and will be used in other programs. We need to put it someplace that is easy to access. Because *delay( )* is based on the *getticks( )* function, which in turn uses the ROM BIOS, we will add both of these functions to the bios library. And, of course, *timer.h* takes a permanent home in *include**local.*

Audible Feedback

We now turn our attention to sound generation. The first thing to notice about sound is that it irritates some users. Also, sound is totally inappropriate in some settings. Therefore, we must provide a way for the user to disable sound. The programs in this book will use a variable, usually the global variable *Silent*, to record the user's preference regarding sound. If *Silent* is logically *TRUE*, our program will be mute.

The shaded boxes in Figure 6-4 on page 143 show the PC sound system. Notice how the sound system is built upon channel 2 of the timer subsystem and a couple of I/O ports in the 8255-5 programmable peripheral interface (PPI) device. The timer/counter produces squarewave signals that are amplified and filtered, then passed to the speaker. The AND gate ahead of the driver is controlled by bit 1 of the PPI port 61 hex. In addition, bit 0 of the same port controls the gate lead of timer channel 2. Thus, the PPI can be used to turn sound on (both bits a logical 1) or off (either bit a logical 0). The advantage of using the timer to produce sound is that the sound plays in the "background," and does not steal precious cycles from the CPU.

Alternatively, we can disable the timer by setting port 61 hex, bit 0 low, and pulse the speaker directly under program control via bit 1. The problem with this approach is that the program can do nothing else while it attends to the speaker. We will not use this approach.

The file *sound.h,* also in *include**local,* is the header file for our sound routines. It contains definitions and macros used to control the speaker's state. *SPKR_ON* sets the low two bits in the peripheral interface port to logical 1s. This enables the timer and passes signals through to the speaker. The *SPKR_OFF* macro sets both bits low, turning the speaker off by robbing it of input signals.

```
/*
 *      sound.h -- header for sound routines
 */

#define PPI        0x61
#define SPKR       0x03
#define SPKR_ON    outp(PPI, inp(PPI) | SPKR)
#define SPKR_OFF   outp(PPI, inp(PPI) & ~SPKR)
```

As noted already, the speaker can operate independently, letting us put sounds in the background. We can demonstrate this with a simple control program, SPKR. This program turns the speaker off if it is called with no arguments and on if it receives any other number of arguments. The source for this test driver is contained in *spkr.c* (on the following page).

```
/*
 *      spkr -- turn speaker ON/OFF
 *
 *              no args => OFF
 *              any arg(s) => ON
 */

#include <local\sound.h>

main(argc, argv)
int argc;
char **argv;
{
        /* turn speaker on or off */
        if (argc == 1)
                SPKR_OFF;
        else
                SPKR_ON;
        exit(0);
}
```

The program has one problem—it does not set the pitch of the tone the speaker emits. This must be done by another program, TONE, a simple test driver that lets us set the pitch from the DOS command line. TONE takes a single argument that specifies the desired frequency in hertz. The usable range for the PC's internal speaker is about 40 Hz to a little more than 6 KHz. Higher frequencies can also be used; however, these may cause some speakers to produce barely audible tones or clicking sounds. TONE calls upon a low-level routine, *setfreq( )*, to calculate the needed divisor for the specified frequency and to set up the timer's channel 2, from which the speaker derives its input. The *setfreq( )* function includes the *timer.h* header file which contains the declarations for the port addresses and values needed to set the frequency of the timer.

The code for TONE and *setfreq( )* follow:

```
/*
 *      tone -- set the frequency of the sound generator
 */

#include <stdio.h>
```

(continued)

```
main(argc, argv)
int argc;
char **argv;
{
        extern void setfreq(unsigned int);

        if (argc != 2) {
                fprintf(stderr, "Usage: tone hertz\n");
                exit(1);
        }

        /* set the frequency in hertz */
        setfreq(atoi(*++argv));
        exit(0);
}
```

```
/*
 *      setfreq -- sets PC's tone generator to run
 *      continuously at the specified frequency
 */

#include <conio.h>
#include <local\timer.h>

void
setfreq(f)
unsigned f;      /* frequency in hertz (approximate) */
{
        unsigned divisor = TIMER_CLK / f;

        outp(TIMER_CTRL, TIMER_PREP);        /* prepare timer */
        outp(TIMER_COUNT, (divisor & 0xFF));  /* low byte of divisor */
        outp(TIMER_COUNT, (divisor >> 8));    /* high byte of divisor */
}
```

To use these programs to demonstrate some of the capabilities of the sound system, compile and link them, and then type

```
TONE 1000
SPKR ON
```

This sets an audible pitch and turns on the speaker. You can do other work and the tone will continue to play unless some other program turns off the speaker. Typing

SPKR

without any arguments turns off the speaker.

You can simulate a burglar alarm sound if you have a perverse nature. Key in the code for *sweep.c,* compile it and link it with the *setfreq.obj* file, and type

SWEEP

To stop the sound before the police arrive, press any key.

```c
/*
 *      sweep -- produce a sound that sweeps from
 *      a low to a high frequency repeatedly until a
 *      key is pressed
 */

#include <conio.h>
#include <local\sound.h>

main()
{
        unsigned int f;
        int d, n;
        extern void setfreq(unsigned int);

        SPKR_ON;
        while (1) {
                /* give the user a way out */
                if (kbhit())
                        break;
                n = 10;
                for (f = 100; f <= 5000; f += n) {
                        setfreq(f);
                        d = 1000;
                        /* fake a short delay (machine dependent) */
                        while (d-- > 0)
                                ;
                        n += 10;
                }
        }
```

(continued)

```
        SPKR_OFF;
        exit(0);
}
```

All this noise making is wonderful for something, I'm sure, but we will want finer control of the sound subsystem in our programs. We obtain that control via the *sound( )* function, our high-level sound interface function. Using *sound( )*, we can produce distinctive sounds such as a confirmation signal (*confirm( )*), a warning signal (*warn( )*), and many others. The source for the *sound( )* function is contained in *sound.c.*

```
/*
 *        sound -- produce a constant tone for a specified duration
 */

#include <conio.h>
#include <local\sound.h>


void
sound(f, dur)
unsigned int f; /* frequency of pitch in hertz */
float dur;      /* in seconds and tenths of seconds */
{
        extern void setfreq(unsigned int);
        extern void delay(float);

        /* set the frequency in hertz */
        setfreq(f);

        /* turn the speaker on for specified duration */
        SPKR_ON;
        delay(dur);
        SPKR_OFF;
}
```

Notice that the speaker is turned on, continues to sound during the specified interval, and is then turned off for each tone being generated. Earlier demonstration programs turned on the speaker once, issued a series of pitch changes, and then turned off the speaker. Either way is OK, but the approach used by the *sound( )* function is more versatile for our purposes.

The program SOUNDS contains a few sample audible signals selected via a simple menu. You can use these as a starting point and create some of your own.

```
/*
 *      sounds -- make various sounds on demand
 */

#include <stdio.h>
#include <conio.h>
#include <math.h>

#define ESC     27

extern void sound(unsigned int, float);

main()
{
        int ch;

        fprintf(stderr, "1=warble 2=error 3=confirm 4=warn\n");
        fprintf(stderr, "Esc=quit\n");
        while ((ch = getch()) != ESC)
                switch (ch) {
                case '1':
                        warble();
                        break;
                case '2':
                        error();
                        break;
                case '3':
                        confirm();
                        break;
                case '4':
                        warn();
                        break;
                }
        exit(0);
```

(continued)

```
}

#define CYCLES  3
#define LOTONE  600
#define HITONE  1200
#define PERIOD  0.1

warble()
{
        int i;

        for (i = 0; i < 2 * CYCLES; ++i)
                if (i % 2)
                        sound(LOTONE, PERIOD);
                else
                        sound(HITONE, PERIOD);
}

error()
{
        float d = 0.1;

        sound(440, d);
        sound(220, d);
}

confirm()
{
        float d = 0.1;

        sound(440, d);
        sound(880, d);
}

warn()
{
        float d = 0.2;

        sound(100, d);
}
```

Don't forget to check the user's preference before "making a joyful noise." Give the user a command-line argument to disable sound: Use -s, for example, to set *Silent* to *TRUE* if it is Boolean, or to a nonzero value if it is a simple integer. Then a simple conditional such as

```
if (Silent == FALSE)
     warn();
```

will prevent the sound produced by *warn()* from being heard by an ungrateful audience!

Getting User Input

Next we turn our attention to the topic of getting input from the user. In our programs, we sometimes need to ask the user for a filename, a drive letter, or some other piece of important information. The goal of our next task is to design a general purpose input routine that prompts the user with a brief instruction and gathers a reply. It sounds simple enough: Just use *printf()* to display the prompt and *scanf()* to collect the response. This may sound reasonable, but this approach has some unnecessary limitations and some really serious problems.

The *scanf()* function is not appropriate because it is designed for use with formatted data—the kind that is produced automatically by a program, not entered by hand. Besides, users are notorious for breaking things, accidentally or on purpose, and *scanf()* can be easily broken, even by the well-intentioned user who simply makes a typing mistake. We need something more versatile.

Programs that have a lot of information on the screen may run short of screen space, so to make things interesting, we will require that the response field be able to take a response that is larger than the displayable field width. The response field must, therefore, be a window onto the user's response and must scroll sideways to permit the user to view and edit the response text.

Figures 6-5A and 6-5B depict what we are trying to do in terms of screen presentation. We will use the BIOS video routines developed in

Chapter 5 to control screen appearance and the DOS keyboard routines
(also Chapter 5) to gather the user's input. Editing operations include the
usual destructive backspace (←) and single-character delete (Del). A character is inserted into the buffer by pushing all characters from the cursor
to the end of the line, to the right one position, and by putting the input
character in the vacated spot. The cursor moves to the right one position.

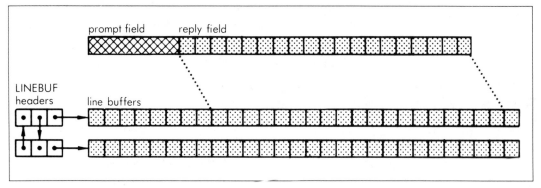

FIGURE 6-5A | *Memory and screen of*
getreply( )

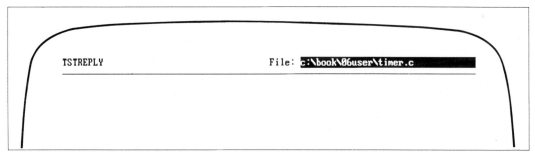

FIGURE 6-5B | *Sample screen: Getting a*
pathname

Cursor motions include moving to the beginning of text (Home), to the end of text (End), and left and right by one character (left and right arrows). Pressing Esc aborts the input operation and causes *getreply( )* to return a *NULL* pointer to the calling function; pressing Enter anywhere in the line returns a pointer to the reply string. The calling function is responsible for validating the reply it receives.

If *getreply( )* is to be used more than once for a given reply field in a form or an interactive program, it would be wonderful if it could recall the most recent response, or better yet, scroll back and forth through a list of previous responses. Rather than put all of the complications associated with list management into *getreply( )*, we will have the calling function pass a pointer to an array of line buffers that it sets up. Then *getreply( )* permits the user to scan up and down the list of line buffers by using the up and down arrow keys.

This design may seem to be a tall order to fill, but it is actually not that difficult. Several cooperating functions give us a very nice user interface routine and teach us a few things about windows and editing, too. We will name the routine *getreply( )* and try to generalize it enough to make it useful in many programs.

We will call on the standard library to help us with a few tasks. The memory function, *memcpy( )*, copies strings within a single segment. The source and destination strings will be allowed to overlap to permit sideways scrolling. The *memcpy( )* function guarantees that no characters will be lost in an overlapping copy operation. The reply string buffer within *getreply( )* is initialized to null bytes (\0) before it is allowed to receive any user data. This action guarantees that the resulting string will be properly terminated.

After getting a preliminary version of *getreply( )* working and grousing over a few of its idiosyncracies, I arrived at the following sources for the function, which behaves rather well when challenged by even the most hostile users. The line buffer data structure is defined in *linebuf.h*, and the source for the *getreply( )* function is in *getreply.c*.

```
/*
 * linebuf.h
 */

typedef struct lb_st {
        struct lb_st *l_next;
        struct lb_st *l_prev;
        char *l_buf;
} LINEBUF;
```

```
/*
 *      getreply -- display a message and wait for a reply
 */

#include <stdio.h>
#include <stdlib.h>
#include <memory.h>
#include <ctype.h>
#include <local\std.h>
#include <local\keydefs.h>
#include "linebuf.h"

char *
getreply(row, col, width, mesg, lp, size, attr, pg)
short row, col, width;  /* window location and width */
char *mesg;             /* message text */
LINEBUF *lp;            /* line pointer */
short size;             /* size of line buffer */
short attr;             /* video attribute for response field */
short pg;               /* active display page */
{
        int n, k, len;
        short mfw;      /* message field width */
        short rfw;      /* response field width */
        short ccol;     /* visible cursor column */
        int msgflag;    /* non-zero after a message is displayed */
        char *cp;       /* character pointer */
        char *wp;       /* pointer to window start */
        char *tmp;      /* temporary char pointer */

        extern int writemsg(short, short, short, char *, char *, short);
```

(continued)

```
/* display the prompt string and calculate response field width */
putcur(row, col, pg);
mfw = writemsg(row, col, width, mesg, NULL, pg);
rfw = width - mfw;
writea(attr, rfw, pg);

/* collect the user's response */
memset(lp->l_buf, '\0', size);
wp = cp = lp->l_buf;
putcur(row, col + mfw, pg);
msgflag = 0;
while ((k = getkey()) != K_RETURN) {
        if (msgflag) {
                /* clear old messages */
                errmsg("");
                putcur(row, ccol, pg);
                msgflag = 0;
        }
        if (isascii(k) && isprint(k)) {
                len = strlen(cp);
                if (cp + len - lp->l_buf < size - 1) {
                        memcpy(cp + 1, cp, len);
                        *cp = k;
                        ++cp;
                }
                else {
                        errmsg("input buffer full");
                        ++msgflag;
                }
        }
        else
                switch (k) {
                case K_LEFT:
                        /* move left one character */
                        if (cp > lp->l_buf)
                                --cp;
                        break;
                case K_RIGHT:
                        /* move right one character */
                        if (*cp != '\0')
                                ++cp;
                        break;
```

(continued)

```
        case K_UP:
                /* pop a line off the stack */
                if (lp->l_prev != NULL) {
                        lp = lp->l_prev;
                        wp = cp = lp->l_buf;
                }
                break;
        case K_DOWN:
                /* push a line onto the stack */
                if (lp->l_next != NULL) {
                        lp = lp->l_next;
                        wp = cp = lp->l_buf;
                }
                break;
        case K_HOME:
                /* beginning of buffer */
                cp = lp->l_buf;
                break;
        case K_END:
                /* end of buffer */
                while (*cp != '\0')
                        ++cp;
                break;
        case K_CTRLH:
                if (cp > lp->l_buf) {
                        tmp = cp - 1;
                        memcpy(tmp, cp, strlen(tmp));
                        --cp;
                }
                break;
        case K_DEL:
                /* delete character at cursor */
                memcpy(cp, cp + 1, strlen(cp));
                break;
        case K_ESC:
                /* cancel current input */
                lp->l_buf[0] = '\0';
                putcur(row, col, pg);
                writec(' ', width, pg);
                return (NULL);
```

(continued)

```
                    default:
                            errmsg("unknown command");
                            ++msgflag;
                            break;
                    }

            /* adjust the window pointer if necessary */
            if (cp < wp)
                    wp = cp;
            else if (cp >= wp + rfw)
                    wp = cp + 1 - rfw;

            /* display the reply window */
            ccol = col + mfw;
            writemsg(row, ccol, rfw, wp, NULL, pg);

            /* reposition the cursor */
            ccol = col + mfw + (cp - wp);
            putcur(row, ccol, pg);
    }
    putcur(row, col, pg);
    writec(' ', width, pg); /* blank message area */
    return (lp->l_buf);
}
```

A few parts of the code appear to be a bit dense and need some explanation. The dimension of the reply field is calculated by subtracting the prompt field width from the working area allowed to *getreply( )* by the calling function. Values are not error-checked, so be sure to pass something that makes sense.

The bulk of the work is done in the *while* statement that loops as long as the Return key (or Enter as IBM prefers to call it) is not pressed. If a key is a printable ASCII character, it is inserted into the buffer. If not, it is checked to see whether it is an editing or cursor movement command. Valid commands are executed and invalid keypresses evoke an error response.

Controlling the window position relative to the input text is handled by a pair of pointers. The character pointer *cp* tracks the current input/editing position in the buffer, and *wp,* also a character pointer, points to the first character in the buffer that will be displayed in the reply field window. A test within the loop assures that the editing/input position is always within the displayed reply window.

The *getreply( )* function uses an external error message routine. This practice assures the calling routine that nothing will be displayed arbitrarily on the screen. The calling function has complete control as to when and where the error message will appear.

One thing that angers me when I use some programs is having old error messages still displayed on the screen. The code for *getreply( )* prevents messages from being displayed past their time. A message flag is set when a new error message is issued and is cleared with the next keystroke. The message handler is sent a null message, which is its hint to clean up the message display area. It can ignore the hint, but it usually should not.

To see *getreply( )* in action, compile and link TSTREPLY, and run it. Although the program does little more than call *getreply( )*, it gives us a way to test *getreply( )* and demonstrate its operation. It also provides all of the code necessary to set up a message handler and manage a line buffer array. The C source is in *tstreply.c*:

```
/*
 *      tstreply -- test the getreply function
 */

#include <stdio.h>
#include <string.h>
#include <local\std.h>
#include <local\video.h>
#include "linebuf.h"

#define INPUT_ROW       0
#define INPUT_COL       40
#define WIDTH           40

int Apage = 0;
BOOLEAN Silent = FALSE;

main(argc, argv)
int argc;
char *argv[];
```

(continued)

```
{
        unsigned int r, c, ch, attr, revattr;
        char reply[MAXPATH + 1];
        LINEBUF buf;

        extern char *getreply(short, short, short,
                char *, LINEBUF *, short, short, short);

        /* process command line */
        if (argc == 2 && strcmp(argv[1], "-s") == 0)
                Silent = TRUE;
        else if (argc > 2) {
                fprintf(stderr, "Usage: tstreply [-s]\n");
                exit(1);
        }

        /* initial setup */
        getstate();
        readca(&ch, &attr, Apage);
        revattr = ((attr << 4) | (attr >> 4)) & 0x77;
        clrscrn(attr);
        putcur(0, 0, Apage);
        writestr("TSTREPLY", Apage);
        putcur(1, 0, Apage);
        writec(HLINE, Maxcol[Vmode] - 1, Apage);
        buf.l_buf = reply;
        buf.l_next = buf.l_prev = (LINEBUF *)NULL;

        /* demo getreply() */

        if (getreply(INPUT_ROW, INPUT_COL, WIDTH, "File: ", &buf,
                MAXPATH, revattr, 0) == NULL) {
                putcur(INPUT_ROW, INPUT_COL, Apage);
                writeca(' ', attr, WIDTH, Apage);
                putcur(2, 0, Apage);
                fprintf(stderr, "input aborted\n");
                exit(1);
        }
        putcur(INPUT_ROW, INPUT_COL, Apage);
        writeca(' ', attr, WIDTH, Apage);
        putcur(2, 0, Apage);
        fprintf(stderr, "reply = %s\n", reply);
        exit(0);
```

(continued)

```
}

#define MSG_ROW 24
#define MSG_COL 0

int errmsg(mesg)
char *mesg;
{
        int n;
        extern void sound(unsigned int, float);

        putcur(MSG_ROW, MSG_COL, Apage);
        if ((n = strlen(mesg)) > 0) {
                writestr(mesg, Apage);
                if (Silent == FALSE)
                        sound(100, 0.2);
        }
        else
                writec(' ', Maxcol[Vmode] - 1 - MSG_COL, Apage);
        return (n);
}
```

Automatic Program Configuration 7

We saw in Chapters 3 and 6 how programs can be given optional arguments to control their behavior in order to meet special needs. In the case of CAT in Chapter 6, for example, the -s option causes CAT to remain silent about missing files. The use of such a command-line option is a manual means of configuring a program.

However, the use of command-line options is often an impractical approach, particularly if a program uses many options. Users often will avoid reading the manual page and therefore may give up on a perfectly good program. What can be done about this?

One solution is to treat an additional program feature as you would an extra nose on your face—avoid it if you can. No sense cluttering up a simple and effective program with lots of little gargoyle-like appendages. Try to keep a program simple and geared to doing a single task as well as possible. If you believe that a program needs another feature to round out its capabilities, see whether other users of the program agree. But avoid the temptation to put in every feature requested by every user; the result will usually be a program that nobody uses.

Assuming that there is no way to avoid adding that slick new feature to your program, let's at least look at ways of automating things to make using your software product easier for the "liveware." We can provide automatic program configuration in several tidy, user-controlled ways, including, but not limited to, using the program name and using external configuration files.

Using the Program Name

As we learned earlier, the name used to invoke a program under DOS version 3.00 and later is available to the program. We could, therefore, use a program's name to alter its behavior. For example, if some additional code were put into our CAT program from the previous chapter, we could cause the program to become a "silent" CAT simply by making a copy of CAT.EXE with the name SCAT.EXE. Then the command

```
C> scat filename
```

would have the same effect as the command

```
C> cat -s filename
```

used in our current design.

All we need to do is add these lines to *cat.c* just after line 46, following the optional argument-processing loop:

```
if (strcmp(pgm, "SCAT") = = 0)
        Silent = TRUE;
```

Many other programs lend themselves to this form of configuration. Under UNIX and XENIX, giving a program another name adds only a link to the original file. No additional space is required for the program file's contents. However, there is a price for doing this under DOS. Every additional name for the same program file requires an additional directory entry, a file allocation table entry, and storage space. Using aliases, then, is not recommended except in rare situations in which the convenience outweighs the lost disk space.

Using Configuration Files

There is another convenient way to configure a program. Like the use of the program's name, it too provides automatic operation. Although it also requires additional disk space, it typically uses only a single cluster, not a complete duplication of the original program file.

In this method, variables and values are read from a file and are used to initialize or update selected program variables at any time during the operation of the program. Several levels of configuration files may be used. An arrangement that works well in practice uses a global data file that is located in a directory pointed to by a DOS environment variable.

For example, on my hard-disk-based systems, I use a single subdirectory called *c:\config* as a convenient location for all configuration files for the programs that accept external configuration. Each of these files bears the name of the program it configures plus a .CNF extension. Thus, *c:\config\progname.cnf* contains the configuration data for the PROGNAME program. The DOS variable CONFIG is defined by the statement

```
set config = c:\config
```

in my AUTOEXEC.BAT file.

A local configuration file—one located in the current directory—may override the global file. This permits directory-by-directory control over program behavior. For instance, a user of a program that prints the contents of a text file may want one type of behavior for program-source files and quite another for a "dumb-things-I-gotta-do" list.

The pseudocode for handling the configuration layers just described is as follows:

```
initialize program control variables to built-in values
if (local configuration file is found)
        overlay defaults with local configuration values
else if (specified DOS variable found)
        if (global configuration file found)
                overlay defaults with global values
else
        return NULL file pointer
update variables per command-line instructions, if any
```

It is not an error for either the local or the global configuration file, or both, to be missing, but it is an error for program-control variables not to be initialized by the program before they are used. The responsibility for the first step in the process—providing default initialization—is left to the main program. The local and global steps can be performed by a new addition to our utility library, the *fconfig( )* function. We still permit command-line arguments to override other settings on a per-invocation basis, as indicated by the last step in the process described by the pseudocode.

Here is the C source code for the *fconfig( )* function, which seeks a configuration file and, if it finds one, returns a *FILE* pointer to the file, which is open and ready to read from the top.

```
/*
 *      fconfig -- return a FILE pointer to a local or
 *      global configuration file, or NULL if none found
 */

#include <stdio.h>
#include <stdlib.h>
#include <string.h>
#include <ctype.h>
#include <local\std.h>

FILE *
fconfig(varname, fname)
char *varname;
char *fname;
{
        FILE *fp;
        char pname[MAXPATH + 1];
        char *p;

        /* look for a local configuration file */
        if ((fp = fopen(fname, "r")) != NULL)
                return (fp);

        /* look for a directory variable */
        if ((p = getenv(strupr(varname))) != NULL) {
                strcpy(pname, p);
                strcat(pname, "\\");
                strcat(pname, fname);
                if ((fp = fopen(pname, "r")) != NULL)
                        return (fp);
        }

        /* didn't find anything to read */
        return (NULL);
}
```

The calling function must specify the name of an environment variable, which may contain a global-configuration directory name, and the name of the configuration data file itself.

The name of the DOS variable that may hold a configuration-directory pathname is passed as a parameter to *fconfig( )*, not hard-coded into the function. This gives a calling program the latitude of specifying any environment-variable name it wants. The *pname* string variable within *fconfig( )* is large enough (*MAXPATH* plus room for a terminating null byte) to hold the longest pathname permissible under DOS.

The environment variable, if it exists, holds the pathname that represents the chain of directories leading up to the place where the global configuration file would be located. The *fconfig( )* function still must append a backslash and the filename to complete the full pathname of the configuration file. (Because the backslash is the C "escape" character, two backslashes are needed to get one out, the first turning off the special meaning of the second.)

Nothing we've done so far places any restrictions on the type of data that can be stored in and read from the configuration data file. The best format is highly dependent on the amount of data and what will be done with it. If a lot of Boolean flags are used to control a program, the best approach might be to use a binary format with all bits significant. If the data will be typed in by a casual user, the best approach might be to use strictly ASCII text. In practice, it turns out that the ordinary text file is best because it is more easily transported from one system to another without concerns about the native size of data words or the ordering of bytes within data words.

All data read into a program from a configuration file should be qualified in some way before being used to update program data. Data files created by mere mortals often will contain errors, such as typos, incorrect data types, out-of-range values, or too many or too few values. Data files created by a custom-designed setup program are less prone to such problems; however, checking all data wastes little time compared with the time it takes to reboot a system that chokes on its input.

Printer Control Functions

Now we'll look at an example of program configuration that nearly every PC user has a need for at one time or another. In this section of the chapter, we will develop a set of printer-interface routines that are aimed primarily at controlling the fonts of Epson and IBM dot-matrix printers. Then, in the next section, we will use the printer routines as the basis of a printer-control program that enables us to control the printer from the DOS command line and from batch files.

Let's begin with a look at Epson and compatible printers, including the original IBM PC printer. Many other printers use Epson-compatible control codes, so the following routines are applicable without change to a wide range of printers. For those printers that are not Epson compatible, our interface accepts user-supplied configuration data from a file.

To simplify matters a bit, we will make a few rules. First, the printer must be able to produce emphasized text without having to backspace and retype the text repeatedly. Second, the printer must be able to underline without having to back up and restrike the text with underscores. Third, if the printer does not offer a particular mode (double-strike, compressed, or expanded, for example), initializing the control codes for the mode to null strings ("") must effectively turn off the mode in the interface routines; no attempt is made to synthesize a mode from combinations of other modes.

Limitations such as these would be deadly to a commercial printer-control program, but they are acceptable here in our demonstration of printer control because they simplify our task and make it more manageable. If you need something more elaborate, you can use this program as a base and add controls for paper length, top-of-form position, line-to-line spacing, and many other features. The principles are the same as for the font-control set described here.

The file *printer.h* in the *include**local* directory contains the default values for Epson MX/FX-series printers and a set of printer variables used by the interface routines.

```
/*
 *      printer.h -- header for printer-control functions
 */



/* ASCII codes used for Epson MX/FX-series printer-control */
#define DC2     18      /* cancel condensed type mode */
#define DC4     20      /* cancel expanded type mode */
```

(continued)

```
#define ESC      27      /* signal start of printer-control sequences */
#define FF       12      /* top of page next page */
#define SO       14      /* start expanded type mode */
#define SI       15      /* start condensed type mode */

/* font types */
#define NORMAL          0x00
#define CONDENSED       0x01
#define DOUBLE          0x02
#define EMPHASIZED      0x04
#define EXPANDED        0x08
#define ITALICS         0x10
#define UNDERLINE       0x20

/* miscellaneous constants */
#define MAXPSTR 32       /* maximum printer-control string length */

/* primary printer-control data structure */
typedef struct printer_st {
        /* hardware initialize/reset */
        char p_init[MAXPSTR];

        /* set option strings and codes */
        char p_bold[MAXPSTR];    /* bold (emphasized) on */
        char p_cmp[MAXPSTR];     /* compressed on */
        char p_ds[MAXPSTR];      /* double strike on */
        char p_exp[MAXPSTR];     /* expanded (double width) on */
        char p_ul[MAXPSTR];      /* underline on */
        char p_ital[MAXPSTR];    /* italic on */

        /* reset option strings and codes */
        char p_norm[MAXPSTR];    /* restore normal font */
        char p_xbold[MAXPSTR];   /* bold (emphasized) off */
        char p_xcmp[MAXPSTR];    /* compressed off */
        char p_xds[MAXPSTR];     /* double strike off */
        char p_xexp[MAXPSTR];    /* expanded (double width) off */
        char p_xul[MAXPSTR];     /* underline off */
        char p_xital[MAXPSTR];   /* italic off */
} PRINTER;
```

The ASCII codes are used directly to control printer modes (SO, SI, and so forth) or to build up control-code strings (ESC in conjunction with other characters).

A set of font-type constants is defined so that each font type is mapped to a single bit. This permits fonts to be "stacked" to form composite fonts by using the bitwise OR. For example, *ITALICS | UNDERLINE* combines the values 0x10 and 0x20 to request an underlined italic font.

The file *printer.c* contains a set of three related printer-control functions: *setprnt( )*, *clrprnt( )*, and *setfont( )*. These functions use the variables defined in *printer.h* to determine what control strings to send to the printer. Here is the text of *printer.c*:

```
/*
 *      printer -- interface functions for printer
 */


#include <stdio.h>
#include <stdlib.h>
#include <string.h>
#include <local\std.h>
#include <local\printer.h>


PRINTER prt;    /* printer data */


/*
 *      setprnt -- install printer codes from configuration
 *      file for printer (defaults to Epson MX/FX series)
 */


#define NSELEM  13


int
setprnt()
{
        int n;
        char *s, line[MAXLINE];
        FILE *fp, *fconfig(char *, char *);

        /* use local or global config file, if any */
        if ((fp = fconfig("CONFIG", "printer.cnf")) != NULL) {
                n = 0;
                while (fgets(line, MAXLINE, fp) != NULL) {
                        if ((s = strtok(line, " \t\n")) == NULL)
                                return (-1);
```

(continued)

```
switch (n) {
case 0:
        strcpy(prt.p_init, s);
        break;
case 1:
        strcpy(prt.p_bold, s);
        break;
case 2:
        strcpy(prt.p_ds, s);
        break;
case 3:
        strcpy(prt.p_ital, s);
        break;
case 4:
        strcpy(prt.p_cmp, s);
        break;
case 5:
        strcpy(prt.p_exp, s);
        break;
case 6:
        strcpy(prt.p_ul, s);
        break;
case 7:
        strcpy(prt.p_xbold, s);
        break;
case 8:
        strcpy(prt.p_xds, s);
        break;
case 9:
        strcpy(prt.p_xital, s);
        break;
case 10:
        strcpy(prt.p_xcmp, s);
        break;
case 11:
        strcpy(prt.p_xexp, s);
        break;
case 12:
        strcpy(prt.p_xul, s);
        break;
default:
        /* too many lines */
        return (-1);
}
```

(continued)

```
                            ++n;
                    }
            if (n != NSELEM)
                        /* probably not enough lines */
                        return (-1);
        }

        /* or use Epson defaults */
        strcpy(prt.p_init, "\033ə");        /* hardware reset */
        strcpy(prt.p_bold, "\033E");        /* emphasized mode */
        strcpy(prt.p_ds, "\033G");          /* double-strike mode */
        strcpy(prt.p_ital, "\0334");        /* italic mode */
        strcpy(prt.p_cmp, "\017");          /* condensed mode */
        strcpy(prt.p_exp, "\016");          /* expanded mode */
        strcpy(prt.p_ul, "\033-1");         /* underline mode */
        strcpy(prt.p_xbold, "\033F");       /* cancel emphasized mode */
        strcpy(prt.p_xds, "\033H");         /* cancel double-strike mode *
        strcpy(prt.p_xital, "\0335");       /* cancel italic mode */
        strcpy(prt.p_xcmp, "\022");         /* cancel condensed mode */
        strcpy(prt.p_xexp, "\024");         /* cancel expanded mode */
        strcpy(prt.p_xul, "\033-0");        /* cancel underline mode */


        return (0);
}


/*
 *      clrprnt -- clear printer options to default values
 *      (clears individual options to avoid the "paper creep"
 *      that occurs with repeated printer resets and to avoid
 *      changing the printer's notion of top-of-form position)
 */
int
clrprnt(fout)
FILE *fout;
{
        fputs(prt.p_xbold, fout);          /* cancel emphasized mode */
        fputs(prt.p_xds, fout);            /* cancel double-strike mode */
        fputs(prt.p_xital, fout);          /* cancel italic mode */
        fputs(prt.p_xcmp, fout);           /* cancel condensed mode */
        fputs(prt.p_xexp, fout);           /* cancel expanded mode */
        fputs(prt.p_xul, fout);            /* cancel underline mode */
} /* end clrprnt() */
```

(continued)

```
/*
 *      setfont -- set the printing font to the type specified
 *      by the argument (may be a compound font specification)
 */

int
setfont(ftype, fout)
int ftype;      /* font type specifier */
FILE *fout;     /* output stream */
{
        clrprnt(fout);
        if ((ftype & CONDENSED) == CONDENSED)
                if ((ftype & DOUBLE) == DOUBLE ||
                        (ftype & EMPHASIZED) == EMPHASIZED)
                        return FAILURE;
                else if (*prt.p_cmp)
                        fputs(prt.p_cmp, fout);
        if (*prt.p_ds && (ftype & DOUBLE) == DOUBLE)
                fputs(prt.p_ds, fout);
        if (*prt.p_bold && (ftype & EMPHASIZED) == EMPHASIZED)
                fputs(prt.p_bold, fout);
        if (*prt.p_exp && (ftype & EXPANDED) == EXPANDED)
                fputs(prt.p_exp, fout);
        if (*prt.p_ital && (ftype & ITALICS) == ITALICS)
                fputs(prt.p_ital, fout);
        if (*prt.p_ul && (ftype & UNDERLINE) == UNDERLINE)
                fputs(prt.p_ul, fout);

        return SUCCESS;
} /* end setfont() */
```

The *setprnt( )* function has the Epson default-control strings hard-coded into it. However, if the user wishes to use some other printer, *setprnt( )* calls *fconfig( )* to look for a local or global *printer.cnf* file to override these values. If a configuration file is found, each line is read in and assigned to the next printer control-code variable. If too many or too few codes are obtained, an error is indicated by a return value of −1. A return value of 0 tells the caller all went well, but it is still possible that the codes were received in the wrong sequence or that bad codes were given in the configuration file. The *setprnt( )* function cannot detect such errors; the printer will simply not operate correctly if it gets bad control strings.

The next function, *clrprnt( )*, resets the printer to the normal font. It does so by turning off each special font individually rather than by using the hardware reset-control string. The hardware reset on most printers resets the top-of-form and causes the paper to creep a bit each time it is called. Because of this, I have elected to avoid using the reset command entirely, although its value is contained in the configuration data structure for possible future use. The *clrprnt( )* function calls upon the standard library function *fputs( )* with the control strings needed to turn off each printer font mode. It sends the strings to the output stream specified by its only argument.

The *setfont( )* function accepts two arguments: one specifies the desired font combination, and the other specifies the destination stream. The first thing *setfont( )* does is call *clrprnt( )* to cancel all currently active print modes. Then it issues control strings for each of the desired modes.

Most print-mode combinations are legal, but a few are not. In this design, two font combinations are excluded. The *setfont( )* function returns a FAILURE indication if the caller requests the compressed mode combined with either a double-strike or emphasized mode. Epson printers don't allow these, but some other printers might. All other combinations of supported fonts and print modes are permitted.

The control strings are emitted one at a time for each requested mode. Thus the request

    setfont(EMPHASIZED | EXPANDED);

in a program results in the control string for emphasized mode being sent to the destination stream, followed by the control string for expanded mode.

To permit ready access to the printer interface, we will compile it by typing

    msc print;

and then add the *print.obj* file to our utility library using the command

    lib\lib\local\util +print;

Now we can proceed to an example of how to use this simple but effective printer interface.

Printer Control Program

My original purpose in designing the printer interface just described was to gain some control over the printer from within my C programs. (Chapter 9 is devoted to a general-purpose printer program that uses this interface.) The approach I took gave me reasonable printer control from C programs, and, with the small amount of extra work that we'll do next, from the DOS command line and from batch files as well.

We now have the tools needed to control print modes, but getting access to the printer from DOS involves one additional step: packaging the basic control functions in a DOS program file that accepts option flags to set desired modes. In addition, we will write a supplementary program that allows us to send arbitrary text strings to the printer.

The MX program, originally named for its use with my trusty old MX-80 printer, controls the basic print modes via command-line arguments. The program also works nicely with the Epson FX- and JX-series printers and with many other compatible printers. The configurability of MX permits its use with many other printers, too. A look at the manual page (Figure 7-1) and source listing for MX shows that it is simple to use and equally simple to program.

NAME

　　　MX—control printer modes

SYNOPSIS

　　　mx -*option(s)*

DESCRIPTION

　　　The MX program sends mode-setting control strings to a printer
　　　under control of options. Most of the modes may be set
　　　individually or in combinations of two or more. It should be
　　　obvious that *normal* (-n) should be used by itself. Less obvious is
　　　that *condensed* (-c) and either *bold* (-b) or *double-strike* (-d)
　　　cannot be used together. Within the limitations noted above,
　　　options listed below may be used singly or combined in any
　　　order:

FIGURE 7-1 | *Manual page for MX*　　　　　　　　　　　　　*(continued)*

Option	Meaning
-b	Select bold (emphasized) mode
-c	Select compressed mode
-d	Select double-strike mode
-e	Select expanded mode
-i	Select italic font
-n	Select normal font. This command option clears all special font and print-mode selections.
-o *file*	Use the specified output file or stream
-p	Preview output on screen (may be redirected)
-r	Issue a hardware reset command. This clears all attributes and establishes the current position as the new top-of-form reference.
-t	Eject a page (top-of-form command) by issuing a formfeed
-u	Select underline mode

The *reset* (-r) and *top-of-form* (-t) options have temporal priority over any other options invoked in the same call to MX. *Reset* is done first, then *formfeed,* then *font selection.* Printer configuration can be controlled via optional local and global configuration files (local overrides global).

EXAMPLES

Request compressed and italicized printing:

mx -ci

Eject a page:

mx -t

FIGURE 7-1 | *continued*

```
/*
 *     mx -- control Epson MX-series printer
 */

#include <stdio.h>
#include <stdlib.h>
#include <local\std.h>
```

(continued)

```
#include <local\printer.h>

extern PRINTER prt;        /* printer data */

main(argc, argv)
int argc;
char **argv;
{
        int ch, font;
        BOOLEAN errflag;           /* option error */
        BOOLEAN clrflag;           /* clear special fonts */
        BOOLEAN rflag;             /* hardware reset */
        BOOLEAN tflag;             /* top-of-form */
        FILE *fout;
        static char pgm[MAXNAME + 1] = { "mx" };
        extern void getpname(char *, char*);
        extern int getopt(int, char **, char *);
        extern char *optarg;
        extern int optind, opterr;
        extern int setprnt();
        extern int clrprnt(FILE *);
        extern int setfont(int, FILE *);

        if (_osmajor >= 3)
                getpname(*argv, pgm);

        if (setprnt() == -1) {
                fprintf(stderr, "%s: Bad printer configuration\n", pgm);
                exit(1);
        }

        /* interpret command line */
        errflag = clrflag = rflag = tflag = FALSE;
        font = 0;
        fout = stdprn;
        while ((ch = getopt(argc, argv, "bcdefino:prtu")) != EOF) {
                switch (ch) {
                case 'b':
                        /* set bold */
                        font |= EMPHASIZED;
                        break;
                case 'c':
                        /* set compressed */
                        font |= CONDENSED;
                        break;
```

(continued)

```
        case 'd':
                /* set double strike */
                font |= DOUBLE;
                break;
        case 'e':
                /* set double strike */
                font |= EXPANDED;
                break;
        case 'i':
                /* set italic */
                font |= ITALICS;
                break;
        case 'n':
                /* set normal (clear all special fonts) */
                clrflag = TRUE;
                break;
        case 'o':
                /* use specified output stream */
                if ((fout = fopen(optarg, "w")) == NULL)
                        fatal(pgm, "cannot open output stream");
                break;
        case 'p':
                /* preview control strings on stdout */
                fout = stdout;
                break;
        case 'r':
                /* hardware reset */
                rflag = TRUE;
                break;
        case 't':
                /* top of form */
                tflag = TRUE;
                break;
        case 'u':
                /* set underline */
                font |= UNDERLINE;
                break;
        case '?':
                /* unknown option */
                errflag = TRUE;
                break;
        }
}
```

(continued)

```
        /* report errors, if any */
        if (errflag == TRUE || argc == 1) {
                fprintf(stderr, "Usage: %s -option\n", pgm);
                fprintf(stderr,
                        "b=bold, c=compressed, d=double strike, e=expanded\n");
                fprintf(stderr,
                        "i=italic, n=normal, o file=output to file\n");
                fprintf(stderr,
                        "p=preview, r=reset, t=top-of-form, u=underline\n");
                exit(2);
        }
        /* do hardware reset and formfeed first */
        if (rflag == TRUE)
                fputs(prt.p_init, fout);
        else if (tflag == TRUE)
                fputc('\f', fout);

        /* clear or set the aggregate font */
        if (clrflag == TRUE)
                clrprnt(fout);
        else if (setfont(font, fout) == FAILURE) {
                fprintf(stderr, "%s: Bad font spec\n", pgm);
                exit(3);
        }

        exit(0);
}
```

Each time MX is invoked, it checks for a configuration file. This can take a little time on a floppy disk-only system. If you will be using MX with nothing but Epson-compatible printers on a floppy-based system, you may want to bypass the configuration step and build in the Epson default-control strings for faster execution.

MX uses *getopt( )*, which is now part of our utility library, plus all of the printer-interface routines in the *printer* object file. Most of the option flags are obvious; however, two require some explanation. The -o option takes as an argument the name of a destination stream, presumably a disk file, to be used in place of the standard output stream. This allows us to capture the output of MX for diagnostic purposes or to create files that can drive the printer directly as formatting scripts.

The -t option uses the ASCII formfeed character to eject a page (go to top-of-form). This will work on nearly all modern printers. To accommodate all printers, you may instead want to permit the use of a series of newlines to get to the top of the next page. The PR program described in Chapter 9 shows how to use either control mechanism.

The text of *mx.mk* tells the Microsoft MAKE command how to assemble the MX program.

```
# makefile for mx program

LINC=c:\include\local
LLIB=c:\lib\local

mx.obj:       mx.c $(LINC)
        msc $*;

mx.exe:       mx.obj $(LLIB)\util.lib
        link $*, $*,, $(LLIB)\util;
```

The PRTSTR program is an auxiliary program that prints an arbitrary string. PRTSTR also permits optional newline suppression, which gives users the ability to construct printed lines in a mixture of print modes to obtain various textual effects. The default for PRTSTR is to end the string with a newline, which causes the printer to return to the beginning of the current line and then move down one line. In addition, if it receives no arguments, PRTSTR issues a single newline. Think of PRTSTR as an intelligent substitute for the DOS ECHO command. The only advantage that ECHO has over PRTSTR is that ECHO is built into the DOS COMMAND processor, so it operates faster. However, because printers tend to move like molasses in the Arctic, PRTSTR poses no problem in typical uses.

The manual page for PRTSTR (Figure 7-2) describes its operation and application. The source code and makefile (*prtstr.mk*) are, by now, quite predictable.

NAME

PRTSTR—print string(s) on standard printer

SYNOPSIS

prtstr [*options*] [*string* . . .]

DESCRIPTION

Use PRTSTR to send a string or group of strings given as arguments to the standard printer device (*stdprn*). PRTSTR appends one space after each argument and issues a newline to terminate the line. Use quotes to protect embedded special characters, such as tabs or spaces, in the text-argument list. The following options may be used separately or together to alter the default behavior:

Option	Meaning
-n	Suppress newline and trailing space.
-p	Preview output on screen (may be redirected).

EXAMPLES

Send the line *C is a fantastic language!* to the standard printer device (notice that no quotes are needed):

prtstr C is a fantastic language!

Send the string *BASEBALL* to a file:

prtstr -p BASEBALL > baseball.txt

Print some text and stop on the same line:

prtstr -n "This is a test: "

FIGURE 7-2 | *Manual page for PRTSTR*

```
/*
 *       prtstr -- send text string(s) to standard printer
 */

#include <stdio.h>
#include <stdlib.h>
#include <local\std.h>

main(argc, argv)
int argc;
char **argv;
{
        int ch;
        BOOLEAN errflag, lineflag;
        static char pgm[MAXNAME + 1] = { "prtstr" };
        FILE *fout;

        extern void getpname(char *, char*);
        extern int getopt(int, char **, char *);
        extern int optind, opterr;
        extern char *optarg;

        if (_osmajor >= 3)
                getpname(*argv, pgm);

        errflag = FALSE;        /* process options, if any */
        lineflag = TRUE;
        fout = stdprn;
        while ((ch = getopt(argc, argv, "np")) != EOF)
                switch (ch) {
                case 'n':       /* don't emit the trailing newline */
                        lineflag = FALSE;
                        break;
                case 'p':       /* preview on stdout */
                        fout = stdout;
                        break;
                case '?':       /* bad option */
                        errflag = TRUE;
                        break;
                }
        if (errflag == TRUE) {
                fprintf(stderr, "Usage: %s [-np] [string...]\n", pgm);
                exit(1);
```

(continued)

```
        }

        /* print the string(s) */
        argc -= optind;
        argv += optind;
        while (argc-- > 1 ) {
                fputs(*argv++, fout);
                fputc(' ', fout);
        }
        fputs(*argv++, fout);
        if (lineflag == TRUE)
                fputc(' ', fout);
        if (lineflag == TRUE)
                fputc('\n', fout);

        exit(0);
}
```

This very simple program has only one wrinkle that requires close examination. When the newline-suppression option is selected, we suppress not only the trailing newline, but also the single space that follows the last argument string. This permits us to mix print modes within text strings. We could, for example, print part of a word in boldface and another part in italics to distinguish the fixed and variable parts of a user's response.

```
# makefile for prtstr program

LINC=c:\include\local
LLIB=c:\lib\local

prtstr.obj:     prtstr.c $(LINC)
        msc $*;

prtstr.exe:     prtstr.obj $(LLIB)\util.lib
        link $*, $*,, $(LLIB)\util;
```

The SAMPLE.BAT file is a demonstration of printer control from a DOS batch file. The sample text (Figure 7-3 on the next page) shows off some of the many text combinations that can easily be obtained with simple commands. Note the use of mixed print modes in some of the lines.

```
echo off
mx -n
prtstr This is normal text.
mx -b
prtstr This is bold (emphasized) text.
mx -n
prtstr We can mix fonts, too.
mx -be
prtstr This is bold and expanded together.
mx -n
prtstr -n We can mix fonts in a line also:
mx -b
prtstr -n " bold"
mx -i
prtstr -n " and "
mx -e
prtstr expanded.
mx -u
prtstr This is underlined text...
mx -i
prtstr ... this is italicized.
mx -n
prtstr And finally back to normal type.
```

```
This is normal text.
This is bold (emphasized) text.
We can mix fonts, too.
This   is   bold   and   expanded   together.
We can mix fonts in a line also; bold and expanded.
This is underlined text...
...this is italicized.
And finally back to normal type.
```

FIGURE 7-3 | *Output from SAMPLE.BAT*

Please keep in mind that this is a minimal printer interface intended to demonstrate means of automatic program configuration. Modern dot-matrix and ink-jet printers offer many additional font and print-mode selections, and laser printers permit even greater selections. Have fun making the most of them!

Selection Functions

In configuring programs, some types of input require fairly elaborate processing to get the input data into an internal form that is suitable for program use. For example, the file *select.c* contains several functions that work together to manage input data presented in the form of lists.

The next section of this chapter uses the SELECT package to process tab settings. Our objective is to take the user-supplied list of columns that represents tab stops and convert it into an array of integers that can be used by a program to initialize its internal tab stops to something other than the hardware tabs that occur at multiples of eight columns, starting in column one (1, 9, 17, and so on). (Users generally count the leftmost column as one, not zero.) The SELECT routines can be used to process other types of lists, too. For instance, the routines will be used in Chapter 9 to select pages to be printed by the PR program.

By way of example, one of our programs might receive a list such as 6, 20, 71–80 as a command-line argument. To be used by the program, the data must be extracted from the list, which is a character string, converted to integer form, and stored somehow for easy access. We'll deal with internal data access soon. For now, let's just worry about the process of extracting and converting the data.

The example specification shown has twelve members. Technically speaking, each entry in the list represents a range, although some ranges have the same minimum and maximum values. Thus the 6 entry may be represented internally as *min = 6, max = 6*, whereas the *71–80* entry is represented as *min = 71, max = 80*. We will use an array of structures to hold these values in data storage that is private to the routines within the SELECT module.

The SELECT module contains three related functions: *mkslist( )* creates a selection list from user data; *save_range( )* is an internal function (*static*) called by *mkslist( )* to extract starting and ending values from explicit and implicit range specifications; and *selected( )* returns a nonzero value to its caller to indicate that a given value is contained in the selection list.

The routines in the SELECT module communicate through a global data structure, *Slist*, which is defined as

```
struct slist_st {
        long int s_min;
        long int s_max;
} Slist[NRANGES + 1];
```

This allocates an array of *NRANGES + 1* structures, each of which can hold a minimum and a maximum value for a single range. *NRANGES* is currently defined to be 10, but any reasonable number may be used. I have had no need to specify more than 10 ranges in a list. *Slist* is declared globally here for testing and demonstration purposes, but in practice it should be declared *static* so that only the functions in the SELECT module can access it.

The pseudocode description of *mkslist( )* shows how a selection list is parsed. The manifest constant *BIGGEST* is defined in *local**std.h* to be the largest number (65535) that can be stored in an unsigned integer. A global variable, *Highest,* is initially 0 and is updated to the highest value received in the list.

```
if (list in null)
        set min = 0
        set max = BIGGEST
else
        while (next token of list is not NULL)
                save_range(token)
        set min in next to -1 (terminate list)
```

The *save_range( )* function could be coded right in *mkslist( )* because it is only called once. However, by separating out the task of converting a string token to a range of numbers, the apparent complexity of *mkslist( )* is reduced. The *save_range( )* function is described as follows:

```
copy first number to a buffer
convert to long int
if (only one number received)
        set max = min
else
        if (second number is null)
                set max = BIGGEST
```

(continued)

```
        else
                copy second number into buffer
                convert to long int
                save in max
    return (max)
```

This design lets the user specify open ranges such as *40–*, which gives a firm minimum number but lets the maximum default to a large number. This is handy for telling a program to operate on all lines starting at 40 and continuing until the last line (of unknown number) is reached.

To determine whether a number is a member of the selection list, we can call the function *selected( )*, which returns a nonzero value if the specified entry is a member of a range in the list. The *selected( )* function scans the selection list (*Slist*) one array element at a time until it finds a range that contains its argument or until it finds a -1 flag that terminates the list.

The source code for the selection functions is contained in *select.c*:

```
/*
 *      select -- functions to create a selection table and
 *      to determine whether an item is an entry in the table
 */

#include <stdio.h>
#include <stdlib.h>
#include <string.h>
#include <local\std.h>

#define NRANGES 10
#define NDIGITS 5

struct slist_st {
        long int s_min;
        long int s_max;
} Slist[NRANGES + 1];

long Highest = 0;

/*
 *      mkslist -- create the selection lookup table
 */
```

(continued)

```
int
mkslist(list)
char *list;
{
        int i;
        char *listp, *s;
        long tmp;
        static long save_range();

        if (*list == '\0') {           /* fill in table of selected items */
                Slist[0].s_min = 0;      /* if no list, select all */
                Slist[0].s_max = Highest = BIGGEST;
                Slist[1].s_min = -1;
        }
        else {
                listp = list;
                for (i = 0; i < NRANGES; ++i) {
                        if ((s = strtok(listp, ", \t")) == NULL)
                                break;
                        if ((tmp = save_range(i, s)) > Highest)
                                Highest = tmp;
                        listp = NULL;
                }
                Slist[i].s_min = -1;
        }
        return (0);
} /* end mkslist() */


/*
 *      selected -- return non-zero value if the number
 *      argument is a member of the selection list
 */

int
selected(n)
long n;
{
        int i;

        /* look for converted number in selection list */
        for (i = 0; Slist[i].s_min != -1; ++i)
                if (n >= Slist[i].s_min && n <= Slist[i].s_max)
                        return (1);
```

(continued)

```
                return (0);
        } /* end selected() */


        /*
         *      save_range -- convert a string number spec to a
         *      numeric range in the selection table and return
         *      the highest number in the range
         */

        static long
        save_range(n, s)
        int n;
        char *s;
        {
                int radix = 10;
                char *cp, num[NDIGITS + 1];

                /* get the first (and possibly only) number */
                cp = num;
                while (*s != '\0' && *s != '-')
                        *cp++ = *s++;
                *cp = '\0';
                Slist[n].s_min = atol(num);
                if (*s == '\0')
                        /* pretty narrow range, huh? */
                        return (Slist[n].s_max = Slist[n].s_min);

                /* get the second number */
                if (*++s == '\0')
                        /* unspecified top end of range */
                        Slist[n].s_max = BIGGEST;
                else {
                        cp = num;
                        while (*s != '\0')
                                *cp++ = *s++;
                        *cp = '\0';
                        Slist[n].s_max = atol(num);
                }
                return (Slist[n].s_max);
        } /* end save_range() */
```

In *mkslist()*, *strtok()* is called with a pointer that is initially set to the
start of the user-supplied list, to extract the first (possibly the only) token.

The pointer is then set to *NULL* for subsequent calls to *strtok( )* to extract additional tokens, if any, from the list. Acceptable separators are comma, space, and tab. This gives the list-maker considerable flexibility in forming the list string. If the list contains embedded spaces or tabs, it must be quoted, so that DOS sees it as a single argument. A range specification must not have any white space around the hyphen (-), so that *strtok( )* can parse it as a single token.

TSTSEL is a program that I used to debug the SELECT functions. It accesses the *Slist* data structure directly, so that we can see what gets stored in there for various list specifications. The operation of this program is straightforward.

```
/*
 *      tstsel -- test driver for the "select" functions
 */

#include <stdio.h>
#include <local\std.h>

#define MAXTEST 20
#define NRANGES 10
#define NDIGITS 5

extern struct slist_st {
        long int s_min;
        long int s_max;
} Slist[NRANGES + 1];

main (argc, argv)
int argc;
char **argv;
{
        int i;
        extern int mkslist(char *);
        extern int selected(unsigned int);
        static void showlist();

        if (argc != 2) {
                fprintf(stderr, "Usage: tstsel list\n");
                exit(1);
        }
```

(continued)

```
        printf("argv[1] = %s\n", argv[1]);
        mkslist(argv[1]);
        showlist();
        for (i = 0; i < MAXTEST; ++i)
                printf("%2d -> %s\n", i, selected(i) ? "YES" : "NO");
        exit(0);
}


/*
 *      showlist -- display the contents of the select list
 */

static void
showlist()
{
        int i;

        /* scan the selection list and display values */
        for (i = 0; i <= NRANGES; ++i)
                printf("%2d %5ld %5ld\n", i, Slist[i].s_min, Slist[i].s_max);
}
```

The TSTSEL program produced the following output for one of my
test runs invoked with the command line

```
tstsel 1,2,3,5-10
```

```
argv[1] = 1,2,3,5-10
  0    1    1
  1    2    2
  2    3    3
  3    5   10
  4   -1    0
  5    0    0
  6    0    0
  7    0    0
  8    0    0
  9    0    0
 10    0    0
  0 -> NO
  1 -> YES
  2 -> YES
```

(continued)

```
 3 -> YES
 4 -> NO
 5 -> YES
 6 -> YES
 7 -> YES
 8 -> YES
 9 -> YES
10 -> YES
11 -> NO
12 -> NO
13 -> NO
14 -> NO
15 -> NO
16 -> NO
17 -> NO
18 -> NO
19 -> NO
```

The first line shows the argument containing the user's list. The next block of lines displays the contents of the select list, *Slist*. Note the -1 sentinel that marks the list's end. The next block of lines shows the results when *selected( )* is used to query the select list to determine if a value is a member of a range. We have shown the results as YES/NO strings.

Setting Tab Stops

In processing files that contain text, it is sometimes necessary or desirable to alter tab-stop positions, or to convert tabs to spaces or the reverse.

The formula for determining regular tab-stop positions is $1 + kn$, where k is the requested interval and n is an integer in the range of 0 through some maximum number determined by the line length. Thus, for the value k = 8, tabs fall at 1, 9, 17, and so on.

Variable tab stops are a bit more difficult to set up, but they have their uses. We might appreciate being able to set the tab stops for a FORTRAN program source file to 1, 7, 11, 15, 19, and 23, for example. We can apply the selection-list technique just described to the setting of tab stops at variable column positions in a line.

The file *tabs.c* contains the source code for three functions used to set and test tab stops. A private array of characters holds the tab-stop data. Each character represents a column position in a line and contains 1 if the associated column is a tab stop and 0 if it is not.

Two of the functions in the TABS module are used to set the tab stops. The *fixtabs( )* function installs tab stops at regular (fixed) intervals. The interval is given as an integer argument to *fixtabs( )*. The *vartabs( )* function works from a list to set tabs at variable intervals. We use the SELECT functions to gather data from a user-supplied list and then convert it to the needed form. A third function, *tabstop( )*, is used to query the *Tabstops* array.

```
/*
 *       tabs -- a group of cooperating functions that set
 *       and report the settings of "tabstops"
 */

#include <local\std.h>

static char Tabstops[MAXLINE];

/*
 *       fixtabs -- set up fixed-interval tabstops
 */
void
fixtabs(interval)
register int interval;
{
        register int i;

        for (i = 0; i < MAXLINE; i++)
                Tabstops[i] = (i % interval == 0) ? 1 : 0;
} /* end fixtabs() */

/*
 *       vartabs -- set up variable tabstops from an array
 *       integers terminated by a -1 entry
 */
void
vartabs(list)
int *list;
```

(continued)

```
{
        register int i;

        /* initialize the tabstop array */
        for (i = 0; i < MAXLINE; ++i)
                Tabstops[i] = 0;

        /* set user-specified tabstops */
        while (*list != -1)
                Tabstops[*++list] = 1;
} /* end vartabs() */

/*
 *      tabstop -- return non-zero if col is a tabstop
 */
int
tabstop(col)
register int col;
{
        return (col >= MAXLINE ? 1 : Tabstops[col]);
} /* end tabstop() */
```

The TABS module uses C's natural base of 0 as the first element of an array; therefore, all calculations are based on 0 as the leftmost column. We accommodate the difference between the TABS module's view of the world and the user's view of the world in the programs that handle the collection and presentation of tab data.

The best way to see how this all works is to demonstrate it. The *showtabs.mk* file tells MAKE how to put it all together. The SHOWTABS program gets a user specification of the needed tab stops. A -f option flag means SHOWTABS is getting a fixed interval specification, and a -v option flag signals a variable tab list. These options are mutually exclusive, and the parsing of the command-line options enforces the use of only one of them.

```
#makefile for SHOWTABS program

LLIB=c:\lib\local

tabs.obj:        tabs.c
     msc $*;

select.obj:      select.c
     msc $*;

showtabs.obj:    showtabs.c
     msc $*;

showtabs.exe:    showtabs.obj select.obj tabs.obj $(LLIB)\util.lib
     link $* select tabs, $*, , $(LLIB)\util;
```

```c
/*
 *      showtabs -- graphically display tabstop settings
 */

#include <stdio.h>
#include <stdlib.h>
#include <local\std.h>

#define MAXCOL    80
#define TABWIDTH  8

extern long Highest;

main(argc, argv)
int argc;
char *argv[];
{
     int ch, i;
     int interval, tablist[MAXLINE + 1], *p;
     char *tabstr;
     BOOLEAN errflag, fflag, vflag;
     static char pgm[MAXNAME + 1] = { "showtabs" };

     extern char *getpname(char *, char *);
     extern int getopt(int, char **, char *);
```

(continued)

```
extern char *optarg;
extern int optind, opterr;
extern int mkslist(char *);
extern int selected(long);
extern void fixtabs(int);
extern void vartabs(int *);
extern int tabstop(int);


if (_osmajor >= 3)
        getpname(*argv, pgm);


/* process command-line options */
errflag = fflag = vflag = FALSE;
interval = 0;
while ((ch = getopt(argc, argv, "f:v:")) != EOF) {
        switch (ch) {
        case 'f':
                /* used fixed tabbing interval */
                if (vflag == FALSE) {
                        fflag = TRUE;
                        interval = atoi(optarg);
                }
                break;
        case 'v':
                /* use list of tabs */
                if (fflag == FALSE) {
                        vflag = TRUE;
                        strcpy(tabstr, optarg);
                }
                break;
        case '?':
                errflag = TRUE;
                break;
        }
}
if (errflag == TRUE) {
        fprintf(stderr, "Usage: %s [-f interval | -v tablist]\n", pgm);
        exit(2);
}


/* set the tabstops */
if (vflag == TRUE) {
        /* user-supplied variable tab list */
```

(continued)

```
                mkslist(tabstr);
                p = tablist;
                for (i = 0; i < MAXLINE && i < Highest; ++i)
                        *p++ = selected((long)i + 1) ? i : 0;
                *p = -1;            /* terminate the list */
                vartabs(tablist);
        }
        else if (fflag == TRUE)
                /* user-supplied fixed tabbing interval */
                fixtabs(interval);
        else
                /* hardware default tabbing interval*/
                fixtabs(TABWIDTH);

        /* display current tabs settings */
        for (i = 0; i < MAXCOL; ++i)
                if (tabstop(i))
                        fputc('T', stdout);
                else if ((i + 1) % 10 == 0)
                        fputc('+', stdout);
                else
                        fputc('-', stdout);
        fputc('\n', stdout);

        exit(0);
}
```

If SHOWTABS receives a variable list, it calls the SELECT functions to do the necessary conversion from the string form of the program argument to an array of integers that *vartabs( )* understands. In the case of a -f option, SHOWTABS uses *atoi( )* to produce a single number, which is taken to be a fixed interval specifier that is passed to *fixtabs( )*.

Once the *Tabstops* array is populated, SHOWTABS calls upon *tabstop( )* to display the status of every column in the first 80 columns of a line. A plus sign (+) in the display marks columns that are nonzero multiples of 10. A T marks a tab stop, and a minus sign (−) marks all other positions. Figure 7-4 on the next page shows the results of various tab-setting calls to SHOWTABS.

```
C) showtabs -v 1,9,17,61-68
T-------T+------T--+----------+----------+----------+----------+TTTTTTTT-+----------+


C)
```

FIGURE 7-4 | *Output from SHOWTABS*

Because the functions in both the SELECT and TABS modules are generally useful, we will add *select.obj* and *tabs.obj* to *util.lib* in \ *lib* \ *local.*

In the next chapter, we will develop a group of utilities for DOS that emulate some of the UNIX utilities; this will help ease the transition of new users from one system to the other and will help those who are constantly moving between the two operating systems, as is the case for many software developers.

SECTION III

File-Oriented Programs

Basic File Utilities 8

This chapter presents a set of file-oriented utilities that satisfy two primary goals. First, the commands give programmers who divide their time between UNIX/XENIX and DOS a set of programs that make it easier to switch back and forth between the two environments. The programs essentially implement a UNIX/XENIX-style interface under DOS. Second, the programs serve as models for other utility programs that you might like to add to your toolkit. The programs employ many of the functions and techniques we have developed thus far in the book plus a few that are new.

The programs in this set include the following utilities:

UTILITY	ACTION
TOUCH	update the modification times of files
TEE	split a stream into two separate streams
PWD	print the working directory pathname
RM	remove files
LS	list the files in a directory

Some of these programs perform functions already provided by DOS, but in a way that is more familiar to UNIX/XENIX users. LS is similar to the DOS DIR command. PWD does the job of the DOS CD command, when CD is typed without an argument. The RM command provides some enhancements over the standard DOS ERASE/DEL command. Other programs in this set are tools used by programmers that have no DOS equivalents.

Update File Modification Time (TOUCH)

We have been using the MAKE command to assist us in creating and maintaining programs. The MAKE command uses a file's last modification time and instructions in a "makefile" as the basis of its decision-making process. MAKE compares the modification time of an object with that of its sources (specified in a dependency list in the makefile) to determine whether an object is older than one or more of its respective sources. So, when we modify a source file, every object that lists that source file in its dependency list will be remade.

At times, we may want to force an object to be remade. We can do this in several ways. We can edit a source file; even if we make no changes to the file, the act of saving the file with an editor updates its modification time. The source will then be newer than the object that is created from it, so the object will be remade.

Another way to force an object to be remade is to remove it. MAKE will discover that the object does not exist and will remake it from the recipe in the makefile.

A third way is to use a program called TOUCH to update the file modification time of the source file without making any other changes to it. This will also cause MAKE to remake the object. TOUCH is particularly handy when you want to force all the files in an entire project or subproject to be remade. A single TOUCH command does the work of many separate DEL or editor commands.

The following pseudocode describes how TOUCH works.

```
for (each named file)
        update time
        if (update not successful)
                increment error count
                if (verbose)
                        print error message
        else
                if (verbose)
                        print confirmation message
```

The manual page for TOUCH is presented in Figure 8-1.

NAME

TOUCH — update file modification time(s)

SYNOPSIS

touch [-cv] file . . .

DESCRIPTION

The TOUCH command updates the file modification times associated with a file or files. Under DOS, the last modification time (and last access time for DOS version 3.00 and later) maintained in the directory entry for a file are identical. TOUCH sets the file time to the current DOS time. TOUCH accepts the following command-line options, singly or in combination:

Option	Meaning
-c	Control file creation. TOUCH usually creates a named file if it does not exist. This option tells TOUCH not to create files.
-v	Verbose mode. Tells TOUCH to send information to the standard error stream about file times that have been successfully updated, about files that were created, and so forth.

EXAMPLES

Update the modification times of all C source files in the current directory and tell the user what's going on:

touch -v *.c

Create a set of empty files in the current directory (assumes these files do not exist yet):

touch file1.c file2.c file3.c

FIGURE 8-1 | *Manual Page for TOUCH*

The source code for the TOUCH program is in the file *touch.c*.

```
/*
 *      touch -- update modification time of file(s)
 */

#include <stdio.h>
#include <stdlib.h>
#include <ctype.h>
#include <sys\types.h>
#include <sys\stat.h>
#include <sys\utime.h>
#include <io.h>
#include <errno.h>
#include <local\std.h>

/* error return -- big enough not to be mistaken for a bad file count */
#define ERR     0x7FFF

main(argc, argv)
int argc;
char *argv[];
{
        int ch;
        int i;
        int badcount;           /* # of files that can't be updated */
        struct stat statbuf;    /* buffer for stat results */
        BOOLEAN errflag,        /* error flag */
                cflag,          /* creation flag */
                vflag;          /* verbose flag */
        FILE *fp;

        static char pgm[MAXNAME + 1] = { "touch" };
        extern int getopt(int, char **, char *);
        extern int optind, opterr;
        extern char *optarg;
        extern void getpname(char *, char *);
        static void usage(char *);

        /* get program name from DOS (version 3.00 and later) */
        if (_osmajor >= 3)
                getpname(argv[0], pgm);

        /* process optional arguments first */
        errflag = cflag = vflag = FALSE;
```

(continued)

```
        badcount = 0;
        while ((ch = getopt(argc, argv, "cv")) != EOF)
                switch (ch) {
                case 'c':
                        /* don't create files */
                        cflag = TRUE;
                        break;
                case 'v':
                        /* verbose -- report activity */
                        vflag = TRUE;
                        break;
                case '?':
                        errflag = TRUE;
                        break;
                }
        argc -= optind;
        argv += optind;

        /* check for errors including no file names */
        if (errflag == TRUE || argc <= 0) {
                usage(pgm);
                exit(ERR);
        }

        /* update modification times of files */
        for (; argc-- > 0; ++argv) {
                if (stat(*argv, &statbuf) == -1) {
                        /* file doesn't exist */
                        if (cflag == TRUE) {
                                /* don't create it */
                                ++badcount;
                                continue;
                        }
                        else if ((fp = fopen(*argv, "w")) == NULL) {
                                fprintf(stderr, "%s: Cannot create %s\n",
                                        pgm, *argv);
                                ++badcount;
                                continue;
                        }
                        else {
                                if (fclose(fp) == EOF) {
                                        perror("Error closing file");
                                        exit(ERR);
```

(continued)

```
                                    }
                                    if (stat(*argv, &statbuf) == -1) {
                                            fprintf(stderr, "%s: Cannot stat %s\n",
                                                    pgm, *argv);
                                            ++badcount;
                                            continue;
                                    }
                            }
                    }
                    if (utime(*argv, NULL) == -1) {
                            ++badcount;
                            perror("Error updating date/time stamp");
                            continue;
                    }
                    if (vflag == TRUE)
                            fprintf(stderr, "Touched file %s\n", *argv);
            }

        exit(badcount);
} /* end main() */


/*
 *      usage -- display an informative usage message
 */

static void
usage(pname)
char *pname;
{
        fprintf(stderr, "Usage: %s [-cv] file ...\n", pname);
        fprintf(stderr, "\t-c  Do not create any files\n");
        fprintf(stderr, "\t-v  Verbose mode -- report activities\n");
} /* end usage() */


/*
 *      dummy functions to show how to save a little space
 */

_setenvp()
{
}

#ifndef DEBUG
```

(continued)

```
_nullcheck()
{
}
#endif
```

Note the use of two dummy functions, _setenvp( ) and _nullcheck( ). These functions reduce the final program code size slightly by eliminating the code for environment processing and for checking attempts to reference data through null pointers. The _nullcheck( ) function is inside a preprocessor directive block that includes the code during debugging and omits it when the program is finally compiled.

If we are really serious about minimizing code size, we will also eliminate calls to *printf*-family functions because the formatting code is rather large (about 2.5–8 KB, depending on the compiler and memory model used). Using *fputs( )* and *fputc( )* to synthesize the *fprintf( )* function, when it is used to process only strings, will save several kilobytes in the executable program. But be on the lookout for "hidden" formatting. Depending on how the compiler supplier implements *perror( ),* for example, you may find that a call to *fprintf( )* gets dragged in anyway, even though you didn't use one directly in your code.

Tapping a Pipeline (TEE)

The TEE program is often called the "pipefitters' dream." The manual page for TEE (Figure 8-2 on the next page) tells you why.

TEE always writes a copy of its input to the standard output stream. In addition, TEE attempts to open for writing any files given as command-line arguments. If the option -a is given, TEE attempts to open the files in append mode instead of write mode. By naming output files, the user creates a multi-way split and sends copies of the same input stream to two or more output streams. The pseudocode for TEE is

```
set file mode string
for (each name file)
        open file per mode string
for each character received from stdin
        copy the character to all open output streams
close all streams
```

NAME

TEE—split a stream into multiple streams

SYNOPSIS

tee [-a] [file . . .]

DESCRIPTION

TEE copies its standard input onto its standard output. If any files are named, they too become destinations for the output of TEE. The files are created if necessary. If they already exist, their prior contents are lost unless the -a option (append) is given on the command line.

EXAMPLES

Display the contents of a file (FILE1) and simultaneously copy it to another file (FILE2):

type *file1* | tee *file2*

Use CAT to display the file *timer.c* on the console and append a copy of the output to two existing files (SRCFILE1 and SRCFILE2):

cat timer.c | tee -a *srcfile1 srcfile2*

NOTES

TEE does not work with files that contain binary data. As designed, it handles only ASCII text.

The number of destination files is limited by the operating system and by the use of the value _NFILE in the *stdio.h* header file (_NFILE is typically 20). There are five opened files (*stdin, stdout, stderr, stdaux,* and *stdprn*) when a program starts executing, which reduces the number of files you can open.

FIGURE 8-2 | *Manual page for TEE*

TEE is especially useful in debugging programs. I use it to view the output of a program on the screen while capturing a copy of the data stream in a file for detailed inspection using DUMP (Chapter 10) or a text editor. It is surprising what kind of garbage finds its way into the output data stream of an ill-behaved program.

```
/*
 *      tee -- a "pipe fitter" for DOS
 */

#include <stdio.h>
#include <stdlib.h>
#include <string.h>
#include <local\std.h>

main(argc, argv)
int argc;
char *argv[];
{
        register int ch, n;
        static char openmode[] = { "w" };
        static char pgm[MAXPATH + 1] = { "tee" };
        FILE *fp[_NFILE];       /* array of file pointers */

        extern int getopt(int, char **, char *);
        extern int optind, opterr;
        extern char *optarg;
        extern void getpname(char *, char *);

        /* check for an alias */
        if (_osmajor >= 3)
                getpname(argv[0], pgm);

        /* process command-line options, if any */
        while ((ch = getopt(argc, argv, "a")) != EOF)
                switch (ch) {
                case 'a':
                        strcpy(openmode, "a");
                        break;
                case '?':
                        break;
                }
        n = argc -= optind;
        argv += optind;

        /* check for errors */
        if (argc > _NFILE) {
                fprintf(stderr, "Too many files (max = %d)\n", _NFILE);
                exit(1);
```

(continued)

```
        }

        /* open the output file(s) */
        for (n = 0; n < argc; ++n) {
                if ((fp[n] = fopen(argv[n], openmode)) == NULL) {
                        fprintf(stderr, "Cannot open %s\n", argv[n]);
                        continue;
                }
        }

        /* copy input to stdout plus opened file(s) */
        while ((ch = getchar()) != EOF) {
                putchar(ch);
                for (n = 0; n < argc; ++n)
                        if (fp[n] != NULL)
                                fputc(ch, fp[n]);
        }

        /* close file(s) */
        if (fcloseall() == -1) {
                fprintf(stderr, "Error closing a file\n");
                exit(2);
        }

        exit(0);
}
```

The source code for TEE introduces the use of the standard library function *fcloseall( )*, which can be used to shut down all open streams except the standard streams that were opened for you by the C run-time startup system. The function returns -1 in the event that it cannot close a stream. We report this to the operating system via the *exit( )* function. The ERRORLEVEL feature of batch files can be used to test the return value, but DOS ignores it.

Print Working Directory Path (PWD)

The manual page for PWD (Figure 8-3) says all you need to know about "what" but may leave you wondering "why." What's wrong with typing CD without an argument to find out the name of the current directory?

Nothing, really. But those of us who switch back and forth between DOS and UNIX/XENIX have certain reflex reactions that cause problems. Under UNIX/XENIX, a bare CD command reports nothing. Instead, it takes you back to your "home" directory from anywhere in the directory hierarchy. The PWD command is used to display the current directory pathname. I wrote a DOS PWD command to make the two environments a bit more alike for some often-used commands.

NAME

    PWD—print working directory

SYNOPSIS

    pwd

DESCRIPTION

    PWD displays the full pathname of the current ("working") directory. It is designed to ease the transition between UNIX/ XENIX and DOS. It provides the same function as the DOS command CD if CD is typed without a pathname argument.

EXAMPLE

    Display the current directory pathname:

    pwd

NOTES

    Under UNIX and XENIX, the CD command typed without a pathname argument moves the user's context to the "home" directory, which might surprise an experienced DOS user trying to get the current pathname by the standard technique.

FIGURE 8-3 | *Manual page for PWD*

The source for PWD, *pwd.c,* uses the standard library function *getcwd( )* to get the current "working" directory pathname. The first argument can be the address of a user-supplied buffer that is long enough to hold a DOS pathname (64 characters). If *NULL* is used instead, *getcwd( )* creates its own buffer, the length of which is specified by the second argument.

```
/*
 *      pwd -- print (display actually) the current directory pathname
 */

#include <stdio.h>
#include <direct.h>
#include <local\std.h>

main()
{
        char *path;

        if ((path = getcwd(NULL, MAXPATH)) == NULL) {
                perror("Error getting current directory");
                exit(1);
        }
        printf("%s\n", path);
        exit(0);
}

_setargv()
{
}

_setenvp()
{
}

_nullcheck()
{
}
```

Remove Files (RM)

One of the limitations of the DOS ERASE/DEL command is that it accepts only a single file specification; if we want to remove several different types of files, a series of ERASE commands must be issued. Another limitation is the lack of an interactive deletion feature. RM does the job of ERASE while adding these two useful features.

The manual page for RM is presented in Figure 8-4. The basic behavior of RM is the same as ERASE except that you may provide any number of exact and ambiguous filename specifications up to the limits imposed by the DOS command line. Each command-line argument (following command options, if any) is expanded if necessary. The -i option, when used, puts RM into an interactive mode that is a great help in avoiding the unwanted loss of files. Each deletion must be confirmed by a Y response and a Return—more work for the user, but safer.

NAME

      RM—remove file(s)

SYNOPSIS

      rm [-i] file . . .

DESCRIPTION

      RM removes a file or a group of files. Each file specification may be a full or relative pathname and may contain wildcards to name files ambiguously.

      The -i option causes RM to operate in an interactive mode. The program prompts the user to confirm each removal before it is executed. A response that starts with y or Y for "yes" confirms the removal. Any other initial character is interpreted as a "no" response.

EXAMPLES

      Remove all backup files in the current directory:

      rm *.bak

      Remove object files and "map" files in the current directory interactively:

      rm -i *.obj *.map

FIGURE 8-4 | *Manual page for RM*

The pseudocode for the heart of RM is

```
for each file
        if (interactive mode selected)
                print file name
```

(continued)

```
            prompt user for reply (y/n)
            read a line of input
            if (no)
                    break
    else
            unlink file
    if (error occurred)
            print error message
```

The source for RM is composed of three functions: *main( )*, *do_rm( )*, and *affirm( )*. The return value of the call to *unlink( )*, a standard library function, is compared to -1, which flags an error condition. The *perror( )* library function is used to print an error message. There is no exit made at this point because other files may still need to be removed.

The most likely error is an attempt to remove a non-existent file. Also likely is the typical failure caused by attempts to access a floppy drive that has no disk or has its door open. RM simply reports about non-existent files; it lets the DOS error handler deal with drive problems.

```
/*
 *      rm -- remove file(s)
 */

#include <stdio.h>
#include <stdlib.h>
#include <sys\types.h>
#include <sys\stat.h>
#include <ctype.h>
#include <io.h>
#include <local\std.h>

main(argc, argv)
int argc;
char *argv[];
{
        int ch;
        BOOLEAN errflag,
                iflag;
```

(continued)

```
        static char pgm[MAXNAME + 1] = { "rm" };
        extern void getpname(char *, char *);
        static void do_rm(char *, char *, BOOLEAN);
        extern int getopt(int, char **, char *);
        extern int optind, opterr;
        extern char *optarg;

        /* get program name from DOS (version 3.00 and later) */
        if (_osmajor >= 3)
                getpname(*argv, pgm);

        /* process optional arguments first */
        errflag = iflag = FALSE;
        while ((ch = getopt(argc, argv, "i")) != EOF)
                switch (ch) {
                case 'i':
                        /* interactive -- requires confirmation */
                        iflag = TRUE;
                        break;
                case '?':
                        /* say what? */
                        errflag = TRUE;
                        break;
                }
        argc -= optind;
        argv += optind;

        if (argc <= 0 || errflag == TRUE) {
                fprintf(stderr, "%s [-i] file(s)\n", pgm);
                exit(1);
        }

        /* process remaining arguments */
        for (; argc-- > 0; ++argv)
                do_rm(pgm, *argv, iflag);

        exit(0);
} /* end main() */

/*
 *      do_rm -- remove a file
 */
```

(continued)

```
static void
do_rm(pname, fname, iflag)
char *pname, *fname;
BOOLEAN iflag;
{
        int result = 0;
        struct stat statbuf;
        static BOOLEAN affirm();

        if (iflag == TRUE) {
                fprintf(stderr, "%s (y/n): ", fname);
                if (affirm() == FALSE)
                        return;
        }
        if ((result = unlink(fname)) == -1) {
                fprintf(stderr, "%s: ", pname);
                perror(fname);
        }
        return;
}


/*
 *      affirm -- return TRUE if the first character of the
 *      user's response is 'y' or FALSE otherwise
 */

#define MAXSTR  64

static BOOLEAN
affirm()
{
        char line[MAXSTR + 1];
        char *response;

        response = fgets(line, MAXSTR, stdin);
        return (tolower(*response) == 'y' ? TRUE : FALSE);
}
```

That's it for the easy utilities. The next is more powerful and useful than the utilities we have just written and is appropriately more complicated and more difficult to write as well. As the weight lifters say, "No pain, no gain."

List Directories (LS)

Let's start with the manual page for LS (Figure 8-5 on the next page); it shows us where we are headed. Note that this LS command has six options. That may sound like a lot, but the UNIX/XENIX *ls* command has more than three times as many! To keep things simple and usable, I elected to leave many bells and whistles out of LS. Anyone who wants another 15 options is free to put them in.

The pseudocode for LS only hints at the complications of doing this job in a DOS environment. Ignoring startup tasks (version control, option parsing, setting up a Ctrl-Break handler, and so forth), LS follows this general blueprint:

```
allocate a buffer for file data
allocate a buffer for directory data
if (no arguments)
        get current directory pathname
else
        for each named item
                if (it's a directory)
                        add directory name to directory buffer
                else if (it's a file)
                        add file name and data to file buffer
if (any files in file buffer)
        sort entries
        send file list to output
if (any directories in directory buffer)
        for (each directory)
                expand it to a list of files
                sort entries
                output list
```

The LS program resides in several files that are devoted exclusively to LS-related chores. In addition, several DOS functions of more far-reaching application are used. These are new, and will be added to the local DOS library that we created in Chapter 5.

The header file, *ls.h*, shows the data structures that describe file data and the manifest constants needed to request and interpret file data. Note that the LS program deals with information about files, rather than the information that is in them.

NAME

LS—list information about a directory

SYNOPSIS

ls [-aCFlrt] [filespec]

DESCRIPTION

The LS command is a general-purpose directory lister. It has
enough features to be useful without being threateningly
complex. The most common use of LS is to find out what files
are in the current directory. This requires no argument on the
command line. To get greater amounts of detail or to modify the
output of LS in some way, use one or more of the following
options separately or grouped in any meaningful combination.

Option	Meaning
-a	All files in the named directory are listed, even those marked hidden or system. The default is to shield hidden and system files from view.
-C	Produce multi-column output with items sorted down each column. Without this option, single-column output is employed. This option causes output to be in the largest number of columns possible (determined by the length of the longest item name).
-F	Show file type in the output listing. Directories are marked by a trailing backslash (*mydir* \).
-l	Produce a single-column "long" listing, including a summary of mode bits, file date and time stamp, and file size in bytes. This option overrides the -C and -F options.
-r	Reverse the sorting order. Works for the default sorting of file and directory names and for the sort on file modification time data (see -t option).
-t	Sort by file time rather than name. The default is oldest first, but most-recent-first may be obtained by combining this option with -r.

FIGURE 8-5 | *Manual page for LS*   *(continued)*

EXAMPLES

Display a long list of the current directory:

ls -l

Display a multi-column listing of the root directory on the
current disk from anywhere in the directory hierarchy:

ls -C \

FIGURE 8-5 | *continued*

```
/*
 *      ls.h -- header file for ls program
 */


/* structure definition for output buffer elements */
struct OUTBUF {
        unsigned short o_mode;  /* file mode (attributes) */
        long o_size;            /* file size in bytes */
        unsigned int o_date;    /* file modification date */
        unsigned int o_time;    /* file modification time */
        char *o_name;           /* DOS filespec */
};


/* constants for DOS file-matching routines */
#define FILESPEC        13      /* maximum filespec + NUL */
#define RNBYTES         21      /* bytes reserved for next_fm() calls */


/* file modes (attributes) */
#define READONLY        0x0001
#define HIDDEN          0x0002
#define SYSTEM          0x0004
#define VOLUME          0x0008
#define SUBDIR          0x0010
#define ARCHIVE         0x0020


/* structure definition for DOS file-matching routines */
struct DTA {
        unsigned char d_reserved[RNBYTES];      /* buffer for next_fm */
        unsigned char d_attr;                   /* file attribute (type) byte */
```

(continued)

```
        unsigned d_mtime;                /* time of last modification */
        unsigned d_mdate;                /* date of last modification */
        long d_fsize;                    /* file size in bytes */
        char d_fname[FILESPEC];          /* file spec (filename.ext + NUL) */
};
```

The OUTBUF structure template is used to allocate storage for an output buffer that contains the name of a file, its modification data and time, the file size in bytes, and the file mode for each file in the default directory and any named directories.

The basic substance of the LS program is in the file *ls.c*. It contains a slew of *include* file directives, a set of global configuration variables, the *main( )* function, and a Ctrl-Break handler function. LS can produce mountains of output; therefore, we must provide a convenient way to break out if the user gets bored or finds the sought-after information part way through the listing.

The *main( )* function orchestrates everything, calling on other functions to do most of the hard work. Its job is to collect the user's requests and preferences and then to parcel out the work of getting file data, expanding directory names to the contents of the directories, and much more. Here is the *ls.c* file. Think what it might look like with 15 additional options!

```
/*
 *      ls -- display a directory listing
 */

#include <stdio.h>
#include <stdlib.h>
#include <string.h>
#include <memory.h>
#include <dos.h>
#include <direct.h>
#include <signal.h>
#include <search.h>
#include <local\std.h>
#include <local\doslib.h>
#include "ls.h"
```

(continued)

```
/* allocation quantities */
#define N_FILES 256
#define N_DIRS  16

/* global data */
int Multicol = 0;
int Filetype = 0;
int Hidden = 0;
int Longlist = 0;
int Reverse = 0;
int Modtime = 0;

main(argc, argv)
int argc;
char *argv[];
{
        int ch, i;
        int errflag;            /* error flag */
        char *ep;               /* environment pointer */
        int status = 0;         /* return status value */
        int fileattr;           /* file attribute number */
        struct DTA buf;         /* private disk buffer */
        char path[MAXPATH + 1]; /* working pathname */
        struct OUTBUF *fp, *fq; /* pointers to file array */
        char **dp, **dq;        /* pointer to directory pointer array */
        int fbc = 1;            /* file memory block allocation count */
        int dbc = 1;            /* directory memory block allocation count */
        int nfiles;             /* number of file elements */
        int ndirs;              /* number of directory elements */

        static char pgm[MAXNAME + 1] = { "ls" };

        /* function prototypes */
        extern void getpname(char *, char*);
        extern int getopt(int, char **, char *);
        extern int optind, opterr;
        extern char *optarg;
        extern char *drvpath(char *);
        extern void fatal(char *, char *, int);
        extern void setdta(char *);
        extern int first_fm(char *, int);
        extern int next_fm();
        extern int ls_fcomp(struct OUTBUF *, struct OUTBUF *);
```

(continued)

```
extern int ls_dcomp(char *, char *);
extern int ls_single(struct OUTBUF *, int);
extern int ls_multi(struct OUTBUF *, int);
extern int ls_dirx(char *, char *);
int bailout();

/* guarantee that needed DOS services are available */
if (_osmajor < 2)
        fatal(pgm, "ls requires DOS 2.00 or later", 1);

/* get program name from DOS (version 3.00 and later) */
if (_osmajor >= 3)
        getpname(*argv, pgm);

/* useful aliases (DOS version 3.00 and later) */
if (strcmp(pgm, "lc") == 0)
        ++Multicol;
if (strcmp(pgm, "lf") == 0) {
        ++Multicol;
        ++Filetype;
}

/* prepare for emergencies */
if (signal(SIGINT, bailout) == (int(*)())-1) {
        perror("Can't set SIGINT");
        exit(2);
}

/* process optional arguments first */
errflag = 0;
while ((ch = getopt(argc, argv, "aCFlrt")) != EOF)
        switch (ch) {
        case 'a':
                /* all files (hidden, system, etc.) */
                ++Hidden;
                break;
        case 'C':
                ++Multicol;
                break;
        case 'F':
                /* show file types (/=directory, *=executable) */
                ++Filetype;
                break;
```

(continued)

```
            case 'l':
                    /* long list (overrides multicolumn) */
                    ++Longlist;
                    break;
            case 'r':
                    /* reverse sort */
                    ++Reverse;
                    break;
            case 't':
                    /* sort by file modification time */
                    ++Modtime;
                    break;
            case '?':
                    errflag = TRUE;
                    break;
        }
argc -= optind;
argv += optind;

/* check for command-line errors */
if (argc < 0 || errflag) {
        fprintf(stderr, "Usage: %s [-aCFlrt] [pathname ...]", pgm);
        exit(3);
}

/* allocate initial file and directory storage areas */
dp = dq = (char **)malloc(N_DIRS * sizeof (char *));
if (dp == NULL)
        fatal(pgm, "Out of memory", 4);
fp = fq = (struct OUTBUF *)malloc(N_FILES * sizeof (struct OUTBUF));
if (fp == NULL)
        fatal(pgm, "Out of memory", 4);
nfiles = ndirs = 0;

/* use current directory if no args */
if (argc == 0) {
        if (getcwd(path, MAXPATH) == NULL)
                fatal(pgm, "Cannot get current directory", 5);
        *dq = path;
        ndirs = 1;
}
else {
        /* use arguments as file and directory names */
```

(continued)

```
        for ( ; argc-- > 0; ++argv) {
                strcpy(path, *argv);
                if (path[0] == '\\') {
                        /* prepend default drive name */
                        memcpy(path + 2, path, strlen(path) + 1);
                        path[0] = 'a' + getdrive();
                        path[1] = ':';
                }
                if (path[1] == ':' && path[2] == '\0' && drvpath(path) == NULL) {
                        fprintf(stderr, "%s: Cannot get drive path", pgm);
                        continue;
                }


                /* establish private disk transfer area */
                setdta((char *)&buf);

                /* set file attribute for search */
                if (Hidden)
                        fileattr = SUBDIR | HIDDEN | SYSTEM | READONLY;
                else
                        fileattr = SUBDIR;
                if (first_fm(path, fileattr) != 0 && path[3] != '\0') {
                        fprintf(stderr, "%s -- No such file or directory\n", path);
                        continue;
                }
                if ((buf.d_attr & SUBDIR) == SUBDIR || path[3] == '\0') {
                        /* path is a (sub)directory */
                        *dq = strdup(path);
                        if (++ndirs == dbc * N_DIRS) {
                                ++dbc;  /* increase space requirement */
                                dp = (char **)realloc(dp, dbc * N_DIRS
                                        * sizeof (char *));
                                if (dp == NULL)
                                        fatal(pgm, "Out of memory", 4);
                                dq = dp + dbc * N_DIRS;
                        }
                        else
                                ++dq;
                }
                else {
                        fq->o_name = strdup(path);
                        fq->o_mode = buf.d_attr;
                        fq->o_date = buf.d_mdate;
```

(continued)

```
                              fq->o_time = buf.d_mtime;
                              fq->o_size = buf.d_fsize;
                              if (++nfiles == fbc * N_FILES) {
                                      ++fbc;
                                      fp = (struct OUTBUF *)realloc(fp,
                                              fbc * N_FILES * sizeof (struct OUTBUF));
                                      if (fp == NULL)
                                              fatal(pgm, "Out of memory", 4);
                                      fq = fp + fbc * N_FILES;
                              }
                              else
                                      ++fq;
                      }
              }
      }


      /* output file list, if any */
      if (nfiles > 0) {
              qsort(fp, nfiles, sizeof(struct OUTBUF), ls_fcomp);
              if (Longlist)
                      ls_long(fp, nfiles);
              else if (Multicol)
                      ls_multi(fp, nfiles);
              else
                      ls_single(fp, nfiles);
              putchar('\n');
      }
      free(fp);


      /* output directory lists, if any */
      if (ndirs == 1 && nfiles == 0) {
              /* expand directory and output without header */
              if (ls_dirx(pgm, *dp))
                      fprintf(stderr, "%s -- empty directory\n", strlwr(*dp));
      }
      else if (ndirs > 0) {
              /* expand each directory and output with headers */
              dq = dp;
              qsort(dp, ndirs, sizeof(char *), ls_dcomp);
              while (ndirs-- > 0) {
                      fprintf(stdout, "%s:\n", strlwr(*dq));
                      if (ls_dirx(pgm, *dq++))
                              fprintf(stderr, "%s -- empty directory\n",
```

(continued)

```
                                        strlwr(*dq));
                        putchar('\n');
                }
        }

        exit(0);
}

/*
 *      bailout -- optionally terminate upon interrupt
 */
int
bailout()
{
        char ch;

        signal(SIGINT, bailout);
        printf("\nTerminate directory listing? ");
        scanf("%1s", &ch);
        if (ch == 'y' || ch == 'Y')
                exit(1);
}
```

Global variables are used to hold control information that is needed by other functions in the LS program. Global variables should not be used to pass data between functions.

The *main( )* function calls on *malloc( )* to allocate memory for the file data structure and for an array of pointers to directory names. The technique used here allocates a fixed amount. If that amount proves to be too small to handle the job, additional space is obtained from *realloc( )*. This guarantees that the expanded allocation is contiguous with the earlier allocation (even if the whole block has to be moved to a new location in memory), which makes it possible to use pointers and array indexes to access elements in the data areas.

Two DOS functions, *getdrive( )* and *drvpath( )*, are called by *main( )*. The first gets the current drive number (0 = A, 1 = B, and so forth), and the second appends to a copy of the current pathname onto a drive specification.

```
/*
 *      getdrive -- return the number of the default drive
 */

#include <dos.h>
#include <local\doslib.h>

int getdrive()
{
        return (bdos(CURRENT_DISK));
}
```

```
/*
 *      drvpath -- convert a drive name to a full pathname
 */

#include <stdio.h>
#include <dos.h>
#include <string.h>
#include <ctype.h>
#include <local\doslib.h>

char *
drvpath(path)
char path[];    /* path string */
                /* must be large enough to hold a full DOS path + NUL */
{
        union REGS inregs, outregs;
        static int drive(char);

        /* patch root directory onto drive name */
        strcat(path, "\\");

        /* set current directory path for drive from DOS */
        inregs.h.ah = GET_CUR_DIR;
        inregs.h.dl = drive(path[0]);           /* convert to drive number */
        inregs.x.si = (unsigned)&path[3];       /* start of return string */
        intdos(&inregs, &outregs);

        return (outregs.x.cflag ? (char *)NULL : path);
```

(continued)

```
}

static int
drive(dltr)
char dltr;          /* drive letter */
{
        /* 'A' (or 'a') => 1, 'B' (or 'b') => 2, etc. */
        return (tolower(dltr) - 'a' + 1);
}
```

These two files should be compiled and the resulting object files should be added to the *dos.lib* in the \ *lib* \ *local* directory.

After the file and directory buffers have been filled, *main( )* sequences the outputting of the data. All file data goes out first, followed by the file and directory names associated with each named directory. The simplest case is a list of files produced by a request like

ls

which produces a one-column listing of the file and directory names in the current directory. The output is done in a multi-column format if the *MULTICOLUMN* variable is set to the value of logical 1 by using -C on the command line or by renaming the LS program to either LC or LF under DOS version 3.00 or later.

The output of LS is directed to the standard output stream, so it appears on the screen unless it is redirected.

A default of 80 columns maximum is used to determine line length. This fits easily on most display screens and printers. You might want to add a feature that allows the line length to be controlled, either from the command line or by a configuration file or an environment variable.

Output lists are sorted lexically by default. Options allow the user to select reverse sorting (-r) and sorting by last modification time (-t). The standard library sort routine, *qsort( )*, does the sorting and calls on *ls_fcomp( )* to compare items being sorted. The file *ls_fcomp.c* contains the source for the comparison function.

```
/*
 *       ls_fcomp -- file and directory comparison functions
 */

#include <string.h>
#include "ls.h"

extern int Modtime;
extern int Reverse;


/*
 *       ls_fcomp -- compare two "file" items
 */

int
ls_fcomp(s1, s2)
struct OUTBUF *s1, *s2;
{
        int result;

        if (Modtime) {
                if ((result = s1->o_date - s2->o_date) == 0)
                        result = s1->o_time - s2->o_time;
        }
        else
                result = strcmp(s1->o_name, s2->o_name);

        return (Reverse ? -result : result);
} /* end_fcomp() */


/*
 *       dcomp -- compare two "directory" items
 */

int
ls_dcomp(s1, s2)
char *s1, *s2;
{
        int result;

        result = strcmp(s1, s2);

        return (Reverse ? -result : result);
} /* end ls_dcomp() */
```

After lists are sorted, they are sent to the output device by functions in the *ls_list* module. Single-column output is done by *ls_single( )*. Multi-column output is handled by *ls_multi( )*. The latter function is the more interesting one. First, here is the source:

```
/*
 *      ls_list -- list functions (long, single, multi) for ls
 */

#include <stdio.h>
#include <string.h>
#include "ls.h"

#define MAXCOL          80
#define MONTH_SHIFT     5
#define MONTH_MASK      0x0F
#define DAY_MASK        0x1F
#define YEAR_SHIFT      9
#define DOS_EPOCH       80
#define HOUR_SHIFT      11
#define HOUR_MASK       0x1F
#define MINUTE_SHIFT    5
#define MINUTE_MASK     0x3F

extern int Filetype;

/*
 *      ls_long -- list items in "long" format (mode time size name)
 */

int
ls_long(buf, nelem)
struct OUTBUF *buf;
int nelem;
{
        int n = 0;
        char modebuf[5];
        static void modestr(unsigned short, char *);

        while (nelem-- > 0) {
                /* convert mode number to a string */
                modestr(buf->o_mode, modebuf);
                printf("%s ", modebuf);
```

(continued)

```
                /* display file size in bytes */
                printf("%7ld ", buf->o_size);

                /* convert date and time values to formatted presentation */
                printf("%02d-%02d-%02d ", (buf->o_date >> MONTH_SHIFT) & MONTH_MASK,
                        buf->o_date & DAY_MASK, (buf->o_date >> YEAR_SHIFT) + DOS_EPOCH);
                printf("%02d:%02d ", (buf->o_time >> HOUR_SHIFT) & HOUR_MASK,
                        (buf->o_time >> MINUTE_SHIFT) & MINUTE_MASK);

                /* display filenames as lowercase strings */
                printf("%s\n", strlwr(buf->o_name));

                ++buf;
                ++n;
        }

        /* tell caller how many entries were printed */
        return (n);
} /* end ls_long() */


/*
 *      ls_single -- list items in a single column
 */

int
ls_single(buf, nelem)
struct OUTBUF *buf;
int nelem;
{
        int n = 0;

        while (nelem-- > 0) {
                printf("%s", strlwr(buf->o_name));
                if (Filetype && (buf->o_mode & SUBDIR) == SUBDIR)
                        putchar('\\');
                putchar('\n');
                ++buf;
                ++n;
        }

        /* tell caller how many entries were printed */
        return (n);
```

(continued)

```
} /* end ls_single() */


/*
 *      ls_multi -- list items in multiple columns that
 *      vary in width and number based on longest item size
 */

int
ls_multi(buf, nelem)
struct OUTBUF *buf;
int nelem;
{
        int i, j;
        int errcount = 0;
        struct OUTBUF *tmp;     /* temporary buffer pointer */
        struct OUTBUF *base;    /* buffer pointer for multi-col output */
        int n;                  /* number of items in list */
        int len, maxlen;        /* pathname lengths */
        int ncols;              /* number of columns to output */
        int nlines;             /* number of lines to output */

        /*
         * get length of longest pathname and calculate number
         * of columns and lines (col width = maxlen + 1)
         */
        tmp = buf;
        n = 0;
        maxlen = 0;
        for (tmp = buf, n = 0; n < nelem; ++tmp, ++n)
                if ((len = strlen(tmp->o_name)) > maxlen)
                        maxlen = len;
        /*
         * use width of screen - 1 to allow for newline at end of
         * line and leave two spaces between entries (one for optional
         * file type flag)
         */
        ncols = (MAXCOL - 1) / (maxlen + 2);
        nlines = n / ncols;
        if (n % ncols)
                ++nlines;


        /* output multi-column list */
        base = buf;
```

(continued)

```
            for (i = 0; i < nlines; ++i) {
                    tmp = base;
                    for (j = 0; j < ncols; ++j) {
                            len = maxlen + 2;
                            len -= printf("%s", strlwr(tmp->o_name));
                            if (Filetype && (tmp->o_mode & SUBDIR) == SUBDIR) {
                                    putchar('\\');
                                    --len;
                            }
                            while (len-- > 0)
                                    putchar(' ');
                            tmp += nlines;
                            if (tmp - buf >= nelem)
                                    break;
                    }
                    putchar('\n');
                    ++base;
            }

        return (errcount);
} /* end ls_multi() */


static void
modestr(mode, s)
unsigned short mode;    /* file mode number */
char s[];               /* mode string buffer */
{

        /* fill in the mode string to show what's set */
        s[0] = (mode & SUBDIR) == SUBDIR ? 'd' : '-';
        s[1] = (mode & HIDDEN) == HIDDEN ? 'h' : '-';
        s[2] = (mode & SYSTEM) == SYSTEM ? 's' : '-';
        s[3] = (mode & READONLY) == READONLY ? 'r' : '-';
        s[4] = '\0';
} /* end modestr() */
```

The *ls_multi( )* function receives a sorted list of names, scans it once
to find the length of the longest name, and then outputs the list in columns. The number of columns depends on the file data. Optimal column
width and number of columns are determined by the length of the longest
filename or subdirectory name to be output, thus maximizing the number
of columns output and minimizing the number of lines used. All names

are output in lowercase. Most people find words in all uppercase letters difficult to read; if you don't, feel free to leave out the call to *strlwr( )*.

The next function, *ls_dirx( )*, is the workhorse to which falls the task of expanding a directory name into a list of its subordinate file and subdirectory names. This is not a trivial task. The file system under DOS is fractured—part residing in a fixed directory at the "root" level of a disk, and the rest in dynamically allocated subdirectories that are simply special files in the file system. In addition, we must be concerned with the use of a drive name (A, for example) as an alias for the current directory on that drive. *Note:* The drive name is not an alias for the root directory.

```
/*
 *      ls_dirx -- expand the contents of a directory using
 *      the DOS first/next matching file functions
 */

#include <stdio.h>
#include <stdlib.h>
#include <string.h>
#include <malloc.h>
#include <dos.h>
#include <direct.h>
#include <signal.h>
#include <search.h>
#include <local\std.h>
#include <local\doslib.h>
#include "ls.h"

#define NFILES  1024

extern int Recursive;
extern int Longlist;
extern int Multicol;
extern int Hidden;

int
ls_dirx(pname, namep)
char *pname;
```

(continued)

```
char *namep;
{
        int status = 0;                 /* function return value */
        int n;                          /* number of items found */
        int fileattr;                   /* attributes of file-matching */
        struct DTA buf;                 /* disk transfer area */
        struct OUTBUF *bp, *bq;         /* output buffer pointers */
        char path[MAXPATH + 1];         /* working path string */

        extern void setdta(char *);
        extern int first_fm(char *, int);
        extern int next_fm();
        extern int ls_fcomp(struct OUTBUF *, struct OUTBUF *);
        extern char last_ch(char *);

        /* allocate a buffer */
        bp = bq = (struct OUTBUF *)malloc(NFILES * sizeof(struct OUTBUF));
        if (bp == NULL)
                fatal(pname, "Out of memory");

        /* form name for directory search */
        strcpy(path, namep);
        if (last_ch(path) != '\\')
                strcat(path, "\\");
        strcat(path, "*.*");

        /* list the files found */
        n = 0;
        /* establish a private DTA */
        setdta((char *)&buf);
        /* select file attributes */
        if (Hidden)
                fileattr = SUBDIR | HIDDEN | SYSTEM | READONLY;
        else
                fileattr = SUBDIR;
        if (first_fm(path, fileattr) == 0) {
                /* add file or directory to the buffer */
                do {
                        if (!Hidden && buf.d_fname[0] == '.')
                                continue;
                        bq->o_name = strdup(buf.d_fname);
```

(continued)

```
                        bq->o_mode = buf.d_attr;
                        bq->o_size = buf.d_fsize;
                        bq->o_date = buf.d_mdate;
                        bq->o_time = buf.d_mtime;
                        ++bq;
                        ++n;
                        setdta((char *)&buf);    /* reset to our DTA */
                } while (next_fm() == 0);

                if (n > 0) {
                        /* got some -- sort and list them */
                        qsort(bp, n, sizeof(struct OUTBUF), ls_fcomp);
                        if (Longlist)
                                ls_long(bp, n);
                        else if (Multicol)
                                ls_multi(bp, n);
                        else
                                ls_single(bp, n);
                }
        }
        else
                ++status;
        free(bp);

        return (status);
}
```

To get the data it needs from DOS, *ls_dirx( )* calls on three DOS functions: *setdta( )* to establish a disk transfer area in memory; *first_fm( )* to obtain the name of the first file that matches an ambiguous filename specification; and *next_fm( )* to get any subsequent matches to the same specification. We will compile these three functions and add the object modules to the DOS library.

```
/*
 *      setdta -- tell DOS where to do disk transfers
 */

#include <dos.h>
#include <local\doslib.h>

void
setdta(bp)
char *bp;        /* pointer to byte-aligned disk transfer area */
{
        union REGS inregs, outregs;

        inregs.h.ah = SET_DTA;
        inregs.x.dx = (unsigned int)bp;
        (void)intdos(&inregs, &outregs);
}
```

```
/*
 *      first_fm - find first file match in work directory
 */

#include <dos.h>
#include <local\doslib.h>

int
first_fm(path, fa)
char *path;     /* pathname of directory */
int fa;         /* attribute(s) of file to match */
{
        union REGS inregs, outregs;

        /* find first matching file */
        inregs.h.ah = FIND_FIRST;
        inregs.x.cx = fa;
        inregs.x.dx = (unsigned int)path;
        (void)intdos(&inregs, &outregs);

        return (outregs.x.cflag);
}
```

(continued)

```
/*
 *      next_fm - find next file match in work directory
 */

#include <dos.h>
#include <local\doslib.h>

int
next_fm()
{
        union REGS inregs, outregs;

        /* find next matching file */
        inregs.h.ah = FIND_NEXT;
        (void)intdos(&inregs, &outregs);

        return (outregs.x.cflag);
}
```

In addition, *ls_dirx( )* calls *last_ch( )* to examine the last character in the pathname. If the last character is not a \, a \ is appended to the pathname. The *last_ch( )* function is added to the *lib**local**util.lib* library.

```
/*
 *      last_ch -- return a copy of the last character
 *      before the NUL byte in a string
 */

char
last_ch(s)
char *s;
{
        register char *cp;

        /* find end of s */
        cp = s;
        while (*cp != '\0')
                ++cp;

        /* return previous character */
        --cp;
        return (*cp);
}
```

To assist you in producing and maintaining the LS program, here is a makefile, *ls.mk*:

```
# makefile for the LS program

LIB=c:\lib
LLIB=c:\lib\local

first_fm.obj:    first_fm.c
        msc $*;
        lib $(LLIB)\dos -+ $*;

next_fm.obj:    next_fm.c
        msc $*;
        lib $(LLIB)\dos -+ $*;

setdta.obj:      setdta.c
        msc $*;
        lib $(LLIB)\dos -+ $*;

getdrive.obj:   getdrive.c
        msc $*;
        lib $(LLIB)\dos -+ $*;

drvpath.obj:     drvpath.c
        msc $*;
        lib $(LLIB)\dos -+ $*;

ls_fcomp.obj:   ls_fcomp.c ls.h
        msc $*;

ls_dirx.obj:    ls_dirx.c ls.h
        msc $*;

ls_list.obj:    ls_list.c ls.h
        msc $*;

ls.obj:          ls.c ls.h
        msc $*;

ls.exe:          ls.obj ls_dirx.obj ls_fcomp.obj ls_list.obj \
                 $(LLIB)\util.lib $(LLIB)\dos.lib
        link $* ls_dirx ls_fcomp ls_list $(LIB)\ssetargv, $*,, $(LLIB)\util $(LLIB)\dos;
```

The temptation to add features to LS is great. It (and its equivalents, such as DIR) is a high-use program, typically accounting for some 30 to 40 percent of command executions on a given system. Perhaps because of its visibility, it is a frequent target for enhancements. Try to avoid turning LS into a program that no one uses because it is too complicated.

File Printing 9

One essential programmer's tool is a program that displays or prints the contents of text files—program source files, debugging listings, program "map" files, and so on. The PR program developed in this chapter to take care of this task is patterned after the UNIX utility of the same name. It is designed to be flexible yet not encumbered with unnecessary features. It provides a basic file-printing capability supplemented by a collection of helpful options.

By default, PR produces output suitable for a generic line printer. It uses only the standard format-effector codes (carriage return and line-feed) and normal displayable characters (including space). The options enable you to use special features of the Epson and Epson-compatible printers, sequentially number lines, print a list of pages from a file, and control basic page layout. Many options of PR allow the program to be used as a filter, reading from its standard input and producing formatted pages on its standard output or other output streams.

Program Specification

Figure 9-1 on the next page is the manual page that describes the features and applications of PR. During the development of the program, the manual page served as a wish list. A prototype of PR, based on an earlier version of the manual page, was tested on some "friendly users." Their feedback led to changes in the manual page and subsequent revisions of the program that eventually resulted in the final program presented here.

NAME

PR — print file(s)

SYNOPSIS

pr [*options*] [*file . . .*]

DESCRIPTION

The PR program takes a list of filenames and sends the contents of each in turn to the standard output. Formatting of the output "pages" is controlled via built-in defaults and may be modified by external configuration files and command-line options. If no filenames are specified, PR reads from its standard input (usually the keyboard, unless input is redirected).

Each page starts with a header composed of the filename, the file-relative page number, and the file's modification date and time. When reading from the standard input, the filename is omitted and the current date and time are used.

Long lines are folded onto the next line rather than being truncated. The line count is not affected by this. PR continues to track the number of logical lines in the source file, not the number of physical lines printed.

The options listed below may be used singly or combined in any order.

Option	Action
-e	Toggle the Epson-compatible printer mode
-f	Use a formfeed to eject a page (the default is spaces)
-h *hdr*	Replace the filename part of the header with the text given in *hdr* (must be quoted if it contains white space)
-l *len*	Set the page length to *len* lines (the default is 66)
-n	Enable the line-numbering feature (the initial setting is off)
-o *cols*	Set offset to *cols* columns from left edge of the paper
-p	Preview output on screen (may be redirected)
-s *list*	Output only those lines selected by the comma-separated *list* (must be quoted if it contains any white space)
-w *cols*	Set the output line width to *cols* columns

FIGURE 9-1 | *Manual page for PR*   *(continued)*

Program configuration may be controlled via optional local and global configuration files (local overrides global). Most settings established by configuration files may be altered by the user via the command-line arguments listed above. The following listing (comments are optional—only the numbers and strings at the beginning of each line are required) is the default global configuration file, which, if it exists, must reside in a subdirectory pointed to by the CONFIG environment variable:

```
2     top1
2     top2
3     bottom
132   width
5     left margin
3     right margin
66    lines per page
6     lines per inch
1     printer mode (Epson)
1     line number enabled
1     use formfeeds
8     standard tabs
PRN   output destination
```

EXAMPLES

Print all of the C source files in the current directory, with line-numbering turned on, to an Epson printer attached to the standard printer port:

`pr -en *.c`

Display the contents of the \ *include* \ *std.h* header file with an offset of 10 columns and a text file:

`pr -o10 \ include \ std.h`

Print the file *myprog.pas* on the default printer starting at page 4 and continuing up to and including page 10:

`pr -s4,10 myprog.pas`

FIGURE 9-1 | *continued*

I will describe the program's basic features and its options in detail as the PR functions are presented, but before doing that, we need to define just what is meant by a "page" of output.

Figure 9-2 is a proposed page layout. The assumption that governs choices of default values is that standard document paper is used. A sheet of letter-sized paper is 8½ inches wide by 11 inches long. (An additional half-inch on either side of a sheet of pin-fed paper contains the holes for the tractor feed, resulting in a raw page size of 9½ by 11 inches.) A good guideline regarding page appearance is that at least ½ inch of unused space should be left on both sides and at the top and bottom. Using less white space tends to make a printed page look too crowded.

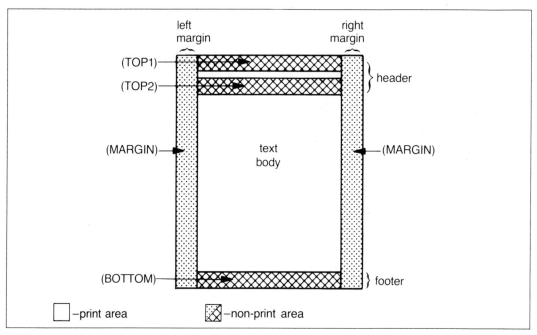

FIGURE 9-2 | *Proposed page layout*

The left side of a page may need to be punched for ring binding, so some additional clear space might be needed there. For most purposes, however, I find that the default of ½ inch is enough. This indentation or offset is obtained by spacing in five columns for a 10-pitch font. Condensed type, such as that produced by an Epson printer in condensed mode, requires a larger number of columns (about eight) to obtain the same physical offset.

Given the specification presented in the manual page and the values obtained from the proposed page layout, we can now design a program to produce nicely formatted listings of text files. We can start by noting that PR follows a pattern of behavior that is similar to CAT: It takes some input, applies some transformation, and produces some output. However, we will have to treat lines a bit differently to accommodate optional line-numbering, page offset, and other aspects of format.

If our design is done well, we should have enough flexibility to handle 90 percent of all the printing needs of a programmer. The behavior of the PR program will be controlled by reasonable built-in defaults that may be modified by configuration files located in the current directory or in a directory selected by the user and by command-line options.

After analyzing the requirements for PR and trying several simple prototypes to investigate ways of implementing the features, I settled on an organization for the program. Each program module is packaged in a separate file, usually with one function per file. The program has the following functions and calling hierarchy:

```
main()
        getpname()
        pr_gcnf()
                fconfig()
        getopt()
        pr_help()
        pr_file()
                pr_cpy()
                        mkslist()
                        pr_getln()
                        fit()
                        lines()
                        spaces()
                        setfont()
                        selected()
                        pr_line()
        exit()
```

As you can see, many functions that we developed in earlier chapters are called by functions used in PR. These external names are resolved by the linker, using *util.lib* as one of the searched libraries.

If the user gives an erroneous option, *main( )* calls *pr_help( )* to display an abbreviated manual page on the *stderr* channel. The C source for *pr_help( )* is:

```
/*
 *      pr_help -- display an abbreviated manual page
 */

#include <stdio.h>
#include <local\std.h>

void
pr_help(pname)
char *pname;
{
        static char *m_str[] = {
                "The following options may be used singly or in combination:",
                "-e\t set Epson-compatible mode",
                "-f\t use formfeed to eject a page (default is newlines)",
                "-g\t use generic printer mode",
                "-h hdr\t use specified header instead of filename",
                "-l len\t set page length in lines (default = 66)",
                "-n\t enable line-numbering (default = off)",
                "-o cols\t offset from left edge in columns (default = 5)",
                "-p\t preview output on screen (may be redirected)",
                "-s list\t print only selected pages",
                "-w cols\t line width in columns (default = 80)"
        };
        int i, n = sizeof (m_str)/ sizeof (char *);

        fprintf(stderr, "Usage: %s [options] file...\n\n", pname);
        for (i = 0; i < n; ++i)
                fprintf(stderr, "%s\n", m_str[i]);

        return;
}
```

The function uses a *static* array of string pointers to message lines. The calculation in the line

n = sizeof (m_str) / sizeof (char *)

sets n to the number of message lines in a way that lets us add message lines without having to count them and declare how many are used. This makes it easier to modify the function as the program evolves, as most programs do.

To achieve the desired flexibility, we will use a global data structure to hold the values of the important formatting and program-operation control variables used by the program's various modules. Only those modules that need to know about the data will be given access to the data structure. Here is the header file, *print.h,* that contains the data structure definition and some manifest constants used to initialize the program:

```
/*
 *      print.h -- header information for print programs
 */

/* default printing format information */
#define BOTTOM  3       /* blank lines at bottom of page */
#define MARGIN  5       /* default margin width in columns */
#define MAXPCOL 80      /* maximum number of printed columns per line */
#define MAXPSTR 64      /* maximum characters in a string variable */
#define PAGELEN 66      /* default page length (at 6 lines per inch) */
#define LPI     6       /* default lines per inch */
#define TABSPEC 8       /* default tab separation */
#define TOP1    2       /* blank lines above header line */
#define TOP2    2       /* blank lines below header line */


/* primary data structure for printer programs */
typedef struct pr_st {
        /* numeric variables */
        int p_top1;     /* lines above header */
        int p_top2;     /* lines below header */
        int p_btm;      /* lines in footer */
        int p_wid;      /* width in columns */
        int p_lmarg;    /* left margin */
        int p_rmarg;    /* right margin */
        int p_len;      /* lines per page */
        int p_lpi;      /* lines per inch */
```

(continued)

```
    int p_lnum;      /* nonzero turns line-numbering on */
    int p_mode;      /* zero for generic printer */
    int p_font;      /* font number when in nongeneric mode */
    int p_ff;        /* nonzero uses formfeed to eject page */
    int p_tabint;    /* tab interval */

    /* string variables */
    char p_hdr[MAXPSTR];
    char p_dest[MAXPSTR];
} PRINT;
```

A *typedef* is used to create a synonym, *PRINT*, for the *struct pr_st* data structure. The structure contains about a dozen integer-sized variable definitions and two string variable definitions. The header file defines the *printer* data structure, but it does not declare any storage for it. That is done in the configuration function, *pr_gcnf( )*, which we'll examine shortly. First, let's take a look at PR from the top.

The *main( )* function is contained in the file *pr.c.* It declares and initializes global variables, establishes the default output channel, processes command-line arguments, and calls *pr_file( )* with a list of files named as input by the user. If no filenames are specified, PR uses the standard input channel so that data can be routed through PR from a redirected input or from a pipeline. Thus, PR fits the description of a filter in the same way as the DOS programs MORE and SORT, except that PR can be configured to send its output to someplace other than the standard output. In such cases, PR is referred to as a *sink* instead of a filter, because it is a termination point for data flow.

```
/*
 *      pr -- file printer
 */

#include <stdio.h>
#include <stdlib.h>
#include <dos.h>
#include <local\std.h>
#include "print.h"


char Pagelist[MAXLINE];
```

(continued)

```
main(argc, argv)
int argc;
char **argv;
{
        int ch;
        BOOLEAN errflag;
        extern PRINT pcnf;
        static char pgm[MAXNAME + 1] = { "pr" };

        extern void getpname(char *, char*);
        extern int getopt(int, char **, char *);
        extern char *optarg;
        extern int optind, opterr;
        extern int pr_gcnf(char *);
        extern pr_file(char *, int, char **);
        extern void pr_help(char *);
        extern void fixtabs(int);
        extern int setprnt();

        if (_osmajor >= 3)
                getpname(*argv, pgm);

        /* do configuration */
        if (pr_gcnf(pgm) != 0) {
                fprintf(stderr, "%s: Configuration error", pgm);
                exit(2);
        }
        if (setprnt() == -1) {
                fprintf(stderr, "%s: Bad printer configuration\n", pgm);
                exit(1);
        }
        fixtabs(pcnf.p_tabint);

        /* process command-line arguments */
        while ((ch = getopt(argc, argv, "efgh:l:no:ps:w:")) != EOF) {
                switch (ch) {
                case 'e':
                        /* force "Epson-compatible " printer mode */
                        pcnf.p_mode = 1;
                        break;
                case 'f':
                        /* use formfeed to eject a page */
```

(continued)

```
                    pcnf.p_ff = 1;
                    break;
            case 'g':
                    /* force "generic" printer mode */
                    pcnf.p_mode = 0;
                    break;
            case 'h':
                    /* use specified header */
                    strcpy(pcnf.p_hdr, optarg);
                    break;
            case 'l':
                    /* set lines per page */
                    pcnf.p_len = atoi(optarg);
                    break;
            case 'n':
                    /* enable line-numbering */
                    pcnf.p_lnum = 1;
                    break;
            case 'o':
                    /* set left margin */
                    pcnf.p_lmarg = atoi(optarg);
                    break;
            case 'p':
                    /* preview output on screen */
                    strcpy(pcnf.p_dest, "");
                    break;
            case 's':
                    /* output selected pages */
                    strcpy(Pagelist, optarg);
                    break;
            case 'w':
                    /* set page width in columns */
                    pcnf.p_wid = atoi(optarg);
                    break;
            case '?':
                    /* unknown option */
                    errflag = TRUE;
                    break;
            }
    }
    if (errflag == TRUE) {
            pr_help(pgm);
```

(continued)

```
            exit(3);
    }

    /* print the files */
    pr_file(pgm, argc - optind, argv += optind);

    exit(0);
}
```

The *main( )* function calls *getpname( )* to get the program name and then calls *pr_gcnf( )* to get the configuration data needed to initialize the program. Next, it uses *getopt( )* to process user-supplied options, if any, and finally it passes a list of filenames (possibly none) to *pr_file( )*. We have seen the use of *getpname( )* and *getopt( )* before. There should be no surprises here.

Option Handling

The *pr_gcnf( )* function is specific to PR, but the design can be applied to other programs. The pseudocode for this function is

```
if (a configuration file exists)
        open the file
        read numeric data
        read string data
        if (data good)
                set flag
        close file
if (flag is set)
        initialize to values just read
else
        use defaults from the header file
```

Here is the source code for pr_gcnf( ):

```
/*
 *      pr_gcnf -- get configuration for pr program
 */

#include <stdio.h>
#include <string.h>
#include <local\std.h>
```

(continued)

```
#include <local\printer.h>
#include "print.h"

/* expected number of configuration items */
#define N_NBR    12

PRINT pcnf;

int
pr_gcnf(pname)
char *pname;
{
        char line[MAXLINE];
        char *s;
        int cnf[N_NBR];
        int n, errcount, good;
        FILE *fp, *fconfig(char *, char *);

        /* get configuration file values, if any */
        n = good = errcount = 0;
        if ((fp = fconfig("CONFIG", "pr.cnf")) != NULL) {
                while (n < N_NBR && (s = fgets(line, MAXLINE, fp)) != NULL) {
                        cnf[n] = atoi(s);
                        ++n;
                }
                if ((s = fgets(line, MAXLINE, fp)) == NULL)
                        ++errcount;
                else
                        strcpy(pcnf.p_dest, strtok(line, " \t\n"));
                if (n != N_NBR)
                        ++errcount;
                if (errcount == 0)
                        good = 1;
                if (fclose(fp) == -1)
                        fatal(pname, "cannot close config file", 1);
        }

        /* use config data is good; use defaults otherwise */
        pcnf.p_top1 = good ? cnf[0] : TOP1;
        pcnf.p_top2 = good ? cnf[1] : TOP2;
        pcnf.p_btm = good ? cnf[2] : BOTTOM;
        pcnf.p_wid = good ? cnf[3] : MAXPCOL;
        pcnf.p_lmarg = good ? cnf[4] : MARGIN;
```

(continued)

```
        pcnf.p_rmarg = good ? cnf[5] : MARGIN;
        pcnf.p_len = good ? cnf[6] : PAGELEN;
        pcnf.p_lpi = good ? cnf[7] : LPI;
        pcnf.p_mode = good ? cnf[8] : 0;
        pcnf.p_lnum = good ? cnf[9] : 0;
        pcnf.p_ff = good ? cnf[10] : 0;
        pcnf.p_tabint = good ? cnf[11] : TABSPEC;
        if (!good)
                strcpy(pcnf.p_dest, "PRN");
        if (pcnf.p_mode == 1)
                pcnf.p_font = CONDENSED;
        strcpy(pcnf.p_hdr, "");

        return (errcount);
}
```

The *PRINT* type is used to declare a global data structure for the
printer, *pcnf*, which stands for printer configuration. Any other source file
that needs access to *pcnf* must declare it as external data.

If no configuration file is found, *pr_gcnf( )* falls through to the default
assignments. The *fconfig( )* function we created in Chapter 7 is used to
query DOS for an external configuration file. A *NULL* result indicates that
none was found. If a configuration file is found, it is read in a line at a time.

Numeric values are obtained by converting the character representations in the file to integers by using the standard library function *atoi( )*.
Because *atoi( )* accepts only characters that can be considered part of a
number, we can add comments to the lines. Thus, when the line

66 number of lines per page

is retrieved from the configuration file and is given as the string argument
to *atoi( )*, the function merely assigns the integer value 66 to a temporary
array.

String arguments are handled similarly. A line is read in and the
library function *strtok( )* extracts the first token, which is the string value
we need to save. The remaining characters on the line, if any, are ignored.

An example of a string variable is *p_dest*, which determines where
PR's output will go. This variable is a member of *pcnf* and is accessed using

the dot operator as in *pcnf.p_dest*. Each line of output is sent by default to the device specified in *p_dest*. If *p_dest* is set to CON, or if it is null (""), output is directed to the standard output channel and will be displayed on the user's console screen unless program output is redirected. (MS-DOS and UNIX permit the standard output of a program to be redirected using the greater-than (>) symbol—see Chapter 3 or your DOS manual for details. Thus, output that would otherwise be displayed on the system console or a terminal screen may be sent to a printer port or captured in another file.)

In this presentation of the PR program, I have set *p_dest* to PRN, the default printer device, because that is where I usually want the output to go. We can still send the output to the screen by selecting the -p (preview) option, which uses CON as the destination for a single invocation of PR.

To display the contents of a file named *myfile.txt* on the system console, you would type

```
pr -p myfile.txt
```

To send the output to a printer that is attached to the default printer port, you would instead type

```
pr myfile.txt
```

If PR is compiled with *ssetargv.obj* included in the linker object list (as shown in the makefile, *pr.mk)*, PR permits the use of wildcards in filenames, letting you use abbreviated command lines to specify print jobs. For example, to print hard copies of all the header files in the *include* subdirectory and in the *include\sys* subdirectory, type

```
pr \include\*.h \include\sys\*.h
```

If you have a hardware or software print spooler on line (such as the one provided with Microsoft Windows), you can turn your attention to something productive while your printer dumps a mound of paper on the floor. Otherwise, you'll have to mark time for a while.

File Handling

The processing loop in *pr_file( )* receives a list of files and tries to get each file formatted and printed. The function must handle errors

gracefully. If, for example, a user specifies a file that does not exist or one
that cannot be opened, the program sends an error message to the standard error channel and then continues looking for more files to print. The
standard error channel is used because messages sent to it will appear on
the console screen even when normal program output is directed elsewhere. The standard input channel is used as a data source if no files are
named on the command line.

The *pr_file* function is also responsible for connecting the output of
PR to the required stream. If the user has configured PR to send output to
one of the standard output channels (*sdtout, stdprn,* or *stdaux*), there is
no need to open the stream, because DOS has already done so when PR
started running. Other destinations, such as a named file, must be explicitly opened for writing.

The source code for *pr_file( )* is:

```
/*
 *      pr_file -- process each filename or standard input
 */

#include <stdio.h>
#include <stdlib.h>
#include <string.h>
#include <local\std.h>
#include "print.h"

int pr_file(pname, ac, av)
char *pname;
int ac;
char **av;
{
        int ch, errcount = 0;
        FILE *fin, *fout;
        extern PRINT pcnf;

        extern void fatal(char *, char *, int);
        extern int pr_cpy(FILE *, FILE *, char *);

        /* open output stream only if not already open */
        if (*pcnf.p_dest == '\0' || strcmp(pcnf.p_dest, "CON") == 0)
                fout = stdout;
```

(continued)

```
        else if (strcmp(pcnf.p_dest, "PRN") == 0)
                fout = stdprn;
        else if (strcmp(pcnf.p_dest, "AUX") == 0)
                fout = stdaux;
        else
                if ((fout = fopen(pcnf.p_dest, "w")) == NULL)
                        fatal(pname, "Error open destination stream", 1);

        /* prepare input stream */
        if (ac == 0)
                pr_cpy(stdin, fout, "");
        else {
                for (; ac > 0; --ac, ++av) {
                        if ((fin = fopen(*av, "r")) == NULL) {
                                fprintf(stderr, "%s: Error opening %s\n",
                                        pname, *av);
                                continue;
                        }
                        if (pr_cpy(fin, fout, *av) == -1) {
                                fprintf(stderr, "%s: Cannot stat %s\n",
                                        pname, *av);
                                continue;
                        }
                        if (fclose(fin) == EOF)
                                fatal(pname, "Error closing input file", 1);
                }
        }
        return (errcount);
}
```

Notice the message "Cannot stat (*filename*)" after the call to
pr_cpy( ) (described next). This tells the user that file statistics could not
be obtained for the named file even though it was found and opened. This
flags a possible error with the disk directory and should inspire the user to
find out why the error occurred. It could be that a bad sector is developing
or that a disk formatting or updating problem has occurred.

What's My Line?

The work of orchestrating the formatting and copying of text pages
falls to *pr_cpy( )*. A line in a text file may be thought of as a single logical

line that may be represented as one or more physical lines of output. Long lines of output—those that exceed the width of the printable or display-able area—may be handled in at least three ways. We can:

▶ let the line run long and leave the treatment up to the printer and its driver software. This approach can result in some bizarre-looking output.

▶ "fold" a long line so that what cannot be displayed or printed on the current line is moved to the next output line.

▶ truncate the input so that anything on a line that would have to be displayed past the last column is effectively lost.

The PR program has been designed to fold lines so that nothing is lost on output. If line-numbering is turned on, a logical line number is displayed at the beginning of each line. If a line has to be folded, as shown in Figure 9-3, the additional physical lines needed to print or display it are indented as usual, but they do not have a number field associated with them. Logical lines are numbered starting with one. The number of a line indicates its relative offset from the beginning of the file.

```
           .
           .
           .
     46          /* process command-line arguments */
     47          while ((ch = getopt(argc, argv, "efgh:l:no:ps:w:")) !=
EOF) {
     48                  switch (ch) {
     49                  case 'e':
           .
           .
           .
```

FIGURE 9-3 | *A folded line, as displayed by PR*

Before going any further, here are the pseudocode and C source code for *pr_cpy( )*.

```
set up source and destination streams
if (source is stdin)
        get current time
else
        get file modification time
for each line in source file or stream
```

(continued)

```
        if (line won't fit on page OR formfeed)
                eject page
        if (at top of a page)
                print header
        print the logical line
    if (not at top of page)
            eject page
```

```
/*
 *      pr_cpy -- copy input stream to output stream
 */

#include <stdio.h>
#include <string.h>
#include <local\std.h>
#include <local\printer.h>
#include <sys\types.h>
#include <sys\stat.h>
#include <time.h>
#include "print.h"

extern PRINT pcnf;
extern char Pagelist[MAXLINE];
extern long Highest;

int
pr_cpy(fin, fout, fname)
FILE *fin;
FILE *fout;
char *fname;
{
        int errcount = 0;
        unsigned int p_line;     /* page-relative line number */
        long f_line;             /* file-relative line number */
        long f_page;             /* file-relative page number */
        int lnlen;               /* line length */
        char line[MAXLINE];      /* input line buffer */
        struct stat tbuf;        /* file information */
        long ltime;              /* date and time */
        FILE *fnull, *fx;        /* additional output file pointers */

        extern void mkslist(char *);     /* make a selection list */
        extern int selected(long);       /* is item in the list? */
        extern int spaces(int, FILE *);  /* emit string of spaces */
```

(continued)

```
extern int setfont(int, FILE *);/* set printer font type */
extern int clrprnt(FILE *);      /* clear special fonts */
extern int lines(int, FILE *);   /* emit string of blank lines */
static int fit(int, int);        /* will line fit on page? */
extern int pr_line(char *, FILE *, unsigned int);

/* install page selection list, if any */
if (Pagelist[0] != '\0') {
        /* open the NUL device for dumping output */
        if ((fnull = fopen("NUL", "w")) == NULL) {
                perror("Error opening NUL device");
                exit(1);
        }
        mkslist(Pagelist);
}
else
        Highest = BIGGEST;
/* get date and time stamp */
if (*fname == '\0')
        /* using stdin -- use today's date and time */
        ltime = time(NULL);
else {
        if (stat(fname, &tbuf) == -1)
                return (-1);
        /* use file's modification time */
        ltime = tbuf.st_mtime;
}
p_line = 0;
f_line = 1;
f_page = 1;
while ((lnlen = pr_getln(line, MAXLINE, fin)) > 0 ) {
        /* if formfeed or no room for line, eject page */
        if (line[0] == '\f' || !fit(lnlen, p_line)) {
                /* to top of next page */
                if (pcnf.p_ff == 0)
                        lines(pcnf.p_len - p_line, fx);
                else
                        fputc('\f', fx);
                p_line = 0;
        }

        /* if at top of page, print the header */
        if (p_line == 0) {
```

(continued)

```
                    if (f_page > Highest)
                            break;
                    fx = selected(f_page) ? fout : fnull;
                    p_line += lines(pcnf.p_top1, fx);
                    if (pcnf.p_mode != 0)
                            setfont(EMPHASIZED, fx);
                    spaces(pcnf.p_lmarg, fx);
                    if (*pcnf.p_hdr != '\0')
                            fprintf(fx, "%s ", pcnf.p_hdr);
                    else if (*fname != '\0')
                            fprintf(fx, "%s ", strupr(fname));
                    fprintf(fx, "Page %u ", f_page++);
                    fputs(ctime(&ltime), fx);
                    ++p_line;
                    if (pcnf.p_mode != 0)
                            setfont(pcnf.p_font, fx);
                    p_line += lines(pcnf.p_top2, fx);
                }

                /* OK to output the line */
                if (line[0] != '\f')
                        p_line += pr_line(line, fx, f_line++);
        }
        if (ferror(fin) != 0)
                ++errcount;
        if (p_line > 0 && p_line < pcnf.p_len)
                if (pcnf.p_ff == 0)
                        lines(pcnf.p_len - p_line, fx);
                else
                        fputc('\f', fx);

        if (pcnf.p_mode != 0)
                clrprnt(fx);
        return (errcount);
}


/*
 *      fit -- return nonzero value if enough physical
 *      lines are available on the current page to take
 *      the current logical line of text
 */

#define NFLDWIDTH  8    /* width of number field */
```

(continued)

```
static int
fit(len, ln)
int len, ln;
{
        int need, left; /* physical lines */
        int cols;       /* columns of actual output */
        int lw;         /* displayable line width */

        /* total need (columns -> physical lines) */
        cols = len + (pcnf.p_lnum > 0 ? NFLDWIDTH : 0);
        lw = pcnf.p_wid - pcnf.p_lmarg - pcnf.p_rmarg;
        need = 1 + cols / lw;

        /* lines remaining on page */
        left = pcnf.p_len - ln - pcnf.p_btm;

        return (need <= left ? 1 : 0);
}
```

The *pr_cpy( )* function handles a few other tasks in addition to fold-ing long lines. It detects that an input stream has ended before the output page is full and emits enough extra blank lines to get back to the top of a fresh page. That's so the next file will start printing in the right place. It makes sure that there is enough room remaining on a page to accept the next logical line. The *static* function *fit( )* within the *pr_cpy.c* file does the needed calculations.

The function also needs to handle a special situation that results from a fairly widespread practice. Programmers often create source files with two or more functions in them. Sometimes a literal formfeed control character (Ctrl-L) is placed between functions. This causes most printers to eject a page and to begin printing anew at the top of the next page. Care must be taken to keep the file-relative line and page numbers accurate.

The functions *mkslist( )* and *selected( )* obtain a selection list and de-termine whether an item is in the list; they were explained fully in Chap-ter 7. These functions are called by *pr_cpy( )* to process a list of selected pages, the *Pagelist* variable, to be formatted and printed by PR. The spe-cial page number BIGGEST is used to supply the high end of an open range specification (like 20–), which causes PR to print all pages between 20 and the end of the file.

The *pr_getln( )* function obtains a line of text from the input stream and expands it while reading it into the line array. The expansion alluded to here is that of converting each tab character in the input into the right number of output spaces so that column alignments are retained. The expansion is necessary because we will be doing indenting (page offset) and other formatting operations upon output, and because some older printers do not handle tabs correctly. All positions in the line array that are used to hold the text must be filled with characters that have a single unit of displacement in the output. This facilitates character counting so that *fit( )* can determine how much space is required for the expanded line.

This is the source code for *pr_getln( )*:

```
/*
 *      pr_getln -- get a line of text while expanding tabs;
 *      put text into an array and return the length of the line
 *      including termination to the calling function.
 */

#include <stdio.h>
#include <stdlib.h>
#include <local\std.h>

int
pr_getln(s, lim, fin)
char *s;
int lim;
FILE *fin;
{
        int ch;
        register char *cp;

        extern int tabstop();    /* query tabstop array */

        cp = s;
        while (--lim > 0 && (ch = fgetc(fin)) != EOF && ch != '\n' && ch != '\f') {
                if (ch == '\t')
                        /* loop and store spaces until next tabstop */
                        do
                                *cp++ = ' ';
                        while (--lim > 0 && tabstop(cp - s) == 0);
                else
```

(continued)

```
                        *cp++ = ch;
        }
        if (ch == EOF && cp - s == 0)
                ;
        else if (ch == EOF || ch == '\n')
                *cp++ = '\n';   /* assure correct line termination */
        else if (ch == '\f' && cp - s == 0) {
                *cp++ = '\f';
                fgetc(fin);       /* toss the trailing newline */
        }
        *cp = '\0';

        return (cp - s);
}
```

The tab expansion is done by the functions in *tabs.c* that were described in Chapter 7.

Top-of-page processing is done directly by *pr_cpy( )*, which prints the page header composed of some blank lines, a header line that contains the name of the current file (or a substitute text string), the output page number, and the date and time when the file was created or last modified. The blank lines are produced by a call to *lines( )*, a function that emits a series of newlines to the specified stream.

```
/*
 *      lines -- send newlines to the output stream
 */

#include <stdio.h>
#include <stdlib.h>

int
lines(n, fp)
int n;
FILE *fp;
{
        register int i;

        for (i = 0; i < n; ++i)
                if (putc('\n', fp) == EOF && ferror(fp))
                        break;
```

(continued)

```
        /* return number of newlines emitted */
        return (i);
}
```

The filename as typed by the user is converted to uppercase. This is
done because DOS automatically converts filenamcs returned in response
to an ambiguous specification (using wildcards) in uppercase letters. We
could just as easily convert everything to lowercase.

The formatting of the header line differs from the text body when
the Epson-compatible mode is selected. The *setprnt( )*, *setfont( )*, and
clrprnt( ) functions described in Chapter 7 are employed to control the
printer so that headers may be printed in a different typeface than the
main text. (Although not a necessary feature, this demonstrates a practical use of different typefaces on a single page.) The text body can be
printed in a compressed form, to permit long lines (up to about 137
characters) to be printed on standard letter-sized paper.

The function *pr_line( )* is called to output a logical line of text composed of two or three parts: a left margin produced by a call to *spaces( )*,
an optional file-relative line-number field, and finally the text of the expanded line. If additional physical lines are needed, *spaces( )* is called at
the beginning of each to obtain a uniform page offset.

Here is the source code for *pr_line( ):*

```
/*
 *      pr_line -- ouput a buffered logical line and
 *      return a count of physical lines produced
 */

#include <stdio.h>
#include <stdlib.h>
#include <local\std.h>
#include "print.h"

int
pr_line(s, fout, rline)
```

(continued)

```
char *s;                /* buffered line of text */
FILE *fout;             /* output stream */
unsigned int rline;     /* file-relative line number */
{
        int c_cnt;      /* character position in output line */
        int nlines;     /* number of lines output */
        extern PRINT pcnf;

        extern int spaces(int, FILE *); /* emit string of spaces */

        nlines = 1;
        c_cnt = 0;

        /* output the left indentation, if any */
        c_cnt += spaces(pcnf.p_lmarg, fout);

        /* output the line number if numbering enabled */
        if (pcnf.p_lnum != 0)
                c_cnt += fprintf(fout, "%6u ", rline);

        /* output the text of the line */
        while (*s != '\0') {
                if (c_cnt > (pcnf.p_wid - pcnf.p_rmarg)) {
                        fputc('\n', fout);
                        ++nlines;
                        c_cnt = 0;
                        c_cnt = spaces(pcnf.p_lmarg, fout);
                }
                fputc(*s, fout);
                ++s;
                ++c_cnt;
        }

        return (nlines);
}
```

The *pr_line( )* function returns the number of physical lines that were used to print the single logical input line.

The *spaces( )* function (on the next page) is almost identical to *lines( )*, except for the character that it emits (space instead of newline).

```
/*
 *       spaces -- send spaces (blanks) to the output stream
 */

#include <stdio.h>
#include <stdlib.h>

int
spaces(n, fp)
int n;
FILE *fp;
{
        register int i;

        for (i = 0; i < n; ++i)
                if (putc(' ', fp) == EOF && ferror(fp))
                        break;

        /* return number of spaces emitted */
        return (i);
}
```

Since the tasks performed by *lines( )* and *spaces( )* are needed frequently in programs that send text to the screen or some other output device, we will add the object files *lines.obj* and *spaces.obj* to our utility library, *util.lib*, by compiling them and using the command

lib util + lines spaces;

Remember to copy the updated library into the \ *lib* \ *local* subdirectory so that LINK can find it.

Program Maintenance

A special-purpose library called *prlib.lib* contains all but a few of the object modules that comprise the PR program. The *pr.obj* file, which contains the *main( )* function, is kept separate from the rest because of the way the DOS linker, LINK, works. The executable filename defaults to the name of the first object module specified in the link list, and at least one module must be named.

The makefile script for PR is in *pr.mk*. It automatically keeps the needed objects and the *prlib.lib* file up to date as changes are made to the program source files. Here is the text of *pr.mk:*

```
# makefile for the pr program

LINC=c:\include\local
LIB=c:\lib
LLIB=c:\lib\local

pr_cpy.obj:      pr_cpy.c print.h $(LINC)\printer.h
        msc  $*;
        lib prlib -+$*;

pr_file.obj:     pr_file.c print.h
        msc  $*;
        lib prlib -+$*;

pr_getln.obj:   pr_getln.c
        msc  $*;
        lib prlib -+$*;

pr_help.obj:    pr_help.c
        msc  $*;
        lib prlib -+$*;

pr_gcnf.obj:    pr_gcnf.c print.h $(LINC)\printer.h
        msc  $*;
        lib prlib -+$*;

pr_line.obj:    pr_line.c print.h
        msc  $*;
        lib prlib -+$*;

pr.obj:          pr.c print.h
        msc  $*;

pr.exe:         pr.obj prlib.lib $(LLIB)\util.lib
        link $* $(LIB)\ssetargv, $*,, prlib $(LLIB)\util;
```

Possible Enhancements

As well endowed as PR is already, there is always some new wrinkle or feature that some user would like to see. In trying to avoid making PR into a program that serves everyone in every way but no one particularly well in any way, I have chosen to stick with the feature set provided.

However, some users of PR have requested the following features, which you may want to consider adding. First, it might be helpful to have a multi-column output feature. This would take lines from a file and present them in columns across the page. Each line would be truncated if it exceeded the column width minus one character position for a separator. It would be necessary to format an entire page in memory before sending anything to the output.

Another feature of interest to some users is a more elaborate way of controlling the appearance of the header and footer. This, to me, smacks of word processing, and I have elected to use Microsoft Word if I need such control over the output.

The addition of single-sheet control might be useful to some users. I always use pin-fed, fan-fold paper, so I have not felt a compelling need for this feature. It can be added easily by introducing a new numeric (actually a Boolean) variable in the PRINT data structure and testing it before outputting a new page.

One additional feature may make it into my next version of PR. Some users would like to be able to do side-by-side printing of multiple files. This is a kind of visual file comparison. It can also be used to generate, in a somewhat restricted way, scripts for plays and motion pictures. This could be done either a line at a time or by doing full-page makeup before generating output.

Next, we will devise a program that lets us peer into nontext files that cause PR and DOS text-file programs (TYPE, for example) to produce strange and not particularly useful output.

Displaying Non-ASCII Text 10

Our kit of programmer's utilities now contains some pretty useful tools: the CAT program for concatenating files and PR to print them out on paper; LS to list a directory in a variety of display formats; TOUCH to assist the MAKE command in building programs; and RM to help us clean up our disk directories easily. In addition, we have a raft of low-level and mid-level routines to help us create other tools.

Thus far, we have been concerned only with text files and tools that permit us to view and manipulate them. However, one of the essential tools that a programmer needs to have at the ready is a utility that permits the inspection of nontext files. Nontext files are produced by compilers, tokenizing interpreters (such as Microsoft interpretive BASIC), assemblers, program configurators (see Chapter 7), and many commercial word processors, database-management systems, and spreadsheets.

If you were asked to convert a file produced by a word processor that you do not have to a form that is acceptable to one that you do, how would you go about it? Ignoring the possibility of buying the needed word processor, we will have to do some detective work, which is what makes the computer business such a lot of fun for some and such a pain in the neck for others.

The form and content of the data file would have to be determined so that it could be converted to a suitable form for the target word processor. A straight ASCII text file would suffice as data to be merged into the input stream of most word processors, so we would first attempt to remove any non-ASCII characters from the data file and save the results of the conversion in an intermediate file for later processing.

But how would we examine the data file? Our current tools are suitable only for text files, so we need something else. In this chapter, we will develop a program called DUMP that takes any file and produces an output listing that looks like the dump output of the DOS DEBUG program.

Each line of the output listing includes a hexadecimal offset in the leftmost column, a hexadecimal display of 16 (10 hex) bytes from the data file in the center, and the equivalent data in extended ASCII in the rightmost column. A character code that would cause problems on the display and on a printer is converted to a dot (.) before being displayed. These filtered codes include newline, carriage return, and most other control codes.

The reason for developing a stand-alone program is that DUMP will allow us to capture the converted output in a file or on paper for easy examination. Our design will also permit DUMP to be used as a filter in pipeline commands.

Before designing and programming DUMP, let's review some of the most common data-presentation formats and prepare some functions to do needed conversions.

Some Useful Conversion Functions

The primary data-presentation formats for numbers are the binary, octal, decimal, and hexadecimal notations. While we humans take more or less naturally to decimal (something to do with fingers and toes), our machines tend to favor binary, in which things are on or off (1 or 0). The octal (base 8) and hexadecimal (base 16) formats are simply notations that make binary data more palatable to us. Octal number representations were widely used for many years and still are in some quarters, but octal notation has lost favor with the majority of programmers, who use hexadecimal notation instead. All characters in the computer are represented internally as binary numbers, however. That's all the computer "understands." Our task is to receive data, convert it to the desired form, and send it to the standard output. The output will be displayed on the computer or terminal screen, or sent to some other device if *stdout* is redirected.

Our programs will need to convert the computer's internal representation of numbers into decimal, hexadecimal, or character forms, depending upon what we are trying to see. We will use two functions to do this. They are used in DUMP and will be placed in the utility library (*util.lib*) for use by other programs. The first function, *byte2hex( )*, converts a byte-sized (8-bit) quantity to hexadecimal. The second, *word2hex( )*, performs the same job on a word-sized (16-bit) quantity. These sizes are appropriate for the IBM PC and other 16-bit machines, but they are not universal, so portability to other machines is not guaranteed.

Both *byte2hex( )* and *word2hex( )* are packaged in a single source file named *hex.c*, which has the following contents:

```
/*
 *      hex.c -- hex conversions routines
 */


#define NIBBLE  0x000F
#define BYTE    0x00FF
#define WORD    0xFFFF

char hextab[] = {
        '0', '1', '2', '3', '4', '5', '6', '7',
        '8', '9', 'A', 'B', 'C', 'D', 'E', 'F'
};

/*
 *      byte2hex -- convert a byte to a string
 *      representation of its hexadecimal value
 */

char *
byte2hex(data, buf)
unsigned char data;
char *buf;
{
        char *cp;
        unsigned int d;

        d = data & BYTE;
```

(continued)

```
        cp = buf;
        *cp++ = hextab[(d >> 4) & NIBBLE];
        *cp++ = hextab[d & NIBBLE];
        *cp = '\0';

        return (buf);
}


/*
 *      word2hex -- convert a word to a string
 *      representation of its hexadecimal value
 */

char *
word2hex(data, buf)
unsigned int data;
char *buf;
{
        char *cp;
        unsigned int d;

        d = data & WORD;
        cp = buf;
        *cp++ = hextab[(d >> 12) & NIBBLE];
        *cp++ = hextab[(d >> 8) & NIBBLE];
        *cp++ = hextab[(d >> 4) & NIBBLE];
        *cp++ = hextab[d & NIBBLE];
        *cp = '\0';

        return (buf);
}
```

The *hextab* array is a conversion lookup table. It uses a number in
the range of 0 through 15 as an index into the table, where the correspond-
ing character constant (number or letter) is found. Hence, the numeral 3
is represented by a character constant of 3 (ASCII code 51—be sure you
know the difference), and the number 10 is represented by an A. These
half-byte quantities are comically referred to as "nibbles" because they're
smaller than bytes. The symbolic constant *NIBBLE* is defined as 0x000F.

It is used to mask off all but the four bits of interest in each conversion step. Right-shift operations are used to pull the needed bits into the correct position for conversion to a hexadecimal digit.

A byte can be conveniently expressed as two hex characters (two nibbles) that represent values in the range of 0 (00 hex) through 255 (FF hex). The same range in binary is 00000000 through 11111111, which obviously lacks notational convenience. The hex notation is more compact, requiring only two characters to represent any value in the range.

Now that we have a simple means of displaying data in hexadecimal, we can move on to the development of the DUMP program.

A DEBUG-style File-dump Program

The design of DUMP is strongly influenced by the expectation that its output will be easy to feed to other programs and to a generic printer. We want to build in enough flexibility to permit DUMP to be used as a filter or as a stand-alone program. In stand-alone operation, DUMP takes a list of files as arguments and produces the hex/ASCII output for each in sequence on its standard output. As a filter, it receives a stream of arbitrary characters and transforms it to the hex/ASCII output stream.

The proposed format of DUMP's output looks a lot like that of DEBUG. One difference is that the offset of each block of 16 bytes will be shown relative to the start of the displayed file. We won't know where the file is located in memory, so the offset value will stand alone. Another difference is more subtle. DEBUG converts all non-ASCII characters in the text display area to dots. DUMP will display all standard ASCII characters plus the IBM extended ASCII character set when output is directed to the screen. A command-line option will allow us to strip all nonprintable characters from the output stream so that we can use any type of printer as an output device.

Figure 10-1 on the next page is the manual page for DUMP. Note the overall simplicity of the program. Therein lies its power, because it can be used in a wide range of situations without change.

NAME

DUMP—dump file in hexadecimal and text formats

SYNOPSIS

dump [-sv] [*file ...*]

DESCRIPTION

The DUMP program is a stand-alone program that can be used as a filter. It receives a stream of data and transforms it into a combined hexadecimal and text output stream. Each line of output contains three fields: an offset from the start of the incoming stream; a hexadecimal display of a 16-byte block of data; and a text representation of the same block of bytes.

The output of DUMP contains non-ASCII characters that may confuse printers and other output devices. The -s option causes these to be stripped out of the output stream and replaced by dots (.). When this option is used, the output of DUMP may be safely sent to any other program that can read from its standard input, and to any device that can accept an ASCII text stream.

The -v option tells DUMP to be verbose. For each file given as a command-line argument, DUMP outputs a blank line, then the name of the file being dumped, and then moves to a new line before outputting the formatted file dump. When the standard input is the data source, the verbose option is ignored.

EXAMPLES

Display the converted contents of *hex.obj* on the screen:

dump hex.obj

Print the converted contents of PROG.COM:

dump prog.com > prn

FIGURE 10-1 | *Manual page for DUMP*

The code for DUMP is straightforward. DUMP follows the pattern established in Chapter 8, where file-oriented utility programs used similar command-line options to control program operation and write to the standard output channel. Here is the pseudocode description of the *main( )* function of DUMP, excluding the generic items, such as getting the program name from DOS and error checking at each step:

```
if (no files named)
        hexdump(stdin)
else
        for each file
                open(file)
                hexdump(file)
                close(file)
```

The *hexdump( )* function does the work of transforming the input into the desired presentation format:

```
for each block of input [BUFSIZ]
        for each block of bytes [NBYTES]
                copy byte offset into output buffer
                        [word2hex()]
                copy hex values into output buffer
                        [byte2hex()]
                copy ASCII values into output buffer
                copy output buffer to stdout
```

The *main( )* function of DUMP uses *getopt( )* to scan the command line for optional arguments and filename arguments. If the -s option is found, the Boolean variable *sflag* is set to *TRUE* to indicate that non-ASCII characters should be stripped. If the -v option is found, the Boolean variable *vflag* (verbose) is set to *TRUE* and a header consisting of a blank line followed by the name of the file being dumped is output before the formatted data for each file is listed. You may want to add other data to the verbose output, such as file date and time, character count, and so on. If no filenames are specified, DUMP reads from its standard input and the verbose option is ignored because no name is associated with the data stream.

```
/*
 *      dump -- display contents of non-ASCII files in hex byte and
 *      ASCII character forms (like the DOS debug dump option)
 */

#include <stdio.h>
#include <stdlib.h>
#include <fcntl.h>
#include <sys\types.h>
#include <sys\stat.h>
```

(continued)

```
#include <io.h>
#include <local\std.h>

#define STDINPUT        0
#define LINEWIDTH       80

main(argc,argv)
int argc;
char *argv[];
{
        int ch;
        BOOLEAN sflag = FALSE,
                vflag = FALSE,
                errflag = FALSE;
        int fd;
        static char pgm[MAXNAME + 1] = { "dump" };

        extern int getopt(int, char **, char *);
        extern char *optarg;
        extern int optind, opterr;
        extern void getpname(char *, char *);
        extern int hexdump(int, BOOLEAN);
        extern void fatal(char *, char *, int);

        if (_osmajor >= 3)
                getpname(*argv, pgm);

        while ((ch = getopt(argc, argv, "sv")) != EOF)
                switch (ch) {
                case 's': /* strip -- convert all non-ASCII to '.' */
                        sflag = TRUE;
                        break;
                case 'v': /* verbose -- tell user what's happening */
                        vflag = TRUE;
                        break;
                case '?': /* bad option */
                        errflag = TRUE;
                        break;
                }

        if (errflag == TRUE) {
```

(continued)

```
                fprintf(stderr, "Usage: %s [-sv] [file...]\n", pgm);
                exit(1);
        }

        if (optind == argc) {
                if (setmode(STDINPUT, O_BINARY) == -1)
                        fatal(pgm, "Cannot set binary mode", 2);
                hexdump(STDINPUT, sflag);
                exit(0);
        }

        for ( ; optind < argc; ++optind) {
                if ((fd = open(argv[optind], O_BINARY | O_RDONLY)) == -1) {
                        fprintf(stderr,
                                "%s: Error opening %s -- ", pgm, argv[optind]);
                        perror("");
                        continue;
                }
                if (vflag == TRUE)
                        fprintf(stdout, "\n%s:\n", argv[optind]);
                if (hexdump(fd, sflag) == FAILURE) {
                        fprintf(stderr,
                                "%s: Error reading %s -- ", pgm, argv[optind]);
                        perror("");
                }
                if (close(fd) == -1)
                        fatal(pgm, "Error closing input file", 3);
        }

        exit(0);
}
```

One or more filenames can be specified either directly or by wildcard specifications. Like CAT and PR, DUMP will operate sequentially on a list of files in the order in which they are presented. Ambiguous filenames under Microsoft C are expanded in lexical order, not directory order.

Files are opened in binary mode, not translated mode, because we will most likely be reading nontext files. Even if we read a text file, we want to be able to see all characters, so the translation of the CR/LF and Ctrl-Z codes is inappropriate.

The *hexdump( )* function uses an internal buffer, *outbuf,* to form a
line in memory before outputting it with the *fputs( )* library function. Although the buffering is not essential, it collects the writing operation into
a single function call instead of having five separate calls to several different library routines. This buffering approach makes it easier to change the
output code if we decide to use a different means of writing the output
to the screen.

```c
/*
 *       hexdump -- read data from an open file and "dump"
 *       it in side-by-side hex and ASCII to standard output
 */

#include <stdio.h>
#include <stdlib.h>
#include <ctype.h>
#include <local\std.h>

#define LINEWIDTH       80
#define NBYTES          16
#define WORD            0xFFFF
#define RGHTMARK        179
#define LEFTMARK        179
#define DEL             0x7F

int hexdump(fd, strip)
int fd;
BOOLEAN strip;
{
        unsigned char i;
        int n;                  /* bytes per read operation */
        unsigned long offset;   /* bytes from start of file */
        char inbuf[BUFSIZ + 1], outbuf[LINEWIDTH + 1];
        char hexbuf[5];
        register char *inp, *outp;

        extern char *byte2hex(unsigned char, char *);
        extern char *word2hex(unsigned int, char *);

        offset = 0;
        while ((n = read(fd, inbuf, BUFSIZ)) != 0) {
```

(continued)

```
                if (n == -1)
                        return FAILURE;
                inp = inbuf;
                while (inp < inbuf + n) {
                        outp = outbuf;

                        /* offset in hex */
                        outp += sprintf(outp, "%08lX",
                                offset + (unsigned long)(inp - inbuf));
                        *outp++ = ' ';

                        /* block of bytes in hex */
                        for (i = 0; i < NBYTES; ++i) {
                                *outp++ = ' ';
                                strcpy(outp, byte2hex(*inp++, hexbuf));
                                outp += 2;
                        }
                        *outp++ = ' ';
                        *outp++ = ' ';
                        *outp++ = (strip == TRUE) ? '|' : LEFTMARK;

                        /* same block of bytes in ASCII */
                        inp -= NBYTES;
                        for (i = 0; i < NBYTES; ++i) {
                                if (strip == TRUE && (*inp < ' ' || *inp >= DEL))
                                        *outp = '.';
                                else if (iscntrl(*inp))
                                        *outp = '.';
                                else
                                        *outp = *inp;
                                ++inp;
                                ++outp;
                        }
                        *outp++ = (strip == TRUE) ? '|' : RGHTMARK;
                        *outp++ = '\n';
                        *outp = '\0';
                        fputs(outbuf, stdout);
                }
                offset += n;
        }
        return SUCCESS;
}
```

Figure 10-2 on the next page is a sample of the output produced by DUMP. The figure shows the hexadecimal and equivalent text output

produced by DUMP when it uses the *hex.obj* object file as input. DUMP was
not instructed to strip all nonprintable characters from the output listing.

```
00000000  80 07 00 05 68 65 78 2E 43 BE 88 07 00 00 00 4D  Ç...hex.C¹ê....M
00000010  53 20 43 6E 88 05 00 00 9F 45 4D 42 88 09 00 00  S Cnê...ƒEMBê...
00000020  9F 53 4C 49 42 46 50 10 88 08 00 00 9F 53 4C 49  ƒSLIBFP.ê...ƒSLI
00000030  42 43 64 88 07 00 00 9F 4C 49 42 48 B3 88 06 00  BCdê...ƒLIBH|ê..
00000040  00 9D 30 73 4F E3 88 06 00 00 A1 01 43 56 37 96  .¥0sOnê...í.CV7û
00000050  2E 00 00 06 44 47 52 4F 55 50 05 5F 54 45 58 54  ....DGROUP._TEXT
00000060  04 43 4F 44 45 05 5F 44 41 54 41 04 44 41 54 41  .CODE._DATA.DATA
00000070  05 43 4F 4E 53 54 04 5F 42 53 53 03 42 53 53 3F  .CONST._BSS.BSS?
00000080  98 07 00 28 CA 00 03 04 01 67 98 07 00 48 10 00  ÿ..(╨...gÿ..H..
00000090  05 06 01 FD 98 07 00 48 00 00 07 07 01 0A 98 07  ...²ÿ..H......ÿ.
000000A0  00 48 00 00 08 09 01 07 9A 08 00 02 FF 03 FF 04  .H......ü... . .
000000B0  FF 02 56 9C 0D 00 00 03 01 02 02 01 03 04 40 01  .V£.........@.
000000C0  45 01 C0 8C 2D 00 0A 5F 5F 61 63 72 74 75 73 65  E.└î-.._acrtuse
000000D0  64 00 09 5F 62 79 74 65 32 68 65 78 00 09 5F 77  d.._byte2hex.._w
000000E0  6F 72 64 32 68 65 78 00 08 5F 5F 63 68 6B 73 74  ord2hex.._chkst
000000F0  6B 00 A8 A0 14 00 02 00 00 30 31 32 33 34 35 36  k.¿á.....0123456
00000100  37 38 39 41 42 43 44 45 46 A8 A0 CE 00 01 00 00  789ABCDEF¿á╬....
00000110  55 8B EC B8 04 00 E8 00 00 56 8A 46 04 2A E4 89  Uï∞¸..è..VèF.*Σë
00000120  46 FE 8B 46 06 89 46 FC 8B D8 FF 46 FC 8B 76 FE  F■ïF.ëFⁿïⁿ F■ïv■
00000130  B1 04 D3 EE 81 E6 0F 00 8A 84 00 00 88 07 8B 5E  ▓.╙∩.èä..ê.ï^
00000140  FC FF 46 FC 8B 76 FE 81 E6 0F 00 8A 84 00 00 88  ⁿ F■ïvⁿüⁿ..èä..ê
00000150  07 8B 5E FC C6 07 00 8B 46 06 5E 8B E5 5D C3 55  .ï^ⁿ├..ïF.^ïσ].U
00000160  8B EC B8 04 00 E8 00 00 56 8B 46 04 89 46 FE 8B  Uï∞¸..è..VïF.ëF■ï
00000170  46 06 89 46 FC 8B D8 FF 46 FC 8B 76 FE B1 0C D3  F.ëFⁿïⁿ F■ïvⁿ▓.╙
00000180  EE 81 E6 0F 00 8A 84 00 00 88 07 8B 5E FC FF 46  ∩.èⁿ..èä..ê.ï^ⁿ F
```

FIGURE 10-2 | *Hex dump sample*
| *(HEX.DMP)*

When the -s option is selected, the ASCII text display is surrounded
by vertical lines formed from the vertical bar symbol (|). The normal out-
put, which assumes that the destination device is the PC screen, uses the
IBM drawing character (code 179) for a single vertical line; this looks
pretty on the screen, but cannot be printed correctly by many printers.

The makefile for DUMP is contained in *dump.mk*:

```
# makefile for dump utility

LIB=c:\lib
LLIB=c:\lib\local

dump.obj:        dump.c
        msc $*;
```

(continued)

```
hexdump.obj:      hexdump.c
        msc $*;


dump.exe:         dump.obj hexdump.obj $(LLIB)\util.lib
        link $* hexdump $(LIB)\ssetargv, $*, nul, $(LLIB)\util;
```

To compile DUMP, first compile *hex.c* and add the object file to the utility library (*lib**local**util.lib*); then type

MAKE DUMP.MK

The resulting executable file, DUMP.EXE, should be placed, as usual, in a directory that is accessible to DOS via the PATH variable, so that it can be called from anywhere in the directory hierarchy.

The DUMP program can now be used for one of its intended purposes—determining the file format of a special-purpose data file. This will help us build another useful tool, SHOW, which lets us see nonprintable characters in files in an unambiguous way and recover text from specially formatted files.

The SHOW Program

The next program is called SHOW because it shows us things that we might not otherwise see. SHOW closely resembles DUMP in construction and purpose, but its output is very different from DUMP's.

If the task at hand is to retrieve the essential text from a document file, rather than to determine how the formatting was done, we need a tool that filters out the nonprintable codes and emits a stream of ASCII-only text. In some situations, we might also want to see the formatting codes represented visibly.

The SHOW program takes files that may contain special (usually nonprintable) characters in addition to normal text and produces an ASCII text output. Nonprintable codes are converted to their displayable hexadecimal notation—a backslash followed by two hex digits.

Two options allow us to strip out special codes and produce an output that is pure text. The -s option strips all special codes except the usual format effectors (newline, tab, and space).

The -w (word-processor) option strips special codes (by setting the -s
option), but it handles several additional elements of word-processor data
files as well. For example, when forming paragraphs, many word processors use a carriage return as a "soft" return (line break) and a combined
carriage return and linefeed as a "hard" return (paragraph terminator).
For compatibility with such word-processor file formats, the -w option of
SHOW converts a lone carriage return to a newline, thus breaking long
lines into a sequence of shorter ones. Also, some word processors use the
eighth bit of some bytes to signal formatting options (bold, underline,
end-of-word, and so on). To make these bytes visible, SHOW (with the -w
option set) turns off the high bit of all bytes and displays the bytes that
then fall into the printable ASCII range.

The full manual page for SHOW is presented in Figure 10-3. Notice
that SHOW is also a filter: It can read from its standard input channel and
write the transformed output to the standard output channel.

The pseudocode description for SHOW is nearly identical to that of
DUMP. The primary differences are found in the *showit( )* function, which
is described (without options) by the following pseudeocode:

```
for each input character
        if it's ASCII
                if it's printable or a format effector
                        send it to stdout
                else
                        send printable equivalent to stdout
```

The options -s and -w add some minor complications to the description. The effects of the options are best seen in the code for the *main( )*
and *showit( )* functions. In *main( )* (in the file *show.c*), *getopt( )* is once
again used to process command-line options. A variable, *wflag,* controls
whether SHOW attempts to convert word-processing data files. It is initially *FALSE.* The call to *getopt( )* requires the addition of *w* to the allowed
option list. The value of *wflag* is passed to *showit( )* as an argument, rather
than being treated as global data. If SHOW had a lot of functions that
needed to know about *wflag,* we would probably make it a global variable.

NAME

SHOW—make all characters in a stream visible

SYNOPSIS

show [-svw] [*file ...*]

DESCRIPTION

The SHOW program is a stand-alone program that can be used as a filter. It receives a stream of data and transforms it into a straight ASCII output stream. Normal displayable characters pass through unchanged, but most nonprintable characters are converted to a two-digit hexadecimal form.

The -s option strips all control codes and IBM extended ASCII characters from the text stream, except for the primary format effectors (tab and newline). The -v option tells SHOW to be verbose. When the -w (word-processing) option is used, a carriage return that is not paired with a newline is assumed to be a "soft" return and is replaced by a newline. The -w option also causes SHOW to convert all extended codes (eighth bit on) to 7-bit ASCII and outputs those whose converted values fall into the displayable ASCII range.

EXAMPLES

Display the contents of a spreadsheet data file:

show data.wks

Convert a word processor's formatted document file to straight ASCII text and save output in a file:

show -w letter.doc >letter.txt

FIGURE 10-3 | *Manual page for SHOW*

```
/*
 *      show -- a filter that displays the contents of a file
 *      in a way that is guaranteed to be displayable
 */

#include <stdio.h>
#include <stdlib.h>
```

(continued)

```
#include <fcntl.h>
#include <io.h>
#include <local\std.h>

main(argc, argv)
int argc;
char **argv;
{
        int ch;
        FILE *fp;
        BOOLEAN sflag = FALSE;  /* strip non-ASCII characters */
        BOOLEAN vflag = FALSE;  /* verbose mode */
        BOOLEAN wflag = FALSE;  /* filter typical word-processing codes */
        BOOLEAN errflag = FALSE;
        static char pgm[] = { "show" };

        extern int getopt(int, char **, char *);
        extern char *optarg;
        extern int optind, opterr;
        extern int showit(FILE *, BOOLEAN, BOOLEAN);
        extern void fatal(char *, char *, int);

        if (_osmajor >= 3)
                getpname(*argv, pgm);

        while ((ch = getopt(argc, argv, "svw")) != EOF) {
                switch (ch) {
                case 's': /* strip non-ASCII characters */
                        sflag = TRUE;
                        break;
                case 'v': /* verbose */
                        vflag = TRUE;
                        break;
                case 'w': /* use word-processing conventions */
                        wflag = sflag = TRUE;
                        break;
                case '?':
                        errflag = TRUE;
                        break;
                }
        }
```

(continued)

```
        /* check for errors */
        if (errflag == TRUE) {
                fprintf(stderr, "Usage: %s [-sv] [file...]\n", pgm);
                exit(1);
        }

        /* if no file names, use standard input */
        if (optind == argc) {
                if (setmode(fileno(stdin), O_BINARY) == -1)
                        fatal(pgm, "Cannot set binary mode on stdin", 2);
                showit(stdin, sflag, wflag);
                exit(0);
        }

        /* otherwise, process remainder of command line */
        for ( ; optind < argc; ++optind) {
                if ((fp = fopen(argv[optind], "rb")) == NULL) {
                        fprintf(stderr,
                                "%s: Error opening %s\n", pgm, argv[optind]);
                        perror("");
                        continue;
                }
                if (vflag == TRUE)
                        fprintf(stdout, "\n%s:\n", argv[optind]);
                if (showit(fp, sflag, wflag) != 0) {
                        fprintf(stderr,
                                "%s: Error reading %s\n", pgm, argv[optind]);
                        perror("");
                }
                if (fclose(fp) == EOF)
                        fatal(pgm, "Error closing input file", 2);
        }

        exit(0);
}
```

The *showit( )* function receives a *FILE* pointer and the values of *sflag* and *wflag*. If neither of the flags is *TRUE*, *showit( )* passes anything that is printable (including format effectors) to the standard output channel and converts everything else to a displayable hexadecimal byte representation. Thus, the null byte is shown as \00, the ASCII Del character is shown as \7F, and so on. If -s was used on the command line, *sflag* (and therefore *strip*) is *TRUE*, which causes *showit( )* to eliminate the hexadecimal conversions.

Setting the -w option sets the *wp* variable in *showit( )* to *TRUE*, causing the function to alter the default treatment of carriage returns and extended characters.

```
/*
 *        showit -- make non-printable characters in
 *        the stream fp visible (or optionally strip them)
 */

#include <stdio.h>
#include <ctype.h>
#include <local\std.h>

int
showit(fp, strip, wp)
FILE *fp;
BOOLEAN strip;   /* strip non-ASCII codes */
BOOLEAN wp;      /* filter typical word-processing codes */
{
        int ch;

        clearerr(fp);
        while ((ch = getc(fp)) != EOF)
                if (isascii(ch) && (isprint(ch) || isspace(ch)))
                        switch (ch) {
                        case '\r':
                                if (wp == TRUE) {
                                        if ((ch = getc(fp)) != '\n')
                                                ungetc(ch, fp);
                                        putchar('\r');
                                        putchar('\n');
                                }
                                else
                                        putchar(ch);
                                break;
                        default:
                                putchar(ch);
                                break;
                        }
```

(continued)

```
                else if (strip == FALSE)
                        printf("\\%02X", ch);
                else if (wp == TRUE && isprint(ch & ASCII))
                        putchar(ch & ASCII);
        return (ferror(fp));
}
```

The makefile for SHOW is similar to the one for DUMP:

```
# makefile for the show program

LIB=c:\lib
LLIB=c:\lib\local

show.obj:       show.c
        msc $*;

showit.obj:     showit.c
        msc $*;

show.exe:       show.obj showit.obj $(LLIB)\util.lib
        link $* showit $(LIB)\ssetargv, $*, nul, $(LLIB)\util;
```

To see the output of SHOW, try the program on a data file from a word processor or spreadsheet with and without the optional processing features. The results should be at least intriguing and will probably be enlightening to those who have not snooped around in such files before.

In the next section, we move from the line-by-line realm of file-oriented programs to the intensely visually oriented programs that make the PC so popular with the average user.

SECTION IV

Screen-Oriented Programs

Screen Access Routines

11

In this chapter and the next two, we will explore some of the many options available to designers for presenting information on a PC screen. The method of screen access presented in this chapter is relatively easy to implement, produces excellent results, and costs little in terms of program size and complexity. Its use is not recommended for programs that will operate in a windowing environment, however, because it violates one of the primary rules of good behavior: "Thou shalt not write directly to the screen."

We will purposely break this rule at first to show what level of performance we are striving for. In Chapter 12, we will explore some interesting display buffering techniques and show how we can be "good" boys and girls by using BIOS-based screen routines as an alternative to direct access. Then, in Chapter 13, we will seek to be downright virtuous by using the ANSI standard interface that is portable to nearly every PC that runs a version of MS-DOS (and PC-DOS).

Determining the Display System Type

One of the challenges that has always faced PC software designers is writing a program that determines what type of display adapter and monitor is in use before it does anything else. It is unfortunate that many programs ignore this crucial first step.

Many of the offending programs were designed by programmers working on monochrome-only systems. When run on a color/graphics-equipped system, these programs at least alter the user's selected video attributes so that either during or following the program's running, the screen is unpleasant to look at or has a whole new shade of reality. Sometimes, but not too often, the screen gets completely messed up by being left in an inappropriate video mode.

Programs designed for color-only systems can produce similarly unpleasant effects on monochrome systems. For example, light blue is a very pleasing color for text, but it causes everything on a monochrome system to be underlined and intense. Then there's the problem of a program that assumes the needed display adapter is in use and does not check for its presence. This can leave the user with a system that appears to be frozen.

And it isn't just amateur programmers who are guilty of these transgressions. Although most commercial software offerings check the hardware, many supposedly "commercial quality" programs have the bad manners to ignore the user's color preferences, video mode settings, and so on.

We can do something about this situation. Following are some routines and program examples that show how to detect, save, and restore the user's operating conditions. The routines use BIOS functions and simple memory tests to determine what equipment is installed. You can call the functions, as demonstrated in the DSPYTYPE program that follows and the ScreenTest (ST) program later in this chapter, and save the video state at the time your program begins execution. The original operating conditions can then be restored before the program returns control to DOS.

```
/*
 *      dspytype -- determine display adapter type
 */

#include <stdio.h>
#include <dos.h>
#include <local\bioslib.h>
#include <local\video.h>

#define MDA_SEG 0xB000
#define CGA_SEG 0xB800

main()
```

(continued)

```
{
        extern int memchk(unsigned int, unsigned int);
        int mdaflag, egaflag, cgaflag;
        int ega_mem, ega_mode;
        unsigned int features, switches;
        static int memtab[] = {
                64, 128, 192, 256
        };


        mdaflag = egaflag = cgaflag = 0;

        /* look for display adapters */
        if (ega_info(&ega_mem, &ega_mode, &features, &switches))
                ++egaflag;
        fputs("Enhanced graphics adapter ", stdout);
        if (egaflag) {
                fputs("installed\n", stdout);
                fprintf(stdout, "EGA memory size = %d-KB\n", memtab[ega_mem]);
                fprintf(stdout, "EGA is in %s mode\n",
                        ega_mode ? "monochrome" : "color");
        }
        else
                fputs("not installed\n", stdout);


        /* look for IBM monochrome memory */
        if (!egaflag || (egaflag && ega_mode == 0))
                if (memchk(MDA_SEG, 0))
                        ++mdaflag;


        /* look for CGA memory */
        if (!egaflag || (egaflag && ega_mode == 1))
                if (memchk(CGA_SEG, 0))
                        ++cgaflag;
        }
        fputs("Monochrome adapter ", stdout);
        if (mdaflag)
                fputs("installed\n", stdout);
        else
                fputs("not installed\n", stdout);
        fputs("Color/graphics adapter ", stdout);
        if (cgaflag)
```

(continued)

```
                fputs("installed\n", stdout);
        else

                fputs("not installed\n", stdout);

        /* report video settings */
        getstate();
        fprintf(stdout, "mode=%d width=%d page=%d\n", Vmode, Vwidth, Vpage);

        exit(0);
}
```

The DSPYTYPE program is a test driver for the functions *memchk( )*
and *ega_info( )*. These functions supplement the BIOS *equipchk( )* and
getstate( ) functions we saw in Chapter 5. The *memchk( )* function looks
for memory at a specified segment and offset. It is a small-model function
that calls on the library function *movedata( )* to write and read the contents of memory locations. A large-model version of *memchk( )* would use
memcpy( ) in place of *movedata( )*. The *memcpy( )* function takes long
pointers used in large-model programs; *movedata( )* requires segmented
addresses to access far data items in small-model programs.

```
/*
 *      memchk -- look for random-access memory at
 *      a specified location; return nonzero if found
 */

#include <dos.h>
#include <memory.h>

int
memchk(seg, os)
unsigned int seg;
unsigned int os;
{
        unsigned char tstval, oldval, newval;
        unsigned int ds;
        struct SREGS segregs;

        /* get value of current data segment */
        segread(&segregs);
        ds = segregs.ds;
```

(continued)

```
    /* save current contents of test location */
    movedata(seg, os, ds, &oldval, 1);

    /* copy a known value into test location */
    tstval = 0xFC;
    movedata(ds, &tstval, seg, os, 1);

    /* read test value back and compare to value written */
    movedata(seg, os, ds, &newval, 1);
    if (newval != tstval)
            return (0);

    /* restore original contents of test location */
    movedata(ds, &oldval, seg, os, 1);

    return (1);
}
```

The technique used to detect the presence of a monochrome display adapter (MDA) or a color/graphics adapter (CGA) involves a sequence of operations that save, write, read, compare, and restore the contents of a memory location that is known to be in the range of the given adapter. The save and restore operations ensure that the test is non-destructive. The write-read-compare operation determines whether there is any active memory at the test location. The value 55H is a bit pattern of alternating 0s and 1s. Because unoccupied memory locations tend to look like 1s to programs that try to read them, the pattern of the test value used by *memchk( )* is not likely to be duplicated. If you want to feel more sure of the results, use sequential tests at the same address with two or more different values.

But why bother looking at the memory—why not simply read the mode value returned by *getstate( )*? We will probably want to do both in our programs. Use *getstate( )* to find out what the operating video mode is, and look for memory at the other adapter locations. Some PC users (programmers in particular) have both monochrome and color display systems installed in a PC. A program that was designed to work exclusively with a CGA system might find the system in mode 7 (monochrome). The program can respond to this in two ways: It can print a message stating its need for a CGA and quit, or it can look for a CGA system and switch to it if one is found. I favor the first approach because the user may have the color system turned off. He or she can use the DOS MODE command to select the needed display mode (MODE MONO to select monochrome; MODE CO80, MODE CO40, and so on, to select a CGA mode).

The *memchk( )* function has other uses, too, such as looking around for blocks of memory that might be separated from the main memory of a system. It cannot be used to detect the presence of read-only memory (ROM), of course, because ROM cannot be written to and it will fail our tests. You can use *memchk( )* to check memory locations at one-kilobyte increments to count up how much RAM is available to DOS and how much might be noncontiguous. Many add-in memory boards permit split-memory addressing, allowing you to set up stand-alone print spoolers and other special memory allocations. With *memchk( )*, we have a convenient way to find them. Add *memchk( )* to the utility library to make it readily accessible to your programs.

The enhanced graphics adapter (EGA) complicates the video-adapter detection problem a bit. The address space of the EGA nominally starts at segment A000. However, an EGA's addressing modes are very flexible, and the adapter usually masquerades as a CGA or MDA while operating at the DOS command level, setting itself up to start at either the B800 or B000 memory segments. The problem is in determining whether an EGA or some other adapter is installed at a particular location. The function *ega_info( )*, based on information provided by IBM, looks for an EGA by calling the BIOS video interrupt 10H and invoking the Alternate Function Select function AH = 18 (12H), which is an EGA BIOS feature (the EGA BIOS is located at segment C000H). When AL equals 10H upon entry, this function returns EGA information, which includes the EGA mode (color or monochrome) and memory size (64 to 256 KB) in addition to feature and switch-setting information. An EGA display system is absent if *ega_info( )* returns mode values other than 0 and 1 and memory size values outside the range of 0 to 3.

If an EGA is found, checking the video mode returned by *getstate( )* tells us whether it is emulating a CGA or MDA. If we need to know if another adapter is installed, we can use *memchk( )* to do the test. If an EGA is emulating a CGA, you cannot have a real CGA installed, so we need check only for the adapter type not being emulated by the EGA.

```
/*
 *      ega_info -- gather information about an EGA;
 *      return a nonzero value if one is found
 */

#include <dos.h>
#include <local\bioslib.h>

#define EGA_INFO 0x10
#define NMODES  2
#define NMEMSIZ 4

int
ega_info(memsize, mode, features, switches)
int *memsize;           /* EGA memory size indicator: 0 = 64K */
                        /* 1 = 128K; 2 = 192K; 3 = 256K */
int *mode;              /* 0 = color mode; 1 = mono mode */
                        /* use getstate function to find out which mode */
unsigned int
        *features,      /* feature bit settings */
        *switches;      /* EGA switch settings */
{
        int result = 0;
        union REGS inregs, outregs;

        /* request EGA information */
        inregs.h.ah = ALT_FUNCTION;
        inregs.h.bl = EGA_INFO;
        int86(VIDEO_IO, &inregs, &outregs);

        *memsize = outregs.h.bl;
        *mode = outregs.h.bh;
        *features = outregs.h.ch;
        *switches = outregs.h.cl;

        /* return nonzero if EGA installed */
        if (*memsize >= 0 && *memsize < NMEMSIZ && *mode >= 0 && *mode < NMODES)
                result = 1;
        return (result);
}
```

DSPYTYPE is a simple program that calls *ega_info( )* and *memchk( )* to determine what display adapters are installed in a system and to report the results to the user. DSPYTYPE also reports the current video mode, screen width, and screen page number. In practice, we would use the functions to get the video mode and the display adapter configuration, and then set up the needed display conditions for our program or abort with an explanatory message about the lack of needed hardware.

Next we will consider a method of direct screen access for reading and writing that serves as an alternative to using BIOS and DOS methods of screen access. The BIOS and DOS functions automatically deal with the wide variety of display configurations that are possible in a PC system, but they introduce a lot of processing overhead because an adapter test occurs with every character (or dot) that is written or read. The display-adapter detection methods just described are important to direct screen access because they let us do the adapter tests once at program start-up, cutting out a huge amount of processing during subsequent screen read and write operations.

Direct Screen Access

A fast but inherently nonportable way of updating the PC screen is to write directly to its associated memory. Using one or more off-screen buffers in the program's data space to create images before displaying them can produce excellent visual performances. A block-copy routine quickly copies the buffered-memory image to physical display memory, producing an "instant screen" effect. The IBM monochrome display adapter exhibits no problems with this strategy. Neither do the IBM enhanced graphics adapter and many third party monochrome and color/graphics adapters, all of which have been designed to permit simultaneous access to display memory by both the CPU and the display-refresh circuitry.

The original CGA in either 40-column or 80-column text mode poses a problem for designers because, unlike the monochrome adapter, the CGA exhibits visible interference when a program tries to access display memory while the monitor screen is being updated (refreshed) from the same memory. The interference looks like "snow"—an irritating pulsing of short line segments covering all or portions of the screen. Several methods of avoiding the interference have been developed. One is to synchronize the display accesses during both reading and writing operations with the time periods within a display-refresh cycle that are considered "safe." The safe times are the horizontal and vertical retrace periods of each displayed frame. Another method involves blanking (turning off) the raster scan while the display memory is being written to. As we'll see, each approach has advantages and disadvantages.

Display Adapter Basics

We begin with a brief examination of the color/graphics adapter to see why the retrace periods are the only safe times for display memory accesses. This discussion is not applicable to the IBM enhanced graphics adapter because it uses faster memory devices and additional logic that prevent problems that occur when the CPU and video-refresh circuitry try to access the video buffer simultaneously.

The memory on the standard CGA is placed within the address space of the central processor. The CGA memory starts at segment B800H and extends upward for 16 KB, enough memory for one high-resolution graphics screen (128,000 picture elements), or four screen pages in 80-column color text mode. The text mode is the focus of this discussion.

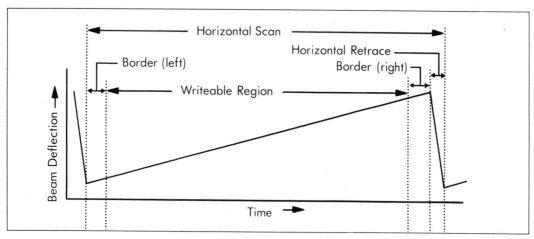

FIGURE 11-1 | *Typical horizontal sweep signal*

Figure 11-1 on the previous page represents the horizontal sweep signal, which is the signal within the display device that is responsible for the horizontal deflection of the electron beam that paints the screen. The figure depicts one horizontal scan period. The dependent (vertical) axis depicts the amount of beam deflection as a function of time shown along the independent (horizontal) axis. On a computer display device, the image on the screen is under-scanned so that the image is completely visible within the normal viewing area, resulting in a framed picture with a visible border. Television sets, on the other hand, use over-scanning to make the image "bleed," leaving no border. The beam is turned off completely (blanked) during retrace to avoid leaving unwanted residue on the screen.

The IBM display is not interlaced, so there are 262.5 horizontal scans per frame (one full screen image), and frames occur at a rate of 60 per second. With 15,750 horizontal scans per second, each one takes about 63.4 microseconds. Only a small portion of a single scan, typically 20 percent or less, is allocated to the horizontal retrace—one of the safe times for display memory accesses, as can be seen in the figure.

The horizontal sweep signal moves the electron beam from side to side, and if it were the only sweep signal affecting the beam, there would be only a single straight line on the display surface. Another kind of sweep signal is needed to move the beam up and down the face of the tube. The vertical sweep has the same basic sawtooth shape as the horizontal sweep, but a slower rate of change. At minimum deflection, the beam is at the top of the screen; it moves toward the bottom with increasing deflection.

There is a vertical retrace period at the end of each frame that occurs during the vertical-sync pulse period. During this time, the electron beam is blanked and moved from the lower right corner of the screen back to the upper left corner. The vertical-sync period (typically a little more than one millisecond for the standard American TV signals used by the CGA) is long enough to permit a block of about 250 data words (2-byte character and attribute pairs) to be transferred to or from display memory without interference. Most video controller designs disable the horizontal sweep during the vertical retrace, but some let it run continuously.

Programming Considerations

A few important choices affect the way programs that interact tightly with the display system are designed and written. There are enough choices at every step in the process of designing a video application so that no two designers are likely to do the job in exactly the same way. The following program implements one way of designing a video interface. It is not the only way. Other methods that are even more intimately tied to specific hardware can run as much as four times faster than the method described here, but they are much less portable to other hardware configurations.

I decided to use a buffered screen interface. This means that the image to be sent to the display is assembled in the program's own data space. When complete, the image is copied in its entirety as quickly as possible to display memory.

Conversely, an unbuffered approach is used by many programs and is adequate for most purposes. In the typical unbuffered scheme, characters are written into display memory via DOS and BIOS routines, but no memory image is retained by the application program. The DOS and BIOS routines can also be used in a buffered screen-management system but will slow things down quite a bit compared to direct methods. As we'll see in the next chapter, careful design can greatly improve the apparent speed of the DOS and BIOS routines under many operating conditions.

The routines described in this chapter assume that programs calling them have already done an equipment inventory and have set up the display system in an 80-column text mode. The *getstate( )* function obtains the current video mode, screen width, and visual display page values. Mode values of 2 or 3 indicate 80-column text modes (monochrome and color, respectively) on a CGA, and a value of 7 indicates a monochrome adapter. The DOS MODE command may be used to select an appropriate video mode before calling programs that require a particular mode.

Alternative Solutions

Available methods of synchronization to avoid visual interference on a CGA depend on the use of the status register at I/O address 3DA hex. This is a read-only register on the CGA that has two bits of interest to the block-copy routine described below. When high (1), bit 0 indicates that a horizontal retrace is in progress. When high, bit 3 indicates that a vertical retrace is in progress.

Another register—a write-only register at I/O address 3D8 hex on the CGA—has a bit that may be reset (made 0) to disable video. Bit 3 must be set to a value of 1 to turn on the beam that paints the screen. Turning off the beam is an effective way to prevent visual interference from reaching the viewer's eye. However, the beam cannot be left off for more than about three character rows' worth of data before a flicker becomes apparent. The BIOS video scroll routines use this technique and are not pleasant to look at if the background color is anything but black. Even normal text on a black background appears to dim somewhat in the upper half on the display when the blanking method is used.

A Synchronized Block-copy Routine

The direct method of screen access uses a memory buffer that holds the same amount of data as one display page on the standard CGA. The block-copy routine, *cpblk( )*, copies the contents of the memory buffer to display memory only during safe times. The memory buffer has a total of 4000 bytes; 2000 bytes are for characters (25 rows by 80 columns), and the other 2000 bytes hold the attributes associated with the characters. Display memory has 4096 bytes per page (four pages in 80-column mode), but the last 96 bytes of each page are unused (except by some programs that hide information in them).

The C-language source for the block-copy routine is *cpblk.c*. An image is copied from application memory to display memory as a series of ten blocks of 200 words each. Each word represents a character and its associated video attribute. (An assembly-language version of this routine is described in my "Instant Screens" article in the June 1986 issue of *PC Tech Journal*. Portions of this chapter are based on that article.)

```
/*
 *      cpblk -- copy a block of characters and attributes
 *      while eliminating "snow" on a standard CGA display
 */
```

(continued)

```
#include <conio.h>
#include <memory.h>

#define BLKCNT   10
#define VSTAT    0x3DA
#define VRBIT    8
#define WRDCNT   200
#define NBYTES   (2 * WRDCNT)

/* macro to synchronize with vertical retrace period */
#define VSYNC    while ((inp(VSTAT) & VRBIT) == VRBIT); \
                 while ((inp(VSTAT) & VRBIT) != VRBIT)

int
cpblk(src_os, src_seg, dest_os, dest_seg)
unsigned int src_os, src_seg, dest_os, dest_seg;
{
        register int i;
        int n;
        register int delta;

        n = 0;
        delta = 0;
        for (i = 0; i < BLKCNT ; ++i) {
                /* copy a block of words during vertical retrace */
                VSYNC;
                movedata(src_seg, src_os + delta,
                        dest_seg, dest_os + delta, NBYTES);
                n += WRDCNT;

                /* adjust buffer offset */
                delta += NBYTES;
        }

        return (n);
}
```

The C version of *cpblk( )* is about 60 percent slower than its
assembly-language counterpart, but it is fast enough for most purposes,
copying an entire screen in about two-tenths of a second. The assembly-
language version uses both horizontal and vertical retrace periods to
reduce the number of blocks needed to six instead of ten. The use of ten
blocks is conservative and will work with nearly all IBM-compatible

display hardware. On all of the IBM machines I tested, eight blocks were sufficient; however, some compatibles required smaller blocks because of differences in the timing of the retrace signal used to determine the safe time for copying data.

Double Buffering

To obtain the snappiest looking performance from a buffered screen-interface technique, programs can use an in-memory screen buffer that is updated out of view of the user and then is copied to display memory as fast as possible. A way of achieving nearly instant CGA updates is shown in Figure 11-2. The technique is called double buffering because two levels of buffers are maintained in the application program and elsewhere in main memory. A two-step process is used to form a composite image in a screen buffer before it is copied to physical display memory.

Data source buffers may be of any size and are usually thought of as being rectangular in shape although they are simply sequences of bytes in memory. They are mapped to the off-screen buffer as needed—a technique that permits windows for help frames, menus, and the like to be easily overlaid onto another image. In the next chapter, we will write a set of library functions that handle the needed operations, such as writing characters, attributes, and strings, scrolling regions, and so on, and demonstrate the technique in a sample program.

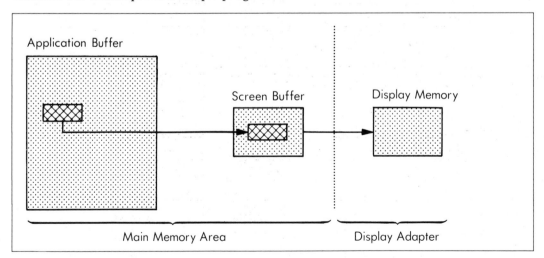

FIGURE 11-2 | *Double buffering*

Once the off-screen buffer has all of its characters and attributes in the right places, the task of getting the data to the visual display is handled by the *cpblk( )* routine described above. If the screen buffer is copied directly to the part of display memory being viewed, the user will see the screen being updated, albeit very quickly. If the contents of the before and after images vary only in small areas, it is difficult to notice that an update occurs.

If, however, there are massive image changes, such as switching background colors, the user will detect the update. For some purposes, the visible updating of screen displays is desirable because it reassures the user that the program is doing something. In other situations, we will want screen images to snap instantly into place. We can have it either way.

Demonstration Program

The file *st.c* contains the C-language source for a test driver program called ST (for ScreenTest). The driver program uses a static screen buffer to hold text images that are copied en masse to display memory after the image is fully constructed.

The *getkey( )* function (see Chapter 5) calls DOS function 7 hex, which returns the next available character in the keyboard buffer. The function waits for a keypress if nothing is ready. The driver program displays a help message for any nonprintable keypress except Esc (the Quit command) and Ctrl-Break (Abort). As each character is keyed in, its value is used to fill the screen buffer. Differing color attributes derived from the character code are used to show the effects of massive color and intensity changes. The attribute for a given character is the code for the character shifted left 8 bit positions. The high bit is masked off to prevent screen blinking.

```
/*
 *      st -- screen test using cpblk function
 */

#include <stdio.h>
#include <stdlib.h>
#include <conio.h>
```

(continued)

```
#include <ctype.h>
#include <dos.h>
#include <local\std.h>
#include <local\video.h>

#define CG_SEG          0xB800
#define MONO_SEG        0xB000
#define NBYTES          0x1000
#define PAGESIZ         (NBYTES / 2)
#define PG0_OS          0
#define PG1_OS          PG0_OS + NBYTES
#define ESC             27
#define MAXSCAN         14


main(argc, argv)
int argc;
char *argv[];
{
        int i;
        int k;                          /* user command character */
        int ca;                         /* character/attribute word */
        int ch;                         /* character value read */
        int row, col;                   /* cursor position upon entry */
        int c_start, c_end;             /* cursor scan lines */
        unsigned char attr;             /* saved video attribute */
        unsigned dseg;                  /* destination buffer segment */
        unsigned os;                    /* page offset in bytes */
        static unsigned sbuf[NBYTES];   /* screen buffer */
        unsigned *bp;                   /* screen element pointer */
        unsigned sseg;                  /* source segment */
        int special;                    /* use special copy routine */
        int apg, vpg;                   /* active and visual display pages */

        /* segment register values */
        struct SREGS segregs;

        extern void swap_int(int *, int *);

        static char pgm[] = { "st" };   /* program name */

        /* save user's current video state */
        getstate();
        readcur(&row, &col, Vpage);
```

(continued)

```
putcur(row - 1, 0, Vpage);
readca(&ch, &attr, Vpage);
getctype(&c_start, &c_end, Vpage);
setctype(MAXSCAN, c_end);
clrscrn(attr);
putcur(1, 1, Vpage);

/* initialize destination segment */
special = 1;
fputs("ScreenTest (ST): ", stderr);
if (Vmode == CGA_C80 || Vmode == CGA_M80) {
        dseg = CG_SEG;
        fprintf(stderr, "Using CGA mode %d", Vmode);
}
else if (Vmode == MDA_M80) {
        dseg = MONO_SEG;
        fprintf(stderr, "Using MDA (mode %d)", Vmode);
        special = 0;
} else
        fprintf(stderr, "%s: Requires 80-column text mode\n", pgm);

/* process command-line arguments */
if (argc > 2) {
        fprintf(stderr, "Usage: %s [x]\n", pgm);
        exit(2);
}
else if (argc == 2)
        special = 0;     /* bypass special block move */

/* get data segment value */
segread(&segregs);
sseg = segregs.ds;

/* set up "active" and "visual" display pages */
apg = 1;        /* page being written to */
vpg = 0;        /* page being viewed */

/* display buffers on the user's command */
fprintf(stderr, " -- Type printable text; Esc=exit");
while ((k = getkey()) != ESC) {
        if (isascii(k) && isprint(k)) {
                /* fill the buffer */
                ca = ((k % 0xEF) << 8) | k;
```

(continued)

```
                    for (bp = sbuf; bp - sbuf < PAGESIZ; ++bp)
                            *bp = ca;
                    if (Vmode == MDA_M80)
                            os = 0;
                    else
                            os = (apg == 0) ? PG0_OS : PG1_OS;
                    if (special)
                            cpblk(sbuf, sseg, os, dseg);
                    else
                            movedata(sseg, sbuf, dseg, os, NBYTES);
                    if (Vmode != MDA_M80) {
                            swap_int(&apg, &vpg);
                            setpage(vpg);
                    }
            }
            else {
                    clrscrn(attr);
                    putcur(0, 0, Vpage);
                    writestr(" Type printable text; Esc = exit ", vpg);
            }
    }

    /* restore user's video conditions and return to DOS */
    setpage(Vpage);
    clrscrn(attr);
    putcur(0, 0, Vpage);
    setctype(c_start, c_end);
    exit(0);
}
```

The driver program uses a trick called "page flipping" to produce the appearance of instant screen displays. It actually takes a few tenths of a second to copy a screen buffer in the application data space to the display adapter using the *cpblk( )* routine. Although this is fast when compared to all other methods that avoid video interference, it is still far from instantaneous. The page flipping method is possible because the CGA has enough display memory to hold multiple screen pages simultaneously.

An illustration of page flipping is presented in Figure 11-3. The method depends on having a means of telling the display system to view one page of display memory while the application program is writing to another. The ROM BIOS video interrupt includes a function (5) that sets the visual page.

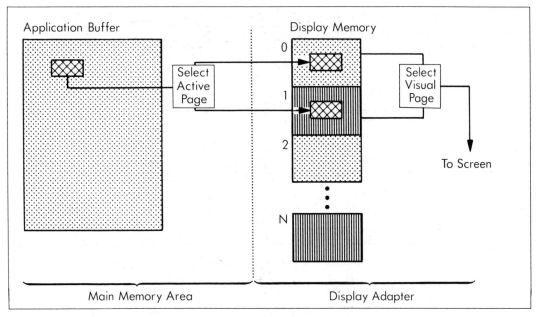

FIGURE 11-3 | *Page flipping*

> ## COMMENT
>
> *Ignore the Technical Reference statement that the function sets the "active" page. To be consistent with the way BASIC describes video pages, the active page should be the one being written and the visual page should be the one being viewed. Most frequently, the visual and active pages are one and the same display page.*

   Notice that the *fprintf( )* standard library function writes to standard error, which appears on the visual page. The *cpblk( )* routine, however, is directed to write to the active page, which is effectively hidden from view. When the active page has been fully written, it is revealed to the user by flipping the pages. The function *swap_int( )* exchanges the values of the *apg* and *vpg* variables. The source for *swap_int( )* is contained in the file *swap_int.c*. The function is useful in other contexts, so we will add it to our utility library.

```
/*
 *      swap_int -- exchange the values of the two integers
 */

void
swap_int(p1, p2)
register int *p1;
register int *p2;
{
        int tmp;

        /* exchange the values */
        tmp = *p1;
        *p1 = *p2;
        *p2 = tmp;
}
```

After building the active page, ST then calls *setpage( )*, another of our *bios* library routines from Chapter 5, to switch to the new visual page. The effect from the computer user's perspective is that of an instant update. There is a short delay while the active page is being updated before the page swap, but it's not noticeable to the user. The screen is repainted in one-sixtieth of a second, far faster than the human eye can follow, and the response to a keypress is usually completed before the key is released.

The special efforts to synchronize with the vertical-retrace signal taken by the *cpblk( )* routine are not needed when an MDA is being used. Therefore, the driver program, ST, checks for mode 7 and uses a standard block-copy routine that invokes the string-copy feature of the 8086/88 processor. A string copy of 4 KB is done very quickly. There is no visible flicker and no apparent delay when this approach is used.

An option on the invocation command line for ST permits a single argument (anything will do) to be given to turn off the special copy feature when operating on an EGA or on a compatible computer that does not experience display interference. Using the command ST x, for example, will tell the program to use a standard block-copy routine instead of the special one. If this option is selected on a system with a standard CGA, visible interference will be quite noticeable, especially if you hold down a key to repeatedly write the same data to the display.

The makefile for ST, *st.mk,* contains the instructions needed by
MAKE to build and maintain the ST programs.

```
# makefile for ScreenTest (ST) program

LLIB=c:\lib\local

swap_int.obj:    swap_int.c

cpblk.obj:       cpblk.c

st.obj:          st.c

st.exe:          st.obj swap_int.obj cpblk.obj $(LLIB)\bios.lib $(LLIB)\dos.lib
         link $* swap_int cpblk, $*, nul, $(LLIB)\bios $(LLIB)\dos;
```

Design Considerations

Because it takes a few tenths of a second to copy data from a screen
buffer to display memory, programs should not attempt to write one character at a time from the keyboard. This would result in a maximum update rate of a few characters per second. Even a very slow typist would
get way ahead of such a program.

A better way to handle this situation is to use a modified *cpblk( )*
function that updates only the changed character or the rectangular region in which changes have been made to the buffer. We could also use
routines based on the BIOS and DOS interrupts to update the visual display page (they do so without causing interference) and use a separate
routine to update the in-memory buffer so that it continues to track what
is being displayed.

The screen-update routines mentioned above can be fashioned from
the *cpblk( )* function. For example, a routine that copies a single line or a
small range of lines, or one that copies a small rectangular region from
a screen buffer to display memory, would be useful in doing selective
screen updates with shorter delays. The next chapter describes screen-
buffer routines that do these and other screen-buffer management tasks.

Remember that the *cpblk( )* routine described here is inherently less portable than the DOS and BIOS calls and thus should be used only when necessary for speed and effect. The symbolic constant that holds the display memory segment could be replaced by a variable. It would then be a simple matter to change the value for machines that put display memory in a nonstandard place, if a reliable method can be developed for determining the identity of the host hardware and its display memory location(s). There is no foolproof method of doing the hardware identity tests; the best we can do is look for copyright notices and company names, but finding out the exact machine type remains an elusive goal. In my programs, I make the assumption that displays are in the standard IBM-specified locations. This works on 90 percent of the machines currently in use. For the other 10 percent I produce customized versions of the programs and charge a little extra to compensate for the added effort.

Buffered Screen-Interface Functions 12

The purpose of this chapter is to extend the screen interface presented in Chapter 11 by building a set of routines that let us directly access a screen buffer as a virtual screen.

A Buffered Screen-Interface Package

We have already seen how a memory image of a text screen can be quickly copied to physical display memory, giving the appearance of instant or at least fast screen updates. Our concern now is how to form the memory image of the desired display. We want to form the images in a way that simplifies the effort needed to manage several distinct areas of the screen. For example, a screen may be divided into viewing areas devoted to user commands, program status, and text. A provision might also be made to display help frames in a region that partially or completely overlays another area of the screen.

While developing the interface presented in this chapter, I wrote a test driver program (SB_TEST) that exercises each interface function to assure correct action. The test program creates several screen regions (or windows) that can be filled, cleared, scrolled, and so on, under control of the user at the keyboard. We'll develop the functions first, then apply the driver to show off some of the capabilities of the screen interface.

An element in display memory consists of two bytes: one representing a character and the other an associated attribute. This design is considerably more flexible than the design used by many low-cost terminals that use a single byte for each screen location. The latter design requires that some screen positions be "wasted" (they appear blank) because they are used to select attributes for all positions that follow until the next attribute-setting position. (The attribute positions are referred to by some as "magic cookies.") The PC design requires twice as much storage but permits attributes to be assigned on a character-by-character basis.

We will form a virtual-screen buffer as a two-dimensional array of "cells," with each cell being represented as a union. This allows our programs to access each cell as individual character and attribute bytes or as a single character/attribute pair. The definitions of a cell, the virtual-screen buffer, and other components of the buffered screen interface are contained in *sbuf.h.*

```
/*
 *       sbuf.h -- header file for buffered screen interface
 */


#define SB_OK   0
#define SB_ERR  (-1)


/* screen-buffer constants */
#define SB_ROWS 25
#define SB_COLS 80
#define SB_SIZ  SB_ROWS * SB_COLS


/* screen character/attribute buffer element definition */
struct BYTEBUF {
        unsigned char ch;       /* character */
        unsigned char attr;     /* attribute */
};


union CELL {
        struct BYTEBUF b;
        unsigned short cap;     /* character/attribute pair */
};


/* screen-buffer control structure */
struct BUFFER {
        /* current position */
        short row, col;
```

(continued)

```
          /* pointer to screen-buffer array */
          union CELL *bp;

          /* changed region per screen-buffer row */
          short lcol[SB_ROWS];   /* left end of changed region */
          short rcol[SB_ROWS];   /* right end of changed region */

          /* buffer status */
          unsigned short flags;
};

/* buffer flags values */
#define SB_DELTA        0x01
#define SB_RAW          0x02
#define SB_DIRECT       0x04
#define SB_SCROLL       0x08

/* coordinates of a window (rectangular region) on the screen buffer */
struct REGION {
          /* current position */
          short row, col;

          /* window boundaries */
          short r0, c0;   /* upper left corner */
          short r1, c1;   /* lower right corner */
          /* scrolling region boundaries */
          short sr0, sc0; /* upper left corner */
          short sr1, sc1; /* lower right corner */

          /* window buffer flags */
          unsigned short wflags;
};
```

Buffer Management Functions

One of the other components referred to above is a definition of a *REGION*, a structure that effectively defines a window, which in this implementation is simply a rectangular region of the screen buffer. To keep things reasonably simple, this interface keeps all screen data (characters and attributes) in the screen-buffer array, which is created by *sb_init( )*. There are no "shadow" buffers for individual windows.

```
/*
 *      sb_init -- initialize the buffered screen interface
 */

#include <stdio.h>
#include <stdlib.h>
#include <string.h>
#include <local\sbuf.h>

/* global data declarations */
struct BUFFER Sbuf;                      /* control information */
union CELL Scrnbuf[SB_ROWS][SB_COLS];    /* screen buffer array */

int
sb_init()
{
        int i;
        char *um;         /* update mode */

        /* set initial parameter values */
        Sbuf.bp = &Scrnbuf[0][0];
        Sbuf.row = Sbuf.col = 0;
        for (i = 0; i < SB_ROWS; ++i) {
                Sbuf.lcol[i] = SB_COLS;
                Sbuf.rcol[i] = 0;
        }
        Sbuf.flags = 0;

        /* set screen update mode */
        um = strupr(getenv("UPDATEMODE"));
        if (um == NULL || strcmp(um, "BIOS") == 0)
                Sbuf.flags &= ~SB_DIRECT;
        else if (strcmp(um, "DIRECT") == 0)
                Sbuf.flags |= SB_DIRECT;
        else
                return SB_ERR;
        return SB_OK;
}
```

The screen buffer is allocated as global data in *sb_init.c*. It has type
union CELL. The declaration

    union CELL Scrnbuf[SB_ROWS][SB_COLS];

uses the constants defined in *sbuf.h* to allocate 4000 bytes of storage for the screen buffer. The *sb_init.c* file also allocates the *Sbuf* structure that holds screen-buffer control information. *Sbuf* is of type *struct BUFFER*. It contains "cursor" row and column position variables, a pointer to the screen-buffer array, 2 bytes (unsigned short) of status flags, and arrays of column positions that mark the beginning and end of changes to each screen-buffer row. The range limits allow the routine that copies the screen buffer to physical-display memory to restrict the number of characters that must actually be written, thus minimizing the time needed to do display updates.

The *sb_show( )* function (in *sb_show.c*) is capable of using several methods to copy the screen-buffer contents to display memory. The buffer-copying method that is actually selected depends upon the user-specified access type (*UPDATEMODE* equal to DIRECT or BIOS access) and the type of display system that is installed in the host machine (IBM monochrome display adapter, or MDA, versus all other types).

```
/*
 *      sb_show -- copy the screen buffer to display memory
 */

#include <stdio.h>
#include <dos.h>
#include <memory.h>
#include <local\sbuf.h>
#include <local\video.h>

#define MDA_SEG 0xB000
#define CGA_SEG 0xB800
#define NBYTES  (2 * SB_COLS)

/* macro to synchronize with vertical retrace period */
#define VSTAT   0x3DA
#define VRBIT   8
#define VSYNC   while ((inp(VSTAT) & VRBIT) == VRBIT); \
                while ((inp(VSTAT) & VRBIT) != VRBIT)

extern struct BUFFER Sbuf;
extern union CELL Scrnbuf[SB_ROWS][SB_COLS];
```

(continued)

```
int
sb_show(pg)
short pg;
{
        register short r, c;
        short n;
        short count, ncols;
        unsigned int src_os, dest_os;
        struct SREGS segregs;

        if ((Sbuf.flags & SB_DIRECT) == SB_DIRECT) {
                /* use the direct-screen interface */
                segread(&segregs);

                /* determine extent of changes */
                n = 0;
                for (r = 0; r < SB_ROWS; ++r)
                        if (Sbuf.lcol[r] <= Sbuf.rcol[r])
                                ++n;
                src_os = dest_os = 0;
                if (n <= 2)
                        /* copy only rows that contain changes */
                        for (r = 0; r < SB_ROWS; ++r) {
                                if (Sbuf.lcol[r] <= Sbuf.rcol[r]) {
                                        /* copy blocks during vertical retrace */
                                        VSYNC;
                                        movedata(segregs.ds, &Scrnbuf[0][0] + src_os,
                                                CGA_SEG, dest_os, NBYTES);
                                        Sbuf.lcol[r] = SB_COLS;
                                        Sbuf.rcol[r] = 0;
                                }
                                src_os += NBYTES;
                                dest_os += NBYTES;
                        }
                else {
                        /* copy the entire buffer */
                        count = 3 * NBYTES;
                        ncols = 3 * NBYTES;
                        for (r = 0; r < SB_ROWS - 1; r += 3) {
                                VSYNC;
                                movedata(segregs.ds, &Scrnbuf[0][0] + src_os,
                                        CGA_SEG, dest_os, count);
```

(continued)

```
                            src_os += ncols;
                            dest_os += count;
                    }
                    VSYNC;
                    movedata(segregs.ds, &Scrnbuf[0][0] + src_os,
                            CGA_SEG, dest_os, NBYTES);
                    for (r = 0; r < SB_ROWS; ++r) {
                            Sbuf.lcol[r] = SB_COLS;
                            Sbuf.rcol[r] = 0;
                    }
            }
    }
    else
            /* use the BIOS video interface */
            for (r = 0; r < SB_ROWS; ++r)
                    /* copy only changed portions of lines */
                    if (Sbuf.lcol[r] < SB_COLS && Sbuf.rcol[r] > 0) {
                            for (c = Sbuf.lcol[r]; c <= Sbuf.rcol[r]; ++c) {
                                    putcur(r, c, pg);
                                    writeca(Scrnbuf[r][c].b.ch,
                                            Scrnbuf[r][c].b.attr, 1, pg);
                            }
                            Sbuf.lcol[r] = SB_COLS;
                            Sbuf.rcol[r] = 0;
                    }

            /* the display now matches the buffer -- clear flag bit */
            Sbuf.flags &= ~SB_DELTA;

            return SB_OK;
}
```

The *sb_show( )* function in DIRECT update mode checks to see how many screen-buffer rows differ from those currently displayed. If there are two or fewer, they are copied individually. Any greater number of changed screen rows causes a block-copy operation (based on the *cpblk( )* function that is described in Chapter 11) to be performed. If the DOS variable *UPDATEMODE* is not set, BIOS is assumed. Adding the line

    set updatemode = direct

to one's AUTOEXEC.BAT file (or typing it on the DOS command line) causes screen updates to use the faster, but less portable, direct-access method.

General Window Functions

Now that we can create a screen buffer and copy it to display memory, we can proceed to prepare functions that place the data to be displaycd into the buffer. The user sees nothing until the image is fully formed and copied. This allows programs to handle overlapping windows and special effects without distracting the user. By writing the least amount of data to the screen, this buffered-screen interface also speeds up the apparent performance of programs. The following functions do the work.

▶ *sb_new( )*. As noted earlier in this chapter, screens are easier to manage if they are divided into separate regions where each region is devoted to a single purpose. The function *sb_new( )* is used to describe a new window by allocating a window-control structure that contains row and column values for two opposite corners (upper left and lower right) of the window and a scrolling region within it, a "cursor" position, and a status flag word. Initially, the scrolling region is set to the same dimensions as the window itself. It can be set to other dimensions by calling *sb_set_scrl( )*.

   Space for the control structure is allocated by a call to *malloc( )*. *NULL* is returned if there is not enough memory to satisfy the request. A successful request results in a pointer to the window-control structure (*struct REGION* *) being returned. All positioning, character and string operations, scrolling, and clearing is done with respect to this window pointer.

```
/*
 *      sb_new -- prepare a new window (rectangular region)
 *      and return a pointer to it
 */

#include <stdio.h>
#include <malloc.h>
#include <local\sbuf.h>

struct REGION *
sb_new(top, left, height, width)
int top;        /* top row */
int left;       /* left column */
int height;     /* total rows */
```

(continued)

```
int width;      /* total columns */
{
        struct REGION *new;

        /* allocate the data-control structure */
        new = (struct REGION *)malloc(sizeof (struct REGION));
        if (new != NULL) {
                new->r0 = new->sr0 = top;
                new->r1 = new->sr1 = top + height - 1;
                new->c0 = new->sc0 = left;
                new->c1 = new->sc1 = left + width - 1;
                new->row = new->col = 0;
                new->wflags = 0;
        }
        return (new);
}
```

▶ *sb_move( )*. This function is used to move the cursor to a specified location within a window. Unreasonable requests (outside window boundaries) elicit an error return code (*SB_ERR*). If the request is in bounds, both the window-relative and buffer-relative cursor row and column values are updated and *SB_OK* is returned.

```
/*
 *      sb_move -- move the screen-buffer "cursor"
 */

#include <local\sbuf.h>

extern struct BUFFER Sbuf;
extern union CELL Scrnbuf[SB_ROWS][SB_COLS];

int
sb_move(win, r, c)
struct REGION *win;     /* window pointer */
register short r, c;    /* buffer row and column */
{
        /* don't change anything if request is out of range */
        if (r < 0 || r > win->r1 - win->r0 || c < 0 || c > win->c1 - win->c0)
                return SB_ERR;
        win->row = r;
```

(continued)

PROFICIENT C

```
        win->col = c;
        Sbuf.row = r + win->r0;
        Sbuf.col = c + win->c0;
        return SB_OK;
}
```

▶ *sb_fill( )*. A window may be filled with a given character and attribute pair by calling *sb_fill( )*. Every cell in the specified window is set equal to the character and attribute values passed as arguments. Two variations on the theme, *sb_filla( )* and *sb_fillc( )*, are used to fill a window with either an attribute or a character while leaving the other component of each cell undisturbed.

```
/*
 *      sb_fill -- fill region routines
 */

#include <local\sbuf.h>

extern struct BUFFER Sbuf;
extern union CELL Scrnbuf[SB_ROWS][SB_COLS];

/*
 *      sb_fill -- set all cells in a specified region
 *      to the same character/attribute value
 */

int
sb_fill(win, ch, attr)
struct REGION *win;
unsigned char ch;          /* fill character */
unsigned char attr;        /* fill attribute */
{
        register int i, j;
        unsigned short ca;

        ca = (attr << 8) | ch;
        for (i = win->sr0; i <= win->sr1; ++i) {
                for (j = win->sc0; j <= win->sc1; ++j)
                        Scrnbuf[i][j].cap = ca;
                if (win->sc0 < Sbuf.lcol[i])
                        Sbuf.lcol[i] = win->sc0;
```

(continued)

```
                    if (win->sc1 > Sbuf.rcol[i])
                            Sbuf.rcol[i] = win->sc1;
            }
            Sbuf.flags |= SB_DELTA;

            return SB_OK;
    }



    /*
     *      sb_fillc -- set all cells in a specified region
     *      to the same character value; leave attributes undisturbed
     */

    int
    sb_fillc(win, ch)
    struct REGION *win;
    unsigned char ch;           /* fill character */
    {
            register int i, j;

            for (i = win->sr0; i <= win->sr1; ++i) {
                    for (j = win->sc0; j <= win->sc1; ++j)
                            Scrnbuf[i][j].b.ch = ch;
                    if (win->sc0 < Sbuf.lcol[i])
                            Sbuf.lcol[i] = win->sc0;
                    if (win->sc1 > Sbuf.rcol[i])
                            Sbuf.rcol[i] = win->sc1;
            }
            Sbuf.flags |= SB_DELTA;

            return SB_OK;
    }



    /*
     *      sb_filla -- set all cells in a specified region
     *      to the same attribute value; leave characters undisturbed
     */

    int
    sb_filla(win, attr)
    struct REGION *win;
```

(continued)

```
unsigned char attr;     /* fill attribute */
{
        register int i, j;

        for (i = win->sr0; i <= win->sr1; ++i) {
                for (j = win->sc0; j <= win->sc1; ++j)
                        Scrnbuf[i][j].b.attr = attr;
                if (win->sc0 < Sbuf.lcol[i])
                        Sbuf.lcol[i] = win->sc0;
                if (win->sc1 > Sbuf.rcol[i])
                        Sbuf.rcol[i] = win->sc1;
        }
        Sbuf.flags |= SB_DELTA;

        return SB_OK;
}
```

▶ *sb_putc( )*. This function puts a character into a window at the current cursor position and advances the cursor. Accommodation is made for wrapping at the end of a window row, and scrolling is forced when a character is written to the last position of the last row of a window. Scrolling can be disabled by clearing the *SB_SCROLL* bit in the window flag word (the default state). Standard format-effector control codes (newline, carriage return, linefeed, and tab) are treated normally.

▶ *sb_puts( )*. A string may be added to a window using *sb_puts( )*, which simply calls *sb_putc( )* to do its work for each character in the string.

```
/*
 *      sb_put -- routines to put characters and strings into the
 *      screen buffer; the cursor location is altered
 */

#include <local\sbuf.h>
#include <ctype.h>

extern struct BUFFER Sbuf;
extern union CELL Scrnbuf[SB_ROWS][SB_COLS];
```

(continued)

```
/*
 *      sb_putc -- put a character into a screen-buffer window
 */

int
sb_putc(win, ch)
struct REGION *win;
unsigned char ch;
{
        short cmax, rmax;
        short lim;
        short noscroll = 0, puterr = 0;

        /* calculate screen-buffer position and limits */
        cmax = win->c1 - win->c0;
        rmax = win->r1 - win->r0;
        Sbuf.row = win->r0 + win->row;
        Sbuf.col = win->c0 + win->col;

        /* process the character */
        switch (ch) {
        case '\b':
                /* non-destructive backspace */
                if (win->col > 0) {
                        --win->col;
                        Sbuf.col = win->c0 + win->col;
                        return SB_OK;
                }
                else
                        return SB_ERR;
        case '\n':
                /* clear trailing line segment */
                while (win->col < cmax)
                        if (sb_putc(win, ' ') == SB_ERR)
                                ++puterr;
                break;
        case '\t':
                /* convert tab to required number of spaces */
                lim = win->col + 8 - (win->col & 0x7);
                while (win->col < lim)
                        if (sb_putc(win, ' ') == SB_ERR)
                                ++puterr;
                break;
```

(continued)

```
        default:
                /* if printable ASCII, place the character in the buffer */
                if (isascii(ch) && isprint(ch))
                        Scrnbuf[Sbuf.row][Sbuf.col].b.ch = ch;
                if (Sbuf.col < Sbuf.lcol[Sbuf.row])
                        Sbuf.lcol[Sbuf.row] = Sbuf.col;
                if (Sbuf.col > Sbuf.rcol[Sbuf.row])
                        Sbuf.rcol[Sbuf.row] = Sbuf.col;
                break;
        }


        /* update the cursor position */
        if (win->col < cmax)
                ++win->col;
        else if (win->row < rmax) {
                win->col = 0;
                ++win->row;
        }
        else if ((win->wflags & SB_SCROLL) == SB_SCROLL) {
                sb_scrl(win, 1);
                win->col = 0;
                win->row = rmax;
        }
        else
                ++noscroll;

        /* update screen-buffer position */
        Sbuf.row = win->r0 + win->row;
        Sbuf.col = win->c0 + win->col;
        Sbuf.flags |= SB_DELTA;

        return ((noscroll || puterr) ? SB_ERR : SB_OK);
} /* end sb_putc() */



/*
 *      sb_puts -- put a string into the screen buffer
 */

int
sb_puts(win, s)
struct REGION *win;
```

(continued)

```
unsigned char *s;
{
        while (*s)
                if (sb_putc(win, *s++) == SB_ERR)
                        return SB_ERR;
        return SB_OK;
} /* end sb_puts() */
```

▶ *sb_rca( )*. Used to read the character and attribute values from
the screen-buffer cell at the current window cursor location. The
functions *sb_ra( )* and *sb_rc( )* read the individual attribute and
character values, respectively. This is a simple task because all the
data is available in the screen buffer. In the case of *sb_rca( )*, an unsigned short quantity is returned. The *sb_ra( )* and *sb_rc( )* functions return an unsigned *char* value.

```
/*
 *      sb_read -- read character/attribute data
 */

#include <local\sbuf.h>

extern struct BUFFER Sbuf;
extern union CELL Scrnbuf[SB_ROWS][SB_COLS];

unsigned char
sb_ra(win)
struct REGION *win;      /* window pointer */
{
        return (Scrnbuf[win->r0 + win->row][win->c0 + win->col].b.attr);
} /* end sb_ra() */


/*
 *      sb_rc -- read character from current location in screen buffer
 */

unsigned char
sb_rc(win)
struct REGION *win;      /* window pointer */
{
        return (Scrnbuf[win->r0 + win->row][win->c0 + win->col].b.ch);
```

(continued)

```
} /* end sb_rc() */


/*
 *      sb_rca -- read character/attribute pair from current
 *      location in screen buffer
 */

unsigned short
sb_rca(win)
struct REGION *win;       /* window pointer */
{
        return (Scrnbuf[win->r0 + win->row][win->c0 + win->col].cap);
} /* end sb_rca() */
```

▶ *sb_scrl( )*. To scroll a window vertically, use *sb_scrl( )*. This function scrolls a region within a window. The scrolling region is frequently made smaller than the full window size to allow for a
boxed border and a title line and other such trimmings. A comparable effect can be obtained by defining a window within a window, but then the regions must be managed individually, adding to
program overhead.

```
/*
 *      sb_scrl -- scrolling routines
 */

#include <local\sbuf.h>

extern struct BUFFER Sbuf;
extern union CELL Scrnbuf[SB_ROWS][SB_COLS];


/*
 *      sb_scrl -- scroll the specified window
 *      n lines (direction indicated by sign)
 */
```

(continued)

```
int
sb_scrl(win, n)
struct REGION *win;
short n;                 /* number of rows to scroll */
{
        register short r, c;

        if (n == 0)
                /* clear the entire region to spaces */
                sb_fillc(win, ' ');
        else if (n > 0) {
                /* scroll n rows up */
                for (r = win->sr0; r <= win->sr1 - n; ++r) {
                        for (c = win->sc0; c <= win->sc1; ++c)
                                Scrnbuf[r][c] = Scrnbuf[r + n][c];
                        if (win->sc0 < Sbuf.lcol[r])
                                Sbuf.lcol[r] = win->sc0;
                        if (win->sc1 > Sbuf.rcol[r])
                                Sbuf.rcol[r] = win->sc1;
                }
                for ( ; r <= win->sr1; ++r) {
                        for (c = win->sc0; c <= win->sc1; ++c)
                                Scrnbuf[r][c].b.ch = ' ';
                        if (win->sc0 < Sbuf.lcol[r])
                                Sbuf.lcol[r] = win->sc0;
                        if (win->sc1 > Sbuf.rcol[r])
                                Sbuf.rcol[r] = win->sc1;
                }
        }
        else {
                /* scroll n rows down */
                n = -n;
                for (r = win->sr1; r >= win->sr0 + n; --r) {
                        for (c = win->sc0; c <= win->sc1; ++c)
                                Scrnbuf[r][c] = Scrnbuf[r - n][c];
                        if (win->sc0 < Sbuf.lcol[r])
                                Sbuf.lcol[r] = win->sc0;
                        if (win->sc1 > Sbuf.rcol[r])
                                Sbuf.rcol[r] = win->sc1;
                }
                for ( ; r >= win->sr0; --r) {
                        for (c = win->sc0; c <= win->sc1; ++c)
                                Scrnbuf[r][c].b.ch = ' ';
```

(continued)

```
                              if (win->sc0 < Sbuf.lcol[r])
                                     Sbuf.lcol[r] = win->sc0;
                              if (win->sc1 > Sbuf.rcol[r])
                                     Sbuf.rcol[r] = win->sc1;
                       }
               }
               Sbuf.flags |= SB_DELTA;
               return SB_OK;
        } /* end sb_scrl() */



        /*
         *      sb_set_scrl -- set the scroll region boundaries
         */

        int
        sb_set_scrl(win, top, left, bottom, right)
        struct REGION *win;      /* window pointer */
        short top, left;         /* upper left corner */
        short bottom, right;     /* lower left corner */
        {
               if (top < 0 || left < 0 ||
                       bottom > win->r1 - win->r0 || right > win->c1 - win->c0)
                       return SB_ERR;
               win->sr0 = win->r0 + top;
               win->sc0 = win->c0 + left;
               win->sr1 = win->r0 + bottom - 1;
               win->sc1 = win->c0 + right - 1;
               return SB_OK;
        } /* end sb_set_scrl() */
```

► *sb_wca( )*. The *sb_wca( )* function writes both a character and an attribute to a window at the current cursor position. A repetition count tells the function the extent of the write operation. The cursor position is not changed. The *sb_wa( )* and *sb_wc( )* functions write an attribute and a character, respectively, to a window. Note that *sb_wca( )* combines the two unsigned *char* values into a single word by shifting the attribute left eight positions and bitwise ORing the result with the character value. We could achieve the same result by using separate assignment statements for the attribute and character components of the screen-buffer cell. The "write" routines are useful for such tasks as displaying horizontal portions of character graphics and changing the highlighting of text strings like those used in menu bars and pop-up selection menus.

```
/*
 *      sb_write -- screen-buffer write routines
 */

#include <local\sbuf.h>

extern struct BUFFER Sbuf;
extern union CELL Scrnbuf[SB_ROWS][SB_COLS];

/*
 *      sb_wa -- write an attribute to a region of the screen buffer
 */

int
sb_wa(win, attr, n)
struct REGION *win;       /* window pointer */
unsigned char attr;       /* attribute */
short n;                  /* repetition count */
{
        short i;
        short row;
        short col;

        i = n;
        row = win->r0 + win->row;
        col = win->c0 + win->col;
        while (i--)
                Scrnbuf[row][col + i].b.attr = attr;

        /* marked the changed region */
        if (col < Sbuf.lcol[row])
                Sbuf.lcol[row] = col;
        if (col + n > Sbuf.rcol[row])
                Sbuf.rcol[row] = col + n;
        Sbuf.flags |= SB_DELTA;

        return (i == 0) ? SB_OK : SB_ERR;
} /* end sb_wa() */
```

(continued)

```
/*
 *      sb_wc -- write a character to a region of the screen buffer
 */

int
sb_wc(win, ch, n)
struct REGION *win;     /* window pointer */
unsigned char ch;       /* character */
short n;                /* repetition count */
{
        short i;
        short row;
        short col;
        i = n;
        row = win->r0 + win->row;
        col = win->c0 + win->col;
        while (i--)
                Scrnbuf[row][col + i].b.ch = ch;

        /* marked the changed region */
        if (col < Sbuf.lcol[row])
                Sbuf.lcol[row] = col;
        if (col + n > Sbuf.rcol[row])
                Sbuf.rcol[row] = col + n;
        Sbuf.flags |= SB_DELTA;

        return (i == 0 ? SB_OK : SB_ERR);
} /* end sb_wc() */



/*
 *      sb_wca -- write a character/attribute pair to a region
 *      of the screen buffer
 */

int
sb_wca(win, ch, attr, n)
struct REGION *win;     /* window pointer */
unsigned char ch;       /* character */
unsigned char attr;     /* attribute */
short n;                /* repetition count */
{
        int i;
```

(continued)

```
            short row;
            short col;

            i = n;
            row = win->r0 + win->row;
            col = win->c0 + win->col;
            while (i--)
                    Scrnbuf[row][col + i].cap = (attr << 8) | ch;

            /* marked the changed region */
            if (col < Sbuf.lcol[row])
                    Sbuf.lcol[row] = col;
            if (col + n > Sbuf.rcol[row])
                    Sbuf.rcol[row] = col + n;
            Sbuf.flags |= SB_DELTA;

            return (i == 0 ? SB_OK : SB_ERR);
    } /* end sb_wca() */
```

Box-drawing Functions

A portion of the screen that demands special attention is often high-lighted by drawing a box around it. Some screen designs require that particular areas of the screen be set off by box designs that signify their purposes. For example, a program that displays multiple windows might identify inactive windows by surrounding them with single-line boxes while highlighting the currently active window with a double-line box.

The IBM extended-ASCII character set (codes 128 through 255), which is supported by nearly all PC-compatible computers, includes a group of line-drawing characters that are suitable for drawing boxes and other shapes with various combinations of single and double lines, full and partial blocks, and various regular dot patterns.

The *sb_box()* function can be called to draw a box around the perimeter of a window. The box is drawn entirely within the bounds of the specified window; therefore, to avoid overwriting it, text functions should be instructed to write to an area at least one character within the box. Box corners and edges are formed from characters that match correctly at all junctions. The box types are defined in the *box.h* header file.

```
/*
 *      box.h -- header for box-drawing functions
 */

typedef struct box_st {
        short ul, ur, ll, lr;    /* corners */
        short tbar, bbar;        /* horizontal bars */
        short lbar, rbar;        /* vertical bars */
} BOXTYPE;

/* box types */
#define BOXASCII        0
#define BOX11           1
#define BOX22           2
#define BOX12           3
#define BOX21           4
#define BOXBLK          5
```

```
/*
 *      sb_box -- draw a box around the perimeter of a window
 *      using the appropriate IBM graphics characters
 */

#include <local\sbuf.h>
#include <local\video.h>
#include <local\box.h>


int
sb_box(win, type, attr)
struct REGION *win;
short type;
unsigned char attr;
{
        register short r;        /* row index */
        short x;                 /* interior horizontal line length */
        short maxr, maxc;        /* maximum row and col values */
        BOXTYPE *boxp;           /* pointer to box drawing character struct */
        static BOXTYPE box[] = {
                '+',    '+',    '+',    '+',    '-',    '-',    '|',    '|',
                ULC11, URC11, LLC11, LRC11, HBAR1, HBAR1, VBAR1, VBAR1,
                ULC22, URC22, LLC22, LRC22, HBAR2, HBAR2, VBAR2, VBAR2,
                ULC12, URC12, LLC12, LRC12, HBAR1, HBAR1, VBAR2, VBAR2,
```

(continued)

```
                ULC21, URC21, LLC21, LRC21, HBAR2, HBAR2, VBAR1, VBAR1,
                BLOCK, BLOCK, BLOCK, BLOCK, HBART, HBARB, BLOCK, BLOCK
        };

        boxp = &box[type];
        maxc = win->c1 - win->c0;
        maxr = win->r1 - win->r0;
        x = maxc - 1;

        /* draw top row */
        sb_move(win, 0, 0);
        sb_wca(win, boxp->ul, attr, 1);
        sb_move(win, 0, 1);
        sb_wca(win, boxp->tbar, attr, x);
        sb_move(win, 0, maxc);
        sb_wca(win, boxp->ur, attr, 1);

        /* draw left and right sides */
        for (r = 1; r < maxr; ++r) {
                sb_move(win, r, 0);
                sb_wca(win, boxp->lbar, attr, 1);
                sb_move(win, r, maxc);
                sb_wca(win, boxp->rbar, attr, 1);
        }

        /* draw bottom row */
        sb_move(win, maxr, 0);
        sb_wca(win, boxp->ll, attr, 1);
        sb_move(win, maxr, 1);
        sb_wca(win, boxp->bbar, attr, x);
        sb_move(win, maxr, maxc);
        sb_wca(win, boxp->lr, attr, 1);

        return SB_OK;
}
```

The Screen-Buffer Library

The *sbuf.lib* is a library that contains the object modules for each of the screen-buffer functions just described. The library has wide applicability to screen-oriented programs. It will reside in the *lib**local* subdirectory for easy access by our programs. The makefile, *sbuf.mk,* using the inference rules in *tools.ini,* keeps all objects and the library file current and puts files in the required places. If you use a different directory scheme, you should modify the makefile to accommodate the differences.

```
# makefile for SBUF.LIB (screen-buffer library)

LLIB = c:\lib\local
LINC = c:\include\local

OBJS = sb_box.obj sb_fill.obj sb_init.obj sb_move.obj sb_new.obj \
sb_put.obj sb_read.obj sb_scrl.obj sb_show.obj sb_write.obj

MODS = sb_box sb_fill sb_init sb_move sb_new.obj sb_put sb_read \
sb_scrl sb_show sb_write

$(LINC)\sbuf.h: sbuf.h
        copy sbuf.h $(LINC)\sbuf.h

$(LINC)\box.h:  box.h
        copy box.h $(LINC)\box.h

sb_box.obj:     sb_box.c $(LINC)\sbuf.h $(LINC)\video.h $(LINC)\box.h

sb_fill.obj:    sb_fill.c $(LINC)\sbuf.h

sb_init.obj:    sb_init.c $(LINC)\sbuf.h

sb_move.obj:    sb_move.c $(LINC)\sbuf.h

sb_new.obj:     sb_new.c $(LINC)\sbuf.h

sb_put.obj:     sb_put.c $(LINC)\sbuf.h

sb_read.obj:    sb_read.c $(LINC)\sbuf.h

sb_scrl.obj:    sb_scrl.c $(LINC)\sbuf.h

sb_show.obj:    sb_show.c $(LINC)\sbuf.h

sb_write.obj:   sb_write.c $(LINC)\sbuf.h
```

(continued)

```
sbuf.lib:        $(OBJS)
        del sbuf.lib
        lib sbuf +$(MODS);
        copy sbuf.lib $(LLIB)
```

```
# inference rules for SB_TEST program
# (small model with function prototyping enabled)

[make]
.c.obj:
        msc -DLINT_ARGS $*;
```

A Test Driver Program

The SB_TEST program (sources are in files *sb_test.c* and *sb_test.h*) alluded to earlier is one of several programs I used to test the *SBUF* library functions as they were being developed. The makefile *(sb_test.mk)* presumes that the screen-buffer function library is up to date. To use the test driver program, simply type its name at the DOS prompt.

SB_TEST creates several windows and places some text in each. On a color display, each window sports its own color scheme. On a monochrome display, the status window displays in reverse video and the help window contains bold text; the other windows display normal text.

```
/*
 *      sb_test.h -- header for sb_test program
 */

/* dimensions of the display windows */
#define CMND_ROW        0
#define CMND_COL        0
#define CMND_HT         1
#define CMND_WID        SB_COLS
#define STAT_ROW        CMND_HT
#define STAT_COL        0
#define STAT_HT         1
#define STAT_WID        SB_COLS
#define TEXT_ROW        (CMND_HT + STAT_HT)
#define TEXT_COL        0
```

(continued)

```
#define TEXT_HT          (SB_ROWS - TEXT_ROW)
#define TEXT_WID         SB_COLS
#define HELP_ROW         5
#define HELP_COL         5
#define HELP_HT          18
#define HELP_WID         70
```

```
/*
 *        sb_test -- driver for screen-buffer interface functions
 */

#include <stdio.h>
#include <stdlib.h>
#include <conio.h>
#include <local\std.h>
#include <local\keydefs.h>
#include <local\sbuf.h>
#include <local\video.h>
#include <local\box.h>
#include "sb_test.h"

#define BEL 7

extern struct BUFFER Sbuf;

main(argc, argv)
int argc;
char *argv[];
{
        char *s, line[MAXLINE];
        int k;
        short i;
        FILE *fp;
        char fname[MAXPATH];
        struct REGION *cmnd, *stat, *text, *help, *curwin;
        unsigned char cmndattr, statattr, textattr, helpattr, curattr;
        unsigned char ch, userattr;

        /* function prototypes */
        int sb_init();
        int sb_move(struct REGION *, short, short);
```

(continued)

```
struct REGION *sb_new(short, short, short, short);
int sb_putc(struct REGION *, unsigned char);
int sb_puts(struct REGION *, char *);
int sb_show(short);
int sb_fill(struct REGION *, unsigned char, unsigned char);
char *get_fname(struct REGION *, char *, short);

getstate();
readca(&ch, &userattr, Vpage);

/* set up the screen buffer */
if (sb_init() == SB_ERR) {
        fprintf(stderr, "Bad UPDATEMODE value in environment\n");
        exit(1);
}


/* set up windows and scrolling regions */
cmnd = sb_new(CMND_ROW, CMND_COL, CMND_HT, CMND_WID);
stat = sb_new(STAT_ROW, STAT_COL, STAT_HT, STAT_WID);
text = sb_new(TEXT_ROW, TEXT_COL, TEXT_HT, TEXT_WID);
help = sb_new(HELP_ROW, HELP_COL, HELP_HT, HELP_WID);
text->wflags |= SB_SCROLL;
sb_set_scrl(help, 1, 1, HELP_HT - 1, HELP_WID - 1);

/* display each primary window in its own attribute */
cmndattr = GRN;
statattr = (WHT << 4) | BLK;
textattr = (BLU << 4) | CYAN;
helpattr = (GRN << 4) | YEL;
sb_fill(cmnd, ' ', cmndattr);
if (sb_move(cmnd, 0, 0) == SB_OK)
        sb_puts(cmnd, "SB_TEST (Version 1.0)");
sb_fill(stat, ' ', statattr);
if (sb_move(stat, 0, 0) == SB_OK)
        sb_puts(stat, "*** STATUS AREA ***");
for (i = 0; i <= text->r1 - text->r0; ++i) {
        sb_move(text, i, 0);
        sb_wca(text, i + 'a', textattr,
                text->c1 - text->c0 + 1);
}
if (sb_move(text, 10, 25) == SB_OK)
        sb_puts(text, " *** TEXT DISPLAY AREA *** ");
```

(continued)

```
        sb_show(Vpage);
        curwin = text;
        curattr = textattr;

        /* respond to user commands */
        while ((k = getkey()) != K_ESC) {
                switch (k) {
                case K_UP:
                        sb_scrl(curwin, 1);
                        break;
                case K_DOWN:
                        sb_scrl(curwin, -1);
                        break;
                case K_PGUP:
                        sb_scrl(curwin, curwin->sr1 - curwin->sr0);
                        break;
                case K_PGDN:
                        sb_scrl(curwin, -(curwin->sr1 - curwin->sr0));
                        break;
                case K_ALTC:
                        /* clear the current window */
                        sb_fill(curwin, ' ', curattr);
                        break;
                case K_ALTH:
                        /* display help */
                        curwin = help;
                        curattr = helpattr;
                        for (i = 0; i < help->r1 - help->r0; ++i) {
                                sb_move(help, i, 0);
                                sb_wca(help, i + 'a', helpattr,
                                        help->c1 - help->c0 + 1);
                        }
                        sb_box(help, BOXBLK, helpattr);
                        break;
                case K_ALTS:
                        /* fill the command area with letters */
                        curwin = stat;
                        curattr = statattr;
                        sb_fill(stat, 's', statattr);
                        break;
                case K_ALTT:
                        /* fill the text area */
                        curwin = text;
```

(continued)

```
            curattr = textattr;
            for (i = 0; i <= text->r1 - text->r0; ++i) {
                    sb_move(text, i, 0);
                    sb_wca(text, i + 'a', textattr,
                            text->c1 - text->c0 + 1);
            }
            break;
case K_ALTR:
            /* read a file into the current window */
            sb_fill(stat, ' ', statattr);
            sb_move(stat, 0, 0);
            sb_puts(stat, "File to read: ");
            sb_show(Vpage);
            (void)get_fname(stat, fname, MAXPATH);
            if ((fp = fopen(fname, "r")) == NULL) {
                    sb_fill(stat, ' ', statattr);
                    sb_move(stat, 0, 0);
                    sb_puts(stat, "Cannot open ");
                    sb_puts(stat, fname);
            }
            else {
                    sb_fill(stat, ' ', statattr);
                    sb_move(stat, 0, 0);
                    sb_puts(stat, "File: ");
                    sb_puts(stat, fname);
                    sb_show(Vpage);
                    sb_fill(text, ' ', textattr);
                    sb_move(text, 0, 0);
                    putcur(text->r0, text->c0, Vpage);
                    while ((s = fgets(line, MAXLINE, fp)) != NULL) {
                            if (sb_puts(text, s) == SB_ERR) {
                                    clrscrn(userattr);
                                    putcur(0, 0, Vpage);
                                    fprintf(stderr, "puts error\n");
                                    exit(1);
                            }
                            sb_show(Vpage);
                    }
                    if (ferror(fp)) {
                            putcur(text->r0, text->c0, Vpage);
                            fprintf(stderr, "Error reading file\n");
                    }
                    fclose(fp);
```

(continued)

```
                    }
                    break;
            default:
                    /* say what? */
                    fputc(BEL, stderr);
                    continue;
            }
            if ((Sbuf.flags & SB_DELTA) == SB_DELTA)
                    sb_show(Vpage);
      }

      clrscrn(userattr);
      putcur(0, 0, Vpage);
      exit(0);
}

/*
 *      get_fname -- get a filename from the user
 */

char *
get_fname(win, path, lim)
struct REGION *win;
char *path;
short lim;
{
      int ch;
      char *s;

      s = path;
      sb_show(Vpage);
      while ((ch = getch()) != K_RETURN) {
            if (ch == '\b')
                    --s;
            else {
                    sb_putc(win, ch);
                    *s++ = ch;
            }
            sb_show(Vpage);
      }
      *s = '\0';
      return (path);
}
```

```
# makefile for SB_TEST driver program

LLIB = c:\lib\local
LINC = c:\include\local

sb_test.obj:    sb_test.c $(LINC)\sbuf.h sb_test.h

sb_test.exe:    sb_test.obj $(LLIB)\sbuf.lib $(LLIB)\bios.lib $(LLIB)\dos.lib
        link $*, $*, nul, $(LLIB)\sbuf $(LLIB)\bios $(LLIB)\dos;
```

After compiling and linking the program, try using scrolling and clearing commands in the help and text windows to see how the command actions are implemented. Of course, a real program would display real text rather than the repeated sequences of letters that are produced by the test driver.

The commands are described in the following table:

COMMAND	DESCRIPTION
Up and down arrows	Scroll up and down by one row
PgUp, PgDn	Scroll up and down by one page (a window-ful minus one row)
Alt-c	Clear the current window
Alt-h	Display a help frame
Alt-s	Fill the status window
Alt-r	Read in a text file
Alt-t	Fill the text area
Esc	Clean up the display and quit

The file-reading operation in SB_TEST demonstrates how implicit scrolling works. The scroll is called by the *sb_putc( )* function, called either directly or indirectly by *sb_puts( )*.

When used in the BIOS update mode, the screen-buffer function library is reasonably portable. Direct mode is, of course, portable only to highly PC-compatible computers. In the next chapter, we will look at the most portable of the screen management tools: the ANSI device driver.

The ANSI Device Driver 13

DOS versions 2.00 and later can be extended to use peripheral devices not planned for in the basic design of DOS. The use of installable device drivers is the basis of this extendability. ANSI.SYS, the best known of these device drivers, is supplied with DOS to handle special keyboard and screen features. This chapter focuses on ANSI.SYS and its uses.

ANSI Basics

The American National Standards Institute (ANSI), long before becoming involved in efforts to standardize the C programming language, proposed terminal and computer-equipment standards that have since become adopted by the computer industry. Adherence to the standards is voluntary, but terminal and computer manufacturers who choose to ignore them do so at their own peril. Nearly all terminal equipment built since the late 1970s conforms, more or less, to the ANSI standards.

Conformance to the ANSI standards can be claimed as long as functions that are implemented use the specified codes to invoke them; it is not necessary to implement every function and capability described by the standards. In addition, the ANSI standards permit the implementation of *private* functions that are invoked by codes outside the range of those specified. Thus, a Digital Equipment Corporation VT100 terminal, which does not have insert- and delete-line capabilities, and which has many private capabilities, is considered to be an ANSI-conforming terminal.

The standard that concerns us most directly with regard to our program designs is X3.64–1979. (The number following the dash represents the year in which the standard became effective or was last revised.) This standard defines a set of "additional controls" for use with the ASCII character set defined in X3.4–1977 (a revision of X3.4–1968) and the code extensions defined in X3.41–1974. The additional controls are invoked by using control-function sequences and strings, which are commonly referred to as *escape sequences* because the ASCII escape code (ESC, 27 decimal, 16 hex) is used as the initial character. The escape code is the signal that identifies the codes that follow as control information rather than ordinary graphic symbols.

The uses of ANSI control sequences are primarily those of screen and keyboard handling, but other control tasks, such as switching to alternate character sets and responding to requests for terminal type identification ("Who are you?"), are covered. The standard accommodates change with built-in mechanisms for adding controls and with periodic review and revision as circumstances dictate.

ANSI control sequences have the general form shown in Figure 13-1. The ASCII escape (shown as ESC— a single code, not three characters) is the *introducer*. It is followed by a string called the *intermediate bit combinations*, usually a mixture of numeric and alphabetic characters, and a *final character* that represents the command to be executed.

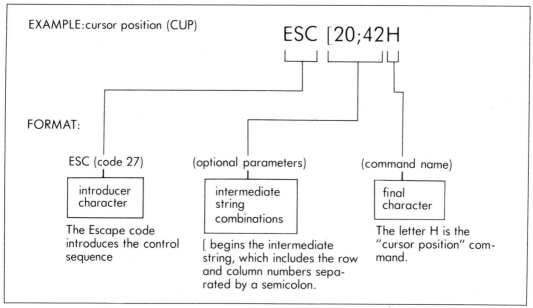

FIGURE 13-1 | *ANSI control sequence formation*

The string in the middle of a control sequence provides variable data that modifies the behavior of the basic command. For example, the sequence for moving the cursor forward (CUF) is ESC[#C. The sharp sign (pound sign or octothorpe, if you prefer) is a replaceable numeric parameter. If a value is given, it specifies the number of columns to move the cursor. If the value is zero or not specified, the default value of one is used. Attempts to move past the end of the line are ignored.

The example given in Figure 13-1 shows how to form the sequence that moves the cursor to an absolute position on the screen. Impossible requests are simply ignored.

Display Memory

Figure 13-2 shows how a character and its associated attribute are stored in a PC's display memory. In a 25-line by 80-column text mode, each display-screen image requires a total of 4000 bytes of memory, half devoted to characters and half to attributes. The even-numbered byte (starting at zero) of each display-memory word holds the code for the character. The odd-numbered byte holds the attribute.

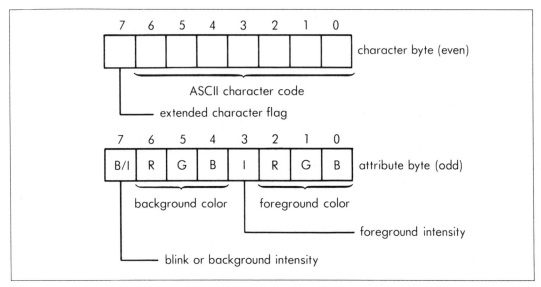

FIGURE 13-2 | *Character and attribute bytes*

The low seven bits (0–6) of a character byte uniquely specify one of the possible 128 character codes (0–127) defined in the ASCII character set.

The most significant bit of the character byte, when set (1), indicates an *extended-ASCII code*, one that falls in the range 128 through 255. On an IBM PC and most compatibles, these are foreign alphabetics, block graphics, and other special characters.

The attribute byte is used to control monochrome and color attributes for each character on an individual basis. As Figure 13-2 shows, bits 0 through 2 specify the foreground color, and bit 3 indicates the intensity level of the foreground. Together, these four bits determine the color value of the character, providing a range of 16 colors. On an IBM monochrome adapter, only three of the values produce unique results (0 = black, 1 = underlined, and 7 = white). All other values below 7 produce normal white, while values between 8 and 15 produce "bright" versions of their respective values in the low range. Thus, the value 15 produces a bright white foreground.

The background color (or grey level) of each character cell is specified by bits 4 through 6. The background can have one of only eight colors.

Bit 7 serves one of two purposes depending on whether blinking is enabled or disabled. When the blink feature is enabled, setting background values above 7 (bit 7 set) produces quite an obnoxious blink in the foreground of the associated character. Disabling the blink produces a far more pleasing result: a stable background that can be any of 16 different colors on suitable display equipment. Chapter 5 presents routines for controlling the blink feature.

ANSI.SYS

As mentioned previously, the ANSI.SYS file provided with DOS versions 2.00 and later is an installable device driver that provides a subset of ANSI-standard screen and keyboard control functions. When loaded into the computer's memory, the ANSI driver monitors keyboard input and screen output data streams.

For screen output, when one of the escape sequences handled by the ANSI driver is received, the driver performs the associated action, such as moving the cursor or setting a display attribute. During keyboard operations, individual keys and combinations of keys can be intercepted and converted into customized character strings. Most codes are simply passed on without anything being done to them.

ANSI escape sequences can be called from within our C programs or even from DOS batch files. The SetColor program described later in this chapter is an example of a C program that uses the ANSI driver to do most of the work involved in controlling the attributes of a color text display.

Installing ANSI.SYS

Installation of ANSI.SYS is trivial. DOS uses the file CONFIG.SYS to configure the system when it is started. If the ANSI.SYS file is in the directory c:\dos, for example, adding the line

device = c: \ dos \ ansi.sys

to CONFIG.SYS will cause DOS to load the ANSI device driver each time the system is turned on ("cold boot") or restarted using Ctrl-Alt-Del ("warm boot").

A program that depends on the ANSI device driver should test for its presence. If the ANSI driver is not loaded into memory, the program should abort and provide instructions to the user about installing it. A method of testing for the presence of the device driver is presented in the next section of this chapter.

The ANSI Control Codes

Figure 13-3 (on the next page) summarizes the ANSI standard control capabilities and indicates which are supported by the DOS ANSI device driver. Note that some of the supported capabilities (for example, erase in display, ED) are implemented in a simplified way, and that others (for example, set mode, SM, and reset mode, RM) are decidedly implementation-dependent, being tied intimately to the IBM PC hardware architecture.

The following descriptions are intended to supplement the information presented in the documentation provided with DOS, particularly with respect to usage guidelines. The subsequent section of this chapter develops an interface package to the ANSI driver and provides practical examples of these codes in use.

CONTROL SEQUENCES WITH NUMERIC PARAMETERS		
ANSI.SYS	*Mnemonic*	*Description*
No	CBT	Cursor Backward Tabulation
No	CHA	Cursor Horizontal Absolute
No	CHT	Cursor Horizontal Tabulation
No	CNL	Cursor Next Line
No	CPL	Cursor Preceding Line
Yes	CPR	Cursor Position Report
Yes	CUB	Cursor Backward
Yes	CUD	Cursor Down
Yes	CUF	Cursor Forward
Yes	CUP	Cursor Position
Yes	CUU	Cursor Up
No	CVT	Cursor Vertical Tabulation
No	DA	Device Attributes
No	DCH	Delete Character
No	DL	Delete Line
No	ECH	Erase Character
No	FNT	Font Selection
No	GSM	Graphic Size Modification
No	GSS	Graphic Size Selection
No	HPA	Horizontal Position Absolute
No	HPR	Horizontal Position Relative
Yes	HVP	Horizontal and Vertical Position
No	ICH	Insert Character
No	IL	Insert Line
No	NP	Next Page
No	PP	Preceding Page
No	REP	Repeat
No	SD	Scroll Down
No	SL	Scroll Left
No	SPI	Spacing Increment
No	SR	Scroll Right
No	SU	Scroll Up
No	TSS	Thin Space Specification
No	VPA	Vertical Position Absolute
No	VPR	Vertical Position Relative

FIGURE 13-3 | *ANSI control sequences*   *(continued)*

CONTROL SEQUENCES WITH SELECTIVE PARAMETERS

ANSI.SYS	Mnemonic	Description
No	CTC	Cursor Tabulation Control
No	DAQ	Define Area Qualification
Yes	DSR	Device Status Report
No	EA	Erase in Area
Yes	ED	Erase in Display
No	EF	Erase in Field
Yes	EL	Erase in Line
No	JFY	Justify
No	MC	Media Copy
No	QUAD	QUAD
Yes	RM	Reset Mode
No	SEM	Select Editing Extent Mode
Yes	SGR	Set Graphic Rendition
Yes	SM	Set Mode
No	TBC	Tabulation Clear

FIGURE 13-3 | *continued*

Cursor Position (CUP)   ESC[#;#H
Horizontal and Vertical Position (HVP)   ESC[#;#f

These two control sequences do the same job. They move the cursor to the position designated by the parameters: the row (the first #) and the column. Illegal requests are ignored. The upper left corner of the screen is designated row 1, column 1. Missing or zero-valued parameters default to 1; therefore, a CUP or HVP sequence with no stated parameters is a synonym for "homing" the cursor.

Cursor Up (CUU)   ESC[#A
Cursor Down (CUD)   ESC[#B
Cursor Forward (CUF)   ESC[#C
Cursor Backward (CUB)   ESC[#D

Each of these control sequences moves the cursor by # positions (the default is 1) in the specified direction. Attempts to move beyond either end of a row or off the top or bottom of the screen are ignored. For example, if a request to move the cursor down exceeds the number of rows between the one containing the cursor and the bottom row of the screen, the cursor is deposited on the bottom row. No scrolling occurs.

Device Status Report (DSR)   ESC[6n
Save Cursor Position (SCP)   ESC[s
Restore Cursor Position (RCP)   ESC[u

These three control sequences are designed to assist in cursor control. The first two determine where the cursor is located, and the third returns the cursor to a saved location. The DSR request causes the ANSI driver to place a string, in the form *ESC[#;#R* plus a trailing carriage return, into the keyboard buffer. The position parameters are stored as two-character representations of the numbers, so the string contains a total of nine characters. The *ansi_cpr( )* function described in the next section can be used to retrieve the row and column data.

The SCP/RCP pair of control sequences can be used to save a cursor position so that it can be restored after an intervening operation moves the cursor from the saved position. Only one position can be saved for subsequent restoration. If multiple calls are made to SCP, a call to RCP will restore the cursor position obtained by the most recent call to SCP.

Erase in Display (ED)   ESC[2J
Erase in Line (EL)   ESC[K

The ED control sequence erases the entire screen by displaying blanks in the prevailing video attribute (see SGR). The cursor is deposited at the upper left corner of the screen. EL erases the characters from the cursor position to the end of the current row. The "erased" positions are set to blanks in the prevailing attribute, and the cursor is left at its current position.

CAUTION

Some versions of the ANSI device driver provided with MS-DOS (for example, MS-DOS 2.11 for the AT&T PC6300) erase by setting characters to blanks in the normal (white on black) attribute rather than the attribute set by SGR.

Set Graphic Rendition (SGR)   ESC[#; . . . ;#m   A *graphic rendition* is the visual style of displaying a graphic symbol (number, letter, punctuation mark, and so forth), which in the IBM PC context translates into the attribute associated with a character. The ANSI driver uses the SGR control sequence to set the intensity, blink status, and color attributes of characters on a color adapter. On a monochrome system, SGR can be used to set intensity, blink status, and underlining. Some IBM-compatible machines (COMPAQ and AT&T are two examples) permit grey-scale settings on monochrome monitors in response to color attribute requests.

SGR can take a series of numeric parameters in a single call. The effect of a single call to SGR with multiple parameters is the same as that produced by a series of calls to SGR with one parameter per call, but the former will be faster because of reduced function-call overhead.

Set Mode (SM)   ESC[= #h
Reset Mode (RM)   ESC[= #l

The mode control sequences that are supported by the ANSI driver set the IBM PC and compatible hardware-dependent video modes for the color/graphics adapter and a "wrap-at-end-of-line" mode. The driver does not support switching to a monochrome adapter from a color/graphics adapter. Both SM and RM can be used to set a video mode with the parameters 0 through 6. Setting a different video mode clears the current mode. Using SM with a parameter of 7 enables wrap; RM given the same value disables wrap.

Pros and Cons of ANSI.SYS

The primary reasons for using the ANSI device driver are simplified programming and portability of programs to other versions of MS-DOS and PC-DOS and to the machines that run DOS. The amount of programming effort required to do many screen operations is reduced to simple calls to ANSI control sequences. Compare the short cursor-positioning macro shown in the next section to the BIOS-interrupt-based function presented in Chapter 5; both do the same job.

Unfortunately, some limitations of the ANSI driver make it unsuitable for many applications. For some purposes—full-screen text editing is a good example—it is simply too slow. In addition, ANSI.SYS implements only a very limited subset of ANSI X3.64. It has no concept of fields, protected display areas, display regions (useful for windowing), and many other important capabilities.

An ANSI Interface Package

In spite of its limitations, the ANSI driver has its place. It comprises a useful but limited subset of ANSI capabilities that can do a surprising amount of work. The interface to the ANSI driver described here uses mostly macros in a header file to accomplish the tasks of moving the cursor, finding its position, setting video attributes, clearing the display, and setting video modes. A few supporting C functions built on the ANSI driver take care of some higher level tasks, such as testing to see whether the driver is installed.

The macros and definitions of the video attributes and modes are contained in the header file *ansi.h*, which resides in the \include\local directory. You should #*include* the file in any C program or function that will need to access the keyboard or screen through the ANSI device driver.

```
/*
 *      ansi.h -- header file for ANSI driver information and
 *      macro versions of the ANSI control sequences
 */

/*****************/
/** ANSI macros **/
/*****************/

/* cursor position */
#define ANSI_CUP(r, c)  printf("\x1B[%d;%dH", r, c)
#define ANSI_HVP(r, c)  printf("\x1B[%d;%df", r, c)

/* cursor up, down, forward, back */
#define ANSI_CUU(n)     printf("\x1B[%dA", n)
#define ANSI_CUD(n)     printf("\x1B[%dB", n)
#define ANSI_CUF(n)     printf("\x1B[%dC", n)
#define ANSI_CUB(n)     printf("\x1B[%dD", n)
```

(continued)

```
/* device status report (dumps position data into keyboard buffer) */
#define ANSI_DSR        printf("\x1B[6n")

/* save and restore cursor position */
#define ANSI_SCP        fputs("\x1B[s", stdout)
#define ANSI_RCP        fputs("\x1B[u", stdout)

/* erase display and line */
#define ANSI_ED         fputs("\x1B[2J", stdout);
#define ANSI_EL         fputs("\x1B[K", stdout)

/* set graphic rendition */
#define ANSI_SGR(a)     printf("\x1B[%dm", a)

/* set and reset modes */
#define ANSI_SM(m)      printf("\x1B[=%dh", m)
#define ANSI_RM(m)      printf("\x1B[=%dl", m)


/*********************/
/** ANSI color codes **/
/*********************/

/* special settings */
#define ANSI_NORMAL     0
#define ANSI_BOLD       1
#define ANSI_BLINK      5
#define ANSI_REVERSE    7
#define ANSI_INVISIBLE  8

/* shift values */
#define ANSI_FOREGROUND 30
#define ANSI_BACKGROUND 40

/* basic colors */
#define ANSI_BLACK      0
#define ANSI_RED        1
#define ANSI_GREEN      2
#define ANSI_BROWN      3
#define ANSI_BLUE       4
#define ANSI_MAGENTA    5
#define ANSI_CYAN       6
#define ANSI_WHITE      7
```

(continued)

```
/*****************************/
/** modes for set and reset **/
/*****************************/

#define ANSI_M40        0
#define ANSI_C40        1
#define ANSI_M80        2
#define ANSI_C80        3
#define ANSI_C320       4
#define ANSI_M320       5
#define ANSI_M640       6
#define ANSI_WRAP       7

/* attribute "position" type */
typedef enum {
        FGND, BKGND, BDR
} POSITION;
```

ANSI color attributes follow a different sequence from the standard IBM attribute set. The *ansi.h* file contains definitions for the basic colors and "shift" values (offsets) for foreground and background attribute specifications. In addition, there are definitions for normal, bright, blink, reverse, and invisible attributes. The normal attribute effectively clears all other special attributes. Thus, to set the foreground to bright green, one uses the statements

```
ANSI_SGR(ANSI_GREEN + ANSI_FOREGROUND);
ANSI_SGR(ANSI_BRIGHT);
```

which will cause all subsequent characters sent to the screen to be displayed in the requested attribute until a new specification is given.

A *typedef* is used to create a *POSITION* data type that is used by some of the functions in the SetColor program to keep track of which color attribute position (foreground, background, or border) is being attended to in the processing of attribute specifications. Each position must be handled in its own special way, as we'll see shortly.

In addition to the macros defined in *ansi.h*, our interface employs several functions. The *ansi_cpr( )* function is used to request a *device status report* (*ANSI_DSR*) and then to read the cursor-position data stored in the keyboard buffer. The format of the response is a string of nine characters, starting with ESC and ending with a carriage return. This is called the *cursor position report*, hence the name *ansi_cpr( )* for the function.

The *ansi_cpr( )* function calls *getkey( )*, a DOS interrupt-based routine (INT 21H) that was defined in Chapter 5, to gather input from the keyboard buffer. Here is the code for *ansi_cpr( )*:

```
/*
 *      cpr -- report where the cursor is located
 *      The position information is placed in the keyboard buffer in the
 *      form ESC[rr;ccR, where ESC is the value of the ESCAPE character
 *      and r and c represent decimal values of row and column data.
 */

#include <local\ansi.h>

void ansi_cpr(row, col)
int     *row,
        *col;
{
        int i;

        /* request a cursor position report */
        ANSI_DSR;

        /* toss the ESC and '[' */
        (void) getkey();
        (void) getkey();

        /* read the row number */
        *row = 10 * (getkey() - '0');
        *row = *row + getkey() - '0';

        /* toss the ';' separator */
        (void) getkey();

        /* read the column number */
        *col = 10 * (getkey() - '0');
        *col = *col + getkey() - '0';

        /* toss the trailing ('R') and return */
        (void) getkey();
        (void) getkey();
        return;
}
```

Because the characters are placed in the buffer in a reasonable order, successive keyboard read calls can be used to gather and process the numeric values easily. We must read every character in the string, even though we're really interested in only four of them, so that no residue is left behind to befuddle other parts of our program's input processing. The formal parameters *row* and *col* are pointers to storage outside the function.

A character representation of the tens digit of a number (row or column) is obtained by a call to *getkey( )*. It is converted to its numeric representation by subtracting 0 (decimal 48) and then multiplying by ten (its numeric weight). The value is then added to the converted value of the next character obtained by *getkey( )*, which is the units digit, to produce the needed number in integer format.

We now have the ability to determine the cursor's position and to save it or pass the information on to other parts of our programs. But, if the ANSI device driver is not already loaded into memory, calling *ansi_cpr( )* will cause the computer to appear to lock up. We need to be sure the driver is installed before calling functions that depend on its presence. The function *ansi_tst( )* calls *ANSI_CUP*, which sets the cursor to a known location, and then calls our *bios* library function *readcur( )* to read the cursor location. If the row and column positions match, the driver is probably loaded. I say "probably" because the routine will falsely claim the driver is loaded if the cursor happens to be at the test location before the *ANSI_CUP* call. (However, this is not likely for the test values used.) To be certain, a series of two tests at differing locations could be used.

```
/*
 *      ansi_tst -- verify that the ANSI.SYS driver is loaded
 *      (prints message and exits if ANSI driver not working)
 */

#include <stdio.h>
#include <local\ansi.h>
#include <local\video.h>

#define TST_ROW 2
#define TST_COL 75
```

(continued)

```
void
ansi_tst()
{
        int row, col;
        static char *help[] = {
                "\n",
                "ANSI.SYS device driver not loaded:\n",
                " 1. Copy ANSI.SYS to your system disk.\n",
                " 2. Add the line device=ansi.sys to your\n",
                "    CONFIG.SYS file and reboot your machine.\n",
                NULL
        };
        char **msg;

        extern int getstate();
        extern int readcur(int *, int *, int);

        getstate();
        ANSI_CUP(TST_ROW, TST_COL);
        readcur(&row, &col, Vpage);
        if (row != TST_ROW - 1 || col != TST_COL - 1) {
                for (msg = help; *msg != NULL; ++msg)
                        fputs(*msg, stderr);
                exit(1);
        }

        return;
}
```

The code for *ansi_tst( )* aborts with an error message and instructions to the user about installing the ANSI driver. An alternative design might simply return a true/false response and let the program deal with the lack of a driver in some other way, such as switching to a mode of operation that does not depend on the ANSI driver being loaded. The file *ansi.mk* is the makefile to compile the separate components of the ANSI interface package.

```
# makefile for the ANSI library

LINC=c:\include\local
LLIB=c:\lib\local
```

(continued)

```
ansi_cpr.obj:   ansi_cpr.c $(LINC)\ansi.h
        msc $*;
        lib $(LLIB)\ansi -+$*;


ansi_tst.obj:   ansi_tst.c $(LINC)\ansi.h $(LINC)\video.h
        msc $*;
        lib $(LLIB)\ansi -+$*;
```

The SetColor Program

Now we'll do something useful with the ANSI interface. SetColor, invoked as *SC* to save keystrokes (in the UNIX tradition), is designed to be used with a computer that has a color display system. With minor modifications it can be used in a limited way with monochrome systems, too.

Figure 13-4 is the manual page for SetColor. The program sets foreground and background attributes via ANSI control sequences. The ANSI driver provides no way to control the border attribute, so we resort to a BIOS routine, *palette( )*, developed in Chapter 5, to do that job. The use of *palette( )* may make the program nonportable to some nominally IBM-compatible equipment.

NAME

SC—control video attributes

SYNOPSIS

sc [*attribute*]

sc [*foreground* [*background* [*border*]]]

DESCRIPTION

The SetColor program may be used in either batch mode or interactive mode to set the foreground, background, and border attributes of a color display system. The interactive mode, invoked by typing *SC* with no arguments, uses on-screen instructions to guide the user in selecting attributes via function keys. The display is updated with each keypress to reflect the current selections.

FIGURE 13-14 | *Manual page for SetColor*   *(continued)*

The attribute selections in batch mode can be formed from the following list of argument values. Only the first three letters are significant and case is not relevant.

Values For Attribute	Values For Foreground, Background and Border	
Normal	Black	Red
Reverse	Blue	Magenta
	Green	Brown
	Cyan	White

All color specifications can be modified by prefixing bold, bright, or light to obtain high-intensity values of the base color. Yellow may be used as a synonym for bold brown. If "blink" is enabled (the default), selecting a high-intensity background will cause the background to be a low-intensity color and the foreground will blink.

EXAMPLES

Run SetColor in the interactive mode:

sc

Request bright white on a blue background with a cyan border:

sc bold white blue cyan

Set up a reverse video screen:

sc reverse

NOTES

The ANSI.SYS device driver must be loaded into memory. This requires DOS version 2.00 or later and the line

device = ansi.sys

in the CONFIG.SYS file.

The border cannot be set on some machines, notably the AT&T PC6300. Also, the ANSI.SYS device driver supplied with MS-DOS version 2.11 erases to Normal attribute (white on black) regardless of the specified attribute. However, displayed characters written after the erasure will have the specified attributes.

FIGURE 13-14 | *continued*

The following pseudocode description of SetColor reveals that the program exhibits extreme schizophrenia. On the one hand, it operates in an interactive mode when invoked as *SC* without arguments. The user selects attributes by pressing function keys. Screen updates immediately show the user what the combined attribute selections look like. However, when called with attribute specifications as arguments, SetColor runs in batch mode. All attributes and intensity modifiers, if any, are taken from the command line. In this mode, SetColor can be used to control screen appearance from within DOS batch files.

```
if ANSI driver not loaded
        print message
        exit
if not in color text mode
        print message
        exit
if command-line argument given
        run in batch mode
else
        run in interactive (menu) mode
clear the screen
exit
```

The SetColor program consists of several functions, each packaged in its own file. Some of the functions have general applicability to other tasks and are, therefore, placed in local libraries.

Starting at the top, the source file *sc.c* contains the *main()* function. In *main()*, two tests are made that determine whether the SetColor program runs to completion or quits early. The first test, *ansi_tst()*, checks to see that the ANSI device driver is installed. If not, the program terminates. If the driver is installed, the second function, *iscolor()*, finds out what video mode is in use. Rather than do anything fancy at this point, we opt to simply terminate program execution with a help message if the mode is not a standard color-text mode. The user's selection of batch or interactive operation, based upon the presence or absence of command-line arguments, is also detected here.

```
/*
 * SetColor (sc) -- set foreground, background, and border attributes
 *               on systems equipped with color display systems
 *
 * Usage:        sc [foreground [background [border]]]
 *               sc [attribute]
 */

#include <stdio.h>
#include <dos.h>
#include <local\std.h>
#include <local\ansi.h>
#include <local\ibmcolor.h>

main(argc, argv)
int argc;
char *argv[];
{
        void ansi_tst();
        BOOLEAN iscolor();
        extern void setattr();
        extern void menumode();

        ansi_tst();
        if (iscolor() == FALSE) {
                fprintf(stderr, "\n\nSystem not in a color text mode.\n");
                fprintf(stderr, "Use the MODE command to set the mode.\n");
                exit(2);
        }

        /* process either batch or interactive commands */
        if (argc > 1)
                /* batch mode processing */
                parse(argc, argv);
        else
                /* no command-line args -- interactive mode */
                menumode();

        ANSI_ED;
        exit (0);
} /* end main() */
```

(continued)

```
/*
 *        iscolor -- return TRUE if a color display system is
 *        in use and is set to one of the text modes
 */

#include <local\std.h>
#include <local\video.h>

BOOLEAN
iscolor()
{
        getstate();
        if (Vmode == CGA_C40) || Vmode == CGA_C80)
                return TRUE;
        return FALSE;
}
```

If attribute arguments are given, the function *parse( )* is called with the argument list obtained by *main( )*. The job of *parse( )* is to analyze each argument and form attribute or color specifications that can be processed by the low-level ANSI interface functions. If no arguments are given, the *menumode( )* function is called. Let's first examine the batch processing functions.

Batch Mode

If *parse( )* receives a single attribute specification, it checks to see whether it is one of the special attributes (normal, reverse, invisible, or blink). None of these takes an optional intensity modifier, and each can be handled easily by a single call to *ANSI_SGR*. If the lone argument is not one of these special attributes or if there are two or more arguments, *parse( )* falls through to a loop that analyzes each argument in turn and creates attribute specifications in a form suitable for processing by the ANSI interface functions.

```
/*
 *        parse -- process a list of attribute specifications
 */
```

(continued)

```
#include <stdio.h>
#include <local\ansi.h>
#include <local\std.h>
#include <local\ibmcolor.h>

/* buffer length for string comparisons */
#define NCHARS  3
#define C_MASK  0x7

void parse(nargs, argvec)
int nargs;      /* number of argument vectors */
char *argvec[]; /* pointer to the argument vector array */
{
        int i, intensity;
        int attribute;
        POSITION pos;
        char str[NCHARS + 1];
        extern int colornum();
        extern void setattr();

        /* clear all attributes */
        ANSI_SGR(ANSI_NORMAL);

        /* look for a single attribute specification */
        if (nargs == 2) {
                attribute = colornum(argvec[1]);
                switch (attribute) {
                case IBM_NORMAL:
                        palette(0, IBM_BLACK);
                        return;
                case IBM_REVERSE:
                        ANSI_SGR(ANSI_REVERSE);
                        palette(0, IBM_WHITE);
                        return;
                case IBM_INVISIBLE:
                        ANSI_SGR(ANSI_INVISIBLE);
                        return;
                case IBM_BLINK:
                        ANSI_SGR(ANSI_BLINK);
                        return;
                }
        }
```

(continued)

```
        /* must be separate attribute specifications */
        pos = FGND;
        intensity = 0;
        for (i = 1; i < nargs; ++i) {
                attribute = colornum(argvec[i]);
                if (attribute == -1) {
                        ANSI_ED;
                        fprintf(stderr, "\nIllegal parameter\n");
                        exit (2);
                }
                if (attribute == IBM_BRIGHT) {
                        intensity = IBM_BRIGHT;
                        continue;
                }
                setattr(pos, attribute | intensity);
                if (pos == FGND)
                        pos = BKGND;
                else if (pos == BKGND)
                        pos = BDR;
                intensity = 0;
        }
        return;
}
```

The basic problem we face is receiving color/attribute specifications as text strings and converting them to numbers. We will also need to account for the differences between the standard IBM attribute numbers and the ANSI attribute numbers described earlier. The IBM attribute numbers are defined in the header file *ibmcolor.h*, which resides in the *include**local* directory.

```
/*
 *      ibmcolor.h
 */

/* basic IBM color codes */
#define IBM_BLACK       0
#define IBM_BLUE        1
#define IBM_GREEN       2
#define IBM_CYAN        3
#define IBM_RED         4
```

(continued)

```
#define IBM_MAGENTA     5
#define IBM_BROWN       6
#define IBM_WHITE       7

/* color modifiers */
#define IBM_BRIGHT      8
#define IBM_BLINK       16

/* special attribute codes */
#define IBM_NORMAL      7
#define IBM_REVERSE     112
#define IBM_INVISIBLE   128
```

The *colornum( )* function converts text strings into these IBM color/ attribute numbers. Given the string *green* as an argument, for example, *colornum( )* returns the defined value *IBM_GREEN*, which is the number 2. Two synonyms for bright (bold and light) are allowed, and yellow is treated as a synonym for bright brown. The following is the source code for *colornum( )* :

```
/*
 *      colornum -- return the IBM number for the color
 *      presented as a string; return -1 if no match.
 */

#include <stdio.h>
#include <string.h>
#include <local\ibmcolor.h>

#define NCHARS  3

int colornum(name)
char *name;
{
        int n;
        static struct color_st {
                char *c_name;
                int c_num;
        } colortab[] = {
                "black",        IBM_BLACK,
                "blue",         IBM_BLUE,
```

(continued)

```
                    "green",        IBM_GREEN,
                    "cyan",         IBM_CYAN,
                    "red",          IBM_RED,
                    "magenta",      IBM_MAGENTA,
                    "brown",        IBM_BROWN,
                    "white",        IBM_WHITE,
                    "normal",       IBM_NORMAL,
                    "bright",       IBM_BRIGHT,
                    "light",        IBM_BRIGHT,
                    "bold",         IBM_BRIGHT,
                    "yellow",       IBM_BROWN + IBM_BRIGHT,
                    "blink",        IBM_BLINK,
                    "reverse",      IBM_REVERSE,
                    "invisible",    IBM_INVISIBLE,
                    NULL,           (-1)
        };

        (void) strlwr(name);
        for (n = 0; colortab[n].c_name != NULL; ++n)
                if ((strncmp(name, colortab[n].c_name, NCHARS)) == 0)
                        return (colortab[n].c_num);
        return (-1);
}
```

The function uses a simple sequential search through a table of string/number pairs that compares the first three letters of the string argument with the table entries. The *strlwr( )* standard library function converts the incoming argument to lowercase before any comparisons are made. Its return type is cast to *void* because the pointer to a character is not used. If no matching string is found, *colornum( )* complains by returning −1 instead of a valid color number.

A color number thus produced may be passed as an argument to *setattr( )*, which takes a position indicator and an attribute value as input. It outputs an ANSI control sequence by applying the *ANSI_SGR* macro to a properly converted attribute number. The process sounds more confusing than it really is. First, the code for *setattr( )*:

```
/*
 *      setattr -- execute an attribute update
 */

#include <stdio.h>
#include <local\ansi.h>
#include <local\ibmcolor.h>

#define C_MASK  0x7

void setattr(pos, attr)
POSITION pos;    /* attribute position */
int attr;        /* composite attribute number (base attr | intensity) */
{
        static int ibm2ansi[] = {
                ANSI_BLACK, ANSI_BLUE, ANSI_GREEN, ANSI_CYAN,
                ANSI_RED, ANSI_MAGENTA, ANSI_BROWN, ANSI_WHITE
        };

        switch (pos) {
        case FGND:
                if (attr & IBM_BRIGHT)
                        ANSI_SGR(ANSI_BOLD);
                ANSI_SGR(ibm2ansi[attr & C_MASK] + ANSI_FOREGROUND);
                break;
        case BKGND:
                if (attr & IBM_BRIGHT)
                        ANSI_SGR(ANSI_BLINK);
                ANSI_SGR(ibm2ansi[attr & C_MASK] + ANSI_BACKGROUND);
                break;
        case BDR:
                palette(0, attr);
                break;
        }
        return;
}
```

The *pos* argument has type *POSITION* (defined in the *ansi.h* header file), and it tells *setattr( )* which rules to apply to the *attr* argument. The attribute argument contains two kinds of information lumped together: The low three bits (0–2) represent the base color or video attribute, and bit 3 indicates the intensity.

An intensity modifier is treated differently when it is applied to a foreground attribute than when it is applied to a background attribute. In the foreground case, bit 3 of the intensity modifier sets the foreground intensity bit in the attribute byte (bit 3). In the background case, it sets the blink bit (bit 7). If blinking is enabled (the default), setting the blink bit causes the foreground to blink and does not change the background intensity, resulting in a useful range of eight background colors. If blinking is disabled, setting the blink bit causes the background intensity to be bright. The full range of 16 background colors can be obtained with blinking disabled. The *setattr( )* function calls *ANSI_SGR* once if *attr* is for normal intensity or twice for high intensity.

A table of foreground and background attribute values in the array *ibm2ansi[ ]* contains the conversions from IBM attributes — represented by the index into the array — to the ANSI values needed by *ANSI_SGR*. Thus, the expression *ibm2ansi[IBM_BLUE]*, where *IBM_BLUE* is defined in *ibmcolor.h* as the number 1, yields the value represented by *ANSI_BLUE*, which is defined in *ansi.h* as the number 4.

The border, on display systems that support it, can be set to any of 16 colors by using *palette( )*. There is no need to separate the intensity information from the rest of the attribute when setting the border because *palette( )* is a BIOS-based function and uses the IBM attribute values directly.

That explains batch-mode processing. The other processing path that can be taken from *main( )* is interactive mode, which is handled by *menumode( )*. The *menumode( )* function calls upon *palette( )*, *setattr( )*, *getkey( )*, and a new function, *sc_cmds( )*, to do the bulk of the work.

Interactive Mode

In interactive mode, attributes are selected by pressing function keys. F1 decrements the foreground color and F2 increments it. The color values wrap around at the boundaries; therefore, a request to increment *foreground = 15* (white) produces *foreground = 0* (black). Similarly, the F3/F4 pair of function keys are used to select the background attribute, and the F5/F6 pair cycle through border attributes.

The *mainmenu( )* function returns control to DOS when the Return key is pressed, leaving the screen cleared to the most recently selected attribute combination.

```
/*
 * menumode -- process user commands interactively
 */

#include <stdio.h>
#include <local\ansi.h>
#include <local\ibmcolor.h>
#include <local\keydefs.h>

/* maximum color number */
#define MAX_CNUM        15

void menumode()
{
        int ch;
        int foreground, background, border;
        extern void setattr();
        extern void sc_cmds();

        /* default attributes */
        foreground = IBM_WHITE;
        background = IBM_BLACK;
        border = IBM_BLACK;

        ANSI_SGR(ANSI_NORMAL);
        setattr(FGND, foreground);
        setattr(BKGND, background);
        ANSI_ED;
        palette(0, border);
        sc_cmds(foreground, background, border);
        while ((ch = getkey()) != K_RETURN) {
                switch (ch) {
                case K_F1:
                        /* decrement foreground color */
                        if (--foreground < 0)
                                foreground = MAX_CNUM;
                        break;
```

(continued)

```
            case K_F2:
                    /* increment foreground color */
                    if (++foreground > MAX_CNUM)
                            foreground = 0;
                    break;
            case K_F3:
                    /* decrement background color */
                    if (--background < 0)
                            background = MAX_CNUM;
                    break;
            case K_F4:
                    /* increment background color */
                    if (++background > MAX_CNUM)
                            background = 0;
                    break;
            case K_F5:
                    /* decrement border color */
                    if (--border < 0)
                            border = MAX_CNUM;
                    break;
            case K_F6:
                    /* increment border color number */
                    if (++border > MAX_CNUM)
                            border = 0;
                    break;
            default:
                    continue;
            }
            ANSI_SGR(ANSI_NORMAL);
            setattr(FGND, foreground);
            setattr(BKGND, background);
            palette(0, border);
            ANSI_ED;
            sc_cmds(foreground, background, border);
        }
    return;
}
```

Because the color/attribute specifications are presented in interactive mode as numbers rather than as text strings, *setattr( )* can process them directly. The process of updating the screen after each set of calls to *setattr( )* means that the list of commands and the current status information must be rewritten following each keypress that affects the foreground or background color. This is done by the function *sc_cmds( )*, which contains a static array that converts IBM color numbers into text strings suitable for humans. All cursor positioning is done via the *ANSI_CUP* macro. Text strings are written to the display by the standard library function *fputs( )*, which is directed to send its output to *stdout*.

```
/*
 *      sc_cmds -- display command summary
 */

#include <stdio.h>
#include <local\ansi.h>

void sc_cmds(fg, bkg, bdr)
int fg, bkg, bdr;
{
        static char *color_xlat[] = {
                "Black (0)", "Blue (1)", "Green (2)", "Cyan (3)",
                "Red (4)", "Magenta (5)", "Brown (6)", "White (7)",
                "Grey (8)", "Light blue (9)", "Light green (10)",
                "Light cyan (11)", "Light red (12)", "Light magenta (13)",
                "Yellow (14)", "Bright white (15)"
        };

        ANSI_CUP(2, 29);
        fputs("*** SetColor (SC) ***", stdout);
        ANSI_CUP(4, 17);
        fputs("Attribute  Decrement  Increment  Current Value", stdout);
        ANSI_CUP(5, 17);
        fputs("---------  ---------  ---------  -------------", stdout);
        ANSI_CUP(6, 17);
        fputs("Foreground    F1         F2", stdout);
        ANSI_CUP(7, 17);
        fputs("Background    F3         F4", stdout);
        ANSI_CUP(8, 17);
        fputs("Border        F5         F6", stdout);
        ANSI_CUP(6, 50);
        fputs(color_xlat[fg], stdout);
        ANSI_CUP(7, 50);
```

(continued)

```
        fputs(color_xlat[bkg], stdout);
        ANSI_CUP(8, 50);
        fputs(color_xlat[bdr], stdout);
        ANSI_CUP(10, 17);
        fputs("Type RETURN to exit. SetColor/Version 2.2", stdout);
        return;
} /* end sc_cmds() */
```

The file *sc.mk* is the makefile for SetColor. It collects several of the
interface functions into a special-purpose library, *color.lib*. This is done to
minimize the number of items that must be specified on the dependency
and link lines that create SC.EXE and keep it up-to-date. A linker-response
file could be used to achieve the same result. To rebuild the SetColor program after any changes are made to its source files or libraries, type

```
make sc.mk
```

```
# makefile for the SC program

LINC=c:\include\local
LLIB=c:\lib\local

iscolor.obj:    iscolor.c
        msc $*;
        lib $(LLIB)\util -+$*;

colornum.obj:   colornum.c $(LINC)\ansi.h $(LINC)\ibmcolor.h
        msc $*;
        lib color -+$*;

sc_cmds.obj:    sc_cmds.c $(LINC)\ansi.h
        msc $*;
        lib color -+$*;

menumode.obj:   menumode.c $(LINC)\ansi.h $(LINC)\ibmcolor.h $(LINC)\keydefs.h
        msc $*;
        lib color -+$*;

parse.obj:      parse.c $(LINC)\ansi.h $(LINC)\ibmcolor.h
        msc $*;
        lib color -+$*;
```

(continued)

```
setattr.obj:    setattr.c $(LINC)\ansi.h $(LINC)\ibmcolor.h
      msc $*;
      lib color -+$*;

sc.obj: sc.c $(LINC)\ansi.h $(LINC)\ibmcolor.h $(LINC)\keydefs.h
      msc $*;

sc.exe: sc.obj color.lib $(LLIB)\ansi.lib $(LLIB)\util.lib
      link $*, $*, nul, color $(LLIB)\ansi $(LLIB)\util $(LLIB)\bios $(LLIB)\dos;
```

Using SetColor

Aside from being a good demonstration of the ANSI device-driver interface, SetColor is a useful program. I use it most frequently in batch files to restore the screen to match my peculiar tastes after some other program has made a mess of things. Most programs, especially those that do full-screen operations, have built-in default settings for video attributes. These programs have no idea what attributes were in use before they were run; therefore, when they exit, they either leave the attributes as they are when the program terminates or set them to white on black.

It would be better to have the colors set to the user's preferences, if possible. This can be achieved in a couple of ways. The first way uses a DOS batch file to intercept the call to a program. The batch file calls the real program and then calls SetColor to make things right again. For example, assume the program in BADPROG.EXE does bad things to the screen when it exits. A batch file called BADPROG.BAT with the lines

```
badprog.exe
sc white blue blue
```

will clear the screen and set the foreground to white on a field of blue when the program returns to DOS.

This can be generalized further by the use of DOS environment variables. If environment variables having the names *FGND*, *BKGND*, and *BORDER* are defined, the batch file can access the values and control the SetColor program automatically. DOS variable values are obtained in batch files by surrounding each variable name with percent signs. The revised batch file looks like this:

```
badprog.exe
sc %fgnd% %bkgnd% %border%
```

Of course, SetColor may be called from the DOS command line with literal attribute specifications. I sometimes change the attributes just to minimize eyestrain during long programming and writing sessions. It's remarkable what a good effect a simple change in screen colors can have (unless it's to something like magenta on red!).

A User-Attribute Function

Here's a way for programmers to be kind to those who will be using their programs. The function *userattr( )* that follows can be used in programs to restore the user's attribute preferences just before the return to DOS. It gets values directly from the DOS environment, just as the batch file in the previous section does. If no attribute variables are defined, *userattr( )* uses some reasonable defaults as parameters. The *userattr( )* function calls on *colornum( )* and *setattr( )* and uses the standard library functions *getenv( )* and *strtok( )* to look for user preferences and parse them into recognizable values.

```
/*
 *      userattr -- set video attributes to user-specified values
 *      (DOS environment parameters) or to reasonable defaults and
 *      return success or a failure indication for bad attributes
 */

#include <stdio.h>
#include <stdlib.h>
#include <string.h>
#include <local\std.h>
#include <local\ansi.h>
#include <local\ibmcolor.h>

int userattr(foreground, background, border)
char *foreground, *background, *border;
{
        char *s;
        static int attrset();

        if ((s = getenv("FGND")) == NULL)
                s = foreground;
```

(continued)

```
        if (attrset(FGND, s) == -1)
                return FAILURE;

        if ((s = getenv("BKGND")) == NULL)
                s = background;
        if (attrset(BKGND, s) == -1)
                return FAILURE;

        if ((s = getenv("BORDER")) == NULL)
                s = border;
        if (attrset(BDR, s) == -1)
                return FAILURE;

        return SUCCESS;
}

/*
 *      attrset -- parse the color spec and try to set it.
 *      return 0 if OK and -1 upon error (bad color number)
 */
static int attrset(apos, str)
POSITION apos;
char *str;
{
        int attr;
        extern int colornum();
        extern void setattr();

        if ((attr = colornum(strtok(str, " \t"))) == IBM_BRIGHT)
                attr |= colornum(strtok(NULL, " \t"));
        if (attr >= 0)
                setattr(apos, attr);
        else
                return (-1);
        return (0);
}
```

The processing of the strings by *strtok( )* is necessary because the attribute specifications may contain an intensity modifier. The *strtok( )* function returns a pointer to a null-terminated string token taken from its first string argument; if no tokens are found, it returns *NULL*. Acceptable token separators are spaces and tabs, in any combination. Subsequent calls to *strtok( )* use *NULL* as the first argument to request further searching in the string given in argument one of the first call. If the first call to *strtok( )* retrieves an intensity modifier, a second call is made to *strtok( )* on the same string to get the second token, which should be a valid attribute specifier. Error-checking code prevents bad attribute names from causing problems.

The next time someone tells you the ANSI.SYS device driver is a worthless piece of software, you can show them how useful it really is!

As a fitting end to this development session, *echo ESC[2J* (look it up).

Viewing Files 14

The next program to be added to our kit of tools is a file viewer. ViewFile, called VF by its close friends and associates, is such a tool.

The design for VF has two objectives: to obtain a convenient window into a file that permits us to look at the file without harming it and to experiment with some programming techniques that we can apply to other tasks. We will apply the linked-list techniques to the management of an in-memory text buffer. In addition, we will use the standard library function *strncmp( )* to implement a simple but fast search capability.

Some trade-offs made in VF's design are noteworthy. First, we sacrifice loading speed to obtain very quick response to user commands. By using an internal buffer, instead of buffering to disk, we provide speedy response to positioning requests but limit files to a size determined by the available memory of the host machine. Fortunately, most PCs these days have lots of memory. Second, VF uses some of the BIOS routines described in Chapter 5 to handle display interactions. It does not use the buffered screen interface described in Chapters 11 and 12. Even so, the display updates are tolerably quick, taking about a second or less for most operations on a standard PC for a typical file.

ViewFile (VF) Features

The features of ViewFile are summarized in the manual page below (Figure 14-1).

NAME

> VF—a full-screen file-viewing program

SYNOPSIS

> vf [-n] file . . .

DESCRIPTION

> ViewFile is a file-viewing program that features fast vertical and horizontal scrolling through any text file. VF uses the PC arrow and special-purpose keys to move around quickly and easily in a file. Most commands have single-letter synonyms.
>
> Absolute go-to-line and search-for-string commands may also be used to seek a position in the file being viewed. Line-numbering is optional; it can be turned on from the command line by using the -n option. Numbering can also be toggled on and off while VF is running by using the N key.
>
> The following commands (and synonyms) are understood by VF:

COMMAND	MEANING
PgUp (U)	Scroll up the file one screen page
PgDn (D)	Scroll down the file one screen page
Up arrow (−)	Scroll up in the file one line
Down arrow (+)	Scroll down in the file one line
Right arrow (>)	Scroll right by 20 columns
Left arrow (<)	Scroll left by 20 columns
Home (B)	Go to beginning of file buffer
End (E)	Go to end of file buffer
Alt-g (G)	Go to a specified line in the buffer
Alt-h (H or ?)	Display the help frame
Alt-n (N)	Toggle line-numbering feature
\ (R)	Reverse search for a literal string
/ (S)	Search forward for a literal string
Esc	Next file from list (quits if none)
Alt-q (Q)	Quit

> This information is also available on-line in the built-in ViewFile help frame.

FIGURE 14-1 | *Manual page for ViewFile* *(continued)*

EXAMPLES

"View" sequentially all of the C source files in the current
directory:

vf -n *.c

FIGURE 14-1 | *continued*

In addition to offering vertical scrolling by screen pages, VF provides
convenient horizontal scrolling as a way of dealing with long lines. VF
accepts lines up to MAXLINE characters (defined as 256 in our *std.h* header
file) including the null-byte terminator. You can make this value larger if
you wish. The horizontal scrolling feature lets you move right and left, 20
columns at a time. The horizontal offset is maintained when vertical
movements are made.

If a list of files is presented to VF, the program will view the files sequentially. Pressing the Escape key tells VF to read the next file in the list,
if any. To quit without viewing any remaining files in the list, type Q
instead. DOS wildcards may be used to specify ambiguous file names.
Therefore, the command

vf \src*.h

forms a list consisting of all header files in the \src directory on the current disk drive. VF then reads in the first matching file and displays the
first screen page of its contents.

The forward and reverse search feature looks through each line in
the buffer for a literal string. VF searches around the end of the buffer,
stopping at the first line that contains a match, or returning to the current
line if no match is found. Searches in either direction may be repeated by
pressing a carriage return in response to the "Search for:" prompt.

VF has a built-in help "frame." When a user types a question mark,
Alt-h, or H, VF overlays the help frame on the text-display area. The next
keypress restores the covered text. Although it is only a brief memory-
jogger, the help frame contains all the information needed to use VF
successfully.

VF should be compiled using the *compact* memory model so that
it can handle large files. Compact model programs are distinguished by

small code space (less than 64 KB) and large data space (whatever available memory permits). Files that exceed the capacity of VF produce the message "File too big to load." To use the compact memory model, you will have to create compact-model versions of the *bios, dos,* and *util* libraries by recompiling all functions with the -AC option. It is probably best to follow the pattern established by Microsoft of having separate library files for each version of a given library. Thus, for example, we might have the files *bios.lib, cbios.lib, lbios.lib,* and so on. The linker gets clues from the object files, so it will use the correct versions of the standard libraries. The makefile, *vf.mk,* contains the instructions required by MAKE. The library of object modules used to construct VF is maintained by *vf.mk,* which enables us to bypass the command-line length limitation imposed by DOS.

```
# makefile for the ViewFile (VF) program
# (compile using "compact" memory model)

LIB = c:\lib
LLIB = c:\lib\local
OBJS = vf_list.obj vf_dspy.obj vf_srch.obj vf_util.obj vf_cmd.obj \
        message.obj getstr.obj

vf_list.obj:    vf_list.c vf.h

vf_dspy.obj:    vf_dspy.c vf.h

vf_srch.obj:    vf_srch.c vf.h

vf_util.obj:    vf_util.c vf.h

vf_cmd.obj:     vf_cmd.c vf.h

getstr.obj:     getstr.c

message.obj:    message.c message.h

cvf.lib:                $(OBJS)
        del cvf.lib
        lib cvf +$(OBJS);
```

(continued)

```
vf.obj: vf.c

vf.exe: vf.obj cvf.lib $(LLIB)\cutil.lib $(LLIB)\cdos.lib $(LLIB)\cbios.lib
        link $* $(LIB)\csetargv, $*, NUL, cvf $(LLIB)\cutil $(LLIB)\cdos \
        $(LLIB)\cbios;
```

The initialization file *tools.ini* in the VF directory instructs MAKE to verify the number and types of function arguments and to use the compact memory model. Renaming or deleting this file causes the default small-model *tools.ini* file to be read for inference rules.

```
# inference rules for VF program make
# enable argument checking and compact memory model

[make]
.c.obj:
        msc -DLINT_ARGS -AC $*;
```

Implementation Details

VF is a modest-sized program. Some of its general-purpose functions are available to other programs.

VF uses an in-memory text buffer. The decision to use an in-memory buffer has a profound impact on how a few of the functions are designed, but virtually no impact on the rest. We should try to keep the number of functions that actually know how the text is stored to a minimum; this permits us to apply them to a wider range of problems. The functions in the message module *message.c*, for example, don't know anything about the text buffer. Therefore, these message functions can be used unchanged in any program that uses the BIOS video routines.

The functions in *vf.c* are also ignorant of the buffer mechanism. The *main( )* function does the customary work of preserving the user's preferences for display type, video attributes, and cursor type. It also aborts the program if the operating environment is a DOS version earlier than 2.00, because VF is designed to accept pathnames in file specifications.

The *main( )* function also clears the screen and sets up the basic display appearance for the VF session. All program and status information, user input, and feedback messages are confined to the top two lines of the screen. The remaining 23 lines are used to display text and optional file-relative line numbers. When help is requested, the help frame is temporarily overlaid on a rectangular portion of the text display area.

Because the cursor is turned off by VF (except during user input operations), it is necessary to restore its shape when the program ends. The *clean( )* function in *vf.c* is called when the program terminates normally or when some condition (out of memory, for example) causes an abnormal termination. The user's original video attribute selection is restored by *clean( )*, and the cursor is then sent to the home position.

```
/*
 *      vf -- view a file using a full-screen window onto
 *      an in-memory text file buffer
 */

#include <stdio.h>
#include <stdlib.h>
#include <string.h>
#include <local\std.h>
#include <local\video.h>
#include "vf.h"

extern int setctype(int, int);
int Startscan, Endscan; /* cursor scan line range */
unsigned char Attr;      /* primary display attribute */
unsigned char Revattr;  /* reverse video for highlighting */
unsigned char Usrattr;  /* user's original attribute */

main(argc, argv)
int argc;
char **argv;
{
        int ch;
        static char pgm[MAXNAME + 1] = { "vf" };
        BOOLEAN errflag;
        BOOLEAN numbers;
```

(continued)

```
        int errcode;
        FILE *fp;
        extern char *optarg;
        extern int optind;

        void clean();

        /* external function prototypes */
        extern void getpname(char *, char *);
        extern void fixtabs(int);
        extern void initmsg(int, int, int, unsigned char, int);
        extern int getopt(int, char **, char *);
        extern int vf_cmd(FILE *, char *, BOOLEAN);
        extern int getctype(int *, int *, int);

        errcode = 0;
        getstate();
        fixtabs(TABWIDTH);

        /* get program name from DOS (version 3.00 and later) */
        if (_osmajor >= 3)
                getpname(*argv, pgm);

        /* be sure we have needed DOS support */
        if (_osmajor < 2) {
                fprintf(stderr, "%s requires DOS 2.00 or later\n", pgm);
                exit(1);
        }

        /* process optional arguments first */
        errflag = numbers = FALSE;
        while ((ch = getopt(argc, argv, "n")) != EOF)
                switch (ch) {
                case 'n':
                        /* turn on line-numbering */
                        numbers = TRUE;
                        break;
                case '?':
                        /* bad option */
                        errflag = TRUE;
                        break;
                }
```

(continued)

```
/* check for command-line errors */
argc -= optind;
argv += optind;
if (errflag == TRUE || argc == 0) {
        fprintf(stderr, "Usage: %s [-n] file...\n", pgm);
        exit(1);
}

/* get current video attribute and set VF attributes */
getstate();
readca(&ch, &Usrattr, Vpage);       /* save user's attribute settings */
Attr = (BLU << 4) | CYAN;           /* basic text attributes */
Revattr = (CYAN << 4) | BLK;        /* reverse video for highlighting */
clrscrn(Attr);

/* save user's cursor shape */
getctype(&Startscan, &Endscan, Vpage);
setctype(MAXSCAN, MAXSCAN);

/* set up the message line manager */
initmsg(MSGROW, MSGCOL, Maxcol[Vmode] - MSGCOL, Attr, Vpage);

/* display first screen page */
putcur(0, 0, Vpage);
putstr("ViewFile/1.0  H=Help Q=Quit Esc=Next", Vpage);
putcur(1, 0, Vpage);
writea(Revattr, Maxcol[Vmode], Vpage);

for (; argc-- > 0; ++argv) {
        if ((fp = fopen(*argv, "r")) == NULL) {
                fprintf(stderr, "%s: cannot open %s -- ", pgm, *argv);
                perror("");
                ++errcode;
                continue;
        }
        if (vf_cmd(fp, *argv, numbers) != 0)
                break;
}
clean();
exit(errcode);
}
```

(continued)

```
/*
 *      clean -- restore the user's original conditions
 */

void
clean()
{
        /* set screen to user's attribute */
        clrscrn(Attr);
        putcur(0, 0, Vpage);

        /* restore user's cursor shape */
        setctype(Startscan, Endscan);
}
```

A set of manifest constants that controls placement of visual elements of the VF display, search direction, and the data structure that defines the text buffer are contained in *vf.h*. The buffer data structure and its application will be described in detail later. The constants determine where the program name and messages to the user appear, which screen line is the "header" row, and how many screen rows of text display and scrolling overlap are to be used. To simplify VF a bit, we do not add automatic configuration to the program. The information and samples in Chapters 7 and 9 give detailed information about configuring programs.

```
/*
 *      vf.h -- header for ViewFile program
 */

#define OVERLAP        2
#define MAXSTR         40
#define MSGROW         0
#define MSGCOL         40
#define HEADROW        1
#define TOPROW         2
#define NROWS          23
#define SHIFTWIDTH     20
#define N_NODES        256
#define TABWIDTH       8
#define MAXSCAN        14
```

(continued)

```
typedef enum {
        FORWARD, BACKWARD
} DIRECTION;

/* doubly-linked list structure */
typedef struct dnode_st {
        struct dnode_st *d_next;
        struct dnode_st *d_prev;
        unsigned int d_lnum;    /* file-relative line number */
        unsigned short d_flags; /* miscellaneous line flags */
        char *d_line;           /* pointer to text buffer */
} DNODE;


/* line flags */
#define STANDOUT        0x1
```

For each file named on the command line (either literally or ambiguously), *main( )* calls *vf_cmd( )*, the ViewFile command module. The *vf_cmd.c* file, which contains the source for *vf_cmd( )* and for the auxiliary function *prtshift( )*, is a large file but it does only a few jobs—all related to controlling and accessing the text buffer. Chief among these jobs is setting up the text buffer for the file that is about to be read. Another major job is handled by the big switch statement within the *while* loop in *vf_cmd( )*, which accepts keypresses as commands. Simple positioning commands are handled directly by *vf_cmd( )*. Commands that require user input are handled by separate functions.

```
/*
 *      vf_cmd -- ViewFile command processor
 */

#include <stdio.h>
#include <stdlib.h>
#include <string.h>
#include <ctype.h>
#include <local\std.h>
#include <local\keydefs.h>
#include <local\video.h>
#include "vf.h"
#include "message.h"
```

(continued)

```
extern unsigned char Attr;

int
vf_cmd(fp, fname, numbers)
FILE *fp;
char *fname;
BOOLEAN numbers;
{
        register int i;            /* general index */
        unsigned int offset;       /* horizontal scroll offset */
        unsigned int n;            /* relative line number */
        int memerr;                /* flag for memory allocation errors */
        char *s, lbuf[MAXLINE];    /* input line buffer and pointer */
        int k;                     /* key code (see keydefs.h) */
        int radix = 10;            /* base for number-to-character conversions */
        char number[17];           /* buffer for conversions */
        int errcount = 0;          /* error counter */
        DNODE *tmp;                /* pointer to buffer control nodes */
        DIRECTION srchdir;         /* search direction */
        char *ss;                  /* pointer to search string */
        static char srchstr[MAXSTR] = { "" };   /* search string buffer */
        DNODE *head;               /* pointer to starting node of text buffer list */
        DNODE *current;            /* pointer to the current node (text line) */
        static DNODE *freelist;    /* pointer to starting node of "free" list */
                                   /* initialized to 0 at runtime; retains value */


        /* function prototypes */
        static void prtshift(int, int);
        extern DNODE *vf_mklst();
        extern DNODE *vf_alloc(int);
        extern DNODE *vf_ins(DNODE *, DNODE *);
        extern DNODE *vf_del(DNODE *, DNODE *);
        extern DNODE *search(DNODE *, DIRECTION, char *);
        extern DNODE *gotoln(DNODE *);
        extern char *getxline(char *, int, FILE *);
        extern char *getsstr(char *);
        extern int clrscrn(unsigned char);
        extern void showhelp(unsigned char);
        extern void clrmsg();
        extern void vf_dspy(DNODE *, DNODE *, int, BOOLEAN);
        extern int putstr(char *, int);
        extern int writec(char, int, int);
        extern char *nlerase(char *);
```

(continued)

```
/* display the file name */
offset = 0;
putcur(HEADROW, 0, Vpage);
writec(' ', Maxcol[Vmode], Vpage);
putstr("File: ", Vpage);
putstr(fname, Vpage);

/* establish the text buffer */
memerr = 0;
if ((head = vf_mklst()) == NULL)
        ++memerr;
if (freelist == NULL && (freelist = vf_alloc(N_NODES)) == NULL)
        ++memerr;
if (memerr) {
        clean();
        fprintf(stderr, "Memory allocation error\n");
        exit(1);
}

/* read the file into the buffer */
current = head;
n = 0;
while ((s = getxline(lbuf, MAXLINE, fp)) != NULL) {
        /* add a node to the list */
        if ((freelist = vf_ins(current, freelist)) == NULL)
                ++memerr;
        current = current->d_next;

        /* save the received text in a line buffer */
        if ((current->d_line = strdup(nlerase(s))) == NULL)
                ++memerr;
        if (memerr) {
                clean();
                fprintf(stderr, "File too big to load\n");
                exit(1);
        }
        current->d_lnum = ++n;
        current->d_flags = 0;
}

/* show the file size as a count of lines */
putstr(" (", Vpage);
```

(continued)

```
putstr(itoa(current->d_lnum, number, radix), Vpage);
putstr(" lines)", Vpage);
prtshift(offset, Vpage);
current = head->d_next;
vf_dspy(head, current, offset, numbers);

/* process user commands */
while ((k = getkey()) != K_ESC) {
        clrmsg();
        switch (k) {
        case 'b':
        case 'B':
        case K_HOME:
                current = head->d_next;
                break;
        case 'e':
        case 'E':
        case K_END:
                current = head->d_prev;
                i = NROWS - 1;
                while (i-- > 0)
                        if (current->d_prev != head->d_next)
                                current = current->d_prev;
                break;
        case K_PGUP:
        case 'u':
        case 'U':
                i = NROWS - OVERLAP;
                while (i-- > 0)
                        if (current != head->d_next)
                                current = current->d_prev;
                break;
        case K_PGDN:
        case 'd':
        case 'D':
                i = NROWS - OVERLAP;
                while (i-- > 0)
                        if (current != head->d_prev)
                                current = current->d_next;
                break;
        case K_UP:
```

(continued)

```
case '-':
        if (current == head->d_next)
                continue;
        current = current->d_prev;
        break;
case K_DOWN:
case '+':
        if (current == head->d_prev)
                continue;
        current = current->d_next;
        break;
case K_RIGHT:
case '>':
case '.':
        if (offset < MAXLINE - SHIFTWIDTH)
                offset += SHIFTWIDTH;
        prtshift(offset, Vpage);
        break;
case K_LEFT:
case '<':
case ',':
        if ((offset -= SHIFTWIDTH) < 0)
                offset = 0;
        prtshift(offset, Vpage);
        break;
case K_ALTG:
case 'g':
case 'G':
        if ((tmp = gotoln(head)) == NULL)
                continue;
        current = tmp;
        break;
case K_ALTH:
case 'h':
case 'H':
case '?':
        showhelp(Attr);
        break;
case K_ALTN:
case 'n':
case 'N':
        numbers = (numbers == TRUE) ? FALSE : TRUE;
        break;
```

(continued)

```
            case K_ALTQ:
            case 'q':
            case 'Q':
                    clrscrn(Attr);
                    putcur(0, 0, Vpage);
                    return (-1);
            case 'r':
            case 'R':
            case '\\':
                    srchdir = BACKWARD;
                    ss = getsstr(srchstr);
                    if (ss == NULL)
                            /* cancel search */
                            break;
                    if (strlen(ss) > 0)
                            strcpy(srchstr, ss);
                    if ((tmp = search(current, srchdir, srchstr)) == NULL)
                            continue;
                    current = tmp;
                    break;
        case 's':
        case 'S':
        case '/':
                    srchdir = FORWARD;
                    ss = getsstr(srchstr);
                    if (ss == NULL)
                            /* cancel search */
                            break;
                    if (strlen(ss) > 0)
                            strcpy(srchstr, ss);
                    if ((tmp = search(current, srchdir, srchstr)) == NULL)
                            continue;
                    current = tmp;
                    break;
        default:
                    /* ignore all other keys */
                    continue;
        }
        vf_dspy(head, current, offset, numbers);
    }
    clrmsg();

    /* release the allocated text buffer memory */
```

(continued)

```
        while (head->d_next != head) {
                /* release text buffer */
                free(head->d_next->d_line);

                /* put node back on the freelist */
                freelist = vf_del(head->d_next, freelist);
        }
        /* release the list header node */
        free((char *)head);

        return (errcount);
}


/*
 *      prtshift -- display the number of columns of horizontal shift
 */

#define SHFTDSP 5

static void
prtshift(amt, pg)
int amt, pg;
{
        char number[17];
        int radix = 10;

        /* clear the shift display area */
        putcur(1, Maxcol[Vmode] - 1 - SHFTDSP, pg);
        writec(' ', SHFTDSP, pg);

        /* display the new shift amount, if any */
        if (amt > 0) {
                putstr(itoa(amt, number, radix), pg);
                putstr("->", pg);
        }
}
```

Within *vf_cmd( )* there are several calls on *putstr( )*. This is a BIOS-based function that displays a string in the prevailing video attribute on a specified screen page. It advances the cursor by the number of characters written. (We could also use the BIOS *writetty( )* function to help us with this task, but *writetty( )* disturbs the video attribute, setting it to the default, which may not be what we want.)

```
/*
 *      putstr -- display a character string in the
 *      prevailing video attribute and return number
 *      characters displayed
 */

int
putstr(s, pg)
register char *s;
int pg;
{
        int r, c, c0;

        readcur(&r, &c, pg);
        for (c0 = c; *s != '\0'; ++s, ++c) {
                putcur(r, c, pg);
                writec(*s, 1, pg);
        }
        putcur(r, c, pg);
        return (c - c0);
}
```

As noted earlier, the *vf.h* header file contains the definition of the buffer node structure. In addition to having forward and backward pointers to other nodes, each node contains a pointer to a character string, a file-relative line number, and a "flag" word. The flag word is not used in this implementation of VF, but it could be used to mark lines for highlighting.

The text buffer management functions are in *vf.list.c*:

```
/*
 *      vf_list -- linked list management functions
 */

#include <stdio.h>
#include <malloc.h>
#include "vf.h"

/*
 *      vf_mklst -- create a new list by allocating a node,
 *      making it point to itself, and setting its values
```

(continued)

```
*       to zero (appropriately cast)
*/

DNODE *
vf_mklst()
{
        DNODE *new;

        new = (DNODE *)malloc(sizeof (DNODE));
        if (new != NULL) {
                new->d_next = new;
                new->d_prev = new;
                new->d_lnum = new->d_flags = 0;
                new->d_line = (char *)NULL;

        }
        return (new);
} /* end vf_mklst() */



/*
 *      vf_alloc -- create a pool of available nodes
 */

DNODE *
vf_alloc(n)
int n;
{
        register DNODE *new;
        register DNODE *tmp;

        /* allocate a block of n nodes */
        new = (DNODE *)malloc(n * sizeof (DNODE));

        /* if allocation OK, string the nodes in one direction */
        if (new != NULL) {
                for (tmp = new; 1 + tmp - new < n; tmp = tmp->d_next)
                        tmp->d_next = tmp + 1;
                tmp->d_next = (DNODE *)NULL;

        }
        return (new);   /* pointer to freelist */
} /* end vf_alloc() */
  /*
   *      vf_ins -- insert a node into a list after the specified node
   */
```

(continued)

```
DNODE *
vf_ins(node, avail)
DNODE *node, *avail;
{
        DNODE *tmp;
        DNODE *vf_alloc(int);

        /*
         *  check freelist -- get another block of nodes
         *  if the list is almost empty
         */
        if (avail->d_next == NULL)
                if ((avail->d_next = vf_alloc(N_NODES)) == NULL)
                        /* not enough memory */
                        return (DNODE *)NULL;

        /* get a node from the freelist */
        tmp = avail;
        avail = avail->d_next;

        /* insert the node into the list after node */
        tmp->d_prev = node;
        tmp->d_next = node->d_next;
        node->d_next->d_prev = tmp;
        node->d_next = tmp;

        /* point to next node in the freelist */
        return (avail);
} /* end vf_ins() */


/*
 *      vf_del -- delete a node from a list
 */

DNODE *
vf_del(node, avail)
DNODE *node, *avail;
{
        /* unlink the node from the list */
        node->d_prev->d_next = node->d_next;
        node->d_next->d_prev = node->d_prev;
```

(continued)

```
        /* return the deleted node to the freelist */
        node->d_next = avail;
        avail = node;

        /* point to the new freelist node */
        return (avail);
} /* end vf_del() */
```

The text buffer used by VF consists of three parts: a group of "control nodes" that form a doubly linked list, pointers to the buffer "head" and the "current" position, and independent character strings for each line in the file being viewed. The node pointed to by *head* is a dummy node that is used to ease the work necessary to set up and maintain the list. Figure 14-2 depicts the text buffer. Note that the control nodes are in a circular list, which makes searching across the buffer boundaries easy. It takes the same amount of time to move backward in the buffer as it does to move forward, because of the use of a doubly linked list. Most other text buffer designs would exact a rather stiff time penalty for scrolling backward in a file.

Figure 14-3 shows another aspect of the text buffer-allocation scheme used by VF. An initial pool of 256 "free" nodes is allocated by a call to *vf_alloc()*; the free nodes are controlled by the symbolic constant *N_NODES*. The list-header node is established by *vf_mklst()*. Both

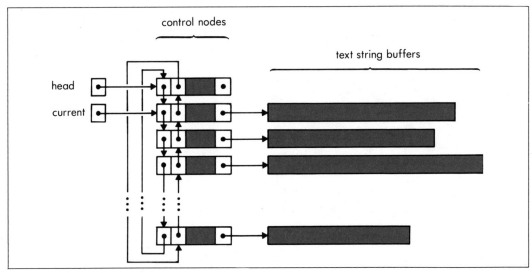

FIGURE 14-2 | *Text buffer management*

vf_mklst( ) and *vf_alloc( )* call the library function *malloc( )* to obtain needed storage.

The header-node pointers are both initially set to point to the header node itself. This constitutes the empty list. The *freelist* pointer points to the chained free nodes. Only the "next" pointers are used for chaining, and the last free node contains a *NULL* next pointer. Each line of text is effectively added to the buffer by the function *vf_ins( )*, which inserts a free node into the list after the position of the current node. When the supply of free nodes is about to be exhausted, another block of nodes is allocated and added to the chain. This process continues as long as there are more lines to read from the file and there is enough memory to satisfy the allocation requests.

Looking at *vf_cmd.c*, we see that after a new node has been inserted into the list by *vf_ins( )*, there is still more work to be done. The Microsoft C standard library function *strdup( )* is used to duplicate the text of the most recently read line from the file. This function also

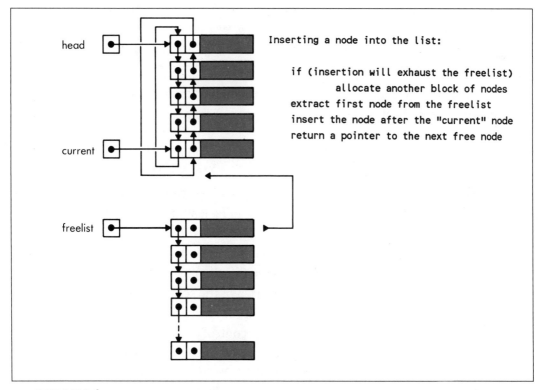

FIGURE 14-3 | *Buffer-allocation scheme*

calls *malloc( )* to obtain an array of characters that is large enough to hold a copy of the received string, including the terminating null byte.

COMMENT

Since strdup( ) *is not a UNIX System V library function, many C compilers may not have it or an equivalent function in their run-time support libraries. You can easily mimic the function using* malloc( ), strlen( ), *and* strcpy( ):

```
#include <stdio.h>
#include <malloc.h>
#include <string.h>


char *
strdup(str)
char *str;
{
        char *buf;

        buf = malloc(strlen(str) + 1)
        return (buf == NULL ? buf : strcpy(buf, str));
}
```

We are careful to check for error returns that let us know if memory is exhausted. VF simply cleans up and quits with an error message if it runs out of memory.

The function *vf_del( )* takes a node out of the list and puts it back on the freelist. We call *vf_del( )*, and *free( )*, a standard library function, when the command loop is terminated by a "next file" (Escape) command. This frees the memory used by the current file, leaving the largest possible amount for the next file in the list. If we do not free the memory, we might eventually receive a "File too big to load" error message.

After any command that affects the current buffer position, *vf_dspy( )* is called to update the text display area of the screen. The version of *vf_dspy( )* presented here uses the *bios* library functions that we constructed in Chapter 5 to position the cursor, control display attributes, and display text and optional line numbers. I elected to use global variables only for the video subsystem based on the BIOS interface. The

Boolean variable *numbers* defaults to *FALSE* but may be set to *TRUE* for the duration of a VF session by using the command-line option -n. The *numbers* variable controls the displaying of line numbers. The initial setting of numbers is passed as an argument from *main( )*, relayed through *vf_cmd( )*, to *vf_dspy( )*. The user may toggle line-numbering on and off while viewing a given file, but the state of line-numbering goes back to the initial setting when the next file from the list is brought into the viewing buffer.

```
/*
 *       vf_dspy -- display a screen page
 */

#include <stdio.h>
#include <stdlib.h>
#include <string.h>
#include <ctype.h>
#include <local\video.h>
#include <local\std.h>
#include <local\bioslib.h>
#include "vf.h"

/* number field width */
#define NFW     8

void
vf_dspy(buf, lp, os, numbers)
DNODE *buf;
register DNODE *lp;
int os;
BOOLEAN numbers;
{
        register int i;
        int j;
        int textwidth;
        char *cp;
        char nbuf[NFW + 1];

        textwidth = Maxcol[Vmode];
        if (numbers == TRUE)
                textwidth -= NFW;
```

(continued)

```
        for (i = 0; i < NROWS; ++i) {
                putcur(TOPROW + i, 0, Vpage);
                cp = lp->d_line;
                if (numbers == TRUE) {
                        sprintf(nbuf, "%6u", lp->d_lnum);
                        putfld(nbuf, NFW, Vpage);
                        putcur(TOPROW + i, NFW, Vpage);
                }
                if (os < strlen(cp))
                        putfld(cp + os, textwidth, Vpage);
                else
                        writec(' ', textwidth, Vpage);
                if (lp == buf->d_prev) {
                        ++i;
                        break;  /* no more displayable lines */
                }
                else
                        lp = lp->d_next;
        }

        /* clear and mark any unused lines */
        for ( ; i < NROWS; ++i) {
                putcur(i + TOPROW, 0, Vpage);
                writec(' ', Maxcol[Vmode], Vpage);
                writec('~', 1, Vpage);
        }
        return;
}
```

The *vf_dspy( )* function updates the text-display area by calling *putfld( )*, which outputs a string of characters to a field starting at the current cursor position. The *putfld( )* function uses a compression technique that is made possible by BIOS. All sequences of repeated characters are output by a single call to *writec( )*. This technique reduces the time needed to update a screen that contains, for example, the large amounts of white space found in C and Pascal source files. Assembly-language source listings, on the other hand, usually do not benefit from this compression technique because they contain long lines and fewer repeated character sequences.

```
/*
 *      putfld -- display a string in the prevailing
 *      video attribute while compressing runs of a
 *      single character, and pad the field to full width
 *      with spaces if necessary
 */

int
putfld(s, w, pg)
register char *s;       /* string to write */
int w;                  /* field width */
int pg;                 /* screen page for writes */
{
        int r, c, cols;
        register int n;

        extern int putcur(int, int, int);
        extern int readcur(int *, int *, int);
        extern int writec(unsigned char, int, int);

        /* get starting (current) position */
        readcur(&r, &c, pg);

        /* write the string */
        for (n = 0; *s != '\0' && n < w; s += cols, n += cols) {
                putcur(r, c + n, pg);
                /* compress runs to a single call on writec() */
                cols = 1;
                while (*(s + cols) == *s && n + cols < w)
                        ++cols;
                writec(*s, cols, pg);
        }

        /* pad the field, if necessary */
        if (n < w) {
                putcur(r, c + n, pg);
                writec(' ', w - n, pg);
        }

        return (w - n);
}
```

This function becomes part of the *bios* library described in Chapter 5. It can be used by any program that uses BIOS to access the PC screen.

We have to watch out for the boundary conditions imposed by physical realities. When there are not enough lines left in the buffer to fill the screen, *vf_dspy( )* must be careful not to leave residue from previous displays. After displaying the last line of the text buffer, *vf_dspy( )* clears each remaining screen line and deposits a tilde in the leftmost column to show that the line is an unused screen line, as opposed to an empty buffer line.

Two utility functions that are specific to VF reside in *vf_util.c.* The first is *gotoln( ),* which implements the absolute go-to-line feature. This function prompts the user for a line number. If the number is within the range of lines in the buffer, the current position is updated and the line sought by the user is brought to the top of the text display area.

The second function is called *showhelp( ).* To assist the user with a brief memory-jogger of command names and actions, *showhelp( )* displays the essence of the manual page at the top of the text display area. When the user has finished reading the help frame, a keypress restores the screen to its former condition by rewriting all of the text lines.

```
/*
 *      vf_util -- utility functions for ViewFile
 */

#include <stdio.h>
#include <stdlib.h>
#include <string.h>
#include <local\std.h>
#include <local\video.h>
#include <local\keydefs.h>
#include "vf.h"

extern int Startscan, Endscan;

#define NDIGITS 6
```

(continued)

```
/*
 *      gotoln -- jump to an absolute line number
 */

DNODE *
gotoln(buf)
DNODE *buf;
{
        register int ln;
        register DNODE *lp;
        char line[NDIGITS + 1];

        extern void showmsg(char *);
        extern char *getstr(char *, int);

        /* get line number from user */
        showmsg("Line number: ");
        setctype(Startscan, Endscan);                      /* cursor on */
        ln = atoi(getstr(line, NDIGITS + 1));
        setctype(MAXSCAN, MAXSCAN);                        /* cursor off */

        /* check boundary conditions */
        if (ln > buf->d_prev->d_lnum || ln <= 0) {
                showmsg("Line out of range");
                return ((DNODE *)NULL);
        }

        /* find the line */
        for (lp = buf->d_next; ln != lp->d_lnum; lp = lp->d_next)
                ;
        return (lp);
}


/*
 *      showhelp -- display a help frame
 */
#define HELPROW TOPROW + 3
#define HELPCOL 10
#define VBORDER 1
#define HBORDER 2
```

(continued)

```
void
showhelp(textattr)
unsigned char textattr; /* attribute of text area */
{
        register int i, n;
        int nlines, ncols;
        unsigned char helpattr;
        static char *help[] = {
                "PgUp (U)        Scroll up in the file one screen page",
                "PgDn (D)        Scroll down in the file one screen page",
                "Up arrow (-)    Scroll up in the file one line",
                "Down arrow (+)  Scroll down in the file one line",
                "Right arrow (>) Scroll right by 20 columns",
                "Left arrow (<)  Scroll left by 20 columns",
                "Home (B)        Go to beginning of file buffer",
                "End (E)         Go to end of file buffer",
                "Alt-g (G)       Go to a specified line in the buffer",
                "Alt-h (H or ?)  Display this help frame",
                "Alt-n (N)       Toggle line-numbering feature",
                "\\ (R)           Reverse search for a literal text string",
                "/ (S)           Search forward for a literal text string",
                "Esc             Next file from list (quits if none)",
                "Alt-q (Q)       Quit",
                "-------------------------------------------------------",
                "              << Press a key to continue >>",
                (char *)NULL
        };

        /* prepare help window */
        ncols = 0;
        for (i = 0; help[i] != (char *)NULL; ++i)
                if ((n = strlen(help[i])) > ncols)
                        ncols = n;
        nlines = i - 1;
        --ncols;
        helpattr = (RED << 4) | BWHT;
        clrw(HELPROW - VBORDER, HELPCOL - HBORDER,
                HELPROW + nlines + VBORDER, HELPCOL + ncols + HBORDER,
                helpattr);
        drawbox(HELPROW - VBORDER, HELPCOL - HBORDER,
                HELPROW + nlines + VBORDER, HELPCOL + ncols + HBORDER,
                Vpage);
```

(continued)

```
            /* display the help text */
            for (i = 0; help[i] != (char *)NULL; ++i) {
                    putcur(HELPROW + i, HELPCOL, Vpage);
                    putstr(help[i], Vpage);
            }
            /* pause until told by a keypress to proceed */
            getkey();

            /* restore help display area to the text attribute */
            clrw(HELPROW - VBORDER, HELPCOL - HBORDER,
                    HELPROW + nlines + VBORDER, HELPCOL + ncols + HBORDER,
                    textattr);
    }
```

The task of gathering the user's input for the *gotoln( )* function falls to *getstr( )*, a function that is constructed from several of the *dos* and *bios* library functions presented in Chapter 5. The *getstr( )* function takes buffer and width parameters as arguments. It echoes keystrokes as it receives them and interprets a few keys as commands rather than as input. The user cancels input by pressing the Escape key, and signals the end of input with a carriage return. Errors may be corrected by pressing Ctrl-H (backspace). All input is in the form of character strings. If a program requires numeric input, such as a line number, it must convert the string to numeric form before using it.

```
/*
 *      getstr -- get a string from the keyboard
 */

#include <stdio.h>
#include <string.h>
#include <local\std.h>
#include <local\video.h>
#include <local\keydefs.h>

char *
getstr(buf, width)
char *buf;
int width;
{
```

(continued)

```
    int row, col;
    char *cp;

    /* function prototypes */
    extern int putcur(int, int, int);
    extern int readcur(int *, int *, int);
    extern int writec(char, int, int);
    extern int getkey();

    /* gather keyboard input into a string buffer */
    cp = buf;
    while ((*cp = getkey()) != K_RETURN && cp - buf < width) {
            switch (*cp) {
            case K_CTRLH:
                    /* destructive backspace */
                    if (cp > buf) {
                            readcur(&row, &col, Vpage);
                            putcur(row, col - 1, Vpage);
                            writec(' ', 1, Vpage);
                            --cp;
                    }
                    continue;
            case K_ESC:
                    /* cancel string input operation */
                    return (char *)NULL;
            }
            put_ch(*cp, Vpage);
            ++cp;
    }
    *cp = '\0';
    return (buf);
}
```

Notice that *getstr( )* is actually a simplified version of the *getreply( )* function that we used in Chapter 6. We don't need a sliding window or other fancy gimmicks, so we took out all the superfluous windowing and editing features, made the prompting external, and eliminated the response stack. What's left is a simple but effective function that collects a string from the keyboard. Two boundary conditions are addressed: First, we don't allow the user to backspace beyond the left column of the response field, and second, we return the response immediately if the user types past the right column of the response field. You may prefer to modify the latter condition to require an explicit carriage return before returning the response.

Additional assistance is provided to the user via the message line on the right half of the top screen line. The simple message-line manager consists of three functions contained in *message.c.* The function *initmsg( )* establishes the message display area by filling in the values called for by the MESSAGE data structure defined in the *message.h* header file. The message line can be placed anywhere on the screen by changing the values presented to *initmsg( ).* The *showmsg( )* function displays a message, and *clrmsg( )* restores the message area to its pristine state. A flag in the message structure is set when a message is displayed and is reset when the message area is cleared. If a call is made to *clrmsg( )* and the flag is not set, no action is taken.

```
/*
 *      message.h -- header for message-line manager
 */

typedef struct msg_st {
        int m_row;
        int m_col;
        int m_wid;
        int m_pg;
        int m_flag;
        unsigned char m_attr;
} MESSAGE;
```

```
/*
 *      message -- routines used to display and clear
 *      messages in a reserved message area
 */

#include "message.h"

MESSAGE Ml;
extern int writec(char, int, int);

/*
 *      set up the message-line manager
 */
```

(continued)

```
void
initmsg(r, c, w, a, pg)
int r;                  /* message row */
int c;                  /* message column */
int w;                  /* width of message field */
unsigned char a;        /* message field video attribute */
int pg;                 /* active page for messages */
{
        MESSAGE *mp;
        void clrmsg();

        mp = &Ml;
        mp->m_row = r;
        mp->m_col = c;
        mp->m_wid = w;
        mp->m_attr = a;
        mp->m_pg = pg;
        mp->m_flag = 1;
        clrmsg();
}

/*
 *      showmsg -- display a message and set the message flag
 */

void
showmsg(msg)
char *msg;
{
        MESSAGE *mp;

        mp = &Ml;
        putcur(mp->m_row, mp->m_col, mp->m_pg);
        writec(' ', mp->m_wid, mp->m_pg);
        putstr(msg, mp->m_pg);
        mp->m_flag = 1;
        return;
}
/*
 *      clrmsg -- erase the message area and reset the message flag
 */
```

(continued)

```
void
clrmsg()
{
        MESSAGE *mp;

        mp = &Ml;
        if (mp->m_flag != 0) {
                putcur(mp->m_row, mp->m_col, mp->m_pg);
                writec(' ', mp->m_wid, mp->m_pg);
                mp->m_flag = 0;
        }
        return;
}
```

The message-line manager functions are based on *bios* library routines. They can be generalized to use either standard library routines or the screen-buffer routines described in Chapters 11 and 12, which permit their use in programs that do not use the BIOS interface.

A simple but useful search feature is implemented by the functions in *vf_srch.c.* The *getsstr( )* function prompts for a search string and reads it using *getstr( ).* The string must be literal in this implementation. The string is presented to *search( ),* which tries to find a line in the specified search direction that contains a match for the search string. Searching starts on the line following the current line (or the preceding line for a reverse search) and continues until a match is found or until *search( )* returns to the current line. The search is circular because of the way the buffer is implemented.

```
/*      vf_srch -- search functions     */

#include <stdio.h>
#include <stdlib.h>
#include <string.h>
#include <local\std.h>
#include "vf.h"

/*      search -- search for a literal string in the buffer     */

DNODE *search(buf, dir, str)
DNODE *buf;
DIRECTION dir;
char *str;
{
```

(continued)

```
        int n;
        register DNODE *lp;
        register char *cp;
        extern void showmsg(char *);

        /* try to find a match -- wraps around buffer boundaries */
        n = strlen(str);
        lp = (dir == FORWARD) ? buf->d_next : buf->d_prev;
        while (lp != buf) {
                if ((cp = lp->d_line) != NULL)  /* skip over header node */
                        while (*cp != '\n' && *cp != '\0') {
                                if (strncmp(cp, str, n) == 0)
                                        return (lp);
                                ++cp;
                        }
                lp = (dir == FORWARD) ? lp->d_next : lp->d_prev;
        }
        showmsg("Not found");
        return ((DNODE *)NULL);
}


/*      getsstr -- prompt the user for a search string      */

extern int Startscan, Endscan;

char *getsstr(str)
char *str;
{
        char line[MAXSTR];
        char *resp;
        extern int putstr(char *, int);
        extern char *getstr(char *, int);
        extern int put_ch(char, int);
        extern void showmsg(char *);
        extern void clrmsg();
        static char prompt[] = { "Search for: " };

        /* get search string */
        showmsg(prompt);
        setctype(Startscan, Endscan);           /* cursor on */
        resp = getstr(line, MAXSTR - strlen(prompt));
        setctype(MAXSCAN, MAXSCAN);              /* cursor off */
        if (resp == NULL)
                return (char *)NULL;
        if (strlen(resp) == 0)
                return (str);
        showmsg(resp);
        return (resp);
}
```

```
/*      nlerase -- replace first newline in a string with a null character     */
char *nlerase(s)
char *s;
{
        register char *cp;

        cp = s;
        while (*cp != '\n' && *cp != '\0')
                ++cp;
        *cp = '\0';
        return (s);
}
```

```
/*      getxline -- get a line of text while expanding tabs, put text into an
 *      array, and return a pointer to the resulting null-terminated line      */

#include <stdio.h>
#include <stdlib.h>
#include <ctype.h>
#include <local\std.h>

char *getxline(buf, size, fin)
char *buf;
int size;
FILE *fin;
{
        register int ch;        /* input character */
        register char *cp;      /* character pointer */
        extern BOOLEAN tabstop(int);

        cp = buf;
        while (--size > 0 && (ch = fgetc(fin)) != EOF) {
                if (ch == '\n') {
                        *cp++ = ch;
                        break;
                }
                else if (ch == '\t')
                        do {
                                *cp = ' ';
                        } while (--size > 0 && (tabstop(++cp - buf) == FALSE));
```

(continued)

```
              else
                      *cp++ = ch & ASCII;
        }
        *cp = '\0';
        return ((ch == EOF && cp == buf) ? NULL : buf);
}
```

Figure 14-4 shows VF in operation.

```
ViewFile/1.0  H=Help Q=Quit Esc=Next
File: vf.c (126 lines)
/*
 *      vf -- view a file using a full-screen window onto
 *
 */        ┌──────────────────────────────────────────────────────┐
           │ PgUp (U)        Scroll up in the file one screen page │
           │ PgDn (D)        Scroll down in the file one screen page│
#include   │ Up arrow (-)    Scroll up in the file one line        │
#include   │ Down arrow (+)  Scroll down in the file one line      │
#include   │ Right arrow ()) Scroll right by 20 columns            │
#include   │ Left arrow (<)  Scroll left by 20 columns             │
#include   │ Home (B)        Go to beginning of file buffer        │
#include   │ End (E)         Go to end of file buffer              │
           │ Alt-g (G)       Go to a specified line in the buffer  │
extern i   │ Alt-h (H or ?)  Display this help frame               │
int Star   │ Alt-n (N)       Toggle line-numbering feature         │
unsigned   │ \ (R)           Reverse search for a literal text string│
unsigned   │ / (S)           Search forward for a literal text string│
unsigned   │ Esc             Next file from list (quits if none)   │
           │ Alt-q (Q)       Quit                                  │
main(arg   │ ──────────────────────────────────────────────────── │
int argc   │             << Press a key to continue >>             │
char **a   └──────────────────────────────────────────────────────┘
{
        int ch;
```

FIGURE 14-4 | *The ViewFile program with the help frame displayed*

Considerations and Alternatives

If you need to view very large files, the use of external storage is the best alternative. A theoretical maximum file size of 32 megabytes can be achieved under current versions of DOS, but some of that space will probably be needed to manage the data storage.

With external storage, a file would be loaded from disk faster than by the current VF because only a small piece of the file need be in memory at one time. However, it's likely that there would be a significant increase in the time needed to access a particular line in the file because the disk must be accessed and read for each new portion of the file that is to be displayed.

An area of the VF design that could use some enhancement is the search feature. Although literal-string searches satisfy most positioning requirements, a regular-expression capability can be extremely handy. Regular expressions are, in essence, text formulas that can be used to form patterns rather than fixed strings.

Another option to consider is an incremental search. As the user types characters, the program accumulates them in the search pattern and moves immediately to a string in the text, if there is one, that matches the accumulated search string. The advantage of the incremental search is that the user need only type enough characters to get the match. You would need to provide an "escape" command to terminate the search when the desired string is found.

The implementation of VF presented in this chapter wraps around the buffer boundaries. In most cases this action is appropriate, but not always. It may be useful to have a "no wrap" option that would terminate the search at the end (or beginning) of the buffer to avoid unwanted repositioning.

SECTION V

Appendixes

Microsoft C Compiler, Version 4.00   **A**

The current version of the Microsoft C Compiler at the time of this writing is version 4.00. The compiler is noted for producing very fast and compact executable program files. It trades compile time for a high degree of optimization and produces object code that is arguably in the same league as that produced by expert assembly-language programmers. "Hand tuning" to improve performance is virtually unnecessary.

Technical Highlights

The following material presents a general overview of the Microsoft C Compiler, version 4.00. The compiler system encompasses a three-pass compiler, extensive runtime library support, and a set of development tools. See Chapter 1 for additional information about the compiler, the impact of the proposed ANSI standard for C, and information about DOS and C compiler programs that assist programmers in the development of programs.

Two compiler drivers are available with the Microsoft C Compiler. The MSC driver executes the preprocessor and compiler passes. The CL driver is similar to the CC driver on XENIX and UNIX, which compiles and links programs automatically. Either driver can take advantage of a variety of compile-time options.

Program Size

The Microsoft C Compiler now provides five distinct memory models—small, medium, compact, large, and huge—plus extensions to produce mixed models.

- ▶ The small model generates tight, efficient code for programs with up to 64 KB of code and up to 64 KB of data.

- ▶ The medium model supports programs with up to 1 MB of code but only 64 KB of data.

- ▶ The compact model handles programs with up to 64 KB of code and up to 1 MB of data.

- ▶ The large model extends program space to 1 MB of code with 1 MB of data.

- ▶ The huge model is similar to the large model, but allows individual arrays to be larger than 64 KB.

Mixed memory models are made possible through the use of *near*, *far*, and *huge* pointers. These pointers change the addressing conventions for one or more elements without changing them for the program as a whole.

Overlays

The Microsoft C Compiler single-level overlay linker allows memory space to be shared in turn by several program modules. Overlays may be called from the "root" program or from another overlay and are automatically loaded when needed.

Multiple Math Libraries

The Microsoft C Compiler offers several options for floating-point operations. If an 8087/80287 math coprocessor is available, the smallest and fastest floating-point library can be used. And even though a math coprocessor may not be present, identical math results can still be obtained from an emulator.

This versatility gives programs the same high degree of precision whether or not a math coprocessor is available. For maximum speed, the emulator routines automatically use the math coprocessor if it is installed.

When full 80-bit precision and consistency with the 8087/80287 math coprocessor are not required, the alternate math package can be selected. Supporting a compatible interface for single- and double-precision IEEE numbers, this math library is optimized for speed.

Network File Sharing

Under MS-DOS version 3.1 or higher with Microsoft Networks version 1.0, or under IBM PC Network, the Microsoft C Compiler supports multi-user network access with both file and record locking.

Direct Interlanguage Calls

Routines written in the Microsoft C Compiler (version 3.00 or higher), Microsoft FORTRAN (version 3.30 or higher), Microsoft Pascal (version 3.30 or higher), or Microsoft Macro Assembler can be linked together. So you can share the investment you've made in developing libraries in a different language.

This interlanguage calling lets you use the best features of each language, or upgrade to a new language while retaining libraries written in the old one. Selected routines can be recoded as needed.

Library Manager

Entire program-development libraries can be built in any mix of C, Pascal, FORTRAN, and assembly language by using the library manager that's included with the Microsoft C Compiler.

Once a library is constructed, the library subroutines can be called directly from your C program. Subroutine calls are resolved when the finished program is linked.

Utility Programs

The Microsoft C Compiler includes several utility programs; two are used to increase the efficiency of .EXE files:

- ▶ EXEPACK removes null characters from .EXE files and optimizes the relocation table. This results in smaller files on disk and faster loading at execution time.

- ▶ EXEMOD allows fine-tuning of file header information usually set by default, such as stack size.

Language Details

This is a summary of data types, keywords, compiler options, pre-processor directives, and other important aspects of the Microsoft C Compiler. Implementation-dependent items are grouped separately. Items that are new in version 4.00 are flagged, as are library routines that are implemented as macros.

KEYWORDS

auto	else	long	switch
break	enum	register	typedef
case	extern	return	union
char	float	short	unsigned
continue	for	signed	void
default	goto	sizeof	while
do	if	static	
double	int	struct	

The keywords const *and* volatile *are reserved for future use.*

IMPLEMENTATION-DEPENDENT KEYWORDS

cdecl	fortran	near	pascal
far	huge		

FUNDAMENTAL TYPES

char	int	signed	void
double	long	unsigned	
float	short		

Enumeration types are also included.

TYPE SPECIFIERS

char	int	struct	unsigned
double	long	typedef *name*	void
enum	short	union	
float	signed		

DATA FORMATS

The standard C data types are implemented as follows:

Type	Length in Bytes	Range
char	1	-128 to 127
double	8	$10** \pm 306$
float	4	$10** \pm 38$
int	2	-32768 to 32767
long	4	$-2**31$ to $2**31-1$
short	2	-32768 to 32767
unsigned char	1	0 to 255
unsigned int	2	0 to 65535
unsigned long	4	0 to $2**32-1$
unsigned short	2	0 to 65535

POINTER SIZES

	Bytes	*Address Arithmetic*
Near Pointer	2	16 bits (offset)
Far Pointer	4	16 bits (offset)
Huge Pointer	4	32 bits (segment offset)

PREPROCESSOR DIRECTIVES

#define	#endif	#ifndef	#pragma
#elif	#if	#include	#undef
#else	#ifdef	#line	

STORAGE CLASSES

auto	extern	register	static

EXTENDED TYPE MODIFIERS

cdecl	fortran	near	pascal
far	huge		

COMPILER STATEMENTS

break	default	for	return
case	do	goto	switch
continue	else	if	while

COMPILER OPTIONS

The Microsoft C Compiler supports a large number of compile-time options.
Here is a partial list.

/A *string*	Sets program memory model
/D*name* [= *text*]	Defines preprocessor macro
/F*x*	Selects listing options for source, object, assembly, and testing
/FP*string*	Selects floating-point options
/G*x*	Specifies options for code generation; generates 8086/8088, 80186/80188, or 80286 instructions; disables stack checking
/I *path*	Adds to #include search path
/O*x*	Controls optimization for speed and size
/W*n*	Sets warning message level
/Z*x*	Selects language options for disabling extensions, emitting debugging information, and structure packing

---

LIBRARY FUNCTIONS

The Microsoft C Compiler contains an extensive set of UNIX System V compatible library routines. This set includes many of the functions included in the emerging ANSI standard. Functions new in this version are designated by a dagger (†) before the function name. Functions implemented as Macros are designated by a double dagger (‡).

Buffer Manipulation

memccpy	memcmp	†memicmp	movedata
memchr	memcpy	memset	

Character Classification and Conversion

‡isalnum	‡isgraph	‡isupper	‡toupper
‡isalpha	‡islower	‡isxdigit	‡_toupper
‡isascii	‡isprint	‡toascii	
‡iscntrl	‡ispunct	‡tolower	
‡isdigit	‡isspace	‡_tolower	

Data Conversion

atof	ecvt	itoa	†strtol
atoi	fcvt	ltoa	ultoa
atol	gcvt	†strtod	

Directory Control

chdir	getcwd	mkdir	rmdir

File Handling

access	fstat	†remove	unmask
chmod	isatty	rename	unlink
chsize	locking	setmode	
filelength	mktemp	stat	

(continued)

I/O Stream Routines

clearerr	fopen	‡getchar	†setvbuf
fclose	fprintf	gets	sprintf
fcloseall	fputc	getw	sscanf
fdopen	fputchar	printf	†tempnam
‡feof	fputs	‡putc	†tmpfile
‡ferror	fread	‡putchar	†tmpnam
fflush	freopen	puts	ungetc
fgetc	fscanf	putw	†vfprintf
fgetchar	fseek	rewind	†vprintf
fgets	ftell	†rmtmp	†vsprintf
‡fileno	fwrite	scanf	
flushall	‡getc	setbuf	

Low-Level Routines

close	dup2	open	tell
creat	eof	read	write
dup	lseek	sopen	

Console and Port I/O Routines

cgets	cscanf	inp	putch
cprintf	getch	kbhit	ungetch
cputs	getche	outp	

Math (Floating Point)

acos	†_control87	frexp	sin
asin	cos	hypot	sinh
atan	cosh	ldexp	sqrt
atan2	exp	log	†_status87
bessel	fabs	log10	tan
cabs	floor	matherr	tanh
ceil	fmod	modf	
†_clear87	†_fpreset	pow	

Memory Allocation

†alloca	†_fmsize	malloc	†_nmsize
calloc	free	†_memavl	realloc
†_expand	†_freect	†_msize	sbrk
†_ffree	†halloc	†_nfree	†stackavail
†_fmalloc	†hfree	†_nmalloc	

MS-DOS Interface

bdos	int86	intdos	segread
dosexterr	int86x	intdosx	

(continued)

Process Control

abort	execve	†onexit	spawnv
execl	execvp	signal	spawnve
execle	†execvpe	spawnl	spawnvp
execlp	exit	spawnle	†spawnvpe
†execlpe	_exit	spawnlp	system
execv	getpid	†spawnlpe	

Searching and Sorting

bsearch	†lfind	†lsearch	qsort

String Manipulation

strcat	strdup	strncmp	strrev
strchr	†strerror	strncpy	strset
strcmp	†stricmp	†strnicmp	strspn
strcmpi	strlen	strnset	†strstr
strcpy	strlwr	strpbrk	strtok
strcspn	strncat	strrchr	strupr

Time

asctime	ftime	localtime	tzset
ctime	gmtime	time	utime
†difftime			

Miscellaneous

‡abs	getenv	perror	setjmp
‡assert	labs	putenv	srand
‡FP_OFF	longjmp	rand	swab
‡FP_SEG			

Other C Compilers   B

There are many C compilers for DOS in today's PC marketplace. If you are in the process of choosing one, I recommend that you read all you can before making a purchase. Price is not the only consideration. Look for features that will make your job easier: a complete standard library of functions and macros; DOS and BIOS interface functions; program-development tools; and product support.

If you are going to produce programs commercially, look for a compiler that produces compact, fast-running programs. Ultimately, it is the user of your programs who will benefit from your choice of a quality product. Using a compiler that compiles faster than others but produces sloppy object code is probably not in your best long-term interest if you intend to make a living by writing programs. It may save you a little development time, but it will penalize your program's users every time they run the program.

Interactive tools such as C interpreters are now available and provide a comfortable testing and experimenting environment that helps a programmer to quickly examine a variety of problem-solving approaches. You may want to use a C interpreter for early development work. The current crop of C interpreters are, however, less appropriate for large programming projects, particularly projects that involve more than one programmer. Analyze your needs carefully before selecting a C compiler or interpreter.

Here are some magazine review articles that may help you decide which C compiler is right for you:

"The State of C," William Hunt, *PC Tech Journal,* January 1986.

"Software Reviews (Department) — 21 C Compilers," S. Leibson, J. Reed, and J. Kyle, *Computer Language,* February 1985 (page 73).

If you already have a C compiler and plan to stick with it, you have a different concern. The task at hand is to use the available compiler features and support tools to produce functioning programs. I have used several C compilers in addition to the Microsoft C Compiler to compile the programs presented in this book. They are the C86 C Compiler (Computer Innovations), The C Programming System (Mark Williams Company), and the MS-DOS C Compiler (Lattice). Each has its own way of doing things, although nearly all C compiler vendors are starting to converge on the proposed ANSI standard for C.

Although it is possible to write source code with conditional compilation directives to accommodate various compilers, I chose not to do so in the source in *Proficient C* because that tends to obscure the meaning of the code and makes the source files nearly unreadable. The following material briefly describes each compiler system, the major observable differences from Microsoft C, and what has to be done to accommodate those differences. Others may exist. The ones mentioned are those relevant to the programs and routines developed in *Proficient C.*

The compilers mentioned here deliver full compatibility with the de facto specification of C presented in the book *The C Programming Language,* by Brian Kernighan and Dennis Ritchie, commonly referred to as "K&R" by the C programming community. Each compiler varies from the others in the level of support for the proposed ANSI standard for C.

Computer Innovations — Optimizing C86, Version 2.3

One of the first C compiler entries into the PC marketplace was Computer Innovations' C86, which was later replaced by Optimizing C86. The compiler features good compatibility with the standard UNIX library (pre-System V), support for many DOS features (all versions), object libraries in MS-DOS object format, and is delivered with all library source (C and assembler) in compressed form on disk.

The compiler is due for an update at the time this is being written to bring it up to System V and DOS (version 3.00 and higher) compatibility. Optimizing C86 differs fundamentally from Microsoft C in that it:

▶ Has no void function return specifier—use a *typedef* of an *int* to get around this.

▶ Has no *enum* keyword—either avoid the use of *enum*s or synthesize a palatable substitute using a *typedef* of an *int*.

▶ Uses the *sysint( )* function instead of *intdos( )* and uses *sysint21( )* instead of *int86( )*. The calling sequence of parameters is different.

▶ Provides *movblock( )* instead of *movedata( )* for segmented address memory moves. The parameter ordering is different.

▶ Has no means of determining the DOS version provided by the compiler—use the *ver( )* function described in Chapter 5.

▶ Has no structure assignment and no passing of entire structures as parameters or function return values.

▶ Has no *perror( )*—use *fprintf( )* and a message of your own making.

Optimizing C86 supports small and large memory models in a way that is consistent with the equivalent Microsoft models. Programs may also be compiled in an 8080 .COM memory model, which is called "compact." It is not the same as the Microsoft compact memory model. There are no equivalents to the Microsoft medium and huge models. No data object can exceed 64 KB in size.

Compiling programs under C86 involves the use of batch files. There are currently no compiler driver programs and no MAKE-like facility to control processing. C86 can be given path information for the default location of header files.

Mark Williams— # The C Programming System, Version 3.0.7

The Mark Williams C Programming System (MWC from now on) is a complete C programming system adapted from the Mark Williams Coherent operating system, a UNIX Version 7 work-alike system. MWC incorporates some of C's newer features such as *enum* and *void* and up-to-date library functions.

The compiler can be told to produce object files in either the Mark Williams or Microsoft object file formats. Libraries for both formats are provided with the compiler. MWC produces both small and large model (32-bit pointers) programs. It offers nothing comparable to the compact, medium, and huge Microsoft models.

A public domain full-screen editor, MicroEMACS, is included in the package along with a good selection of UNIX-style support tools (*make, cc, ld, pr, wc,* and others).

A trimmed-down version of MWC called *Let's C* is also available from Mark Williams. It compiles small-model programs only and is supported by fewer utilities, but it is a full K&R C compiler that is a good entry vehicle for programmers who are new to C.

The primary differences between MWC and Microsoft C are that MWC:

▶ Has no structure assignment and no passing of entire structures as parameters or function return values.

▶ Uses *intcall( )* instead of *intdos( )*. It has no equivalent to the Microsoft *int86( )*, but *intcall( )* with an interrupt number of 21H will do the job (a bit slower, however).

▶ Provides port access via *inb( )* and *outb( )* (equivalent to Microsoft's *inp( )* and *outp( )* routines).

▶ Has no *perror( )*—use *fprintf( )* and a message of your own making. The global variable *errno* produces valid values in connection with math library functions only. It is not generally useful with other standard I/O library routines.

Lattice—MS-DOS C Compiler, Version 3.00H

The Lattice C Compiler, particularly the library support package, has undergone significant changes. The version 3.00 Lattice C compiler is very compatible with Microsoft C, versions 3.00 and 4.00; it differs mostly in minor details:

▶ The standard printer device is called *stdprt* instead of *stdprn*.

▶ The Microsoft *_osmajor* and *_osminor* are handled by the external character variable *_DOS*, which may be accessed as a single character or a two-character array to obtain the DOS major and minor version numbers. You can use the *ver( )* function described in the *Proficient C* DOS library to get the operating system version numbers.

The MS-DOS interface functions emulate virtually all of the PC operating system functions provided by Microsoft C, so calls to *kbhit( )*, *int86( )*, *intdos( )*, and so on require no modifications to compile under Lattice C.

The compiler is accompanied by a library that classifies each function by its "environment" (i.e, origins and compatibility). The following classes are defined by Lattice:

CLASS	DESCRIPTION
ANSI	Conforming to the proposed ANSI standard
UNIX	Conforming to AT&T's UNIX System V standard
XENIX	Compatible with Microsoft XENIX
LATTICE	Available on all systems for which Lattice provides a C compiler
iAPX86	Available only on iAPX32 machines
MS-DOS	Designed for use under generic MS-DOS and compatible with PC-DOS (a superset of MS-DOS)
PC-DOS	For use under PC-DOS but not guaranteed to work under MS-DOS

Lattice offers four memory models: small, program, data, and large. The models are comparable to the Microsoft small, medium, compact, and large models, respectively. Objects are limited to 64 KB in size. There are no equivalents to Microsoft's huge keyword and huge model.

Compiling programs with the latest Lattice C compiler is easier than under previous versions. A compiler driver program, LC, does most of the work of compiling by calling the passes in the correct order and bailing out in the event of compile-time errors. The linking step is still manual and is best handled by batch files tailored to the particular linking task and the selected memory model.

Maintaining Programs

For owners of C compilers that do not provide a MAKE command, several alternatives are available. The first is to use DOS batch files to control compilation and linking steps. The DOS ERRORLEVEL (program exit code) can be used to abort processing when errors occur (if the compiler programs use the error-return facility and you are running DOS version 2.00 or higher). The problem with batch files is that the burden of knowing which program modules have to be remade is left to you.

Another alternative is to use a third-party MAKE utility. An excellent MAKE program called PolyMake is available from Polytron. It is as UNIX-like as any DOS MAKE I have seen and can be made to work with any C compiler via rules placed in a control file. Because PolyMake is closer to the UNIX model that I am familiar with, I prefer to use it rather than the MAKEs provided with most C compilers (with the exception of the Mark Williams MAKE program, which is excellent). Several other MAKE utilities for DOS are available at reasonable cost. *Note:* The makefiles in *Proficient C* are written for the Microsoft version of MAKE. They will probably need to be rewritten to run successfully with other MAKE programs.

Characters and C
Attributes

A character code is a numeric value that is used to represent a character in computer memory and to control peripheral devices such as terminals, the console display screen, and printers. We are interested in two primary character-coding schemes: the ASCII character set, because it is the standard to which most commercial terminal and computer equipment designs adhere, and the IBM extended ASCII character set used by the IBM PC and work-alike computers.

In dealing with terminals and PC console display devices, numeric codes are also used to control the appearance of a displayed character (video attribute), to prevent specified screen regions from being updated (protect), and even to make certain areas of the screen invisible to the user (nondisplay). IBM PCs do not directly support protected fields, although our programs can simulate the effect. On a PC, a nondisplay field is one that carries a special video attribute which sets the foreground color to the same value as the background color.

This appendix is a detailed summary of the characters and attributes available to programmers of the IBM PC family of computers.

ASCII Character Codes

The ASCII (American National Standard Code for Information Interchange) character set is defined as a table of 7-bit codes that represent a collection of control characters and printable characters. In a 7-bit environment all data bits are significant. In the 8-bit environment typical of the IBM PC and similar equipment, the lower seven bits (0 through 6) are used to represent ASCII characters. The high bit (bit 7) is used for IBM code extensions, which are discussed later in this appendix.

Figure C-1 shows the relationship between various character codes and the data bytes that hold them.

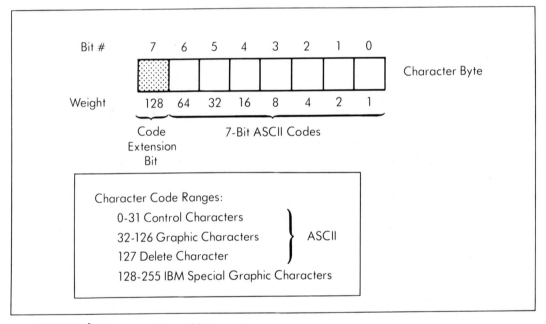

FIGURE C-1 | *Character codes and bytes*

ASCII Control Character Table

ASCII codes 0 through 31 and 127 decimal (shown in Figure C-2, next page) are called control codes because they are used to start, stop, or modify some action. Several of the control characters have meanings that vary with the context of their use, but most can be categorized as being one or more of the following types:

▶ Format Effector (FE)—controls the printed or displayed layout of graphic information

▶ Communications Control (CC)—controls the operation of communication devices and networks

▶ Information Separator (IS)—controls the logical separation of information

It may seem a bit odd to have one control code (DEL = 127) isolated from all the others. This is due to its earliest use with paper-tape punches for which the DEL code means "erase or obliterate" an unwanted character, which on a medium like paper tape could be done only by punching out all seven of the holes (hence code 127 or 7F hex).

In its design of the PC, IBM has attached special meanings to most of the ASCII control codes so that they have displayable graphic content when placed directly into display memory. Thus, the format effector CR (code 13 decimal), in addition to its "carriage return" meaning when embedded in data streams, can also be used to place a musical-note symbol on the display screen. Each of the control codes except NUL (0) have an associated displayable symbol on the IBM PC.

NAME	DESCRIPTION (TYPE)	DEC CODE	HEX CODE	IBM GRAPHIC	KEY
NUL	Null	0	0		nothing
SOH	Start of heading	1	1	☺	^A
STX	Start of text	2	2	☻	^B
ETX	End of text	3	3	♥	^C
EOT	End of transmission	4	4	♦	^D
ENQ	Enquiry	5	5	♣	^E
ACK	Acknowledge	6	6	♠	^F
BEL	Bell	7	7	•	^G
BS	Backspace	8	8	◘	^H
HT	Horizontal tab	9	9	○	^I
LF*	Line feed	10	A	◎	^J
VT	Vertical tab	11	B	♂	^K
FF	Form feed	12	C	♀	^L
CR	Carriage return	13	D	♪	^M
SO	Shift out	14	E	♫	^N
SI	Shift in	15	F	☼	^O
DLE	Data link escape	16	10	►	^P
DC1	Device control 1	17	11	◄	^Q
DC2	Device control 2	18	12	↕	^R
DC3	Device control 3	19	13	‼	^S
DC4	Device control 4	20	14	¶	^T
NAK	Negative acknowledge	21	15	§	^U
SYN	Synchronous idle	22	16	▬	^V
ETB	End transmission block	23	17	↨	^W
CAN	Cancel	24	18	↑	^X
EM	End of medium	25	19	↓	^Y
SUB	Substitute	26	1A	→	^Z
ESC	Escape	27	1B	←	^[
FS	File separator	28	1C	∟	^\
GS	Group separator	29	1D	↔	^]
RS	Record separator	30	1E	▲	^^
US	Unit separator	31	1F	▼	^_
DEL	Delete	127	7F	Δ	Del

* The Line feed character (LF = 10 decimal) can also be interpreted as the New-line (NL) character. Technically, the LF character moves to the next line while holding the same relative column position within the line, if possible. A separate Carriage return (CR = 13 decimal) must be issued to get to the beginning of the line. The alternative NL character interpretation is treated as a combined CR and LF operation, saving one character per line in text streams. The IBM PC uses the CR/LF convention. UNIX and XENIX use the NL convention.

FIGURE C-2 | *ASCII control character table*

Printable Character Table

The ASCII codes in the range of 32 to 126 decimal are designated "graphic" characters to show that they have a visible representation on a display device. Only the meaning of code 32, space (SP), which prints or displays as a blank location in a graphic sequence, is defined by the ASCII standard. All of the remaining graphic characters have meanings that are, in effect, enforced by consensus. We simply accept the fact that code 65 decimal represents the letter 'A', for example.

Nothing in the standard demands that the graphic symbols be shown as Gothic or Roman or any other type style. That decision is left to the terminal/computer maker and usually is determined by whatever type style the producer of the video controller chip supplies. The following table (Figure C-3) shows the accepted definitions of the graphic characters.

ASCII	DEC	HEX	ASCII	DEC	HEX	ASCII	DEC	HEX
\<space\>	32	20	@	64	40		96	60
!	33	21	A	65	41	a	97	61
"	34	22	B	66	42	b	98	62
#	35	23	C	67	43	c	99	63
$	36	24	D	68	44	d	100	64
%	37	25	E	69	45	e	101	65
&	38	26	F	70	46	f	102	66
`	39	27	G	71	47	g	103	67
(	40	28	H	72	48	h	104	68
)	41	29	I	73	49	i	105	69
*	42	2A	J	74	4A	j	106	6A
+	43	2B	K	75	4B	k	107	6B
,	44	2C	L	76	4C	l	108	6C
−	45	2D	M	77	4D	m	109	6D
.	46	2E	N	78	4E	n	110	6E
/	47	2F	O	79	4F	o	111	6F
0	48	30	P	80	50	p	112	70
1	49	31	Q	81	51	q	113	71
2	50	32	R	82	52	r	114	72
3	51	33	S	83	53	s	115	73
4	52	34	T	84	54	t	116	74
5	53	35	U	85	55	u	117	75
6	54	36	V	86	56	v	118	76
7	55	37	W	87	57	w	119	77
8	56	38	X	88	58	x	120	78
9	57	39	Y	89	59	y	121	79
:	58	3A	Z	90	5A	z	122	7A
;	59	3B	[	91	5B	{	123	7B
<	60	3C	\	92	5C	|	124	7C
=	61	3D	]	93	5D	}	125	7D
>	62	3E	^	94	5E	~	126	7E
?	63	3F	_	95	5F			

FIGURE C-3 | The ASCII standard character set

IBM Extended ASCII Codes

Because the ASCII character set is based on a 7-bit code, the high bit of each byte used by the IBM PC is available for other uses. When bit 7 (the high bit) is a logical 1, the character codes range from 128 to 255 decimal

(Figure C-4). IBM uses these extra 128 codes for special characters (international symbols, line-and-block drawing characters, special symbols for mathematics, and so forth).

IBM GRAPHIC	DEC	HEX	IBM GRAPHIC	DEC	HEX	IBM GRAPHIC	DEC	HEX	IBM GRAPHIC	DEC	HEX
Ç	128	80	á	160	A0	└	192	C0	α	224	E0
ü	129	81	í	161	A1	┴	193	C1	β	225	E1
é	130	82	ó	162	A2	┬	194	C2	Γ	226	E2
â	131	83	ú	163	A3	├	195	C3	π	227	E3
ä	132	84	ñ	164	A4	─	196	C4	Σ	228	E4
à	133	85	Ñ	165	A5	┼	197	C5	σ	229	E5
å	134	86	ª	166	A6	╞	198	C6	μ	230	E6
ç	135	87	º	167	A7	╟	199	C7	τ	231	E7
ê	136	88	¿	168	A8	╚	200	C8	Φ	232	E8
ë	137	89	⌐	169	A9	╔	201	C9	Θ	233	E9
è	138	8A	¬	170	AA	╩	202	CA	Ω	234	EA
ï	139	8B	½	171	AB	╦	203	CB	δ	235	EB
î	140	8C	¼	172	AC	╠	204	CC	∞	236	EC
ì	141	8D	¡	173	AD	═	205	CD	φ	237	ED
Ä	142	8E	«	174	AE	╬	206	CE	ε	238	EE
Å	143	8F	»	175	AF	╧	207	CF	∩	239	EF
É	144	90	░	176	B0	╨	208	D0	≡	240	F0
æ	145	91	▒	177	B1	╤	209	D1	±	241	F1
Æ	146	92	▓	178	B2	╥	210	D2	≥	242	F2
ô	147	93	│	179	B3	╙	211	D3	≤	243	F3
ö	148	94	┤	180	B4	╘	212	D4	⌠	244	F4
ò	149	95	╡	181	B5	╒	213	D5	⌡	245	F5
û	150	96	╢	182	B6	╓	214	D6	÷	246	F6
ù	151	97	╖	183	B7	╫	215	D7	≈	247	F7
ÿ	152	98	╕	184	B8	╪	216	D8	°	248	F8
Ö	153	99	╣	185	B9	┘	217	D9	•	249	F9
Ü	154	9A	║	186	BA	┌	218	DA	·	250	FA
¢	155	9B	╗	187	BB	█	219	DB	√	251	FB
£	156	9C	╝	188	BC	▄	220	DC	η	252	FC
¥	157	9D	╜	189	BD	▌	221	DD	²	253	FD
₧	158	9E	╛	190	BE	▐	222	DE	■	254	FE
ƒ	159	9F	┐	191	BF	▀	223	DF		255	FF

FIGURE C-4 | *The IBM extended ASCII character set*

Line-Drawing Characters—Quick Reference

Among the IBM extended ASCII characters are some line-drawing characters that allow us to draw boxes and other shapes that can be

formed from various corners and straight-line segments. The codes are
a bit scattered, so to make them accessible, Figure C-5 visually groups the
codes for single- and double-line drawing characters. The origin of these
design aids can be traced to Rich Schinnell in an item published in *PC
World* (November 1983).

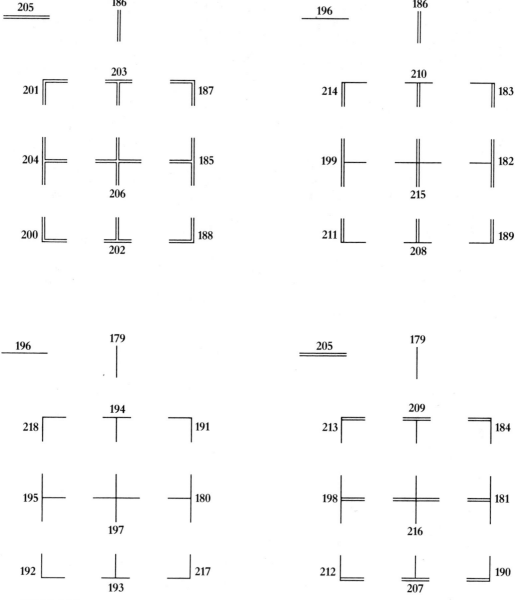

FIGURE C-5 | *Line-drawing character sets*

Block Characters—Quick Reference

The treasure trove of special characters in the IBM extended ASCII character set also contains eight block characters that can be used to good effect in screen displays. They are detailed in Figure C-6.

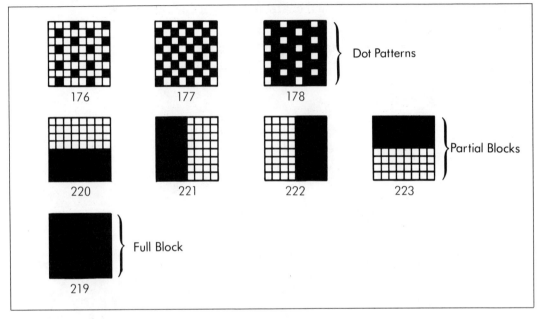

FIGURE C-6 | *Block character sets*

Video Attributes

Both the monochrome and color display systems used with PCs give us a considerable degree of control over the appearance of characters on the screen. Each character byte in memory is accompanied by an attribute byte that specifies the visual characteristics of each displayed character.

Figure C-7 shows how the attribute byte is interpreted.

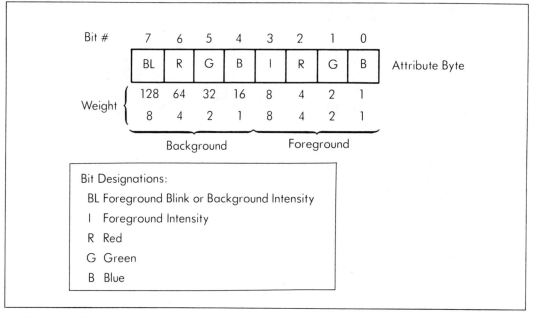

FIGURE C-7 | *Video attribute byte interpretation*

The following table summarizes the text mode attributes for both monochrome and color/graphics systems. The codes between 0 and 7 set the foreground (low 4 bits) or background (high 4 bits) attribute. Thus, storing the code 0x02 in an attribute byte produces a green foreground and a black background.

The high bit in each 4-bit (nibble) attribute component determines the intensity. In the foreground component, setting bit 3 causes the foreground to be high intensity. Setting bit 7 of an attribute byte controls either foreground blinking or background intensity. On a CGA, port 3D8, bit 5 enables foreground blinking when set and disables blinking when cleared. The power-on default is blink (bit 5 = 1). The equivalent MDA port is 3B8.

We can combine attribute values using bit shifting and ORing to produce various compound attributes. The combined code

$$(0x01 << 4) \mid 0x07 \mid 0x08$$

yields a bright white character on a blue background.

PRIMARY ATTRIBUTES

Dec Code	Hex Code	Binary Code	Attribute CGA	Description MDA	MDA BG
0	00	0000	Black	Black	Black
1	01	0001	Blue	White Underline	White
2	02	0010	Green	White	White
3	03	0011	Cyan	White	White
4	04	0100	Red	White	White
5	05	0101	Magenta	White	White
6	06	0110	Brown	White	White
7	07	0111	White	White	White

INTENSITY MODIFIERS

Dec Code	Hex Code	Binary Code	Description
8	08	1000	High Intensity
128	80	10000000	Blinking Foreground (or High Intensity Background). [This is just (0x08 << 4) and is referred to as the "blink" bit or background intensity bit depending upon whether blinking is enabled (default) or disabled.]

Local Library Summary $\quad$ D

Proficient C is largely about stockpiling routines to augment those provided in the standard library. In the course of 14 chapters, we have developed numerous functions and macros for a wide range of purposes. To make the routines accessible to programmers, a brief manual page for each routine is presented here.

The routines are grouped by library category and organized alphabetically within categories. The libraries we developed are the ansi.sys interface (ansi.lib), the operating system interfaces (bios.lib and dos.lib), the buffered screen interface (sbuf.lib), and the utility routines (util.lib).

ANSI LIBRARY

The ANSI device driver is accessed primarily through the macros defined in the ansi.h *header file that resides in* \include\local. *Two additional routines are implemented as functions in* \lib\local\ansi.lib. *The ANSI device driver and this interface are described in Chapter 13.*

Function
 ansi_cpr—cursor position report

Synopsis

```
#include <local\ansi.h>

void ansi_cpr(row, col)
int *row;        /* pointer to row value */
int *col;        /* pointer to column value */
```

Description

Request a cursor position report from the ANSI device driver. The driver must have been previously installed. The cursor position values are saved in the *row* and *col* variables whose addresses are passed as parameters.

Notes

This function will fail (hang the system waiting for keyboard input) if the ANSI device driver is not properly installed.

Macro

ANSI_CUP—position the cursor
ANSI_HVP—horizontal and vertical position

Synopsis

```
#include <local\ansi.h>


ANSI_CUP(r, c)
ANSI_HVP(r, c)
short r, c;     /* row and column */
```

Description

These two macros achieve the same result. They attempt to move the cursor to the specified screen position. Illegal requests are ignored.

Macro

ANSI_CUB—move cursor back (left)
ANSI_CUD—move cursor down
ANSI_CUF—move cursor forward (right)
ANSI_CUU—move cursor up

Synopsis

```
#include <local\ansi.h>

ANSI_CUB(n)
ANSI_CUD(n)
ANSI_CUF(n)
ANSI_CUU(n)
short n;        /* number of repetitions (columns or rows) */
```

Description

These four macros attempt to move the cursor in the specified direction. If *n* is larger than the number of rows or columns remaining in the direction of travel, the cursor is moved to the extreme position.

Macro

ANSI_DSR—request a device status report
ANSI_RCP—restore screen position
ANSI_SCP—save screen position

Synopsis

```
#include <local\ansi.h>

ANSI_DSR
ANSI_RCP
ANSI_SCP
```

Description

A call to *ANSI_DSR* causes the ANSI driver to deposit a string containing the cursor row and column data into the keyboard buffer where it can be read (see the *ansi_cpr( )* function). *ANSI_SCP* and *ANSI_RCP* are cooperating macros that communicate through private storage to save and restore the cursor position.

Macro

ANSI_ED—erase in display (clear screen)
ANSI_EL—erase in line (clear to end of line)

Synopsis

```
#include <local\ansi.h>

ANSI_ED
ANSI_EL
```

Description

ANSI_ED sets all character locations in the display to blanks, effectively clearing the screen. Similarly, *ANSI_EL* sets all character positions from the cursor to the end of the line to blanks.

Notes

Most ANSI drivers use the prevailing video attribute for cleared character positions, but at least the MS-DOS version of the ANSI driver provided for the AT&T 6300 uses the "normal" (white on black) attribute.

Macro

ANSI_RM—reset mode
ANSI_SM—set mode

Synopsis

```
#include <local\ansi.h>

ANSI_RM(m)
ANSI_SM(m)
short m;
```

Description

These two macros are used to set and reset (clear) video modes. In addition to
the usual video modes that can be set from the DOS command line using the
MODE command, ANSI_SM and ANSI_RM permit programs to control
"wrapping" at the end of display lines.

Macro

ANSI_SGR—set graphic rendition (video attribute)

Synopsis

```
#include <local\ansi.h>


ANSI_SGR(a)
unsigned char a;        /* video attribute */
```

Description

ANSI_SGR can be used to set any of the video attributes allowed for text modes.

Function

ansi_tst—check for the presence of *ANSI.SYS*

Synopsis

```
#include <local\ansi.h>


void ansi_tst()
```

Description

Uses cursor positioning and reading to determine whether the ANSI device
driver is installed. If not, the function displays an error message and returns
control to DOS. If the ANSI driver is installed, control is returned to the calling
program.

Notes

This function uses the BIOS *readca( )* function to find out where the cursor is
located because *ansi_cpr( )* cannot be called unless the ANSI driver is known
to be installed. Thus, *ansi_tst( )* may fail on PCs that are not completely BIOS-
compatible with the IBM PC family.

Function

colornum—convert a color string to a number

Synopsis

```
#include <local\ibmcolor.h>


int colornum(name)
char *name;             /* color string */
```

Description

Using a built-in lookup table, *colornum( )* converts a color name in string form, "red" for example, to its IBM numeric equivalent (4 in this case).

Return

A number that specifies the IBM color value for the specified color name.

Function

setattr—set video attribute

Synopsis

```
#include <local\ansi.h>
#include <local\ibmcolor.h>

void setattr(pos, attr)
POSITION pos;
int attr;
```

Description

Using information provided by the caller about the attribute position *(pos)*, *setattr( )* sets the foreground, background, or border attribute to the specified value.

Function

userattr—set a user-specified attribute

Synopsis

```
#include <local\ansi.h>

int userattr(foreground, background, border)
char *foreground, *background, *border;
```

Description

A program can call *userattr( )* just before exiting to set the video attributes to those specified by the user in the DOS environment (using FGND, BKGND, and BORDER DOS variables). The calling function must specify attribute values to be used in the event that none are specified in the environment.

Return

An indication of SUCCESS or FAILURE.

BIOS LIBRARY

The BIOS library is composed of selected routines supported by the PC's ROM BIOS. Primary coverage is given to BIOS video and equipment-determination functions. In addition, keyboard status and some composite video functions are included in the library. Most other needed services can be obtained via routines in the standard libraries provided with nearly all C compilers for DOS.

*Most of the BIOS routines are designed to return the value of the carry flag, which
is a nonzero value if an error occurs duing the interrupt operation. A few use the
return value to pass back the information requested by the calling function.*

Function
> clrscrn—clear the entire screen to spaces
> clrw—clear a "window" region to spaces

Synopsis

```
    int clrscrn(a)
    int clrw(t, l, b, r, a)
    unsigned char a;        /* video attribute */
    int t, l;               /* upper left corner */
    int b, r;               /* lower right corner */
```

Description
> The two functions, *clrscrn( )* and *clrw( )*, set all characters to spaces in the entire
> display memory or a specified region, respectively. The current "visual" page is
> cleared.

Return
> The value of the carry flag.

Function
> delay—provide a machine-independent time delay

Synopsis

```
    void delay(d)
    float d;                /* delay duration */
```

Description
> The *delay( )* function loops to waste the specified number of seconds and
> fractional seconds. The delay has a practical resolution of about .06 seconds.

Function
> drawbox—draw a single-line text graphics box shape

Synopsis

```
    int drawbox(top, lft, btm, rgt, pg)
    int top, lft;           /* upper left corner */
    int btm, rgt;           /* lower right corner */
    int pg;                 /* screen page number */
```

Description
> The *drawbox( )* function draws a fine-rule box (using the IBM single-line
> drawing characters) around the perimeter of the region specified by the corner
> parameters. The *pg* parameter specifies the screen page (active) to draw on. On
> a standard monochrome display adapter, this value must be 0.

Notes

This function is usually not appropriate for use in graphics modes because the special drawing characters are not defined unless you create your own table of "extended" character definitions.

Function

ega_info — gather EGA-related information

Synopsis

```
#include <local\video.h>

int ega_info(memsize, mode, features, switches)
int *memsize;              /* memory size index (0-3) */
int *mode;                 /* color (0)/mono (1) mode */
unsigned int *features;    /* feature bit settings */
unsigned int *switches;    /* EGA switch settings */
```

Description

This function uses an EGA BIOS routine to gather and save EGA-related information including whether an EGA adapter is installed in the system. Memory size is reported by an index (from 0 = 64 KB up to 3 = 256 KB in 64-KB increments) and mode is indicated only as color (0) or monochrome. Use the *getstate( )* function to find out what the video mode number is.

Return

A logical 1 if the reported memory size is valid or 0 otherwise. This is considered by IBM to be an adequate indicator of the presence or absence of an EGA adapter.

Function

equipchk — get equipment list

Synopsis

```
#include <local\equip.h>

int equipchk()
```

Description

The *equipchk( )* function queries the system data areas and fills in the global *Eq* structure to indicate what equipment is installed. The data structure holds the number of logical disk drives, parallel printer ports, and serial ports. It also indicates whether the system has a game port and shows how much of the installed memory is on the system board. In addition, the current video mode is indicated by the BIOS video mode number (see *getstate( )* for details).

Return

The value of the carry flag.

Function
getctype—get the current cursor type

Synopsis

```
#include <local\bioslib.h>

int getctype(start_scan, end_scan, pg)
int *start_scan;        /* starting cursor scan line */
int *end_scan;          /* ending cursor scan line */
int pg;                 /* "visual" page */
```

Description
The *getctype( )* function retrieves the values of the starting and ending cursor scan rows.

Return
The value of the carry flag.

Function
getstate—get the current video state

Synopsis

```
#include <local\video.h>

int getstate()
```

Description
This function queries the system data areas in memory and updates the global video state variables.

Return
The value of the carry flag.

Function
getticks—get the current timer "tick" count

Synopsis

```
long getticks()
```

Description
This function queries the BIOS data area via the time-of-day service to get a value that is the number of timer ticks since midnight. If the rollover flag is set, a full day's worth of ticks is added to the count.

Return
The current timer "tick" count.

Function

kbd_stat—get keyboard status information

Synopsis

```
#include <local\keybdlib.h>

unsigned char kbd_stat()
```

Description

The *kbd_stat( )* function obtains keyboard status information and makes it available to the calling function. Each bit in the status byte is significant and is defined in the *keybdlib.h* file. This function lets the program determine the current state of the shift, control (Ctrl), alternate shift (Alt), and lock (Num, Caps, Scroll) keys.

Return

The value of the AL register, which contains the keyboard status information (bit-significant).

Function

memsize—get memory size in kilobytes

Synopsis

```
int memsize()
```

Description

The *memsize( )* function reads the system data area to determine the total amount of memory installed in the system.

Return

The total memory size (system board plus I/O channel) in kilobytes.

Function

palette—select graphics palette or text border color

Synopsis

```
int palette(id, color)
unsigned int id;        /* palette identifier */
unsigned int color;     /* color number */
```

Description

The *palette( )* function can be used in either graphics or text (alphanumeric) modes. It selects the palette of foreground drawing colors in graphics modes. In text modes, it selects the border color.

Return

The value of the carry flag.

Function
    putcur—move the cursor to a specified row and column

Synopsis

```
int putcur(r, c, pg)
int r, c;              /* row and column */
int pg;                /* "active" screen page */
```

Description
    This function places the cursor at the specified row and column of the active
    page given by *pg*. Illegal requests are silently ignored by the BIOS routine.

Return
    The value of the carry flag.

Function
    putfld—display a string in a field

Synopsis

```
int putfld(s, w, pg)
register char *s;      /* string to write */
int w;                 /* field width */
int pg;                /* screen page for writes */
```

Description
    The *putfld( )* function calls other BIOS functions to display a string within a
    field starting on page *pg* at the current cursor position and extending for *w*
    columns. Runs of a single given character, such as a series of spaces, are com-
    pressed to a single call on *writec( )* to reduce function-call overhead. The field
    is padded with spaces if the string does not completely fill it. The string is trun-
    cated if it is too long to fit in the field. The cursor location is updated to the last
    position written.

Return
    A 0 if all goes well or a nonzero value to flag an error.

Function
    putstr—display a string in the prevailing attribute

Synopsis

```
int putstr(s, pg)
register char *s;      /* string to display */
int pg;                /* "active" screen page */
```

Description
    The *putstr( )* function places the text of the string into display memory and
    advances the cursor position.

Return
Number of characters written.

Notes
Results are undefined if the string is not confined to the current screen row.

Function
put_ch—display a character

Synopsis

```
int put_ch(ch, pg)
register char ch;       /* character to write */
int pg;                 /* "active" screen page */
```

Description
The *put_ch( )* function writes a single character to the display and advances the cursor position.

Return
Always 1 to indicate the number of characters written.

Function
readca—read the character and attribute in a cell

Synopsis

```
int readca(ch, attr, pg)
unsigned char *ch;      /* character */
unsigned char *attr;    /* video attribute */
int pg;                 /* "active" screen page */
```

Description
The *readca( )* function gets the values of the character and video attribute at the current cursor position on the specified active screen page and fills in the *ch* and *attr* variables pointed to by the parameters.

Return
The value of the carry flag.

Function
readcur—get the current cursor row and column

Synopsis

```
int readcur(row, col, pg)
int *row, *col;         /* pointers to cursor values */
int pg;                 /* "active" screen page */
```

Description

The readcur( ) function reports the location of the cursor on the specified screen page by storing the row and column values in the *row* and *col* variables pointed to by the parameters.

Return

The value of the carry flag.

Function

readdot—read the value of a single pixel

Synopsis

```
int readdot(row, col, dcolor)
int row, col;           /* cursor position */
int *dcolor;            /* pointer to dot color */
```

Description

The *readdot( )* function places the color number for the pixel at the row and column position into the variable pointed to by the *dcolor* parameter. The *row* and *col* parameters can be used to address up to 224,000 individual screen pixels in the high resolution mode of the Enhanced Graphics Adapter.

Return

The value of the carry flag.

Function

scroll—scroll a specified screen region vertically

Synopsis

```
int scroll(t, l, b, r, n, a)
int t, l;               /* upper left corner */
int b, r;               /* lower right corner */
int n;                  /* number of rows to scroll */
unsigned char a;        /* video attribute */
```

Description

The *scroll( )* routine clears (initializes) the specified region if *n* is *0*. It scrolls the display image up *n* lines if *n* is a positive nonzero value and down if *n* is negative. Vacated lines are filled with blanks (spaces) in the specified attribute.

Return

The value of the carry flag.

Function

setctype—set the cursor type

Synopsis

```
int setctype(start, end)
int start;              /* starting cursor scan line */
int end;                /* ending cursor scan line */
```

Description

The *setctype( )* function sets the starting and ending scan lines that form the cursor shape. If the starting scan line is greater than the ending scan line, the cursor is split (formed of two parts) on perfectly IBM-compatible machines. Setting the cursor starting scan line to a large value turns the cursor off on many machines, but this is not a reliable method on all hardware.

Return

The value of the carry flag.

Function

setpage—select the "visual" video page

Synopsis

```
int setpage(pg)
int pg;                 /* "visual" screen page */
```

Description

This function sets the "visual" screen page to *pg*. It checks the value of *pg* against the valid page ranges for the current video mode.

Return

The value of the carry flag or -1 if an illegal page request is made.

Function

setvmode—set the video mode

Synopsis

```
int setvmode(vmode)
int vmode;              /* video mode number */
```

Description

The *setvmode( )* function attempts to set the specified video mode. Illegal mode requests are not detected and are usually silently ignored by the BIOS routine.

Return

The value of the carry flag.

Notes

This function cannot be used to switch from one display adapter to another in systems equipped with more than one adapter. Instruct users to run the DOS MODE command to set the mode before entering the program.

Function

writea—write an attribute
writec—write a character
writeca—write a character in a specified attribute

Synopsis

```
int writea(a, count, pg)
int writec(ch, count, pg)
int writeca(ch, attr, count, pg)
unsigned char ch;        /* character */
unsigned char attr;      /* video attribute */
int count;               /* number of repetitions */
int pg;                  /* "active" screen page */
```

Description

These functions write a (possibly) repeated attribute, character, or a combination of the two to the specified screen page. The count specifies the number of characters to write and must fit entirely within the current screen row.

Return

The value of the carry flag.

Function

writedot—write a single pixel

Synopsis

```
int writedot(r, c, color)
int r, c;                /* coordinates of the pixel */
int color;               /* dot color */
```

Description

This function is for use in graphics modes only. It sets the color of the specified pixel to color. Setting the color to the same color as the background effectively erases the pixel.

Return

The value of the carry flag.

Function

writemsg—write a two-part message

Synopsis

```
int writemsg(r, c, w, s1, s2, pg)
int r, c;                /* starting location */
int w;                   /* field width */
char *s1, *s2;           /* components of the string */
int pg;                  /* "active" screen page */
```

Description

The *writemsg( )* function places a two-part message (either or both parts may be empty) on the specified screen page. If the combined string is too long to fit in the field it is truncated. If it does not fill the field exactly, the field is padded with spaces.

Return

The number of characters written.

Function

writetty—write a character using "teletype" style

Synopsis

```
int writetty(ch, attr, pg)
unsigned char ch;        /* character */
unsigned char attr;      /* video attribute */
int pg;                  /* "active" screen page */
```

Description

The *writetty( )* function places a character into the specified screen page and advances the cursor position. The screen is scrolled if necessary to keep the current position within the viewable screen boundaries. The function responds to the usual format effectors (backspace, carriage return, and linefeed) correctly. All other codes, including other control codes, are simply displayed.

Return

The value of the carry flag.

Notes

The attribute specification is honored only in text modes. It is simply ignored in graphics modes.

DOS LIBRARY

Only a very limited set of DOS routines are packaged in the local DOS library because the standard library provides rather complete DOS access to disk files, the console keyboard, DOS date and time, and so on.

Function

drvpath—convert a drive name to a full pathname

Synopsis

```
char *drvpath(path)
char path[];              /* path string buffer */
```

Description

A disk drive designation (d:) is a shorthand notation for the current directory on disk drive d. The *drvpath( )* function accepts a disk drive designation as the initial portion of a character buffer and appends the full pathname of the current directory on that drive to it.

Return

A pointer to a full pathname string starting with the drive letter.

Notes

The user-supplied buffer (path) must be large enough to hold the longest DOS directory pathname (64 characters) plus a terminating NUL.

Function

first_fm—find the first matching filename
next_fm—find the next matching filename

Synopsis

```
int first_fm(path, fa)
int next_fm()
char *path;               /* ambiguous pathname */
int fa;                   /* file attributes */
```

Description

Under DOS, we can specify filenames ambiguously using the * and ? wildcard characters. The *first_fm( )* function finds the first match in directory order to an ambiguous specification. If the first match is found, additional matches, if any, may be found by calling the *next_fm( )* function repeatedly until no match is found.

The file attributes specified by the *fa* parameter determine which files that match the ambiguous name will be matched. If *fa* equals 0, the functions attempt to match only ordinary files. If the volume-label attribute is set, the functions search only for a volume label. Setting *fa* to system, hidden, subdirectory, or any combination of these attributes tells the functions to match files having those attributes in addition to all ordinary files.

Return

Both functions return the value of the carry flag, which is 0 for success or nonzero for failure.

Notes

These functions use a disk transfer area of type struct DTA, which is defined in the header file *ls.h*. The DTA is established by a call to *setdta( )*. If any intervening functions alter the DTA, it must be reset by calling *setdta( )* before making further calls to *next_fm*.

Function

getdrive—return the ID of the default drive

Synopsis

```
int getdrive()
```

Description

The *getdrive( )* function asks DOS for the ID of the current disk drive. The ID is the number used internally by DOS where 0 means drive A, 1 means B, and so on.

Return

The internal drive number of the current disk drive.

Function

getkey—get a keystroke

Synopsis

```
#include <local\keydefs.h>

int getkey()
```

Description

Gets the next available key code from the keyboard buffer. If nothing is ready, *getkey( )* waits for the user to type something. If you do not want a "blocking" read, use *keyready( )* (or *kbhit( )*) to determine whether anything is ready to read before calling *getkey( )*.

Return

The code associated with the oldest item in the keyboard buffer. If the returned value is 256 or more, the input was produced by a special key and the returned value represents an extended key code (*NUL* + scan code).

Notes

Because *getkey( )* uses DOS function 7 (INT 21H), it is immune to Ctrl-Break and it does not echo the typed input to the screen.

Function

keyready—check the keyboard buffer

Synopsis

```
int keyready()
```

Description
Checks the console for a waiting keystroke.

Return
A nonzero value if something is waiting in the keyboard buffer.

Notes
This function performs the same job as the *kbhit( )* function in the standard
Microsoft library. It is presented for those whose C compilers offer no equivalent
function.

Function
setdta—set the disk transfer area (DTA)

Synopsis

```
void setdta(bp)
char *bp;                /* buffer pointer */
```

Description
This function establishes a buffer in memory where disk transfers take place.
There may be multiple DTAs of varying sizes but only one may be active at any
time. If no DTA is established by a program, DOS sets up a 128-byte default DTA
in the program segment prefix (PSP) of the running program.

Function
ver—get the DOS major and minor version numbers

Synopsis

```
int ver()
```

Description
Gets the DOS version major and minor numbers.

Return
The *ver( )* function returns the DOS major version number in the low byte (bits
0–7) and the minor version number in the high byte (bits 8–15).

Notes
These values duplicate the values in the global *_osmajor* and *_osminor* variables
supported by the Microsoft C Compiler. They are here for use with compilers
that support the *bdos( )* function but not the global version variables.

SCREEN-BUFFER LIBRARY

*The screen-buffer library routines are described in Chapter 12. The routines are used
to form a display image in an off-screen buffer and to copy the image in the buffer to
display memory.*

Function

sb_box — draw a box around a window

Synopsis

```
#include <local\sbuf.h>
#include <local\box.h>

int sb_box(win, type, attr)
struct REGION *win;            /* target window */
short type;                    /* line drawing type */
unsigned char attr;            /* video attribute */
```

Description

Draws a box shape around a rectangular region (defined by *win*) in the screen buffer. Types are summarized in the following table:

Type	Description
0	*Default type: + for corners, | for vertical edges, and − for horizontal edges*
1	*Single lines all around*
2	*Double lines all around*
3	*Single horizontal and double vertical lines*
4	*Double horizontal and single vertical lines*
5	*Block shapes for all lines and corners*

Return

SB_OK

Function

sb_fill — fill the scrolling region of a window
sb_filla — fill with an attribute only
sb_fillc — fill with a character only

Synopsis

```
#include <local\sbuf.h>
extern struct BUFFER Sbuf;
extern union CELL Scrnbuf[SB_ROWS][SB_COLS];

int sb_fill(win, ch, attr)
int sb_filla()
int sb_fillc()
struct REGION *win;            /* target window */
unsigned char ch;              /* character */
unsigned char attr;            /* video attribute */
```

Description

These three functions fill the scrolling region of a window (the entire window if not set explicitly). The *sb_fill( )* function takes both a character and an attribute as parameters. The *sb_filla( )* function sets all cells to a common video attribute while leaving the character in each cell undisturbed. And *sb_fillc( )* sets all cells to a common character value while leaving the attribute in each cell undisturbed.

Return

SB_OK

Function

sb_init—initialize the buffered-screen interface

Synopsis

```
int sb_init()
```

Description

Sets up the *Sbuf* buffer control structure and initializes the flag bits and line variables. The *SB_DIRECT* bit is set to a logical 1 if the DOS variable UPDATEMODE is set to DIRECT.

Return

SB_OK if the interface can be initialized and *SB_ERR* if not (due to a bad update mode specification).

Function

sb_move—locate the cursor within a window

Synopsis

```
#include <local\sbuf.h>
extern struct BUFFER Sbuf;
extern union CELL Scrnbuf[SB_ROWS][SB_COLS];

int sb_move(win, r, c)
struct REGION *win;              /* target window */
register short r, c;             /* row and column */
```

Description

The cursor is moved to the specified window-relative row and column (*r, c*). The appropriate data structures are updated to reflect the change.

Return

SB_OK if the cursor location is valid for the window or *SB_ERR* if either *r* or *c* is an invalid value.

Function

sb_new — establish a window (screen-buffer region)

Synopsis

```
#include <local\sbuf.h>

struct REGION *sb_new(top, left, height, width)
int top;                /* top row */
int left;               /* left column */
int height;             /* total rows */
int width;              /* total columns */
```

Description

This function establishes a rectangular region of the screen buffer as a window, defined by the upper left corner position and the height and width values. The scrolling region is initially set to the window values, but may be altered by a call to *sb_set_scrl( )*.

Return

A pointer to a newly allocated window structure or *NULL* if the window could not be established.

Function

sb_putc — put a character into a window
sb_puts — put a string into a window

Synopsis

```
#include <local\sbuf.h>
extern struct BUFFER Sbuf;
extern union CELL Scrnbuf[SB_ROWS][SB_COLS];

int sb_putc(win, ch)
int sb_puts(win, s)
struct REGION *win;      /* target window */
char ch;
unsigned char *s;        /* text string */
```

Description

The *sb_putc( )* function puts the specified character into the screen-buffer array at the current window position and advances the window "cursor." If the character is a newline, the remainder of the current window row is cleared and the cursor advances to the first position of the next row. If scrolling is enabled and is required to keep the cursor inside the window, *sb_scrl( )* is called and the cursor lands in the first position of the last window row.

A call to *sb_puts* is treated as a call to *sb_putc* for each character in the string. A tab is expanded to spaces using a series of calls to *sb_putc( )*. Expansion is limited to the current window row.

Return

    SB_OK or *SB_ERR* if an error occurs.

Function

    sb_ra—read attribute
    sb_rc—read character
    sb_rca—read character and attribute

Synopsis

```
#include <local\sbuf.h>
extern struct BUFFER Sbuf;
extern union CELL Scrnbuf[SB_ROWS][SB_COLS];


unsigned char sb_ra(win)
unsigned char sb_rc(win)
unsigned short sb_rca(win)


union REGION *win;              /* target window */
```

Description

    Each of these functions is passed a window pointer and window-relative row and column values of a cell, and returns information about the specified cell. The *sb_ra( )* function obtains only the video attribute; *sb_rc( )* obtains only the character value. However, *sb_rca( )* gathers both the character and the video attribute of the specified cell.

Return

    The *sb_ra( )* and *sb_rc( )* functions return a byte that contains the attribute or character at the current window cursor position. A word containing both the character and attribute is returned by *sb_rca( )*.

Function

    sb_scrl—scroll a window region
    sb_set_scrl—change the defined scrolling region

Synopsis

```
#include <local\sbuf.h>
extern struct BUFFER Sbuf;
extern union CELL Scrnbuf[SB_ROWS][SB_COLS];


int sb_scrl(win, n)
int sb_set_scrl(win, top, left, bottom, right)


union REGION *win;              /* target window */
short top, left;                /* upper left corner */
short bottom, right;            /* lower right corner */
short n;                        /* number of rows to scroll */
```

Description

If *n* is greater than 0, *sb_scrl( )* scrolls the specified window down by *n* rows. A negative *n* causes upward scrolling. Vacated lines are filled with spaces in the prevailing attribute. If *n* equals 0, the entire scrolling region is set to spaces.

Scrolling occurs within a window's scrolling region. The *sb_set_scrl( )* function defines the scrolling region, which may be any size up to the full window size.

Return

SB_OK. If an illegal scrolling region is specified, *SB_ERR* is returned by *sb_set_scrl( )*.

Function

sb_show — copy the screen buffer to display memory

Synopsis

```
#include <local\sbuf.h>
extern struct BUFFER Sbuf;
extern union CELL Scrnbuf[SB_ROWS][SB_COLS];


int sb_show(pg)
short pg;
```

Description

The screen-buffer array is copied to display memory by *sb_show( )*, which uses either BIOS routines or direct display memory accesses, depending on the value of the variable UPDATEMODE (BIOS or DIRECT) in the DOS environment.

Return

SB_OK

Function

sb_wa — write an attribute
sb_wc — write a character
sb_wca — write a character and attribute

Synopsis

```
#include <local\sbuf.h>
extern struct BUFFER Sbuf;
extern union CELL Scrnbuf[SB_ROWS][SB_COLS];


int sb_wa(win, attr, n)
int sb_wc(win, ch, n)
int sb_wca(win, ch, attr, n)
union REGION *win;              /* target window */
unsigned char ch;              /* character */
unsigned char attr;            /* video attribute */
short n;                       /* number of repetitions */
```

Description

These functions place characters and attributes in the screen-buffer array. The window cursor position is not changed. The repetition number specifies the number of buffer cells that are affected.

Return

SB_OK if the write is successful or *SB_ERR* if an error occurs.

Notes

These functions are valid only within the current row. Behavior is undefined if writes are attempted outside the boundaries of the specified window.

UTILITY LIBRARY

The development of the utility library starts in Chapter 3 and continues throughout the book. These routines are usable in a variety of programming situations and are not easily classified in any of the foregoing categories.

Function

beep—issue a standard terminal beep (Ctrl-G)

Synopsis

```
void beep()
```

Description

Call *beep( )* to sound the PC's internal speaker.

Function

byte2hex—convert a byte value to hexadecimal

Synopsis

```
char *byte2hex(data, buf)
unsigned char data;          /* 1-byte data item */
char *buf;                   /* hex string buffer */
```

Description

The *byte2hex( )* function converts a 1-byte numeric value to a 2-byte hexadecimal representation.

Return

A pointer to the resulting hexadecimal string.

Notes

The calling function must provide a buffer that is large enough to receive the 2-byte string and the terminating null byte.

Function

clrprnt—clear printer to default settings

Synopsis

```
#include <local\printer.h>


int clrprnt(fout)
FILE *fout;
```

Description

The *clrprnt( )* function sends codes needed to set an attached printer back to its power-on default values for the major print modes. It does so by individually clearing each mode rather than sending a printer reset command to avoid "paper creep" and alteration of the top-of-form setting.

Return

SUCCESS if all goes well or *FAILURE* if any attempt at writing to the output stream fails.

Function

fatal—print an error message and exit

Synopsis

```
void fatal(pname, str, errlvl)
char *pname;
char *str;
int errlvl;
```

Description

If an error occurs in a program, *fatal( )* can be called to display an error message and then exit with a status (ERRORLEVEL in DOS terms) other than 0 to indicate an error. The usual error code is 1, but other values can be used if a program can fail in more ways than one.

Function

fcopy—copy input file to output file

Synopsis

```
int fcopy(fin, fout)
FILE *fin, *fout;
```

Description

This function copies an input stream (*FILE* ∗) to an output stream (*FILE* ∗) using the standard library functions *fgets( )* and *fputs( )* and a private buffer of *BUFSIZ* bytes. The *ferror( )* macro is used to check for input errors and testing is done for the unambiguous *EOF* on the output stream.

Return

A successful file copy operation produces a 0 return value. Any input or output error that is detected causes a nonzero return.

Function

fixtabs—set fixed-interval tab stops

Synopsis

```
void fixtabs(interval)
int interval;            /* tabbing interval */
```

Description

A set of fixed tab stops can be set using *fixtabs( )* to initialize the private Tabstops array and then set tab stops at the specified intervals. Internally, the Tabstops array has tab stops at column 0 and repeating at the specified interval. Standard terminal usage has an interval of 8 columns.

Function

getname—extract filename[.ext] from a pathname

Synopsis

```
char *getname(path)
char *path;
```

Description

This function extracts a full filespec (filename[.ext]) from a pathname. It checks to see that the pathname given as a parameter is a valid pathname. Path separators of \ and / are accepted and may be intermixed.

Return

A pointer to a vaild filespec or *NULL* if the path parameter is not a valid pathname.

Function

getopt—get option letters and option arguments

Synopsis

```
extern int optind;
extern int opterr;
extern char *optarg;

int getopt(argc, argv, òpts)
int argc;                /* argument count */
char *argv[];            /* argument vector array */
char *opts;              /* option string */
```

Description

The string variable *opts* is a list of recognized option letters. Option letters that are followed by a colon are expected to take an argument. On each successive call to *getopt( )*, the function returns the next option letter in *argv* that matches a letter in *opts*. The *optarg* variable points to an option argument, if any is expected and found or *NULL* otherwise.

When all options have been processed, *getopt( )* returns *EOF.* The special option "--" (double dash) may be used to mark the end of options. When found, this causes *getopt( )* to skip the special option and return *EOF.*

Return

If an option letter in *argv* is not found in the *opts* string, *getopt( )* returns a question mark and prints an error message. Setting *opterr* to 0 silences *getopt( )*.

Notes

This *getopt( )* is the public domain version that is provided by the AT&T UNIX System Toolchest. It is presented in this book with the permission of AT&T in the interest of promoting a common command-line interface for programs.

Function

getpname—extract a program name from a pathname

Synopsis

```
void getpname(path, pname)
char *path;          /* full or relative pathname */
char *pname;         /* filename part of program name */
```

Description

The *getpname( )* function receives a full or relative pathname. It strips off any leading path information and any trailing extension. This function accepts both \ and / as path separators. It does not check to see that the path parameter is a valid path.

Function

getxline—get an expanded line of text

Synopsis

```
char *getxline(buf, size, fin)
char *buf;           /* output buffer */
int size;            /* maximum number of bytes */
FILE *fin;           /* input stream */
```

Description

The *getxline( )* function receives a line of text as input and "expands" the line by converting each tab to the correct number of spaces. The total character count may thus be altered, but the expanded line appears to be visually identical to the input line when displayed.

Return

A pointer to the buffer that contains the expanded line or *NULL* if an error occurs.

Notes

This function queries the tabstop array, so you must first call either *fixtabs( )* or *vartabs( )* to set tabs.

Function

fconfig—get pointer to a configuration file

Synopsis

```
FILE *fconfig(varname, fname)
char *varname;          /* DOS environment variable name */
char *fname;            /* file name */
```

Description

This function looks for a configuration file by the name *fname*. It looks first in the current directory and then in a directory pointed to by the *varname* DOS variable.

Return

A pointer to the configuration file if one is found or a *NULL* pointer if not.

Function

last_ch—get the last character of a string

Synopsis

```
char last_ch(s)
char *s;                /* source string */
```

Description

The *last_ch( )* function finds the last character of the source string, *s* (just before the *NUL* termination).

Return

The character value or −1 if the string is empty.

Function

lines—send blank lines to an output stream

Synopsis

```
int lines(n, fp)
int n;                  /* number of repetitions */
FILE *fp;               /* output stream */
```

Description

The *lines( )* function places *n* newline characters on the output stream.

Return

The number of newlines actually emitted, which may be less than the number requested if an error occurs on the output stream.

Function

memchk—check for physical memory at an address

Synopsis

```
int memchk(seg, os)
unsigned int seg;        /* segment */
unsigned int os;         /* offset */
```

Description

By sequentially writing and reading the memory location specified by the segmented address, *memchk( )* attempts to determine whether any physical memory is installed. To prevent clobbering needed memory values, the original value is preserved and restored upon completion of the test.

Return

If active memory is found at the specified address, *memchk( )* returns a 1. If no active memory is found, 0 is returned.

Function

mkslist—create a selection list (lookup table)

Synopsis

```
extern long Highest;

int mkslist(list)
char *list;              /* pointer to a list in string form */
```

Description

The *mkslist( )* function extracts tokens from a string representation of a list of numbers, converts the tokens to numeric values, and stores the values as a set of numeric ranges in an array (up to 10 ranges permitted by the current design).

Single numbers are represented as ranges having the same starting and ending number. Open-ended ranges (for example, 3–) are represented as the starting number to some unreasonably high ending value (BIGGEST). The list of ranges is terminated by a −1 starting value in the last array element following the last valid range.

Return

Always zero.

Function

nlerase—erase a newline in a string

Synopsis

```
char *nlerase(s)
char *s;
```

Description

The *nlerase( )* function scans a string and replaces the first newline it finds with a *NUL* (\0) character, effectively terminating the string and erasing the newline.

Return

A pointer to the modified string.

Function

selected—determine whether a number is in a range

Synopsis

```
int selected(n)
long n;                    /* number to test */
```

Description

The *selected( )* function queries the select-list array, *Slist,* which is established by *mkslist( ),* to determine whether the number parameter is a member of one of the ranges in the list.

Return

Returns 1 if the number is in one of the ranges and 0 otherwise.

Function

setfont—select a printer font

Synopsis

```
#include <local\printer.h>

int setfont(ftype, fout)
int ftype;                 /* font specifier */
FILE *fout;                /* output stream */
```

Description

This function is used to select a printer font type. The standard font is a 10 cpi (characters per inch) type and it can be obtained by calling *clrprnt( ).* The special types are chosen from the following list (based on Epson MX/FX-series printer codes):

Symbolic Name	Description
CONDENSED	*A small but very readable type at about 14 cpi (136 characters per line)*
DOUBLE	*Double strike*
EMPHASIZED	*Emboldened by microspacing and restriking*
EXPANDED	*Wider than normal characters (6 cpi)*
ITALICS	*True italic characters (not supported by all Epson-compatible printers)*
UNDERLINE	*Continuous underline (without the need to backspace and restrike the character)*

Return

The *setfont( )* function returns *SUCCESS* to indicate apparent success, or *FAILURE* if an error occurs or an illegal font combination is requested.

Notes

The *CONDENSED* font cannot be used with either *DOUBLE* or *EMPHASIZED* on most Epson-compatible printers, so such combinations are disallowed.

Function

setprnt—install printer codes

Synopsis

```
#include <local\printer.h>

int setprnt()
```

Description

This function installs printer codes from printer configuration files or from internal defaults (for Epson MX/FX series and compatible printers).

Return

The *setprnt( )* function returns *SUCCESS* to indicate apparent success, or *FAILURE* if an error occurs. The only detectable failures are too many or too few lines in a configuration file.

Function

spaces—send spaces to an output stream

Synopsis

```
int spaces(n, fp)
int n;                    /* number of repetitions */
FILE *fp;                 /* output stream */
```

Description

The *spaces( )* function places *n* space (blank) characters on the output stream.

Return

The number of spaces actually emitted, which may be less than the number requested if an error occurs on the output stream.

Function

tabstop—determine whether *col* is a tab stop

Synopsis

```
int tabstop(col)
register int col;
```

Description

The *tabstop( )* function queries the private Tabstops array to determine whether the specified column, *col,* is a tab stop.

Return

A nonzero value if *col* is a tab stop or 0 if it is not.

Function

vartabs—set variable tabs from a list

Synopsis

```
void vartabs(list)
int *list;              /* pointer to an array of tab stops */
```

Description

A set of tab stops can be set from a list using *vartabs( )* to initialize the private Tabstops array and then set the specified tabs.

Function

word2hex—convert a word value to hexadecimal

Synopsis

```
char *word2hex(data, buf)
unsigned short data;    /* 2-byte data item */
char *buf;              /* hex string buffer */
```

Description

The *word2hex( )* function converts a 2-byte numeric value to a 4-byte hexadecimal representation.

Return

A pointer to the resulting hexadecimal string.

Notes

The calling function must provide a buffer that is large enough to receive the 4-byte string and the terminating null byte.

Index

Page numbers for illustrations are in italics

Augie Hansen

Augie Hansen started programming on IBM mainframes more than 20 years ago and since then has been involved with computers and programming at various companies, including General Dynamics, Raytheon Company, and E.G. & G., Inc. In addition, Augie spent 7 years with AT&T Bell Laboratories, specializing in UNIX and C programming. He founded and is the president of Omniware, a company that provides academic and commercial training courses on UNIX, C, and MS/PC-DOS and custom programming consulting. Augie is a contributing editor of *PC Tech Journal* and has written one other book, *vi—The UNIX Screen Editor*, published in 1986 by Brady Books/Prentice-Hall Press.

The manuscript for this book was prepared and submitted to Microsoft Press in electronic form. Text files were processed and formatted using Microsoft Word.

Cover design by Ted Mader & Associates.

Interior text design by the staff of Microsoft Press.

Principal typography by Lisa Iversen.

Text composition by Microsoft Press in Rotation and Rotation Italic, with display in Futura Medium Condensed, using the CCI composition system and the Mergenthaler Linotron 202 digital phototypesetter.